BANNED

In *Banned*, readers are taken on a journey through the intense racial politics surrounding the banning of Mexican American Studies in Tucson, Arizona. This book details the state-sponsored racism that led to the elimination of this highly successful program, and the grassroots and legal resistance that followed. Through extensive research and first-hand narratives, readers will gain a deep understanding of the controversy surrounding this historic case. The legal challenge successfully overturned the Arizona law and became a central symbol in the modern-day Ethnic Studies renaissance. This work is a must-read for anyone interested in understanding the power of community activism, the importance of fighting for educational equity, and why the example of Tucson created an alternative blueprint for how we can challenge states that are currently banning Critical Race Theory (CRT).

Nolan L. Cabrera is a professor at the University of Arizona where he studies race on college campuses. He is a recipient of the National Academy of Education/Spencer postdoctoral fellowship and the author of the award-winning book *White Guys on Campus* (2019).

Robert S. Chang is a professor of law and the founder and executive director of the Fred T. Korematsu Center for Law and Equality at the University of California, Irvine School of Law. He is the author of several books and has an active *pro bono* civil rights practice.

Banned

THE FIGHT FOR MEXICAN AMERICAN STUDIES IN THE STREETS AND IN THE COURTS

NOLAN L. CABRERA
University of Arizona

ROBERT S. CHANG
University of California, Irvine

CAMBRIDGE UNIVERSITY PRESS

Shaftesbury Road, Cambridge CB2 8EA, United Kingdom

One Liberty Plaza, 20th Floor, New York, NY 10006, USA

477 Williamstown Road, Port Melbourne, VIC 3207, Australia

314–321, 3rd Floor, Plot 3, Splendor Forum, Jasola District Centre, New Delhi – 110025, India

103 Penang Road, #05–06/07, Visioncrest Commercial, Singapore 238467

Cambridge University Press is part of Cambridge University Press & Assessment, a department of the University of Cambridge.

We share the University's mission to contribute to society through the pursuit of education, learning and research at the highest international levels of excellence.

www.cambridge.org
Information on this title: www.cambridge.org/9781009563581

DOI: 10.1017/9781009563543

© Nolan L. Cabrera and Robert S. Chang 2025

This publication is in copyright. Subject to statutory exception and to the provisions of relevant collective licensing agreements, no reproduction of any part may take place without the written permission of Cambridge University Press & Assessment.

When citing this work, please include a reference to the DOI 10.1017/9781009563543

First published 2025

A catalogue record for this publication is available from the British Library

A Cataloging-in-Publication data record for this book is available from the Library of Congress

ISBN 978-1-009-56358-1 Hardback
ISBN 978-1-009-56356-7 Paperback

Cambridge University Press & Assessment has no responsibility for the persistence or accuracy of URLs for external or third-party internet websites referred to in this publication and does not guarantee that any content on such websites is, or will remain, accurate or appropriate.

For our children and barrio scholars, past, present, and future.

Contents

List of Figures		*page* ix
Acknowledgments		xi
Chronology of Events		xiii
	Prologue	1
1	Of Course, It's a Different Education, That's the Point: The Formation, Implementation, and Efficacy of MAS	6
2	The Brown Scare	18
3	They Tried to Bury Us, but They Forgot We Were Seeds: Forming the Resistance	30
4	UNIDOS, the Student Movement, Conspiracy Theories, and Militarized School Board Meetings	46
5	Was the Fix In? MAS Goes before an Administrative Law Judge	62
6	Caving to Pressure: Intimidation, Repression, and Absurdity at TUSD	79
7	The Lawsuit: Losing the First Round	97
8	The Appeal: With a Little Help from Friends (and a Community Further Divided)	114
9	A New Hope: A New Legal Team and New Plaintiffs	132
10	Trial!	142
11	Gotcha!: The State Tries (and Fails) to Trip Up the Plaintiffs' Experts	164

12	Doubling Down on Racism: Horne and Huppenthal Take the Stand	185
13	The S.S. Violation and the Close of Trial	204
14	Victory and National Renaissance Amidst Backlash	228
	Epilogue: Children Can Handle the Truth – Children Need the Truth	245
Notes		249
Index		285

Figures

2.1	Silent Protest (© *Arizona Daily Star*)	*page* 21
3.1	*Police State* by Lalo Alcaraz/Go Comics	36
3.2	*Ethnic Studies Book Burn* by Lalo Alcaraz/Go Comics	37
3.3	*Arizona Whitewash* by Lalo Alcaraz/Go Comics	38
4.1	UNIDOS School Board Takeover by Shachaf Polakow	49
4.2	"Batkid" Being Wanded Entering 1010 by Lupita Blancarte	58
6.1	*Librotraficante* by Tony Diaz	82
6.2	School's in Session by George Cabrera	86
6.3	Students and protesters at TUSD board meeting tied themselves together with plastic ties (© Arizona Public Media (AZPM))	92
8.1	Third Amended Complaint Overview by Robert Chang	117
12.1	John Huppenthal Outside of the Courtroom by Bryan Parras	185
13.1	Timeline of ADE's Actions courtesy of Robert Chang	221
13.2	ADE Timeline with Key Testimony courtesy of Robert Chang	222
13.3	Huppenthal Blog Posts courtesy of Robert Chang	223
13.4	*The American Vision*: "Seen in Use" courtesy of Robert Chang	224
13.5	"I'd say it's comparable" courtesy of Robert Chang	224
14.1	The Ethnic Studies Ban Was Racist (© *Arizona Daily Star*)	232
14.2	*Welcome to Arizona* by Lalo Alcaraz/Go Comics	234
14.3	Map of State-Based Ethnic Studies Bills and Requirements by Wayne Au	241

Acknowledgments

We thank the courage of community members who fought to institute the Mexican American Studies (MAS) program at the Tucson Unified School District (TUSD); administrators and teachers who devoted their energy and talent to develop the MAS program at the TUSD; students who took MAS classes, who through their example showed the possibilities of the program; those who fought to keep MAS at TUSD in the face of daunting odds, including the teachers; the Tucson 11, who initially brought a legal challenge to stop HB 2281 (the Arizona bill used to eliminate MAS); as well as the high school students, Nicholas Dominguez, Korina Lopez, Maya Arce, Joseph Gonzalez, Noah González, and Manuel Barcelo who joined the lawsuit. We are grateful also to the parents of the students just mentioned for supporting them in the legal challenge. Special callout to Richard Martinez, the solo practitioner in Tucson, who initiated the legal challenge in 2010 and worked on the case through its resolution in 2017.

Nolan Cabrera would like to thank the Tucson community for continually showing up to fight for MAS and educational self-determination. He would also like to thank his colleagues at the University of Arizona, who supported him doing the MAS work before obtaining tenure when the common sense of higher education is "get tenure, *then* do the controversial work." In particular, he would like to thank Jeff Milem for being such an incredible support, mentor, collaborator, and friend while also being such a strong advocate for equitable education. To Sylvia Hurtado, Cabrera is forever indebted for learning how to do actionable research, which also included the importance of having unimpeachable methods and an almost excruciating attention to detail. To his former dean, Ron Marx, Cabrera is so appreciative of being such a stalwart defender of academic freedom in tumultuous times in addition to being a wonderful co-collaborator. Finally, to Gary Rhoades, thanks for always saying *ad nauseum* and supporting him in embodying the dictum, "Academic freedom is like a muscle. If you don't use it, it atrophies." Most importantly, Cabrera would like to thank his family. He knows it was not easy seeing him go through this, and their unwavering support was foundational to him persisting. Most of all to his little Honey Badger – this struggle was about the future of public education in Tucson and beyond. You and your friends are its legacy.

Robert Chang thanks Anjana Malhotra, the inaugural Korematsu Center clinical teaching fellow, who worked tirelessly on this case while at Seattle University and after she became a clinical law professor at the University of Buffalo School of Law. He also thanks the different cohorts of students in the Korematsu Center's Civil Rights Clinic, who worked on various aspects of this case from 2012 to 2017. He is deeply grateful to *pro bono* counsel at Bingham McCutchen and Morgan Lewis who assisted in the successful Ninth Circuit Appeal. Several Seattle University School of Law faculty members assisted in the appeal, including Lorraine Bannai and Charlotte Garden. He is eternally grateful to *pro bono* counsel and staff at Weil, Gotshal & Manges, who conducted discovery and led the trial presentation, devoting more than four million dollars in attorney hours and hard costs. This included Weil attorneys: Steven Reiss, James Quinn, Luna Barrington, and David Fitzmaurice – and Weil staff: Sirak Biratu, Steve Mangru, and Jorge Martorell.

Chronology of Events

1968	Ethnic Studies strike at San Francisco State University; formation of the Third World Liberation Front
1968	Tucson walkouts – reminiscent of Los Angeles' Chicano Blowouts
1968/1969	Mexican American Studies (MAS) established at the University of Arizona
1996	Community and Neighborhoods for Mexican American Studies (CONMAS) started its struggle for *Raza* Studies (U of A students and community activists)
1998	"Hispanic Studies Department" is created at TUSD
2002	Deputy Superintendent Dr. Becky Montaño appoints Augustine Romero Director (NCLB mandate highlights the White/Latino "Achievement" – or rather *opportunity* – Gap)
2002	Mexican Community Advisory Board – Hispanic is changed to Mexican American/*Raza* Studies
April 3, 2006	Labor leader Dolores Huerta gives a speech at Tucson where she says that based on their legislative agenda (especially the anti-immigrant, draconian HR4437), "Republicans hate Latinos"
May 12, 2006	Margaret Garcia Dugan gives a rebuttal saying that she was an example that Republicans don't hate Latinos; attendance was mandatory, and there was no opportunity for Q&A; students staged a silent protest, and Horne blamed MAS for teaching students to be "disrespectful"
June 11, 2007	Arizona State Superintendent of Public Instruction Tom Horne issues his "An Open Letter to the Citizens of Tucson"
2008	HB 1108 is introduced as part of a Homeland Security Bill as the first attempt to eliminate MAS (failed, supported by Horne, Governor veto)

2009	HB 1069 is drafted by Tom Horne and introduced (Judicial Bill, failed)
February 2010	HB 2281 – Horne drafts a bill to "get rid of the MAS program"; Governor Napolitano (D) becomes part of the Obama administration and Jan Brewer (R) is appointed; 2010 is a midterm election in the middle of a nation-wide recession, and both HB 2281 and the anti-migrant SB 1070 are part of the larger political strategy (passed)
April 2010	Huppenthal amends HB 2281 to delay the effective date to January 1, 2011, giving himself enforcement power if elected State Superintendent of Public Instruction
May 2010	*Three Sonorans* launches a blog that was part of TucsonCitizen.com
Fall 2010	Huppenthal runs for State Superintendent of Public Instruction promising on radio spots that if elected, he would "stop *la raza*"
October 18, 2010	Eleven MAS teachers file suit alleging HB 2281 violates their First and Fourteenth Amendment protections
November 2, 2010	Horne elected Attorney General of the state of Arizona; Huppenthal elected State Superintendent of Public Instruction
December 30, 2010	Horne prematurely issues TUSD findings of noncompliance two days before the statute is enacted
January 1, 2011	Arizona Revised Statutes (A.R.S.) §15-112 goes into effect
January 4, 2011	Huppenthal sworn in as Superintendent Horne sworn in as Attorney General Huppenthal adopts Horne's finding
February 2011	Cambium selected by Superintendent Huppenthal's office to conduct an independent audit of the MAS program
April 26, 2011	TUSD board member Mark Stegeman introduces motion to demote MAS classes to electives, the first step to elimination (Stegeman Resolution); UNIDOS students take over the deices before the meeting begins in an act of civil disobedience that allowed MAS to continue to exist
May 2, 2011	Cambium Audit finds that there were *no observable* violations of the law and that taking MAS classes likely led to increased student academic success
May 3, 2011	Most-attended (500+ community members) and militarized (~150 officers) TUSD board meeting in history again hears the "Stegeman Resolution"; after numerous acts of civil disobedience and arrests, the TUSD board agrees to not pass the Stegeman Resolution
June 15, 2011	Huppenthal rejects Cambium's findings and issues a finding that the MAS program violated A.R.S. §15-112

Chronology of Events xv

August–October 2011	Hearing before Administrative Law Judge Lewis D. Kowal, Appeal by TUSD of Superintendent's Finding of Violation; hearing takes place on four days – August 19, August 23, September 14, and October 17
October 27, 2011	Longtime MAS supporter and TUSD board member Judy Burns passes away unexpectedly
December 27, 2011	Administrative Law Judge Kowal upholds Superintendent's finding of violation and authorizes withholding of 10 percent of monthly apportionment of state funding until TUSD comes into compliance
January 10, 2012	Judge Tashima dismisses plaintiff teachers and MAS Program Director; plaintiff students are not dismissed; denies plaintiffs' motion for preliminary injunction
January 10, 2012	TUSD board votes to eliminate the MAS program (4-1) – halts all MAS activities in classrooms, begins unannounced visits to former MAS teachers to ensure compliance, and bans MAS teaching materials, including books, removing them from classrooms and putting them in storage
January 2012	Hundreds of students walk out of schools throughout TUSD
January 24, 2012	UNIDOS hosts the "School of Ethnic Studies" where students walking out can learn from the outlawed curriculum of MAS
April 2, 2012	TUSD board member Michael Hicks goes on *The Daily Show*
April 2012	*Three Sonorans* kicked off *Tucson Citizen* and goes independent
March 19, 2012	Hearing on plaintiffs' motion for summary judgment on First Amendment grounds and defendants' cross-motion for summary judgment
March 8, 2013	Judge Tashima grants plaintiffs summary judgment in part, finding A.R.S. §15-112 (A)(3) to be unconstitutionally overbroad, but denies the remainder of it and, instead, grants summary judgment to defendants on plaintiffs' First Amendment claims and, *sua sponte*, on plaintiffs' Fourteenth Amendment equal protection and substantive due process claims; except for the portion of the statute found unconstitutional, plaintiffs' claims are dismissed
April 5, 2013	Plaintiffs file the notice of appeal
November 2013	Plaintiffs file the opening brief and are supported by six amicus briefs: (1) authors of books banned from TUSD; (2) National Education Association and Arizona Education Association; (3) Freedom to Read Foundation, American Library Association, American Booksellers Foundation for Free

	Expression, Asian/Pacific American Librarians Association, Black Caucus of the American Library Association, Comic Book Legal Defense Fund, National Association for Ethnic Studies, National Coalition against Censorship, National Council of Teachers of English, and REFORMA; (4) Chief Justice Earl Warren Institute on Law and Social Policy and the Anti-Defamation League; (5) 48 Public School Teachers; and (6) LatCrit, Inc.
January 31, 2014	Defendants file the response and cross-appeal brief
June 2, 2014	Plaintiffs file reply and response to the cross-appeal
June 2014	Superintendent of Public Instruction John Huppenthal is caught anonymously blogging and leaving racist comments on webpages; he weeps during his public apology
July 21, 2014	Defendants file reply
January 2, 2015	John Huppenthal finds TUSD's "Culturally Relevant Courses" as one of his last acts in office
January 12, 2015	Ninth Circuit Court of Appeals hears oral argument in the appeal of Judge Tashima's ruling
July 7, 2015	Ninth Circuit ruling: Judge Tashima's original ruling, affirmed in part, reversed in part, and remanded for trial before Judge Tashima
Summer 2017	Bench trial before Judge Tashima, June 26–30 and July 17–21
August 22, 2017	Judge Tashima finds that A.R.S. §15-112 was enacted and enforced because of racial animus and partisan political gain, violating the First and Fourteenth Amendment rights of Mexican American students in TUSD
December 27, 2017	Judge Tashima issues the final judgment and permanent injunction against the state regarding any enforcement for A.R.S. §15-112
January 27, 2018	Deadline for appeal passes with no appeal by Arizona; case closed

* * *

November 17, 2022	Tom Horne elected Arizona State Superintendent of Public Instruction again, this time promising to "Ban Critical Race Theory"

Prologue

Tell the story. Make it real for those who refuse to believe that such a thing can happen/has happened/is happening here. Bring the suffering to the attention of those who wallow in willful ignorance. In short, shatter the illusion of innocence at every turn and attack all the shibboleths the country holds sacred.

                    Eddie S. Glaude Jr., *Begin Again*

It was a pleasure to burn.

                    Ray Bradbury, *Fahrenheit 451*

In seeking to write this story, we found solace and inspiration in Eddie Glaude's words.[1] He was writing about the context of James Baldwin more than half a century ago, yet his words seem especially relevant for the modern-day civil rights struggle. This book is specifically about that – bearing witness and telling the masses about the truth: the truth of Arizona's ban of Mexican American Studies (MAS); the truth of community suffering and conflict; the truth of collective resistance against the racist acts of state officials. When the controversy first came to a head circa 2010, many people outside of the state continually asked, "How could Arizona be so backwards? How could they be so racist? What's going on there?" Interestingly, these questions tailed off around 2016, which coincided with the election of President Trump. As a candidate, he pledged to keep Muslims from entering the United States. As a candidate, he said that immigrants from Mexico brought crime and were rapists. He began saying the quiet part out loud, and crowds ate it up. His electoral college victory and ascendancy to the presidency were signs that the country caught up with the overt racism of Arizona in the early 2010s.

President Trump's failure to obtain a second term might be thought to be a successful referendum against his "dog-whistle" racial politics of division. The summer of 2020 leading up to the election held such promise as it appeared that the nation had awoken from its stupor to see, finally, the brutality visited by law enforcement upon Black and Brown bodies and to act, finally, to do something about it.

The primary precipitating event was the murder of George Floyd, a Black man, at the hands of Derek Chauvin, a White police officer. Mr. Floyd's murder rekindled attention and furor over the murders of so many other Black people at the hands of the police. Say their names: Elijah McClain,[2] Daunte Wright, Andre Hill, Manuel Ellis, Rayshard Brooks, Daniel Prude, Breonna Taylor, Atatiana Jefferson, Aura Rosser, Stephon Clark, Botham Jean, Philando Castile, Alton Sterling, Freddie Gray, Janisha Fonville, Eric Garner, Michelle Cusseaux, Akai Gurley, Gabriella Nevarez, Tamir Rice, and Tanisha Anderson.[3]

Concurrently, there was a spike in anti-Asian hate crimes spurred by the COVID-19 pandemic and the way the novel coronavirus was racialized by commentators and leaders such as the then-US president who called it the "Chinese Virus" and "Kung Flu."[4]

But the protests and calls for racial justice have produced a predictable backlash. We now find ourselves in the midst of the attacks that are taking place in state legislatures, in school board meetings, and in school classrooms about the teaching of facts as they relate to race and racism in US history. We had thought that winning the high-profile trial in summer 2017 that invalidated Arizona's law against Ethnic Studies would squelch efforts to do the same in other states.

WE WERE WRONG

As of March 1, 2023, legislators in forty-four states have introduced bills, with eighteen states having enacted restrictions through legislation or other government action on the teaching of Critical Race Theory (CRT) (or related banned concepts) in public schools.[5] Two of the most prominent politicians in the Republican Party with national aspirations, Governor Ron DeSantis of Florida and Governor Sarah Huckabee Sanders of Arkansas, have made the banning of CRT a key part of their political profiles, serving up "red meat" to a conservative base receptive to this style of "dog whistle" politics. Another prominent politician and the first after former President Trump to announce her candidacy for the Republican nomination, Nikki Haley, former governor of South Carolina and former US Ambassador to the United Nations, also quickly doubled down on her earlier attacks saying on Twitter, "CRT is un-American."[6]

It is also important to note that politicians are not just seeking to limit what may be said about race in the classroom. Restrictions are also aimed at what may be said about gender and sexual orientation, as well as others aimed at a particularly vulnerable group, transgender students.[7] As politicians trip over each other to outdo themselves, they appear to do so with a glee that reminds us of the opening sentence in Ray Bradbury's classic, *Fahrenheit 451*: "It was a pleasure to burn."[8]

Even Arizona, despite losing the lawsuit that lies at the heart of this book, passed a law in 2021 that banned the teaching of certain concepts associated with CRT and Ethnic Studies.[9] After this law was invalidated by the Arizona Supreme Court on procedural grounds,[10] the legislature passed a new version of the ban, only to have it vetoed by the newly elected Democratic governor, Katie Hobbs.[11] Time will tell if there will be renewed banning efforts at the state level or whether these efforts will be attempted at the local level as they have been in other states. The legal battles are just beginning in other states, and teachers and students are finding themselves caught in the middle. What, if anything, are teachers permitted to teach children about race and racism? What, if anything, are students permitted to ask their teachers or to discuss in their classrooms about race and racism? What books and other materials will students be able to access in their school libraries?

In this book, we bear witness to the incredible story of the banning of MAS and the resistance. We use the term "incredible" in the sense that many of the stories told in this book defy belief. They do not make sense. Yet they happened. We also use the term "incredible" in the sense that this is an extraordinary tale.

Writing this book requires us to make sense of a decade-long struggle regarding MAS in the Tucson Unified School District (TUSD), but how does one translate into the written word the absolute destruction of one of the most successful Ethnic Studies programs in US history? How can we capture the story of a community that under incredible stress turns on itself with these wounds unhealed even to this day? How do we tell the story of a state superintendent of public instruction who said that Mexican American student achievement was an irrelevant issue in this controversy? Regardless, our collective responsibility is, as Glaude and Baldwin as his muse argue, to bear witness.

MAYBE THAT IS THE POINT

We are tasked with making sense out of that which was not supposed to make sense.

Many precious lives were harmed when the highly successful MAS program was eliminated. They gave their all fighting a banning that was found to be implemented out of racial animus and partisan political gain – or more colloquially, the banning was RACIST (or so says a federal judge).

To build to this point, we had to ask several difficult questions, such as: How does one fight state-sponsored, state-sanctioned, and state-enforced racism? How does one identify and challenge racism when its overt expression has been largely driven underground? What are the personal costs of fighting for educational self-determination? What are the consequences of inaction? What internal, community divisions arise when a state cracks down on a locale, and how does one navigate this terrain? How does one act when the path forward is as clear as mud?

These are questions that have informed the work of equity-oriented activists and agitators for centuries, and they were central to the controversy in Tucson, Arizona, where a state law in 2010 banned a highly successful MAS program – a program that at the time of its elimination was the largest K-12 Ethnic Studies program in the country.

These questions are central to the current controversy over the teaching of race and racism in public schools. We offer this account to describe how these questions played out in Arizona, including the lawsuit that overturned the 2010 law.

To begin at the end, on December 27, 2017, Judge Wallace A. Tashima issued his Final Judgment, Declaration, and Permanent Injunction in *González v. Douglas*, bringing this almost decade-long odyssey that began with the filing of a lawsuit on October 18, 2010, by ten teachers and an administrator who challenged HB 2281, the law that was used to terminate the TUSD MAS program. The plaintiffs' names, for the record, were Curtis Acosta, Sean Arce, Maria Federico Brummer, Dolores Carrion, Alexandro Escamilla, Jose Gonzalez, Norma Gonzalez, Lorenzo Lopez, Jr., Rene Martinez, Sally Rusk, and Yolanda Sotelo. For reasons we will explain later, three TUSD students joined the lawsuit in 2011. These students were Maya Arce, Korina Lopez, and Nicholas Dominguez. As time went by and they graduated, they were replaced by other students, Joseph Gonzalez and then Noah González and Manuel Barcelo, so that the case that started out as *Acosta v. Horne*, and then *Arce v. Huppenthal*, concluded as *González v. Douglas*. Even the named defendants changed over time as successor state superintendents of public instruction took office.

This leads to an even more complicated question than the ones previously lodged. When did this protracted controversy begin? Was it when labor leader and civil rights icon Dolores Huerta speculated that the anti-immigrant legislation of Republicans in Congress meant that "Republicans hate Latinos"? Her statement was the immediate catalyst for the legislative efforts that led to HB 2281. Some say the story starts with her. But for her statement and the ensuing controversy, it is possible that the MAS program would not have become the target that it came to be.

Or was it a twenty-eight-year odyssey dating to the first MAS course taught at TUSD? That course was created because teachers and community members were frustrated by the slow pace of the desegregation lawsuit, frustrated because the court's remedies were not addressing the real problems – the fact that schools were not being responsive to or addressing the needs of Mexican American students. MAS was intended to fix that.

Or was it an over 100-year odyssey dating back to the segregation of Mexican American students in Arizona's public schools?

So many beginnings brought in some ways to an end after a historic trial in Courtroom 6B on the sixth floor of the Evo A. Deconcini US Courthouse on 405 W. Congress Street in Tucson, Arizona. But like any ending, it is really just a beginning, and time will tell what changes will come.

But – as the trial in the summer of 2017 wound down, there was, once again, a sweet smell in the air – HOPE – reminding some of that sweet smell that comes from the creosote plant when there is rain in the desert. Time will tell.

* * *

A key feature of this text is reminiscent of the refrain from *Hamilton*, "Who lives, who dies, who tells your story?" An asset and a liability of this text is that it is written by a lawyer on the federal MAS case and one of the expert witnesses who is also a professor at the University of Arizona and a Tucson community member. This gives us firsthand access to important developments in this controversy on the ground level; however, it also means we have had to navigate some very tricky community politics and controversies in order to write this story as we will detail in later chapters. What follows is an account, a narrative rendering, of the community resistance and successful legal challenge to a law that was enacted and enforced to terminate TUSD's MAS Program. Sometimes the truth is stranger than fiction, and you will soon discover from two insider-outsiders the intense racial/political drama that unfolded for years in the city of Tucson. There are times of racial oppression, times of resistance, times of the absurd, times of internal conflict, and times of social transformation that led to the current Ethnic Studies renaissance that is occurring nationally.

What follows is an amazing, heartbreaking, absurd, true story of MAS in Tucson. We tell this story because it needs to be told.

1

Of Course, It's a Different Education, That's the Point

The Formation, Implementation, and Efficacy of MAS

On the first day of the trial, Dr. Curtis Acosta, a former Mexican American Studies (MAS) teacher testified that the materials in his Latino Literature class were intended to operate as windows on the world as well as mirrors in which students could see themselves.[1] To help his students see the broader world as well as to see themselves in it, he included Shakespeare's *Tempest* as well as Ana Castillo's *So Far from God*.[2] He also testified that the program treated students as bringing cultural assets that should be valued rather than denigrated as tends to happen in the rest of their public school education.[3]

If this sounds different from what occurs in most high school English classes, it is because it is. It's a different education. That's the point. Courses developed in Tucson Unified School District's (TUSD's) MAS program were designed to do what decades of federal oversight over TUSD's had failed to accomplish. They were designed to disparities in school discipline, test scores, and graduation rates of Mexican American students.

And it was working, as would be established at trial in 2017.

The fact that it was working may have threatened those in power, especially when Brown students found their voices and advocated for themselves. These Brown students, by speaking up and engaging politically, showed that they had forgotten their subordinate place in society. The MAS program and its teachers were blamed.

The reality of MAS is much different than how its critics and the masses framed it, and this book seeks to set the record straight. There were overtly racist lies told by politicians, media pundits, and right-wing activists about the MAS program, which were largely imagined or severe distortions of the truth. Further, these distortions were intended to equate teaching about racism with the vilification and demonization of White people. It was much like rapper Immortal Technique offered in the song "Young Lords":

> *Banned ethnic studies claimin' our culture will swallow them*
> *But you can't conquer a people,*
> *And build a country on top them.*[4]

Mexican American Studies was created to "do" education differently in order to serve the needs of Chicana/o-Mexican American students in an educational manifestation of what Roberto "Cintli" Rodríguez refers to as *creation resistance*.[5] This involved building a culturally authentic educational program for Chicana/o-Mexican American students in the borderlands to not only serve their specific needs but also to resist the pressures of the dominant, Anglo-centric US culture that continually tells these students that they are foreign, "illegal," and should "go back to Mexico."[6] While there were non-Chicana/o-Mexican American students who took these courses, they were not the original intended audience, even though they still benefited and were never excluded.[7]

This approach to education stems from the history and creation of Ethnic Studies that dramatically reimagined the relationship among communities, education, scholarship, and racial equity. The formation of the MAS program was deeply connected to the radical legacy of the 1960s, particularly the formation of Chicana/o Studies. While we offer the broad strokes of what Chicana/o Studies and Ethnic Studies are historically and how MAS was developed in Tucson, a detailed account of this is beyond the scope of this text. While some have begun to document it,[8] there are many areas left to explore, given the nuances of the MAS program.

THE HISTORICAL LEGACY OF CHICANA/O STUDIES AND ETHNIC STUDIES

Intentional, collective, grassroots agitation during the 1960s Civil Rights Movement led to the creation of Ethnic Studies in general and Chicana/o Studies in particular.[9] Rodolfo "Corky" Gonzales, in *Message to Aztlán*, had a specific message to the educator: "Your responsibility is one of the most important in the Movement. To you lies the task of teaching the truth about our history, our culture, and our contributions to mankind."[10] Chicana/o Studies was born out of struggle, and it continues in the fight for educational self-determination.[11] Few other disciplines stem from that type of institutional history. To our knowledge, there has never had to be a sit-in for a US university to create a Physics Department or a hunger strike that led to the development of a College of Engineering. Ethnic Studies and Chicana/o Studies are unlike any other academic discipline, especially because they were developed from an analysis of deeprooted social inequities while also calling for community-based education.[12] A core guiding document for Chicana/o Studies was *El Plan de Santa Bárbara*[13] stemming from a 1969 gathering. In the opening manifesto of the document, the authors wrote:

> We recognize that without a strategic use of education, an education that places value on what (Chicanos) value, we will not realize our destiny. Chicanos recognize the central importance of institutions of higher learning to modern progress, in this case, tot the development of our community ... For these reasons Chicano Studies represent the total conceptualization of the Chicano community's aspirations that involve higher education.[14]

In the very formation of Chicana/o Studies, there was a larger community purpose explicitly articulated. It both understood that higher education systematically excluded Brown bodies from full participation since its creation, yet these same institutions hold immense potential in developing community self-determination. Essentially, it was a demand to make higher education work for Chicana/o communities instead of making Chicanas/os assimilate into these White institutions.[15]

In addition, the late historian Ronald Takaki offered another rationale for Ethnic Studies in his classic text A *Different Mirror: A History of Multicultural America*: "What happens, to borrow the words of Adrienne Rich, when someone with the authority of a teacher describes our society, and you are not in it? Such an experience can be disorienting – a moment of psychic disequilibrium, as if you looked into a mirror and saw nothing."[16]

This searing critique of monocultural White curriculum was a central component of the push for Ethnic Studies during the Civil Rights Movement of the 1960s. Education has always been a battle over what constitutes "official knowledge" and how it should be taught.[17] Takaki illustrated the negative psychological effects of monocultural education.[18] Chicana/o Studies' scholar/activist Rudy Acuña took it one step further and examined the effects of exclusionary history on society at large. Specifically, he was concerned about the retrenchment he saw occurring within Arizona in the early 2010s, and from his perspective as a critical historian, he offered:

> History matters. It matters when a student reaches full potential. Chicana/o Studies has a rich foundation of knowledge that should be shared with everyone. It holds the key to the dropout problem that Chicano Studies set out to stem. Xenophobia occurs when there is ignorance of others. Ignorance costs... History has been erased, and over fifty years of research on how to teach Mexican Americans has been ignored. It is very similar to the assault on science; it is as if Nicolaus Copernicus never lived... The events of Arizona have returned us to 1965.[19]

Acuña directly related the backlash to Chicana/o Studies to the interrelated issues of xenophobia and the Chicana/o student dropout (or pushout) crisis. Essentially, the more that xenophobia becomes engrained in society, the more Chicana/o Studies is ignored and banned, and the more Chicana/o students are likely to drop out. While the interrelation of these concepts is much more complicated than a simple 1:1 correlation, the overall trends hold true. Essentially, Chicana/o Studies is critically important to Chicana/o student educational advancement; the more that racism is the norm in society, the less that *raza* are able to utilize this community-oriented, community-developed knowledge base.[20]

From this perspective, Ethnic Studies as related to Chicana/o Studies has multiple interrelated purposes. It is meant to be rigorous education for those frequently written off by society as academically incapable.[21] It is meant to offer an alternative account of this country that shows that their communities and histories are not marginal. As Evelyn Hu-DeHart offered: "Ethnic studies seeks to recover and reconstruct the histories of those Americans whom history has neglected; to identify and credit their contributions to the making of U.S. society and culture; to chronicle protest and resistance; and to establish alternative values and visions, institutions and cultures."[22]

The resistance component is central to Ethnic Studies done effectively, for this is an academic discipline that is also rooted in social activism.[23] It centers structured racial oppression in the analysis and then challenges students, teachers, and community members to collectively transform these inequitable conditions.[24]

The interrogation of systemic oppression was one of the central points of contention offered by opponents of the MAS program. Then State Superintendent of Public Instruction and key MAS opponent, Tom Horne, was very direct in his *Open Letter to the Citizens of Tucson*: "Most of these students' parents and grandparents came to this country, legally, because this is the land of opportunity. They trust the public schools with their children. Those students should be taught that this is the land of opportunity, and that if they work hard they can achieve their goals. They should not be taught that they are oppressed."[25]

The last line is key, that students should "not be taught they are oppressed." This begs the question: What if they *are* systemically oppressed? Most of the leading education and sociological literature on race argue that contemporary racism is a social structure of oppression that privileges White people at the expense of people of color.[26] This contemporary form of White supremacy may be accurate from a social science perspective, but it also makes people – White people in particular – very uncomfortable.[27] John Huppenthal, State Superintendent after Horne, repeated this argument many times as he derided the oppressor/oppressed paradigm that he claimed was the framework of the MAS program.[28]

His essential argument was that explicitly engaging oppression in teaching creates blame toward the people who have and continue to benefit from the system. In this case, that means White people. Huppenthal's critique is, however, very common in the everyday ways that people talk about race. Think about the part of town, wherever you might live, that is labeled "bad" or "dangerous." Please be clear, we are not demeaning these areas. We are criticizing how people conceptualize them. In Tucson, for example, it is the Southside that is the proud Brown *barrio*, and it is extremely common for people – especially on the north side of town – to talk about "those poor people in the south side of Tucson," not to be confused with the separate city, South Tucson. Conversely, it is extremely uncommon for these statements to be linked to the affluence in the largely White suburbs also within the Old Pueblo. As Nolan Cabrera offered, "This is akin to saying *up* with no *down*, *good* with no *bad*, *hot* with no *cold*. Unfortunately, this is how a number of contemporary investigations of race occur – engaging racial marginalization without also analyzing advantage."[29] The one-sided analysis of race was all that Horne and Huppenthal would allow as Superintendents of Public Instruction, which could only be countered by a coordinated resistance to their policies and rulings. Fortunately, resistance is in the very DNA of Ethnic Studies.[30]

THE FORMATION OF MEXICAN AMERICAN STUDIES IN TUCSON

Brown v. Board of Education[31] may have declared a formal end to de jure segregation, but active resistance to integration led to de jure segregation persisting; and even when de jure segregation ended or in places where de jure segregation had never existed, residential segregation meant that de facto segregation remained the lived realities of many students throughout the country.[32] In Arizona, this meant keeping Mexican American and other non-White students separate from White students.[33] Within this context, the "all deliberate speed" mandate of *Brown* butted up against Dr. King's argument in *Why We Can't Wait*.[34] That is, if separate is inherently unequal as declared by *Brown*, how long should minoritized students exist in under-resourced schools? This was especially pressing because despite the change in national law, school officials in Arizona continued to forbid interracial dances, implemented multiple programs to "Americanize" students of Mexican origin – especially around issues of language – and increased internal segregation within schools.[35] Arizona officials also turned to English proficiency, actual or perceived, as a proxy for race, justifying the continued segregation of Mexican American students from their White peers.[36]

With this as context, Darius Echeverría argued that in the 1960s "[m]any students began to believe that the political mindset of moderation, accommodation, and reasonable cultural awareness of their parents' generation was ineffective and ultimately passé."[37] While the dramatic images of the East Los Angeles Blowouts of 1968 and the Crystal City walkouts dominate much of Chicano history, there were lesser known, but equally important, efforts underway in Tucson during the same time period fighting for educational justice.[38] As then activist and current US Congressperson Raúl Grijalva (D-AZ) said, reflecting on the need for direct action against the district, "We knew that we had a school board and a superintendent that basically ignored [us] and at best neglected this community and population so it was just a question of time … There was an urgency for us to make a statement here in Tucson and the statement was the walkouts."[39]

In February of 1969, the Mexican American Liberation Committee (MALC) organized a walkout at both Tucson and Pueblo High, majority Chicano schools, resulting in hundreds of students leaving campus and marching throughout the community. Student leaders such as Isabel Garcia, Guadalupe Castillo, and Raúl Grijalva, all of whom continue to be leaders in Tucson to this day, presented the students' demands. One key component was the implementation of Mexican American history courses.[40]

Much of the Tucson organizing was led by college students associated with MALC, such as UA senior Salomón Baldenegro, the less radical Mexican American Student Association (MASA), and the eventual merging of the two into a MEChA (*El Movimiento Estudiantíl Chicanos de Aztlán*) – the last group being the one Tom Horne continually derides as both "racist" and "anti-American."[41] This group of

Chicana/o college students and their allies, through a protracted five-year struggle, were able to get the University of Arizona administration to bend and institute an MAS program.[42] Their demand for the inclusion of Mexican American history classes would have to wait thirty years and the formation of an MAS Department at TUSD.

It should surprise no one that the initial formation of this department at TUSD stemmed from grassroots activism and a lawsuit.[43] A group called the Coalition of Neighbors for Mexican American Studies (CONMAS) comprised of University of Arizona MEChistas, high school students, and community activists spent approximately two years applying political pressure to the TUSD Board, advocating for the establishment of an MAS department.[44] Again, their advocacy began with a critique.

CONMAS members argued that TUSD had African American and Native American studies, so why did the largest ethnic group in the district not have one of their own?[45] In this case, anything related to MAS was subsumed in the Bilingual Education and Hispanic Studies Department. Scholars Conrado Gómez and Margarita Jiménez-Silva reflecting on this controversy argued, however, that while Bilingual Education was well structured, "the Hispanic Studies component had not properly and systematically been addressed."[46] That is, there were few systemic offerings as one would expect from an academic department, and the community activists demanded more. Additionally, equating MAS with bilingual education created the danger of conflating the two in a way that echoed the earlier use of presumed language ability to treat Mexican American students differently.

To further add pressure to the TUSD school board, a lawsuit was filed in US District Court and claimed that the lack of MAS department amounted to race-based educational discrimination.[47] The lead attorney on the case was none other than the Chicana/o Movement icon José Angel Gutiérrez, whose words spoken in a different context would be seized upon decades later by MAS detractors as promoting resentment and fomenting violence. In the 1960s, Gutiérrez was a founding member of both the Mexican American Youth Organization (MAYO) and the electoral third-party organization the *Raza Unida* Party. Thus, the plaintiffs in Tucson were directly connected to the very history of struggle that led to the creation of Chicana/o Studies in the first place.

The combination of strong political pressure with mounting legal fees led TUSD to settle the case, which resulted in the creation of the autonomous Hispanic Studies Department in 1998. Sean Arce, who later became the director of MAS, taught one of the first courses in the program in American History–Chicano Perspectives. The course offerings, though, remained piecemeal initially.[48]

Strangely, MAS in Tucson became a more integrated department in part because of mandates set forth by the second Bush Administration's No Child Left Behind (NCLB) Act. While the act as a whole has rightfully been criticized as being ineffective, harmful, heightening school-based segregation, and providing a public subsidy for private education,[49] there was one component that was somewhat – stress "somewhat" – beneficial. NCLB mandated that data be collected on student achievement and that the data be disaggregated along racial/ethnic lines. The data from TUSD highlighted massive inequities between White and Mexican American students throughout the district.[50]

This led TUSD Deputy Superintendent Dr. Becky Montaño to appoint Augustine ("Auggie") Romero head of the MAS department, bringing together fifteen teachers across the district to coordinate their efforts and offer a radical alternative to the increasingly rigid and formulaic ways education was being offered in the early 2000s under NCLB. This approach included helping students understand their Indigenous roots in this land, helping them develop the ability to critically analyze structured inequality and oppression, while centering issues of race, racism, and other local community issues in the curriculum and pedagogy.[51]

From 2008 until the elimination of the program, Sean Arce served as its director. During the time the department existed, 2002–2012, those in the MAS program were continually focused on using different forms of critical pedagogy while also raising Mexican American student achievement in the district.[52] Many in Arizona, as detailed in Chapter 2, found this approach to education not only inappropriate but also threatening, especially to White people.[53] This White backlash – or Whitelash if you will – has followed Chicana/o Studies since its creation.[54]

Part of this handwringing is that historically, Chicana/o Studies programs have operated differently from nearly all other academic disciplines,[55] and the TUSD MAS program was true to this legacy.[56] As Juan Gomez-Quiñones succinctly argued, "Validity for Chicano Studies is self-knowledge, community knowledge and social change."[57] Thus, and in stark contrast to the images of higher education and the ivory tower, Chicana/o Studies tends to have a strong connection to local communities.[58] Additionally, community knowledge is seen as valid, moving beyond the ways that traditional, White academic work is done.[59] There is frequently an applied nature to the work that is specifically dedicated to working with marginalized communities to challenge oppressive social circumstances and structures.[60] Gomez-Quiñones, writing in 1974, further defined Chicana/o Studies in terms of its liberatory purpose as well as the predictable backlash it provoked: "When authentic to the historical condition and the contemporary state of the Chicano community, Chicano Studies is indeed a mirror and a call to action. Those who do not like the reflection are bothered by the call. They would prefer to break the mirror, stifle the call, or simply play dumb."[61]

His description of the mirror and the reaction that Chicana/o Studies causes could have been taken out of its 1970s Southern California context, put in the late 2000s Tucson one, and have been just as valid. It shows the potential power of Chicana/o Studies as an avenue of community-based, educational self-determination, as well as how that type of work threatens the powers that be.

Chicana/o Studies in general, and MAS in particular, involves a radical redefinition of education as it overtly acknowledged the cultural and political aspects of teaching. To effectively do this type of education, it requires teachers to blur the lines between the school and the community so the educator can truly understand the community context of their students.[62] While this connection to community beyond the ivory tower has been waning in recent years,[63] it is still a foundational component of Chicana/o Studies in particular and Ethnic Studies in general. It was also this general philosophy that led to some of the central features of the MAS program.[64] It was also a curriculum that explicitly centered race and racism among other forms of oppression in an effort to *racismize* the classroom.[65] To this end, works of Critical Race Theory such as Delgado and Stefancic's seminal text *Critical Race Theory: An Introduction* – a text used in many law schools and in education schools throughout the country – was used in some MAS classes and would later be fiercely criticized by the state and banned by the district.[66] As we remarked earlier, the ushering in of the Trump administration propelled much of the rest of the country to catch up to circa 2010 Arizona. Thus, it was not surprising when Trump signed a 2020 order banning federal trainings that employed "divisive concepts"[67] that have been associated with Critical Race Theory. This 2020 Executive Order eerily mirrored the actions of Arizona state legislators in 2010, and though the Biden administration quickly rescinded it,[68] Arizona and other state legislators revived aspects of the "divisive concepts" ban, seeking to forbid them in public education.[69]

It may be surprising to some that the creators of the MAS program would use college-level texts because the students who took these classes tended to be the ones who the district gave up on. Their grades prior to taking the MAS courses were extremely low, hovering around a 2.0 GPA.[70] Instead of lowering expectations for these students, the MAS teachers and administrators resisted the urge to make them "remedial classes" and instead challenged the students. Oddly, this became a point of contention for critics of MAS, whether the texts offered were "age appropriate."[71] If texts are good enough for college students, and sometimes graduate students, why is it a problem if high school students also read them? Nowhere did this central question become more contentious than in the incorporation of Paulo Freire into the MAS program.

THE BRAZILIAN BOOGEYMAN: PAULO FREIRE

The use of the work of the Brazilian critical theorist Paulo Freire[72] became one of the greatest points of contention as critics such as Tom Horne continually criticized the use of Freire's work, even mislabeling the classic text *Pedagogy of the Oppressed*[73] as the "pedagogy of oppression" in a public document while also claiming to have read the book.[74] Horne centered a great deal of his criticism of the MAS program around the use of this text, even as he continued to get the title wrong,[75] including in his widely circulated *Open Letter to the Citizens of Tucson*.[76]

For those not familiar with this book, some context is necessary. First, Paulo Freire is largely considered the second-most important educational theorist of the twentieth century behind only John Dewey.[77] His work is centrally concerned with education that supports radical democratic possibilities as well as human freedom.[78] Freire's work is assigned in the most prestigious colleges of education in the US,[79] but it is worth noting that his work can also be very difficult to read because of its abstract nature and sometimes convoluted writing style.

One of the authors of this book, Cabrera, has lectured on the MAS controversy throughout the country. As part of many lectures, he would tell audience members that in some of the MAS courses, high school students would read *Pedagogy of the Oppressed*, which often prompted a collective gasp among many education scholars and students. An audience member once said, "Shoot, I'm a third-year doc student, and I still struggle to get through that book!" The overall point is that the MAS teachers using this text were teaching graduate-school-level texts in a high school class, challenging students to both read and apply the lessons in their everyday lives.[80] This, in-and-of-itself, is a remarkable educational feat that should be commended and replicated – not condemned.

What, then, did Horne find so objectionable in *Pedagogy of the Oppressed*? He continually referred to Freire as a "Brazilian Marxist," an accurate description that Horne thought ought to be the end of the conversation.[81] For him, and a number of MAS critics, simply saying "Marxist" was a sufficient critique, at least for their political base and readership. Interestingly, they were *not* concerned with Freire's radical humanism rooted in his Catholic faith and the teachings of Jesus.[82] A more accurate description of Freire's work is that it is an unusual melding of Karl Marx and Jesus Christ, with all of the strange, sometimes contradictory, beauty that this union produces. Instead, a large part of the attacks on MAS were rooted in a modern-day McCarthyism – a "Brown Scare," if you will – meant to paint those associated with the program as anti-American, subversive, and dangerous.[83] This is not unexpected because the formation of MAS was directly linked to the activism of the 1960s that created the community demands for Ethnic Studies, and those activists in their time were also attacked in similar ways as Communist, subversive, anti-American, and White hating.[84] From this context, those attacking the program continually argued that student achievement was irrelevant in this controversy, and the primary messenger was the office of the State Superintendent of Public Instruction.

STUDENT ACHIEVEMENT DOESN'T MATTER HERE: PROGRAMMATIC EFFICACY AND OFFICIAL DISMISSAL

Jose Gonzalez, an MAS teacher, described what he and his co-teachers attempted: "What our program did, really, was focus on identity and making sure that students' identify was affirmed. If students have a sense of self, who they are, and they're proud of it, then they do well academically."[85] He knew, at least anecdotally, that his students benefited from the program. However, it was strange that given the existence of Ethnic Studies in K-12 educational settings since the late 1960s, there had not been a thorough, robust, statistical analysis of any program's efficacy to date when the TUSD MAS controversy arose. This was, in large part, because Ethnic Studies courses tended to be standalone offerings, not a coordinated department like the one in Tucson. As Christine Sleeter demonstrated in her review of the literature on the impacts of Ethnic Studies courses, "Only one school district – Tucson Unified Public Schools – has a full-fledged ethnic studies program" and it was eliminated shortly after her review was released.[86] Thus, it makes sense that there was a severe lack of evidence around Ethnic Studies programs because there was concurrently a severe lack of these programs in existence. That said, there is another layer to this issue. Prior to the elimination of the TUSD MAS program in 2010, Dean Ronald Marx, and Associate Dean Jeffrey Milem from the University of Arizona College of Education made an offer to TUSD Superintendent John Pedicone. They would conduct the statistical analyses of the MAS program free of charge. All Dr. Pedicone had to do was agree to release the data. He refused.

Up to this point, there had been several analyses of the TUSD program that pointed to the program's efficacy.[87] However, the statistics provided were descriptive in nature and not capable of actually determining, quantifiably, the program's impact on students who took it. For example, when it was repeatedly shown using descriptive statistics that MAS students passed state standardized tests and graduated at higher rates than their peers,[88] critics of the program would offer questions such as:

- While the students in the MAS program tend to be low-income Mexican Americans, how do we know that the teachers and administrators didn't simply find the best performing students in this demographic and push them to take these courses?
- We know that female students tend to perform better academically than male students. How do we know that the teachers and administrators didn't simply recruit more female students into these classes and that accounts for these results?

From a scholarly perspective, these questions are important and relevant. The difficulty is that they were rarely lodged from a place of concern for rigorous empirical analyses. Rather, they were meant to shut down the debate about programmatic efficacy, even as they raised legitimate points.

Additionally, there was a major political hurdle in this debate about programmatic efficacy. Tom Horne was clear that he thought the possibility that MAS might raise student achievement, in particular for low-income Mexican American students, was *irrelevant*. Specifically, he said the following in the documentary *Precious Knowledge*: "There are better ways to get students to perform academically and wanting them to go into college than trying to infuse them with racial ideas."[89]

He added later: "And, uh, anybody who says kids can't learn unless they're subject (sic) to that kind of militancy is … is … uh … the clearest example of racism that I can think of."[90]

In both quotations, Horne primarily focused on the "radical ideas" in the course that he found objectionable, and he dismissed educational achievement. He went so far as to say that if people believed MAS was the way to educate Mexican American students, this was itself a form of racism.

A consummate politician, Horne wanted the issue of educational achievement out of the MAS debate. The optics are terrible when a State Superintendent of Public Instruction continues to publicly state that educational achievement is irrelevant within an educational controversy. Attempting to bolster his position, Horne commissioned a fatally flawed study that showed no beneficial effect of taking MAS courses,[91] but this was almost an afterthought for him in the debate about MAS. Leading up to the eventual elimination of the classes, more analyses questioning the efficacy of MAS began to emerge. For example, TUSD released a descriptive report whose author argued that the effects of taking MAS classes were the same as participating in extra-curricular activities such as sports or student government.[92]

The timing of this report being conducted and released was curious because it coincided with increased political pressure on TUSD and a hearing before an administrative law judge (ALJ) in which TUSD was claiming that it was not in violation of HB 2281 and therefore should not lose 10 percent of its funding. That is, the very people tasked with defending the program and local control against the racist attacks of the state – TUSD Superintendent Pedicone and data manager/analyst David Scott – were actively participating in undermining the program by undercutting arguments regarding its efficacy. An interesting point about their analysis was that it was also descriptive in nature and, therefore, not capable of assessing impact. This became the larger context for the definitive analysis on the MAS program's educational efficacy, which became the basis for Nolan Cabrera's expert testimony in the federal trial, which we examine in detail in Chapter 11. But at this stage of the story, the overall point is that what ought to have been at the center of this issue – educational opportunities for Mexican American students – was continually dismissed as irrelevant.

RESISTANCE IS IN OUR DNA

Even though the question of programmatic efficacy remained unresolved, students, teachers, and community activists knew there was something special about the MAS program. It was worth fighting for. People in the community were beginning to realize that the classes were not simply facts and trivia, but as what MAS teacher Curtis Acosta refers to as Quetzalcoatl, *precious and beautiful knowledge*.[93] The state's attacks were more than simply the elimination of a set of courses, but rather, criminalizing and erasing community-based knowledge.[94]

Despite the incredible odds against the people of Tucson, the power and resources of the state of Arizona demanding the classes be eliminated – people in the community were not going to simply accept this edict. Instead, they organized.

While the Chicano blowouts in 1960s Los Angeles received the bulk of the historical attention,[95] similar blowouts occurred in Tucson during that time as well.[96] The demands were similar, and the spirit of activism and resistance lives on in the Old Pueblo to this day. Part of the reason for this is that Tucson is small, for a city, and historical memory persists. While this means that people in Tucson are frequently closely connected, it also means that grievances that went unaddressed during this organizing persist to this day like open wounds. Historically, this has been part of radical coalition politics for decades.[97] Despite these tensions, internal issues, and a repressive state demanding the elimination of the program, people resisted. Despite the divides in the community, people showed up at local rallies to support MAS and shouted, in unison, "When our education's under attack, what do we do? Stand up, fight back!!!"

But when Brown people assert themselves, when they speak and demand justice, when they stop knowing their place, it can give a fright to those who had become comfortable with, and benefit from, the status quo.

2

The Brown Scare

> If you're pro-Chicano, you're perceived to be and labeled anti-gringo. Don't fall for this trick of gringo verbal jujitsu being labeled a reverse racist. Being proud of your heritage, your identity, your persona, is very natural and expected.
>
> José Angel Gutiérrez, *A Gringo Manual on How to Handle Mexicans*

In 1995, the late Derrick Bell delivered a lecture entitled, "Who's Afraid of Critical Race Theory?"[1] Bell wrote this during a period when Critical Race Theory (CRT), which emerged in the legal academy, had come under attack by critics. He framed the attack on CRT by noting that "[m]ost of the many race riots [when white people attacked black people, black businesses, and black homes] in this nation's history were sparked by white outrage over black success."[2] Implicit in this framing is that the attack on CRT during this period was motivated, in no small part, by jealousy among certain legal academics that coveted space in prestigious law journals was going to minority scholars writing on race and, in some instances, that certain elite law schools were hiring these same minority scholars. It is no coincidence that one of the leading critiques of CRT was executed by a Black scholar at Harvard Law School, "whose blackness lends his critique a super legitimacy inversely proportional to the illegitimacy bequeathed to critical race theory."[3] As will be seen later, regardless of the sincerity of the critique, conservatives will seek and amplify the voices of minorities who will do their bidding.

This attack on CRT in the 1990s, which took place mostly on the pages of law journals and in faculty hiring and tenure decisions, bears little resemblance to the attacks on CRT in the latest culture wars. The current attacks on CRT, as well as on feminist, gender, and queer studies, are primarily focused on K-12 education, and on public school teachers, who are far more vulnerable than law professors. Today, uncertainty about what they are permitted to say in the classroom as well as clear directives from state officials have educators censoring themselves. An example of the absurdity created by this uncertainty can be seen in a Zoom™ meeting when an Iowa school superintendent said, "'I don't know' if teachers can say 'slavery was wrong.'"[4] The current attacks are driven by fear fomented by conservative politicians, amplified by conservative media, and this same playbook was developed and implemented to attack MAS.

Politicians in Arizona successfully fomented fear of the *other* in the form of "dangerous immigrants" crossing the border and those "already in our midst."[5] Summer 2010 saw the passage of Arizona's SB 1070, the notorious "show your papers" law, one of the most draconian laws directed against migrants, which fostered copycat legislation in a number of other states.[6] Summer 2010 also brought HB 2281, codified as Arizona Revised Statutes (A.R.S.) §15-112, which was used to eliminate the MAS in the TUSD.

Spearheaded by then Superintendent of Public Instruction, Tom Horne, HB 2281 allowed the state to withhold 10 percent of its funding to any school district having a course or class that:

1. Promote the overthrow of the United States government,
2. Promote resentment toward a race or class of people,
3. Are designed primarily for pupils of a particular ethnic group, or
4. Advocate ethnic solidarity instead of the treatment of pupils as individuals.[7]

This was Horne's third attempt to pass the bill, and he was very direct that he intended this piece of legislation to eliminate the MAS program in TUSD. His first failed attempt occurred in 2008 when he attached this language as an amendment to Arizona Senate Bill 1108 – a *Homeland Security Bill*.[8] That is not a typo. Horne cast MAS as the kind of threat that was appropriate to address in a Homeland Security bill.

What was so scary and threatening about these classes that led the Arizona elected officials to pass HB 2281 which would lead to the eventual outlawing of MAS in Tucson? More importantly, how did a small group of teachers, students, community members, scholars, and lawyers successfully challenge this state-sponsored racism? These are the two questions guiding this book, which lead to some very complicated and important answers given the contemporary renaissance of Ethnic Studies in K-12 education.

Some may ask if it is appropriate to refer to this legislation as "state-sponsored racism." After all, how could it *not* be in the interest of the state to outlaw classes that "promote the overthrow of the U.S. government"? Would it not be important to sanction districts with classes that "promote resentment toward a race or class of people"? In the abstract, the answer may appear to be yes, but, in practice, the banned concepts and practices in HB 2281 were so ambiguous that the Superintendent of Public Instruction could enforce them in any way they wanted, including in a racially discriminatory manner. After seven years of litigation and more than a decade of controversy, federal Judge A. Wallace Tashima ruled that racism and partisan politics were at the core of creating and implementing the law. This is the story of both the creation of this racist law and the collective resistance that helped lead to the federal ruling. What unfolded was the highest profile Ethnic Studies case in US history.

This protracted fight, however, began with the creation of the MAS boogeyman, much like the contemporary CRT boogeyman.[9] That is, in order to develop mass opposition to the program, there had to be a strong misinformation campaign. To do this, the MAS opponents engaged in a protracted propaganda effort in what Herman and Chomsky refer to as the *manufacture of consent*.[10] Those demonizing the program knew they had to win in both the court of public opinion and legislative spheres – understanding the two are closely related.[11] While the anti-MAS hysteria required the central actors and their supporters to be interconnected, we will describe them separately with the understanding that the narrative and position of one enhances the narrative and position of the others. Also, once HB 2281 became codified as law, the anti-MAS hysteria picked up exponentially, consistent with Ibram X. Kendi's thesis that racist policy fosters racist thought.[12]

As a foundation for these attacks, the anti-MAS forces were given a gift when civil rights icon Dolores Huerta spoke at a Tucson high school.

DOLORES HUERTA COMES TO TUCSON

In 2006, labor leader Dolores Huerta gave a speech at Tucson Magnet High School and offered some thoughts on anti-Latino politics. In late 2005, and in preparation for the 2006 midterm elections, Jim Sensenbrenner, a Republican congressman from Wisconsin, introduced HR 4437 which not only created harsh, draconian penalties for undocumented people nationally but also went so far as to criminalize those who offered humanitarian aid to the undocumented.[13] The bill was intended to serve as a wedge issue, whipping up anti-immigrant sentiment among the Republican base, thereby driving up voter turnout in the midterm elections throughout the country.[14] Commenting on this, Huerta said that because of their legislative agenda, "Republicans hate Latinos."[15] If a group of people is willing to strip another of their humanity to gain a partisan advantage, "hate" seems an appropriate label.

The right flipped this and framed Huerta's remarks as "hate speech."[16] In particular, State Superintendent of Public Instruction Tom Horne was incensed. He sent his deputy secretary, a Latina named Margaret Garcia Dugan, to Tucson to offer a rebuttal at a school assembly. Essentially, her speech argued, "I am an example that Republicans don't hate Latinos." Attendance for students was mandatory, and they were told they would not be permitted to ask questions of the speaker. As Ms. Dugan began speaking, students in the audience revealed white shirts saying, "You can silence my voice but not my spirit." Many also symbolically placed painters' tape across their mouths as a silent protest in response to the lack of any dialogue with Dugan.[17] Eventually, many walked out (see Figure 2.1).

Superintendent Horne's response was swift and bold:

FIGURE 2.1 Silent Protest (© *Arizona Daily Star*)

[A] small group of *La Raza* Studies students treated [Ms. Dugan] rudely, and when the principal asked them to sit down and listen, they defiantly walked out. By contrast, teenage Republicans listened politely when Delores [sic] Huerta told the entire student body that "Republicans hate Latinos." In hundreds of visits to schools, I've never seen students act rudely and in defiance of authority, except in this one unhappy case. I believe the students did not learn this rudeness at home, but from their *Raza* teachers.[18]

Aside from misspelling civil rights icon *Dolores* Huerta's name (he also incorrectly referred to her at times as "Cesar Chavez's girlfriend"),[19] Horne's statement included certain assumptions. How did he know that these students learned to protest and walkout in a MAS classroom or from MAS teachers? In his public statement and many subsequent ones, he repeated this claim, treating it as an article of faith. When asked at trial about this statement, all he would say is that he knew this because of "a year of investigation, extensive investigation" and that he had spoken at schools throughout the state and students were always polite; the only difference was that the Tucson high school had *La Raza* teachers.[20] He offered no details about these later investigations. He also bristled at the suggestion that he had made a race-based assumption, calling such a charge despicable.[21] Exploring Horne's method was particularly interesting because, as previously alluded to, it required manufacturing a MAS political boogeyman.

(MIS)REPRESENTING *RAZA*: TOM HORNE FOMENTS ANTI-BROWN HYSTERIA IN ARIZONA

On June 11, 2007, Tom Horne issued his now infamous *Open Letter to the Citizens of Tucson*. It was an impressive document from a rhetoric standpoint – appealing to mass, largely unconscious racist nativism[22] throughout the state of Arizona. By *racist nativism*, Pérez Huber and her co-authors meant a type of populist isolationism predicated upon a widespread fear of foreigners – in particular Brown foreigners. This kind of "dog-whistle politics"[23] preys upon racism, ignorance, and xenophobia – largely unconscious – lurking just beneath the surface of modern political life. Those in power who stoke these fires give the masses license to express racist nativism more publicly and to act upon it. Within this context, consider how Horne framed his letter. Before identifying the parts of the TUSD MAS program he took issue with, he offered a classic, pre-emptive mechanism to insulate himself from accusations of racism:

> In the summer of 1963, having recently graduated from high school, I participated in the civil rights march on Washington, in which Martin Luther King stated that he wanted his children to be judged by the content of their character rather than the color of their skin. That has been a fundamental principal for me my entire life, and Ethnic Studies teaches the opposite.[24]

Horne recounted his alleged experience and subsequent philosophy in a number of public statements and appearances regarding the MAS controversy, including in his testimony before various legislative committees. His constant invocation of "the March" seemed rooted in his belief that this somehow inoculated him from charges of racism.

A few on the MAS legal team had a betting pool – how early in his testimony Horne would mention that the 1963 March. The three who participated all thought it would take place within the first hour. Robert Chang was the closest, guessing 42 minutes, with Horne announcing proudly around the 45-minute mark that he was at the March where Dr. King gave his famous speech.

Horne, in his repeated invocation of the March, misrepresented Dr. King's legacy to advocate for exclusively color-blind approaches to education. Horne ignored that Dr. King was a strong proponent of race-conscious policies as a means to get to his "dream."[25] Unfortunately, this message has been corrupted in what Cornel West refers to as the "Santa Claus-ification" of Dr. King's message.[26] That is, instead of understanding Dr. King's radical, race-conscious, democratic socialist messaging and activism,[27] people like Horne co-opt this message for their own political gain. This common strategy is employed by commentators such as Coleman Huges,[28] Dinesh D'Souza,[29] and many others on the political right. They claim to be the keepers of the flame of Dr. King's dream that children "will not be judged by the color of their skin but by the content of their character." It is a simple playbook: (1) The masses love the sanitized memory of Dr. King; (2) I take "content of their character" out of context to inaccurately frame Dr. King as colorblind; and (3) I argue my colorblind work is an extension of Dr. King's, ergo I win.

This was consistently on display in Horne's public appearances. For example, on May 13, 2010, Tom Horne debated Georgetown Professor Michael Eric Dyson on CNN's *Anderson Cooper 360*.[30] Horne repeated his standard talking points:

- I marched on Washington and Dr. King was colorblind;
- MAS is a race-obsessed philosophy;
- Students should not be divided by race;
- MAS is Marxist/Leninist;
- Students should be treated as individuals, not exemplars of their race;
- Students should be taught this is the land of opportunity; and
- MAS is a downer.

Dyson, a prolific scholar who actually knows what he's talking about when it comes to Ethnic Studies, argued that this educational approach tells a fuller, more complete history of the US, and yes, it can be a "downer" if we are being honest about it. However, Dyson was clear that race consciousness was required to address racial inequities, while Horne repeated his talking points.

The same dynamic occurred on March 22, 2011, when Horne debated MAS attorney Richard Martinez at the University of Arizona law school.[31] Horne, two minutes into his opening remarks, mentioned the march on Washington, and he relied on his standard anti-MAS litany. At one point, Horne asked who in the audience thought that White people tend to believe their individual accomplishments stem from their own effort independent of historical racial advantage. He appeared startled when a number of people raised their hands. He stumbled and offered, "This is the effect of Ethnic Studies,"[32] and there was uproarious laughter.

In contrast, Richard Martinez, the Tucson native and a lawyer for the plaintiffs in the MAS case, stood up with his trademark flowing white mane of hair, mustache, and nasal voice, and took issue with Horne's view that critiquing the US meant that you hated it. Instead, Martinez offered, "I'm willing to take on the warts of our country. Not for the purposes of tearing down our country, but for the purposes of us moving forward in a more enlightened way."[33] However, as in the debate with Dyson, Horne was not really talking *to* Martinez but instead repeated his attacks on MAS to build his base. This tactic seemed to work, as Horne continued to increase his popularity after his public appearances.

Along the way, Horne found a former TUSD teacher who taught briefly in the MAS program who joined his campaign against MAS. Though Horne professed to be colorblind, he always made it a point to emphasize that this teacher was Hispanic.

JOHN WARD: WHISTLEBLOWER OR DISGRUNTLED EMPLOYEE?

John Ward served briefly as a "teacher of record" and co-taught American History from a Chicano Perspective with Sean Arce at TUSD.[34] Arce noted that this came about because Ward "expressed an interest in wanting to teach Mexican-American

Studies, so [Arce] came in to ... collaborate with him" and to "provide model instruction for John Ward."[35]

Although December 2002 marked his last involvement with *Raza*/MAS at TUSD,[36] Ward penned an op-ed in 2008 in the *Tucson Citizen* entitled, "*Raza* Studies Gives Rise to Racial Hostility."[37] In his approximately 800-word complaint, Ward laid out a series of allegations against the MAS program and its employees. Ward asserted that history wasn't really being taught, and: "[W]here history was missing from the course, it was filled by controversial and biased curriculum. The basic theme of the curriculum was that Mexican-Americans were and continue to be victims of a racist American society driven by the interests of middle and upper-class whites."[38]

Ward's statement ignores the fact that the history of racism against Mexican Americans by White people is historically, sociologically, and educationally established fact.[39] Ward's statement highlights a central tension of the MAS controversy. While many buy into the ideology of the US as the "land of opportunity," this perspective does not reflect the reality of limited social mobility.[40] Though Ward viewed those critically examining anti-Mexican American racism as "biased," his own worldview reflected a different bias that ignored these realities.

Ward railed against the "biases, racism, and American-hating" he saw in the MAS program. He took issue with MAS teachers using Tucson Unified as a source of curricular material. Specifically, they explored the underrepresentation of Brown kids in AP classes, and Ward disagreed with the conclusion that "there are fewer Mexican-Americans in Tucson Magnet High School's advanced placement courses because their 'white teachers' do not believe they are capable and do not want them to get ahead." Given the widespread adoption of "deficit models of education," which blame the marginalized for their subordinate social position,[41] it seems likely that this is an important component of this underrepresentation. However, Ward took any critique of socially structured inequity as an assault on American values and "reason"; this view is consistent with the way MAS opponents construe any acknowledgment and engagement with anti-Mexican American racism and social inequities as akin to hating America and hating White people.

Ward's narrative then turned to his removal from the MAS class. People in his MAS class claimed that Ward was visibly frustrated with the content of the course, and that it hit a boiling point when he cursed at a student and slammed a book during class time. This led to his removal.[42] Ward instead claimed to be a victim because of his views: "When I raised these concerns, I was told that I was a 'racist,' despite being Hispanic. The culmination of my challenge to the department's curriculum was my removal from that particular class."[43] His self-description of being "Hispanic" is telling and betrays the very colorblindness central to the opposition to MAS and to the views of conservatives that invoke Dr. King's dream.[44] Ward cannot simultaneously challenge the importance of "Hispanic" perspectives in the classroom while invoking his own Hispanic-ness as a defense to any charges of racism. His descriptor instead means that race does not matter until, of course, it does.

Ward's narrative was taken up by the conservative right in Tucson and beyond as the gospel truth. It became the center of anti-MAS organizing, and it led to a $1 million lawsuit filed by Ward against MAS affiliates Sean Arce and Jose Gonzalez. Though Ward's lawsuit was dismissed on February 13, 2013,[45] the damage was already done. The lawsuit drained resources and energy from two of MAS's central proponents, and his op-ed served as a rallying cry for MAS critics, including Doug MacEachern.

DOUG MACEACHERN AND THE *ARIZONA REPUBLIC*

Anti-MAS rhetoric fostered by Tom Horne's claim that the classes are un-American reached a fever pitch when a member of the public, John White, tried to bring a large knife to a TUSD board meeting. After first refusing to relinquish the knife to security, he relented and was allowed into the meeting where he was permitted to speak. He "spewed a diatribe of violence on 'La Raza' calling for a civil war and killing, saying things like 'blood will flow and white flags will mean nothing.'"[46] Political rhetoric has tangible consequences.

One of the key people whipping up anti-MAS hysteria was Doug MacEachern and his op-eds in the *Arizona Republic*, the largest circulation paper in the state.

MacEachern had an axe to grind with the MAS program. Truth be told, he had an axe to grind with anything he considered left-of-center politically. However, his work had a substantial impact. It was frequently cited by Tom Horne and was included in the infamous *Open Letter to the Citizens of Tucson*: "After my confrontation with TUSD over ethnic studies had begun, Doug MacEachern, a columnist for the *Arizona Republic*, ran a series of investigative reports on Ethnic Studies. This is the kind of thing that the *Star* and the *Citizen* should do, but thus far only the *Republic* has done."[47]

In a tight, cyclical (mis)information loop, MacEachern reported on Horne's anti-MAS actions and Horne used MacEachern's reporting to continue his attacks on the program. One of MacEachern's key sources was John Ward.

MacEachern published a series of reports on the MAS program in 2008 through 2013. Though styled as investigative reports, MacEachern's reporting expressed contempt for the program and people associated with it. MacEachern portrayed the program as a "bastion of Marxism"[48] and that it was secretive, tribalistic, anti-American, and anti-White.[49] He also claimed that the program made students see themselves as racial victims.[50] MacEachern, like Horne, never attended any MAS classes, and his reporting frequently relied on questionable sources of information. For example, he took aim at the proclaimed educational efficacy of the program.[51] To create his argument, he relied on the head of the Walton Family-purchased (as in Walmart) University of Arkansas Department of Educational Reform for his analysis. We will provide more details on this corporate-controlled, ideologically driven educational department in Chapter 5.

MacEachern used print media to keep anti-MAS hysteria burning throughout the state, frequently fanning the flames.[52] He was joined by Tucson's right-wing morning talk radio host Jon Justice.

JON JUSTICE, *THE TRUTH*, AND ANTI-MAS RADIO COVERAGE

In the Arizona right-wing echo chamber, the truth about MAS did not matter. The attacks were loud, consistent, and forceful. In Tucson, Jon Justice (real name Jon LoGiudice) was a morning right-wing radio host on 104.1 "The Truth," on the air Monday through Friday. Every morning, people heard "The Truth" from a champion of "Justice."

Justice regularly used his platform to attack the MAS program, continually circulating the arguments of people such as Horne and MacEachern, as well as anyone who would forcefully critique the program, such as Tucson right-wing activist/ journalists John and Loretta Hunnicutt of Tucsonans United For Sound Districts (TU4SD).[53] From notoriety gained locally, Loretta would later garner national attention on Glenn Beck's Fox News show in 2011 when she was invited to explore "indoctrination" within TUSD.[54] This illustrates how misinformation about the MAS program rapidly spread throughout right-wing social networks.

Returning to Justice, he was well-known primarily throughout the Tucson area. The *Tucson Weekly* labeled him our "mini-Rush Limbaugh,"[55] and local journalist Stephen Lemons simply called him a "hate-monger."[56] For many people to the right on the political spectrum in Tucson, he represented a voice of truth – a counterbalance if you will – against multicultural progressivism, in general, and against the MAS program in particular.

For several years, at the crack of dawn, Jon Justice would take to the airwaves in Tucson and attack MAS, its supporters, and anyone associated with the program. On January 1, 2012, after the MAS program was found out of compliance with A.R.S. §15-112 in an administrative law hearing, he commented: "Not coming from a racial standpoint at all. [This controversy has] always been about right and wrong. The interesting thing to me, and we'll get into this in-depth on the air, in regards to this judge ruling, and the inching closer to the end of this anti-American propaganda … indoctrination course."[57]

Justice was direct in his assessment that the MAS program amounted to anti-American propaganda in the schools, and that his opposition was not racist. Throughout the several years he spent attacking the program, the evidence he provided to support these claims was scant at best, but his framing of the issue was consistent and impactful.

Within another segment, Justice highlighted his role in the anti-MAS movement as well as the amount of time and effort it took to engage in this protracted legal and culture war:

Look how long it took. That article from John Ward came out, the former teacher, what in 2008? Or was that 2009?…. It was a constant spreading of the truth. It started with John Ward's article, the exposure on my show to a large degree, that other individuals, uh, Lory Hunnicutt and John Hunnicutt … picked up the mantle and did more of the hard work in getting it out there.[58]

Justice and his followers were some of the most stalwart critics and anti-MAS activists in the local community. He was intentional about recruiting more and more people to his cause under the guise of "spreading the truth." That truth, according to the federal trial ruling, was anti-Mexican American racist propaganda.

Ultimately, his sentiments centered the traditional snarky framing where the fight over MAS was a protracted war with winners and losers. He righteously felt that he was on the right side of history and allowed his premature imagination to declare after an administrative law hearing ruled against MAS supporters:

> Plus, the judge ruling against TUSD on the *Raza Studies*. Essentially, it's not over on the court battle, but the judge basically said that TUSD was in violation based off of the former HB 2281. And that, well, they lost in court. So, to those supporters of the *Raza Studies*, and that's what they are – the *Raza Studies*. Um, so sad. We win, you lose![59]

Even though the MAS program had "Mexican American" in its title, Justice preferred to call it the *"Raza"* program. It was a method that allowed him to continually paint the program racist, anti-American, and subversive – not because people knew what *raza* meant, but precisely because they did not.

It is likely that the overwhelming majority of Justice's audience members were not familiar with Vasconcelos' creation of the concept *la raza cosmica* and what it meant in terms of different races coming together in Latin America.[60] We are also pretty sure that neither Justice nor his followers cared about the historical significance of the term in the Chicano Movement of the 1960s.[61] Instead, they tended to follow the Tom Horne line of reasoning: *raza* means "race" and therefore the curriculum is "racist."[62]

While people like Tom Horne and Jon Justice misrepresented the meaning of the term and used it as a form of *dog-whistle politics*[63] to stoke xenophobic and racist fears, we would like to clarify for our readers that *La Raza* is more appropriately translated as "the people" or "the community" and not "the race," even though there has been a massive right-wing push to use the inaccurate definition.[64] Yes, the term *raza* literally means "race," but in use that is not how speakers and listeners understand it. To use an English example of this, let's say that Bob and Nolan approach each other and Bob says, "What's up?" Nolan is *not* going to look toward the sky to determine what is literally up. He understands that Bob is saying, "Hi!" To offer a more Chicano-specific example, saying, "What's up homes?" does not mean someone is calling his friend a house. This seems like an obvious linguistic point, but it was not part of the conversation when opponents of the MAS program equated *raza* with race and therefore racism.

Returning to the context in Tucson, the continual insistence on using *raza* was meant to frame the supporters of the program as different, subversive, anti-American, and even potentially dangerous. Much like Tom Horne's push to frame supporters of MAS as racist, other conservative commentators on a national level such as Fox News' Sean Hannity have done the same to groups such as *La Raza* Lawyers.[65] The argument goes something like this: would we accept a group of White lawyers creating a group called the "Caucasian Lawyers Association"? This game of false equivalences has been a decades-long attack point by right-wing activists in response to anti-racist activism since the 1960s.[66]

RAGE FOR THE MACHINE

US Supreme Court Justice Louis Brandeis famously declared that states are the "laboratories of democracy."[67] Due to the racist and regressive pieces of legislation coming out of Arizona in the early 2010s specifically targeting Brown people,[68] Jon Stewart – formerly of *The Daily Show* – labeled the state the "meth lab of democracy."[69] HB 2281/A.R.S. §15-112 was a central feature of Arizona's early 2010s national black eye.

While we identified Ward, Horne, MacEachern, and Justice as four key players in the creation of anti-MAS hysteria, it took dozens of co-conspirators extensively spreading anti-MAS propaganda to justify creating a law aimed at one educational program in the state. It took thousands upon thousands of people in the mass public believing this propaganda in order for the hysteria to truly take hold.

For example, while Tom Horne may have been one of the early elected representatives to publicly attack and condemn the MAS program, state representative John Huppenthal followed suit shortly thereafter. When Horne moved on from the State Superintendent of Public Instruction to become Attorney General of the state, John Huppenthal rode anti-MAS hysteria into the position Horne vacated. Huppenthal's campaign materials promised that, if elected, he would "stop *la raza*."[70] Let that sink in – the term *La Raza* was so widely misunderstood in Arizona that politicians could openly campaign by demonizing about 30 percent of the state's population. If any modern-day politician openly campaigned that "When elected, I will stop the Blacks" or "When elected, I will stop the Jews," they would have been disqualified from consideration. The anti-Brown and anti-MAS activists effectively used racialized code words to openly use this slogan and gain office.

As previously mentioned, this situation was eerily similar to Ibram Kendi's historical analysis whereby the implementation of racist law leads to an expansion of racist thought.[71] Many think racist laws pass because of the racist thoughts of the masses, but Kendi argues the opposite is true. In Arizona, there were obviously racist rumblings regarding the MAS program prior to HB 2281, but the frequency and intensity of these attacks grew exponentially after the bill's passage. Ironically, Jon Justice even agreed with part of this sentiment, that anti-MAS sentiment grew after the legislation passed. As the controversy progressed, his platform on both the radio and social media recruited more and more people to the anti-MAS collective.

Chicano Studies scholar Otto Santa Ana argued that the anti-Mexican American hysteria of the 1980s and 1990s in California was fostered, in part, because of the mass media's continual usage of the metaphor, "brown-tide rising."[72] In the MAS case, the brown-tide rising was low-income Chicano kids learning about themselves, educationally succeeding, and unabashedly demanding educational self-determination. It also started to become a form of "red-tide rising" as the MAS program was portrayed as a Marxist and anti-American program. In this situation, facts did not matter for opponents of the program. The larger point was that many in the mass populace believed it regardless of accuracy, and this continual feed of misinformation developed into the highest-profile Ethnic Studies case in the history of the country – costing both untold millions of dollars, student educational opportunities, and leaving a deeply wounded and fractured community in its wake.

That fact did not matter in Arizona during this period, foregrounding the challenge that awaits those now combating the anti-CRT hysteria sweeping the nation. Those facing this hysteria will be particularly interested in Chapter 3, which details the myriad ways teachers, students, activists, lawyers, and artists fought back.

3

They Tried to Bury Us, but They Forgot We Were Seeds

Forming the Resistance

In Chapter 2, we explored how a loosely networked group of anti-MAS politicians and media personalities worked to eliminate the program. A similar dynamic occurred in defense of MAS. In describing the resistance, we were reminded of the words of rapper Immortal Technique:

> *[I]t's like the elders told me*
> *No one person can do everything,*
> *but everyone can do something*
> *So we gotta rep …*[1]

The burden of bringing about change does not fall on any one person. If it did, that burden could be crippling and immobilizing. Rather than trying to do everything yourself, Immortal Technique is telling people to do what they can. With regard to defending MAS, sometimes the people were teachers; sometimes they were artists; sometimes they were videographers, lawyers, or organizers. Sometimes they were present to bear witness, hold a protest sign, create a petition, or write letters. Sometimes they took over a meeting room in an act of civil disobedience to prevent a vote from taking place. It took a loosely coordinated, dedicated collective to defend MAS against the state of Arizona.

Though working toward a common goal, people trying to defend MAS were not always in agreement, and strong, internal divisions emerged. In telling this story, our purpose is not to determine and declare who is right and who is wrong. For taking this stance, we have been accused by some in the community of playing the "neutrality card." While we disagree with this label, we understand the analysis and feeling behind it. Instead, we definitely do take a side – the position that the state was both racist and wrong in its banning of MAS, a position supported by a federal court ruling.

We offer this account and encourage readers to grapple with the tensions that emerge in this and subsequent chapters. Where there is genuine disagreement in analyses of a moral course of action, we explore how messy coalition politics is, especially among critically oriented students, teachers, administrators, activists, and artists, who were facing the constant pressure of the state weighing down on their shoulders.

As demonstrated in Chapter 1, Ethnic Studies from its inception was born out of resistance as a form of community self-determination.[2] Thus, when the state and many in the public attacked the MAS program, its teachers, and its students, a small but determined community was prepared to fight back. Immediately after Governor Brewer signed HB 2281 into law, ten MAS teachers and one administrator filed a lawsuit against the state of Arizona challenging the constitutionality of the law. This group would become known as the "Tucson 11," and their work became a focal point for others in the community and throughout the country to join the resistance against this form of state-sanctioned racism.

THE TEACHERS FIGHT BACK

On a sunny day, October 18, 2010, the Tucson 11 made their case collectively and publicly in a press conference announcing their lawsuit against Superintendent Tom Horne and the Arizona Board of Education.[3] Beginning the press conference, held outside his law office in the Old Pueblo, Tucson attorney Richard Martinez – who debated Tom Horne in Chapter 2 and provided legal counsel to the Tucson 11 – attacked what he considered the state's racial animus in singling out MAS. Flanked by the Tucson 11, Martinez sketched the legal arguments. First, he argued that though the law generally forbade the teaching of Ethnic Studies and did not single out any group, Superintendent Horne, in drafting it and lobbying for its passage targeted one group: "It's been aimed at Hispanics, specifically Mexican American Studies."[4] Martinez elaborated that Horne has not gone after other programs: "So, [Tom Horne has] narrowed it down to … Mexicanos who can't learn about their culture, their language, their art, their contributions, their history."[5] Martinez contrasted that with the fact that Native Americans and Asian Americans are still able to learn their histories in their respective TUSD programs, which have not been targeted. This singling out of Mexican Americans, according to Martinez, would be subjected to strict scrutiny, and the state would have to offer a compelling state interest that explains the different treatment of the different groups.

Next, Martinez stated that HB 2281 infringed teachers' First Amendment rights because Horne has stated that certain material, like Rudy Acuña's *Occupied America*, cannot be used, that certain posters of people Horne takes offense to or is controversial cannot be displayed in classrooms, and that teachers can no longer teach their students to think critically and to actively participate in the political process.[6] Martinez went on to cite the academic successes of the program, claiming that the Tucson 11 were "at the forefront of where we need to go in our public schools"[7] in terms of educating Mexican American students and that Tom Horne was standing in the way of that progress.

A reporter asked about TUSD's stated position that it will comply with the law. Martinez quickly retorted that MAS *is* within state law, meaning compliant, but the problem, in his view, was Tom Horne's *interpretation* of the law. Martinez noted that Horne had already announced that on December 31, 2010, he was going to find the program in violation of the law. Martinez additionally noted how this would affect the teachers and administrator of MAS, and that a finding of violation by Horne would effectively kill the program. To prevent that, Martinez said that his clients would be seeking a temporary restraining order or an injunction to prevent the state from enforcing HB 2281 against TUSD.[8]

The Tucson 11 and Martinez were not the only ones to speak at the press conference. Two TUSD MAS and MEChA students, Sylvia and Angelica, spoke passionately about their plans to protest HB 2281 by marching from Palo Verde to Cholla High School. Angelica explained the purpose of the march: "These classes mean this much to us that we're willing to walk in this heat."[9] She and Sylvia called upon all concerned students to join the march scheduled for the following Sunday beginning at 9 a.m. Sylvia added, "Please come and support. These classes mean *everything* thing to me! The space is just … I can't even explain the words. I mean…. The teachers, I love them…. I love these classes."[10] And Angelica added, "What students can say that about their classes? That they willing to [march in the Tucson heat] for them?"[11] That is an excellent question. When was the last time students marched to preserve an Algebra class? More to the point, when was the last time students *had to* march to preserve an Algebra class?

Upon filing the lawsuit, the website "Save Ethnic Studies" was launched so that concerned citizens could stay informed on the developments of the law, MAS, and the court case. There was debate about what to name the website. Some thought that using "Ethnic Studies" would serve as a stronger rallying cry throughout the country. Some thought the specificity of MAS was more important. In the end, Curtis Acosta, who favored "Save Ethnic Studies," decided things because it was his credit card that was used to buy the domain name. It proved to be a smart choice because it helped to broaden the support of MAS from a national, multiethnic coalition of critical educators and activists. Concurrently, a local blog, *The Three Sonorans*, began to be the epicenter of reporting on the MAS controversy.

THE CREATION OF THE *THREE SONORANS*

In March of 2010, University of Arizona math PhD student David Abie Morales began blogging for the *Tucson Citizen*. The online newspaper created space for locals to have their voices heard, and he was concerned about the wave of anti-Brown legislation coming down the pipeline in early 2010. In addition to the proposed ban on MAS, there was also SB 1070, a draconian anti-immigrant bill, and there was a referendum on the November ballot that, if passed, would eliminate affirmative action in the state. "Abie," as he is frequently known in the Old Pueblo, took to the virtual airwaves and started railing against these racist state policies. He arrived at the name the *Three Sonorans* because of the unique geography and culture of the Tucson region. Sonorans refers to (1) people from the state in Mexico just south of Tucson, (2) the desert in which Tucson resides, and (3) the best type of hot dog ever created, the Sonoran Hotdog (bacon-wrapped with beans). All three factors combined to create the inspiration for *Three Sonorans*.

Abie was unapologetic in his approach to the work. He went after everybody, including centrist Democrats. To our readers in blue states who might not be as familiar with this context, an Arizona "Centrist Democrat" is a California Republican. There was a local joke that Congressional Representative Gabrielle Giffords, a member of the Democratic Party, was the best Republican representative southern Arizona has had in a long time. People stopped saying that joke about her after Jared Loughner went on a shooting spree at a local Safeway during a "meet your rep," hitting Representative Giffords in the head, and turning her into a national hero and prominent gun control advocate. We will return to this shooting in Chapter 7 as it also altered the course of the MAS case.

Returning to the *Three Sonorans*, Abie started blogging, but to do this effectively, he attended most rallies, school board meetings, and community events. His grassroots perspective included video recording many of these events. Because of this commitment, he was present during the UNIDOS takeover of the April 26th school board meeting – the catalyst of Chapter 4. His coverage of the incident immediately went viral and was requested nationally by such outlets as *Democracy Now* and the *Huffington Post*. While the *Three Sonorans* was a stalwart in covering the MAS controversy, the events of April 26 launched Abie into the epicenter of the controversy and his coverage kept the MAS controversy relevant well beyond the typical news cycle. Thus, Abie earned his other moniker in the early moments of the MAS controversy: *The Chicano Huffington Post*. Nationally, many read and saw the coverage of the MAS controversy, and this compelled a nation-wide response by activists, artists, authors, and others who like to make good trouble.

NATIONAL RESPONSE: RUDY ACUÑA

Before the eyes of the nation centered on Tucson and everyone began weighing in on the MAS controversy, Chicanos Studies professor at the University of California, Northridge, Dr. Rodolfo Acuña, was already involved. Dr. Acuña was one of the first high-profile advocates of the program and he came to Tucson in June of 2010. A bit of context is necessary here. He is a longtime Chicano rights activist. His book *Occupied America: A History of Chicanos* is a foundational text of Chicana/o Studies currently in its eighth printing, and Dr. Acuña has been developing, studying, and fighting for the discipline since the late 1960s. His text was taught in the MAS classes, singled out by Tom Horne as "divisive," and would later be banned by TUSD from MAS classrooms. Dr. Acuña is an icon in Chicana/o Studies and he was one of the first high-profile academics to oppose HB 2281 because he saw clearly its implications for Ethnic Studies, race relations, and freedom of speech.

In June of 2010, Dr. Acuña came to Tucson in his trademark sunglasses and polo shirt, while the Tucson community members *guayaberas* and floral print, embroidered dresses were on full display.[12] In a backyard with metal folding chairs throughout, the MAS crew and their affiliates congregated to welcome a Chicano Studies *veterano* to Tucson to aid in the fight and provide guidance against the MAS banning. Community members lined up for photo opportunities and to have their copies of *Occupied America* signed. Despite the pomp and circumstance, Dr. Acuña came to Arizona out of solidarity with the Tucson 11, utilizing his decades of expertise in the trenches to strategize how to effectively oppose the state ban. This included him assisting the teachers and *Save Ethnic Studies* in efforts to raise funds to support the litigation. These efforts paid off, and slowly, more and more people started joining the cause both locally and from afar.

AFTER ACUÑA, OTHER ACADEMICS WEIGH IN

After TUSD eliminated the program, many national organizations and high-profile individuals joined in criticizing this state-sponsored repression. Many professional and academic organizations weighed in, passing resolutions condemning what they saw as the targeted outlawing of MAS. In February 2012, after TUSD terminated the program, the American Educational Research Association (AERA), the largest scholarly education association in the world, passed two parallel resolutions in favor of MAS, using its position as expert educational researchers and concerned educators to oppose the suspension of MAS. One was directed to the Arizona state legislature; the other to the TUSD Board. In both, AERA highlighted the vast social science research demonstrating the positive impact of properly implemented Ethnic Studies programs and referred to the state's ban as "educationally indefensible."[13] In the second resolution, AERA urged the TUSD governing board to offer MAS classes in the district and offered the scholarly expertise of its roughly 25,000 members to assist in making this a reality.[14]

Another major scholarly professional organization, the Modern Languages Association (MLA), passed a resolution. While MLA is neither explicitly rooted in Ethnic Studies nor education, it saw the state banning of MAS as a general threat to scholarly work. Its resolution in part offered:

> We see in these actions a threat to academic freedom and intellectual inquiry. To pursue scholarly inquiries into the histories and cultures of the United States, teachers must be free from legislative and judicial interference. Allowing state officials to declare legitimate branches of history and culture out of bounds – to the point of seizing and sequestering books – is inimical to the principles on which the

United States was founded. And to students in the Tucson Unified School District, such actions send a far more chilling message than anything they might find in the books that have been removed from their classrooms.[15]

It argued in no uncertain terms that banning MAS posed a direct threat to academic freedom, and in its view, created far more harm than any of the alleged issues state representatives had with the program.

The National Association of Chicana and Chicano Studies (NACCS), the oldest and largest professional association for studying Chicanx/Mexican American Studies, had a strong vested interest in this case because the Arizona banning of MAS was a direct attack on their area of study. Instead of just passing a resolution, NACCS filed an amicus brief supporting the plaintiffs in the lawsuit challenging the constitutionality of the MAS ban. While NACCS was at the center of the filing, twenty-six other organizations joined as amici, all weighing in on the academic validity of MAS while criticizing the state's ban. These other organizations included the Hispanic Association of Colleges and Universities, the League of United Latin American Citizens, and the American Studies Association. Because their filing an amicus brief was opposed by the state, they had to explain why their views on the state ban would be useful to the court as it made its decision: "[I]t is critical for the Court to hear the views of those who have been researching and writing and teaching students in these fields for more than 40+ years, along with those other groups supporting and or aligned with the protection of civil rights of Mexican-Americans and other racial and ethnic groups."[16]

The implications of the MAS banning were far-reaching. Many academic organizations saw a potential domino effect if Arizona was allowed to ban MAS. In addition, they also saw the local issues as central to their argument – that students in Tucson should have a right to study their culture and history without interference from the state government.

Joining the academics and professional associations, a number of artists weighed in on the controversy. Few were as consistently vocal as Lalo Alcaraz.

LALO WEIGHS IN ON THE MAS BAN

One artist most consistently critical of the state of Arizona and its MAS ban was Lalo Alcaraz. Lalo is the creator of *La Cucaracha*, the only Chicano-oriented nationally syndicated comic strip in the country. Arizona's MAS ban provided a great deal of material for Lalo to work with as he was fiercely critical of the rash of anti-Mexican American pieces of legislation coming out of the state including the anti-immigrant SB 1070. In an interview for this book, he explained why he continually critiqued Arizona in his editorial cartoons and comic strip: "It was personal for me on a number of levels.... I had been in Tucson, and I had been in Phoenix. I've spoken a lot in Arizona, and I knew what the environment felt like, and it really confirmed all

36 *They Tried to Bury Us, but They Forgot We Were Seeds*

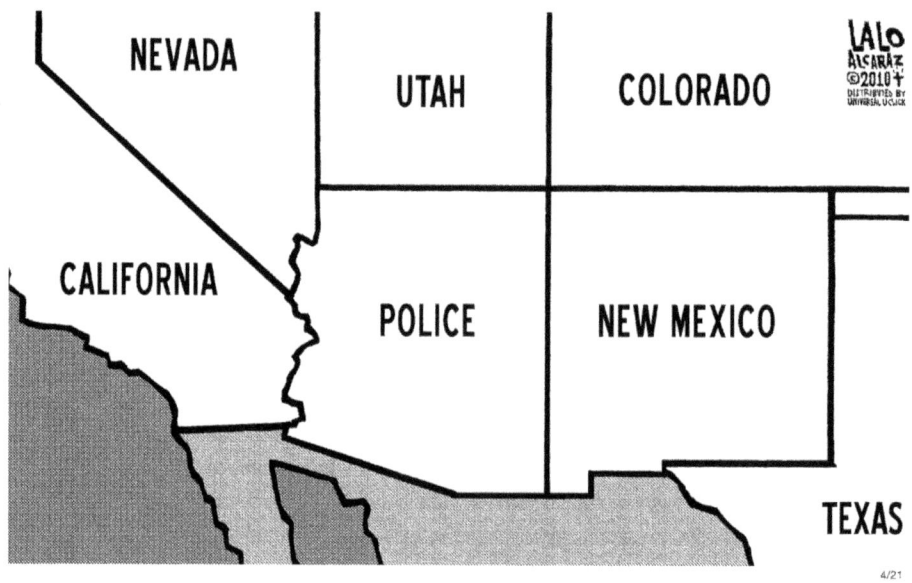

FIGURE 3.1 *Police State* by Lalo Alcaraz/Go Comics

that – that nastiness and racism that's there."[17] He continued that as an artist and author, the banning was particularly personal, but also the racial politics reminded him of the overt racism in California surrounding Prop 187 in 1994. Prop 187 was an anti-Brown immigrant bill that would prevent undocumented persons from accessing public education, non-emergency health care, and other public services. Callously titled "Save Our State," Lalo saw parallels between mid-1990s California and 2010s Arizona and their rampant xenophobia and racist hysteria.

Even though Lalo's work was not banned like some, he empathized and connected with those whose work was. One of his earliest public critiques came in the form of a very simple cartoon where he showed a map of the southwestern United States with the name *Arizona* replaced by *Police*. In particular, he offered that "[w]e're playing wack-a-mole with racism these days, but you've gotta hit the biggest one first."[18] In his mind, Arizona in the early 2010s represented the "biggest one" when it came to state-sanctioned racism, in particular because "it was just so blatant."[19] The not-so-subtle critique was that the crackdown on Brown people, in particular its legalization of racial profiling,[20] amounted to Arizona becoming a police state (see Figure 3.1).

This cartoon was more about the state of Arizona as a whole; however, Lalo also went directly after the MAS banning, and he remained one of the most prominent and consistent national critics of the Arizona legislation. He described his process as, "I am an editorial cartoonist, and I can distill a lot of complicated ideas into direct, blunt images... That's my superpower... I wanted to be as clear and direct as possible!"[21]

FIGURE 3.2 *Ethnic Studies Book Burn* by Lalo Alcaraz/Go Comics

When the actual ban of MAS went into effect, he released the following political cartoon that was both direct and blunt, which became iconic in stature (see Figure 3.2).

This image is so iconic that it serves as this book's cover. He provocatively compared the banning of MAS to book burnings of the past, but the iconography went deeper than that. The law, HB 2281, was seen as the fire that led to the burning of the books – but not just the books. The image evokes the Salem witch trials, drawing a parallel between the MAS ban and a witch hunt. As he described, "Just another day in America, you know, trying to kill off Brown people."[22] Given the scant evidence against the teachers and the district, the metaphor is not far off.

Lalo followed up his *Ethnic Studies Book Burn* image with another very simple yet profound political cartoon that again went after the state as a whole, but very much centered the censoring of Brown folk history. Lalo offered *Arizona Whitewash* (see Figure 3.3).

Within this image, Lalo portrayed the ban on MAS as a literal whitewashing of history. Lalo went directly to the socio-political core of the state, and he argued that the banning was a racist attempt to ban MAS from public education in the state. Lalo may have been one of the most critical, consistent, national voices critiquing HB 2281, but he was not alone.

FIGURE 3.3 *Arizona Whitewash* by Lalo Alcaraz/Go Comics

Many others joined this chorus, and this became increasingly important as the state continually ramped up pressure on TUSD to eliminate the MAS program.

LUIS ALBERTO URREA JOINS IN

As the national reputation of the state of Arizona continued to be tarnished by its combination of rabid anti-immigrant and anti-MAS policies, many authors began to wear it as a badge of honor that their books were banned. That is, if their work was deemed to be offensive by what they perceived as a racist state, they must be doing something right. Luis Alberto Urrea, author of *The Devil's Highway*, became one of the most outspoken writers on the MAS banning. This was, in part, because the banning of MAS led to TUSD banning of his text. In his interview with Bill Moyers, Urrea offered both an impassioned defense of his text and a seething critique of Arizona state policy.[23] His argument stemmed from being ambushed at the Tucson Festival of Books regarding his text where a reporter with no scheduled interview asked him to defend his book because it was being labeled as "anti-American and it had 'devil' in the title."[24]

As a point of context, Urrea's book is his venture into nonfiction where he extensively and heartbreakingly documents the stories of undocumented migrants as they pass through the *devil's highway* – that is, the Sonoran Desert where many people die as they crossed the border seeking a better life in the US. Urrea offered a witty retort to those who thought his book bashed the US, "Anti-American? It's being taught to … to border patrol agents at the academy. So, if it's good enough for the Border Patrol … they're hardly Marxist … invaders."[25] He further elaborated on the title, "And as far as 'devil' in the title, it's on the map. Are you really going to try to change history and remove things you don't like off the map? You can't do that."[26] Through this, he, like Lalo, offered seething social criticism with a twinkle in his eye as he highlighted the absurdity of his work being banned.

The term "book banning" was vehemently rejected by some disregard elected officials. TUSD Superintendent John Pedicone, board member Mark Stegeman, and Superintendent of Public Instruction Tom Horne all denied that there was a book banning in place, with TUSD officials insisting that the books remained available in school libraries.[27] Urrea responded: "They took [the books] out of Brown hands… They took it out of Brown hands… basically… They banned Mexicans. They got rid of Mexican American Studies. All of the books they took away from students, they boxed them away… It's what I call a soft-banning."[28] Urrea would not back down from his public assertion that the Arizona law and the TUSD removal of books amounted to a banning. He did, in the course of the interview, offer a little sympathy for administrators in TUSD because he knew that keeping the books in the classes could mean losing $15 million annually.

Urrea did, however, return to the central issue in the controversy – the effect that the banning had on students in the district. He offered, "It's heartbreaking. They cry."[29] Instead of stopping there, he detailed why Ethnic Studies in general and MAS in particular were vitally important for these students:

> When you come into something like Ethnic Studies or Mexican American Studies, there's a chance you're slightly disenfranchised to begin with. You're in a population that's frowned on by the power structure… You're probably not wealthy. You're often from that 'other side of town' like I was…. And you go to Ethnic Studies that gives you literacy through themes that you understand, and are comfortable with, and it is a gateway.[30]

Urrea continued that if he could have the ear of Governor Brewer, something he acknowledged would never happen, he would argue that Ethnic Studies is a gateway into Americanness. Many Ethnic Studies educators may disagree with this position,[31] and we as authors are sensitive to this issue. Ethnic Studies was created as an educational version of FUBU (For Us, By Us), and it should not need White validation to exist. However, the fight for MAS was waged in the streets, in the courts, in the court of public opinion, and in the classroom. Urrea was speaking to Bill

Moyer's largely White audience and making a compelling case as to why, not only was MAS legitimate education, but why the state was being racist in its banning. His public pronouncement stood in stark contrast to the critics of MAS who continually derided the program as anti-American.

Countless other authors critiqued both the Arizona law and the TUSD banning, and the spotlight on the state's racist policy coupled with TUSD's capitulation was under constant scrutiny. They spoke to numerous audiences, but with the same overall message: (1) MAS is legitimate education and (2) the Arizona/TUSD banning of MAS is unjust. While each individual contribution was important, they are too numerous to recount here. They were invaluable, though, in maintaining pressure on the state and district.

The resistance continued to grow, and Ozomatli added their support.

OZOMATLI: SOCAL ACTIVIST FUNK COMES TO TUCSON

The LA-based, eclectic hip-hop, funk, rock, salsa-inspired, GRAMMY Award-winning band Ozomatli performed at a benefit concert in Tucson.[32] Political activism is central to what the band members stand for as their original name was *"Todos Somos Marcos"* in reference to *Subcomandante Marcos* and the Zapatista uprising in Chiapas, Mexico, circa 1994. As band member Ulises Bella (saxophone/horn player) said in an interview for this book, "[Activism] is kind of engrained in our DNA as a group, trying to use our music and our voices to contribute to something bigger than us."[33] Therefore, it was both welcomed and not surprising that they decided to support the MAS cause. They performed benefit concerts in Arizona due to the intensely anti-immigrant bill SB 1070 as well as the HB 2281 ban on MAS.[34] Ulises elaborated on his outrage about the MAS banning: "Any time people are trying to suppress history and trying to suppress the narratives of people who've been living there forever, I feel it's an attack on reason, an attack on education, an attack on all these values that I feel are important."[35] Thus, Ozomatli opposed this ban and supported the suspended MAS teachers, classes, and students. The concert proceeds went to the group *Save Ethnic Studies*.

It was not just a community fundraiser, but also a community celebration of the *precious knowledge* these classes offered to students – particularly Chicana/o students in Tucson. As Ulises elaborated, "I think music plays a huge role in motivating and inspiring, moving people.... We want to drop our message *and* we wanna make you dance."[36] As the students were the center of the celebration, Ozomatli invited students in the crowd onto the stage and they had a dance party celebrating that which Arizona was trying to ban.

During their set, Ozomatli played a song they frequently play in activist fundraisers, *Cuando Canto*. In this song they offer the following refrain that seemed to perfectly fit the struggle against the Arizona ban on MAS:

Cuando canto mi canción
Quiero inspirar a mi gente con una solución
Cuando despierto en la mañana
Sé que tengo el poder para un día triunfar
Cuando me acuesto en la noche
Puedo mirar a las estrellas que me dan esperanza
Cuando sueño en la madrugada
Ojalá que mi trabajo no sea temporal
Cuando abro mi corazón con mis acciones puedes entender que no soy
    hombre perfecto no soy
Pero trato mucho, trato de decidir lo más mejor para el mundo y lo pongo,
    lo pongo, lo pon en una cancion[*]

The refrain holds so much. First, Ozomatli acknowledges that singing a song does not lead to social transformation. Rather, that their song can help inspire people to do this work. In the same vein, the MAS teachers were planting seeds meant to inspire their students to take intentional action leading to social change. However, Ozomatli also acknowledges that in their activist work, they are imperfect people struggling to do the best for their people. This tension beautifully encompasses the work of the MAS teachers. They, of course, are not perfect people, and despite these limitations, they displayed the courage to develop an innovative and socially transformative way to engage their students. They hoped their work would not be temporary as they dealt with both their idealized vision and their human limitations.

Despite the growing massive popular support for the MAS movement, fractures existed and grew that severely divided the community. We turn now to the most controversial and community-dividing moment of the movement: the documentary *Precious Knowledge*.

THE DOUBLE-EDGED SWORD OF *PRECIOUS KNOWLEDGE*

March 24, 2011, was a watershed moment. On that evening at the historic Fox Theater in downtown Tucson, the documentary *Precious Knowledge* premiered, and it featured an inside look at the classrooms that were under attack from the anti-MAS law.[37] The premiere was sold out with a line up the street, and it was affectionately known to many in the community as "Chican@ prom."[38] Attendees did not mind how stuffy the packed auditorium was as they were entertained by local youth *mariachis* and *ballet folklorico* before the film began. The community

---

[*] The song is beautiful and was meant to be sung/heard in Spanish; however, a rough translation is as follows: When I sing my song/I want to inspire my people with a solution/When I wake up in the morning/I know I have the power to succeed one day/When I lie down at night/I can see stars that give me hope/When I dream in the early morning/I hope that my work is not temporary/When I open my heart through my actions, you can understand that I am not a perfect man, I am not/But I try hard, I try to decide what's best for the world, and I put it, I put it, I put it in a song.

showed up *en masse*, but this was unlike other movie openings because they came to see themselves, their friends, their families, and their school on the big screen. The director, Ari Palos, and producer, Eren McGinnis, gave some opening remarks, and then the lights dimmed. The opening scenes include striking images of the Old Pueblo, both out in the country and cruising through the Southside to the sounds of hip-hop artist Tolteka. There was an indescribable buzz in the air because of the strong connection between people in the audience and the documentary. Even for people who were not in the film, they were seeing a movie about their home area. Periodically, throughout the film you could hear a student shout-whisper "That's my street!"; "That's my school!"; and sometimes, "That's ME!!!" There was a collective joy seeing a community story reaching the big screen and having said community being able to view it together. Of equal importance, the documentary was able to create a public record about the nature of the MAS program, a counternarrative to the propaganda from the state.

The documentary filmed Curtis Acosta's and Jose Gonzalez's classes, and audience members were able to see the way that these master teachers were able to engage their students – especially the students who were continually told by other teachers and the system that they were worthless and just passing through their K-12 years. The images of incredible personal and social transformation had audience members crying throughout the screening. They understood the importance of this work, both for the individual students and the broader community. These images stood in stark contrast to the lies that were being told about the program by people like Tom Horne and John Huppenthal, both of whom were also included in the documentary.

For example, Horne and Huppenthal claimed that a curriculum that critiques racism and helps minoritized students foster a positive sense of self was the "real racism" in the controversy. That makes as much sense as having a doctor diagnose you with cancer and then blaming the doctor for the cancer existing. The documentary showed how these persistent attacks, motivated by a pernicious combination of racism and politics, wore people down and threatened the very existence of the program. Some may wonder how we know that politics and racism drove these critiques. Proving this turned out to be a critical task for the MAS legal team in the federal court litigation. Without giving too much away, the team succeeded and Judge Tashima in the final trial found that a combination of racial animus and partisan politics were central to the attacks on the MAS program. We will return to that in later chapters.

As the screening of *Precious Knowledge* ended, several community members organized talking circles where audience members could debrief and reflect on what they had just seen. There was a collective sigh of relief as people recentered on the critical need to defend the MAS program. Given the barrage of political and racist attacks the Tucson community continued to receive from Horne, Huppenthal, and many others, *Precious Knowledge* was a timely reminder about the importance of the work. It was very easy to become engulfed by the political and racial games, losing sight of the students who should always be at the center of the discussion. This feeling was short-lived as allegations came forth accusing the director of raping one of the former MAS students on the night of the premiere.

* * *

At this point in the story, we as authors and community members have to pump the breaks and walk you, the reader, through a challenge we face in narrating this story. We are not sure what the literary version of breaking the fourth wall is, but that is what we are doing here. We have struggled with how to tell this story, much of which is part of the public record, while also respecting the wishes of the survivor. *Precious Knowledge* was an important component of the evidence presented at the trial, so we cannot tell that story without including the documentary. It was also an important component of the fundraising strategy for the Tucson 11 in their legal challenge to the state law.

We have misgivings, however, about engaging the documentary without mentioning the allegations and subsequent calls for a boycott. Also, the side of the boycott that community members chose resulted in divisions that nearly upended the larger movement. Finally, and most importantly, the survivor has asked to not be mentioned in this book as she believes it is her story to tell, and we respect her wishes by not naming her in this text or detailing specifics. But given the high-profile nature of the allegations, including public accounts by the survivor and a reporter, though her anonymity is impossible, in accord with her wishes, we do not name her here.

* * *

Regardless of one's orientation to the fallout from *Precious Knowledge*, there is general consensus that massive community divisions developed from this controversy. Devon Browne's four-part series on *Medium* entitled *My Other Me* is one of the most extensive explorations of these divisions to date.[39] After the colon, the title read, "A community saves Mexican American Studies. Can Mexican American Studies save a community?" Some interpreted the author's intention – as a reporter far outside of the controversy – that Browne wanted to jumpstart the community healing of some incredibly deep wounds. One person interviewed in the piece, but who requested to be anonymous here, remarked, "That was awfully White of her." That is, what did she expect would come out of her writing? It was informative in terms of setting the community parameters of the controversy, but did she believe that it could help start community healing? Despite this critique, Browne's work documents thoroughly the events and tensions that arose during the MAS controversy, especially the internal community divisions around *Precious Knowledge*.

In contrast, we harbor no illusions that this book will promote community healing. However, this controversy is real and informed many of the dynamics of the overall MAS movement, and we do not know how to tell the story of MAS and the successful legal challenge without including this important issue.

Returning to the specifics of that time, *Precious Knowledge* was already a central feature of the MAS movement, and its role in the national support for MAS would only grow in subsequent months. As the rape allegations surfaced, some community members convened a *tlatocan*, a type of talking circle, to work through the issue. From this convening, the group was unanimous in demanding that the director not film in the community again, but beyond that, the community could not come to a consensus.[40] Some argued that it was necessary to boycott the whole film because the director should not be allowed to profit off alleged rape. The letter making this declaration was never sent because those who were part of the Tucson 11 declined to sign, following the advice of their attorney Richard Martinez, as it might compromise the federal lawsuit challenging the constitutionality of A.R.S. §15-112.[41] Before a community consensus could be reached about a path forward regarding *Precious Knowledge*, UNIDOS members staged the April 26, 2011, takeover of the TUSD board meeting, detailed in Chapter 4. After that point, there was little opportunity for community dialogue. The sides were set and they dug in.

The comedy troupe Culture Clash used to say, "To be 'Chicano' is to be confused and full of rage." Confusion and rage were central components of how people in Tucson dealt with *Precious Knowledge*. In a short amount of time, the Tucson 11 realized that *Precious Knowledge* was a cultural artifact that drew people throughout the country into the struggle around MAS. It was a compelling documentary that helped many outside Tucson understand the social significance of the MAS *movimiento*. Social groups, universities, departments, and school districts were willing to fund members of the Tucson 11 to screen the film and work with people in their locale to develop an MAS-informed pedagogy. It was generally understood among the Tucson 11 that the movie, despite its compromised nature, was one of the most promising avenues to generate enough to fund the legal challenge to the state law used to ban MAS.[42]

As *Precious Knowledge* gained popularity, some in the community felt that there was a culture of silence regarding the rape allegations fostered to "not hurt the movement."[43] All head to work through difficult moral and strategic decisions. For some, it was simple. Anyone who supported the film was essentially supporting rape culture. Either you are on the side of the accused rapist or the survivor. Others disagreed, arguing the movie did not belong to the director and instead belonged to the community. These disagreements ended up becoming deeply personal as friendships of several years began to crumble under the pressure. Regardless of one's stance on *Precious Knowledge*, one issue was clear: the community was fighting the state and itself at the same time.

THE BEGINNING OF THE AFTERMATH

While all this was happening, NACCS again weighed in on the controversy. While NACCS was one of the earliest and strongest advocates in support of the Tucson 11 and against A.R.S. §15-112, its leadership reconsidered their relationship to the movie. In an extended blog post, many members of NACCS offered critical commentaries, beginning with the fact that in their 2011 annual conference, NACCS screened *Precious Knowledge* (AERA did as well). Two years later, the leadership of NACCS was extremely concerned with both the rape allegations and the lack of local response. When they as an organization called for a stronger investigation, they received a letter from the director's lawyer threatening a lawsuit for libel and slander as we will detail further in Chapter 8.[44] This was enough for NACCS to back off formally, but the internal dialogues persisted regarding sexism and the movement. We will elaborate on this issue in Chapter 8. For many, this was simply a replication of the same patriarchal norms that were part of the 1960s Chicano Civil Rights Movement.[45]

In contrast, others thought that the boycott went too far. Under this view, a boycott only made sense if the director of *Precious Knowledge* owns all of the images he captured. Instead, his images were a collective of the efforts of teachers, students, and community, and to cede these images to the director inadvertently means that he owns these parts of the community. Regardless, there were and continue to be passionate and principled arguments, coupled with extreme pain on all sides of this debate. The reputation of the documentary was both tainted locally and renowned nationally. This provoked difficult questions such as: Who owns the images in the film? Does supporting or promoting a film like this mean support of the director? Is any money raised from screening the film forever tainted? How much ownership of the images do the people who are featured in the film retain relative to the director? What other fundraising mechanisms were available for the *Save Ethnic Studies* legal defense fund?[46] Breaking the fourth wall for a second time in this chapter, what would you do?

* * *

Fortunately, the need to fundraise off the film to support the federal lawsuit ended when one of the authors, Robert Chang, joined in 2012 as co-counsel to the plaintiffs in the federal lawsuit. He was able to bring in the resources of the center he directed, the Fred T. Korematsu Center for Law and Equality, then at Seattle University School of Law but now at the University of California, Irvine School of Law, and it brought in additional resources from law firms who joined the case and provided their services pro bono.

But this is getting ahead of ourselves, and before we can turn to the federal lawsuit, the next chapters document the finding by Superintendent Huppenthal that MAS violated the state law, community resistance to efforts to shut down MAS, and the lukewarm defense by TUSD in administrative proceedings to oppose Huppenthal's findings, leading ultimately to the TUSD school board to terminate the program.

4

UNIDOS, the Student Movement, Conspiracy Theories, and Militarized School Board Meetings

In early 2011, the elimination of MAS seemed inevitable. Tom Horne took office as the new Attorney General for the state of Arizona, and John Huppenthal, who had promised to stop *la raza*, took office as the new State Superintendent of Public Instruction. As Tom Horne's last act in office, he issued a finding that TUSD was in violation of all four criteria outlined in A.R.S. §15-112.[1] Oddly, the finding was issued on December 31, 2010, even though the legislation did not go into effect until January 1, 2011. Therefore, all violations alleged by Horne occurred *before* the law went into effect as we previously mentioned. Once Huppenthal was sworn into his new role, one of his first public comments affirmed Horne's findings. Ultimately, Huppenthal chose not to enforce the procedurally defective findings and instead later issued his own finding,[2] something we return to later.

The district stood to lose approximately $15 million annually if Huppenthal's finding held. The under-resourced district, already battling with massive budget shortfalls due to the nationwide recession, found itself under tremendous pressure to eliminate the program. In contrast, a key force supporting MAS was a group of students who named themselves UNIDOS: United Non-Discriminatory Individuals Demanding Our Studies!

THE FORMATION OF UNIDOS

For many in the Tucson community, UNIDOS came out of nowhere. However, it did not spring out of thin air. It was a direct response to the anti-MAS state law, and it was meant to complement the Save Ethnic Studies coalition. Save Ethnic Studies was largely comprised of MAS teachers and an administrator. Future UNIDOS organizers observed this dynamic and said, "teachers couldn't be the only warriors."[3]

UNIDOS grew and developed off this critique – that students needed to also be community warriors – intentionally building in late 2010/early 2011. Taking responsibility for defending their own education, they met on Saturdays in a youth-created, youth-oriented space. They were fascinated by the concept of resistance, and they studied the writings and methods of activists such as the Zapatistas, Black Panthers, and Dr. King.⁴ In particular, they were dedicated to making youth relevant in the MAS debate. As one UNIDOS member described: "The months that followed were spent learning about the dynamics of the public school system and strategies with which we could efficiently combat the impending attacks on our classes. We sought to make the headquarters of Tucson Unified School District a more youth-oriented space where our voices could be heard."⁵

They were sensitive to the fact that teachers, to this point, had largely been carrying the torch, defending the program. They were also critical of the lack of attention and respect youth voices were receiving in this debate. They took up the task of creative reimagination by centering in their activism the issue of what would it take to make 1010 (where TUSD board meetings were held) a more "youth-oriented space."

UNIDOS first announced their presence publicly at a February 8, 2011, press conference held in front of 1010 before a school board meeting. It was a unique press conference, marked by youth culture, as UNIDOS was joined by a DJ, MCs, and live bands.⁶ This then led to their first public engagement with the TUSD Board. Inside the board meeting, they petitioned their elected representatives to meet with them to discuss HB 2281, MAS, and TUSD. Only board members Adelita Grijalva and Judy Burns met with UNIDOS, and they were already the strongest supporters of MAS in that elected body.⁷

A month later, on March 8, "UNIDOS requested a public statement from TUSD that it would protect Mexican American Studies courses. TUSD refused."⁸ Two weeks before the scheduled vote on the Stegeman Resolution, described immediately later, UNIDOS staged a silent protest at a TUSD board meeting by reserving a row of seats and then not sitting in them. The empty seats were meant to represent symbolically the lack of attention that the governing board was giving to student voices and to the data that indicated that taking MAS classes led to greater student achievement.⁹ These events led to April 26, 2011. The protest that took place that day, contrary to popular belief, was the result of months of education, organizing, and building, coupled with the TUSD administration's continued insistence to ignore the youth voice in the MAS controversy.

THE STEGEMAN RESOLUTION: A WATERSHED MOMENT

April 26, 2011, was the date the TUSD Board considered a resolution by board member Mark Stegeman that would make MAS classes no longer count as core graduation requirements. He had many issues with the program including its cost and relatively small size, but the crux of his opposition was what he deemed to be what he viewed as "political bias" in the curriculum. In his resolution to demote the program and move it on the path toward elimination, Stegeman elaborated: "The MAS courses are deliberately founded upon a specific political and educational philosophy. A central component is 'a counter-hegemonic curriculum.' Students who rely on these courses to satisfy core requirements may thus hear, like those who rely on traditional core courses, a relatively narrow range of viewpoints."[10]

Stegeman appeared to believe, unless his statement had a typo, that students in non-MAS courses (traditional core courses) also received a narrow range of viewpoints in their classes. However, he did not seek to demote US History to elective status. Rather, he only targeted MAS courses. Additionally, he publicly argued that he thought the "compromise" of demotion to elective status would alleviate pressure from the state.[11] This statement only makes sense if Stegeman ignored the multiple public statements by Tom Horne that "partial compliance was not possible."[12] It is not clear if his proposal stemmed from a genuine desire to effectuate a compromise or if it reflected political naivete.

Regardless, many in the Tucson community believed that Stegeman would likely be joined by Michael Hicks and Miguel Cuevas in voting to demote the MAS courses to electives.[13] The timing of the Stegeman Resolution was curious because Superintendent Huppenthal's MAS audit was ongoing.[14] Many questions about the MAS program were left unsettled; yet TUSD under the Stegeman Resolution appeared ready to cave to state and public pressure.

As was customary, the TUSD school board was in executive session while the packed room at 1010 was waiting for the public component of the meeting to begin.[15] People overflowed into the lobby; it was truly standing room only. There was tension in the air coupled with notes of resignation as some thought this was the beginning of the end of MAS. The minutes ticked by, and everyone in the audience waited for the school board members to enter the public meeting room. Well, almost everyone. Sitting toward the front of the room, a group, later identified as UNIDOS, stood in unison and made their way to the dais. They speed-walked to the chairs of the individual board members, unveiled chains wrapped around their waists, and padlocked themselves to the chairs. Local attorney and activist Isabel Garcia could be heard telling the security guard who was trying in vain to remove the students, "Don't you hurt our kids!!!"

The students unveiled a banner that read "UNIDOS Presents the Youth Schoolboard" (see Figure 4.1). After being ignored by TUSD leadership for too long, UNIDOS was no longer willing to keep asking and finally demanded that their studies remain intact. UNIDOS members rhythmically pounded their fists against the desk chanting the refrain:

> *Our education's under attack*
> *What do we do?*
> *FIGHT BACK!!*

The powers that be at 1010 were ill-prepared to deal with the takeover, and they scrambled to figure out how to proceed. Those in attendance surrounded the dais as did security guards. People took photographs with their cell phones and called people throughout the community. Local media representatives tried desperately

The Stegeman Resolution: A Watershed Moment 49

FIGURE 4.1 UNIDOS School Board Takeover by Shachaf Polakow

to interview UNIDOS members, asking them what they hoped to accomplish. Meanwhile, the TUSD school board members and superintendent had left the room and were in a closed session trying to figure out how to proceed with the meeting, or even if they could. TUSD security was searching in vain to find bolt cutters. The room became stiflingly hot as everyone waited for the TUSD Board to return.

Superintendent Pedicone, along with board members Michael Hicks, Adelita Grijalva, and the Judy Burns, emerged from executive session and tried to address the crowd. Grijalva and Burns – two of the strongest advocates for the MAS program – spent time with the students at the dais, hearing what they had to say. Board members Stegeman and Cuevas refused to leave the executive chambers. While everyone was waiting for the TUSD Board to decide its course of action, UNIDOS students read, using a bullhorn, a prepared statement about their reasons for the takeover as well as their demands. They unveiled a Ten Point Resolution detailing their demands that included a repeal of HB 2281, an end to TUSD school closures that disproportionately affected low-income Mexican American students, a more accountable TUSD school board, and the preservation of the MAS program.[16]

The minutes ticked by. The tension built. There were rumors that Tucson police were gathering outside the building, and no one knew what would happen next. Would the TUSD Board negotiate? Would the police storm the building and remove people by force?

After a great deal of deliberation, the TUSD Board canceled the remainder of the April 26 meeting in order to allow for more community input on the situation.

Additionally, Superintendent Pedicone agreed not to press charges against the UNIDOS activists. There was an uproar as people cheered this decision, which meant MAS would live to see another day. Some MAS supporters left the building, went to their cars, returned with guitars and an accordion, and began playing on the dais in celebration.[17]

Stegeman was unmoved by the protest; instead, it strengthened his resolve to eliminate MAS. He offered, "Protest is an important American tradition and TUSD has no desire to stop it …. TUSD students' participation in tonight's actions could raise doubts about the methods which we use to teach critical thinking."[18] On the one hand, Stegeman said that TUSD respects protest. On the other, when students actually protested, Stegeman saw it as an indictment of MAS.

The board meeting to discuss the Stegeman Resolution was rescheduled to May 5, 2011 – *Cinco de Mayo*!

PUBLIC OUTCRY, INFANTILIZATION OF UNIDOS, AND CONSPIRACY THEORIES

Both locally and nationally, there was strong and widespread condemnation of UNIDOS' takeover of the board meeting. Most of these critiques were predicated on fundamental misunderstandings of the purpose of protest, and even frequently dovetailed into wild conspiracy theories. The *Arizona Republic* ran an editorial entitled, "Who's in Charge at Tucson Unified?"[19] The seething critique called on adults to "reassert themselves" and their authority within TUSD so that there would not be a repeat of, to use their words, "chaotic political theater." Glenn Beck, who at the time hosted one of the most highly rated shows on *Fox News*, took up the issue on a national stage and framed the protest as juvenile rage and sarcastically offered, "surely those kids who were taught to overthrow their government would behave."[20]

Beck was referring to the first section of A.R.S. §15-112 where districts were not allowed to teach "the overthrow of the U.S. government." Beck's response was precisely what the law's authors hoped for. There was no evidence that MAS teachers sought to promote the overthrow of the US government.[21] If we consider A.R.S. §15-112 as a political instead of legal document, this framing makes sense because it is essentially a form of public accusation. It was Tom Horne's way of saying that TUSD MAS was un-American and therefore dangerous. Beck's coverage aligned with this strategy. Horne made an accusation, some students demonstrated, it made a lot of people uncomfortable, and therefore, the program must be guilty of Horne's accusation. Even without evidence, it provided cover to ignore the complaints and demands of the students.

Perhaps the strongest condemnation of the UNIDOS political protest came from within TUSD in the form of an Op-Ed penned by TUSD Superintendent Pedicone.[22] Given Pedicone's position, his views on the controversy held a great deal of weight. He began by stating, "It is fair to say the situation that occurred at last

Tuesday evening's TUSD Governing Board meeting has caused this school district embarrassment."[23] It was clear Pedicone meant the UNIDOS takeover when he used the euphemistic "situation."

Pedicone continued, "My immediate concern focuses on the events that led up to the decision on the part of a number of adults and students who engaged in an action that interfered with the operation of government." This framing of the UNIDOS school board takeover was odd because it was a youth-led action. He elaborated: "Some would have you believe this action was taken by a group of students who just made a plan to express their dissent. That is not accurate. It is clear adults both helped to plan and influence the outcome of that night."[24]

The evidence Pedicone used to support his claim was that the UNIDOS Ten Point Resolution centered around preserving their studies, eliminating what they viewed as a racist state law, while allowing them their basic human rights guaranteed by the United Nations. Pedicone felt this rhetoric was too closely aligned with certain "adults" in the community, such that the students "must" have had their thinking shaped by outside influences. Despite the lack of direct evidence, Pedicone was forceful in his language as he elaborated, "Students have been exploited and are being used as pawns to serve a political agenda."

One common theory about "adult interference" centered around Loretta Hunnicutt's widely circulated story that longtime MAS supporter and University of Arizona Professor Roberto "Cintli" Rodríguez had given orders to students at the April 26 protest.[25] They believed that Dr. Rodríguez was the ringleader directing students where to go and what to do, like an orchestral conductor. Hunnicutt, a founder of TU4SD, Tucsonans United for Sound Districts, a strong vocal anti-MAS group, went so far as to claim this was a form of "child abuse."[26] Truth continued to be stretched during the MAS controversy.

Pedicone continued his attack by framing the Stegeman Resolution as innocuous, "The simple truth is that one board member suggested having a discussion about changing Mexican American courses from being used to satisfy the state requirement for American Government and American History into electives that will continue to be offered."[27] Unfortunately, there was nothing "simple" nor "truthful" about this statement. As we will later show from the UNIDOS narratives, it was clear that the Stegeman Resolution was the first step to programmatic elimination. It was also a key issue because educational inequality along racial lines has persisted for years nationally, and TUSD was no different.[28] The MAS program was one of the few documented cases where low-income students of color were performing on par with, or even better than, their White and more affluent counterparts.[29] However, Pedicone expressed concern that Tucson locals wished to make MAS "a civil rights issue." It seems rather obvious that educational inequality is a civil rights issue, yet Pedicone was particularly critical of those who framed the MAS program as such, going so far as to claim that this "threatens the district and the community."[30]

A key commonality in these critiques, from Beck to Pedicone, was that they described UNIDOS students as "kids" or "children," infantilizing them and dismissing their grievances while simultaneously paving the way for "adults" to reassert their power and authority. It also meant that the "adults" bore no responsibility for April 26, unless they were the "ringleader(s)." The continual dismissal and disregard of the youth voice and the patronizing "father knows best" attitude created the conditions whereby the only remaining option for UNIDOS was an act of civil disobedience. The adults were not culpable; these "kids" were just being petulant. The infantilization of the UNIDOS members was central to the numerous conspiracy theories that followed, and they only made sense in that context. In order for there to be a puppet master, these students had to be easily influenced and incapable of acting on their own.

The ultimate conspiracy theory centered around Ward Churchill.

CONSPIRACY THEORY OF THE DAY: WARD CHURCHILL, UNIDOS, AND MAS

One conspiracy theory advanced by the aforementioned Doug McEachern blamed Ward Churchill, a former Ethnic Studies professor at the University of Colorado, Boulder, as an instigator of the student actions.[31] Churchill made headlines in 2001 with a controversial essay, "'Some Push Back': On the Justice of Roosting Chickens," in which he claimed that the technocrats who were killed in the 9/11 attacks deserved it because they were complicit in US neo-imperialist foreign policy. He went so far as to call them "little Eichmanns," a reference to Adolf Eichmann, who coordinated much of the Nazi logistics that created the Holocaust.[32] Churchill is definitely a controversial figure, and he happened to be present at the April 26 board meeting.

MAS opponents demanded to know what he was doing in Tucson on April 26. Churchill's presence gained national attention when Glenn Beck did a *Fox News* segment on it.[33] Beck began by drumming up fear that MAS was centered on "social justice" (he used air quotes) and Marxism while centering race in the curriculum. He then told his audience, "America, gotta wake up pretty quickly." This led to his description of the events on April 26. He repeated the conspiracy theory that UA professor Dr. Roberto "Cintli" Rodríguez coached the students before and during the protest and essentially orchestrated the UNIDOS takeover. He took the theory one step further and said that the students were also coached by local community organizers. The term "community organizer" was an important way that Beck framed the issue because it was also one that right-wing critics of President Obama used. It was meant as a way to paint Obama as a radical socialist and anti-American.[34] Beck used the same term to frame the imaginary help the UNIDOS organizers received. He then seized upon Churchill's presence at the board meeting to suggest that he was orchestrating things, saying: "Now, imagine this guy is rounding up little troops in high school. Where's the outrage? Where is it?"[35]

Beck provided an overview of Churchill's previous controversies, showed him at the UNIDOS takeover, and asked, "What's he doing in Tucson? Probably looking for a job."[36] Beck in typical fashion did not explicitly come out and say that Churchill organized the UNIDOS protest. Rather, Beck was just "asking questions," the strong implication being that Churchill was involved in the incident.

MacEachern, whose *Arizona Republic* op-eds we detailed in Chapter 2, demanded to know from Churchill what he was doing in Tucson. MacEachern refused to accept Churchill's responses, as MacEachern sought to connect him with David Morales of the *Three Sonorans*, "Cintli" Rodríguez, and TUSD contacts such as Sean Arce and Auggie Romero.[37] Despite Churchill's denials, MacEachern persisted.[38]

A number of reasons undercut the notion that Churchill was behind the student protest. It is not apparent what MAS proponents would gain by working with Churchill, who is a lightning rod of sorts given his controversial past. The MAS program at this point was hanging on by a thread. The people associated with the program were constantly being accused of being radicals, intent on indoctrinating young minds to their way of thinking.[39] Involving Churchill would have been political suicide for MAS. It was unlikely that a supporter like Dr. Rodríguez and MAS teachers/administrators like Arce and Romero would risk this. This did not deter MacEachern from continuing with his wild speculation. Perhaps most troubling, but not surprising, is that these false conspiracy theories persisted well beyond the aftermath of the April 26 meeting, including in testimony Superintendent Pedicone would give months later during the administrative law hearings.

ASKING UNIDOS: WHY THE STUDENTS ACTUALLY DID IT

A simple method would have helped answer the questions people had about the takeover: asking and listening to understand the views of UNIDOS student organizers. Within Critical Race Theory, a central focus is the power of narrative, especially whose narrative is accepted as the "official story."[40] While there is power in the dominant story, there is also power in counternarratives, which can serve to destabilize the official story.[41] Regarding the student takeover of the school board meeting, the official narrative was clear: these students were acting immaturely, they were likely manipulated by leftists with a radical agenda, and adults need to reassert their authority.

Noticeably absent from these discussions was UNIDOS, and their narratives serve to forcefully destabilize the official narrative. In contrast to the media portrayals of the event, the UNIDOS organizers were very intentional and thoughtful in why they took the dramatic steps of taking over the school board. Theirs was a straightforward calculation. Arizona has open meeting laws, and to pass any resolution, there must be a meeting. If the students took over the room, there could not be a meeting. If there was no meeting, there could be no vote and MAS would live to see another day. Their reasons for taking action were thoughtful and nuanced. First, the students understood that the proposed change, making MAS courses electives instead of core courses, meant that MAS courses would no longer satisfy language arts, history, and government graduation requirements and endangered the long-term viability of the MAS program. As one UNIDOS member elaborated: "If this bill were passed it would dismantle the MAS program in high schools by not allowing them to count as core classes. It was purposed that making them electives was a good idea, but it's not. What student wants to take two history classes and do double the work? It's too much for students."[42]

In other words, if MAS courses were changed to electives, a student wanting to take these courses would have to double up and take the required core course necessary to graduate along with MAS. This is especially important in the context of MAS because the students who took the courses tended to be extremely low-performing *prior* to taking them.[43] This also meant, in part, that many of them may not have wanted to take a non-MAS English course as well as an MAS English course, or a non-MAS History course with an MAS History course. If the resolution passed, students struggling to graduate were likely to focus on taking and passing courses that gave them the core credits they needed to graduate. UNIDOS understood that the Stegeman Resolution had the outward appearance of being supportive of MAS because the courses would remain; they also understood that it was intended to kill the program by drawing students away from MAS.

Both Stegeman and Pedicone publicly insisted that this policy change was *not* the first step to programmatic elimination, but they also never offered why they thought students would keep taking these courses if they did not count as core credit. Their silence on the issue led many in the community, UNIDOS included, to conclude that Stegeman and Pedicone knew it would lead to the death of MAS.

Additionally, UNIDOS and many students throughout the district were upset that their voices were not being heard. This was another central issue that led to the April 26 takeover. When the "adults" in the community refused to take the youth voice seriously, the UNIDOS organizers felt they needed to more proactively assert themselves into the discussion. As one explained:

> I hoped that the school board would stop ignoring us and stop treating us as if issues discussed in school board meetings were not of our concern and should be left up to the "adults" to handle. In fact, every decision made in that room is of huge concern for us as students. I also hoped to make them realize we're not just kids hollering outside buildings for the heck of it. When we say we're defending our classes, we mean business.[44]

UNIDOS organizers framed the MAS controversy as being a "huge concern" for students. This seems obvious and begs the larger question as to why more students were not involved in this decision-making process. This was a consistent critique of how Stegeman decided to offer his resolution. An MAS student, Angelica Peñaran, told him directly that he was not listening to the youth voice. Stegeman tried to reframe the issue:

STEGEMAN: Well, I think we are listening ... We're listening to a very wide range of opinions.
PEÑARAN: But we should be the most important opinion. It's our education.[45]

In one simple and profound statement, Peñaran hit on this key issue. It is the students' education. Why are they not meaningfully at the table? Why should the actions of legislators in Phoenix, following the lead of then-Superintendent Horne and then-Senator Huppenthal, trump the educational needs of Mexican American students in Tucson?

For the UNIDOS activists, the elimination of MAS was about more than simply having particular classes eliminated. Instead, many described the MAS academic endeavors as providing opportunities for self-discovery and self-affirmation. It was one of the first times they were able to learn their true history as Mexican Americans in the borderlands, which led to the following question: What lengths and risks they were willing to incur for the possibility of MAS surviving? One offered:

> We felt that if we didn't do something [on April 26], then our history would be erased. This action was needed to stop the vote and to save our roots from being slashed away. We knew what this action entailed when we decided to go through with it. Arrest was definitely something we knew could happen, but we felt this action was needed. If we didn't stand up for what we believed in, then who would? Our job as citizens is to stop unjust laws or be pushed around unjustly. And we chose to take a stand no matter the consequences.[46]

It was very telling in this quotation that the UNIDOS member not only argued the action was needed but also acknowledged that there would likely be negative repercussions, including possible arrest. They understood that they could be endangering their futures by doing this. Some UNIDOS members were still in high school, applying to college. This mark on their permanent records could adversely affect their long-term goals. Despite this, they were willing to take the risk. As one UNIDOS member said while also critiquing what they saw as the hypocrisy of many adults in the community:

> You have education figures telling students to take charge and become active for their education, to be heard and create change. Then you have youth and community alike act in civil and responsible ways for over a year and still be ignored. Then to have those same figures become angry with the youth for standing up and taking radical action that was youth led, youth empowered, youth organized, is absurd. Not only was [April 26] worth it, it was necessary![47]

The UNIDOS organizer was very direct. Despite the possible repercussions, the takeover was absolutely worth it. Again, in UNIDOS' understanding, the real issue that led to the takeover was the adults in the community continually ignoring the youth voice. The UNIDOS organizer highlighted the hypocrisy of educators continually telling students to be more civically engaged and promote social change; yet when UNIDOS did precisely this, they were ridiculed and infantilized. This attitude was embodied by Stegeman's statement discussed earlier that he was "all for protest," just not this protest.

One of the UNIDOS organizers discussed how, despite nerves, the protesters executed their plan and allowed MAS to exist for one more day:

> [I felt] a mixture of emotions: anxious, nervous, scared, but very hopeful. The reason for this was because everyone up there was risking something. I for example didn't know the reaction my parents would have after they found out; that was scary. The overall experience was all of the above because that moment was do-or-die. Without our actions, the right to our history would be taken.[48]

Again, this organizer was driven by the idea that they did not want their history, or *precious knowledge*, to be removed from the schools and community. To ensure this did not happen, they put themselves at risk – not only legally, but with their parents as well. Despite the fear and anxiety, the UNIDOS organizer remained hopeful. They knew what was at stake, took bold action, and were willing to suffer the consequences to preserve their studies.

MAY 3: SCHOOL BOARD MILITARIZATION BEGINS

It was patently obvious that the TUSD school board and the Tucson Police Department (TPD) did not intend to take seriously the protest actions of April 26. Or rather, they took the protest seriously but disregarded its message. The TUSD and TPD response was to hold a forum at Sunnyside High School. Approximately 300 youth showed up to hear Pedicone lecture them, critiquing the UNIDOS takeover saying, "This type of behavior will not be tolerated."[49] Then Sunnyside Superintendent Manuel Isquierdo chimed in, "The answer is not to chain yourself to a board chair."[50] TPD Chief Roberto Villaseñor also spoke at the meeting and was equally dismissive of the protest, offering, "Some people who protest want to be arrested to make a point."[51] The biting irony of the event was that, in response to UNIDOS students calling for an increased youth voice in the MAS controversy, representatives from TUSD, Sunnyside, and TPD thought it would be a good idea to lecture – to talk *at* – students instead of engaging with them.

In a similar vein, Stegeman penned an open letter that continued his line of argument that he was "all for free speech" just not the UNIDOS version: "I appreciate the sincere passion that many students feel for the Mexican-American Studies (MAS) courses and know the frustration that something which one treasures could change. What occurred on Tuesday, however, went well beyond the exercise of free and passionate speech: the students shut down an elected body by force."[52]

Again, he showed that he could not differentiate between a peaceful act of civil disobedience – one that had potentially dire consequences as the UNIDOS organizers knew – and an act of overt violence. Stegeman was unwilling or unable to understand UNIDOS' message or method. Instead, it was easier to vilify them in the press and move forward with his ill-advised resolution. Despite these efforts to stifle student voices, the UNIDOS protest set off a spark in the community that reignited the energy to defend MAS against the state law.

Realizing the terrible optics if it were to eliminate MAS on *Cinco de Mayo*, the district administration rescheduled the vote for May 3. As there was massive attendance at the April 26 meeting, some community members suggested that the new meeting be moved to a larger venue like Catalina Magnet High School to accommodate a likely even larger crowd.[53] This request was denied, in part, because TUSD administration was concerned about security at an even larger venue, considering how the previous meeting went.

So, the new meeting was set again for 1010, and the line was around the building hours before the meeting was going to begin. Concerned community members were willing to wait in line in 103-degree heat for the possibility of attending this school board meeting. Attendance estimates varied, but they consistently put the crowd seeking entry at over 500 when the meeting room and lobby had a *combined* capacity of 185.[54] The Tucson community seemed galvanized by UNIDOS' civil disobedience at the previous board meeting. More people showed up to have their voices heard. Members of the clergy were also present, arriving at noon to 1010, speaking in front of a banner of *La Virgen de Guadalupe*, and urging the TUSD Board to reject the Stegeman Resolution. The use of this iconography carried echoes of its use during the farmworker strikes of the Civil Rights Movement. They left an altar in front of the building, which the police removed around 3:00 p.m. citing it as a "security threat."

A major difference, however, between this meeting and the one of April 26 was the presence of over 100 police officers, many in riot gear, along with police dogs and a police helicopter.[55] MAS supporters were repeatedly told that the police were "Here for your protection." This statement became questionable as the events of May 3 unfolded. As people waited for TUSD to open the meeting to public, they saw the dogs, the helicopter, and officers on the rooftops whose role was unclear. There were also several plainclothes officers circulating throughout the crowd. They were particularly interested in monitoring UNIDOS. UNIDOS had a table set up outside of 1010 and several news agencies were trying to interview them and get their views on the meeting and the MAS controversy. One plainclothes officer was surveilling these interactions holding a clipboard with information on individual UNIDOS members. Additionally, some of the officers were interviewing students "as part of an investigation that could lead to criminal prosecution."[56]

At approximately 5:30 p.m., the doors opened and new security measures required attendees to proceed single-file and submit to metal-detector security wands, pat

FIGURE 4.2 "Batkid" Being Wanded Entering 1010 by Lupita Blancarte

downs, and bag inspections. Despite the extreme heat, people were not allowed to bring water into the meeting. Again, the rationale for this was "for your protection," which may have been a euphemism for "preemptively trying to stop a protest." One iconic image that got widespread attention on social media is of a child being wanded for contraband by the police before being permitted entry (see Figure 4.2).

TUSD also blocked off the front row seats in the meeting room, claiming they were reserved to allow employees to attend this meeting that was relevant to their work. It seemed like a further attempt to limit the number of people who could attend the meeting and thereby reducing the possibility of another protest.

As the meeting commenced, most of the people who tried to gain entry had to listen to the proceedings through speakers outside the building; roughly 80 percent of the people who waited in line could not get inside, including the TUSD teachers' union president. Superintendent Pedicone's quick appearance at the dais was greeted by chants of "Shame one you Dr. Pedicone. We aren't cattle!" During the meeting, there was the traditional call to the audience where community members had the opportunity to speak, and almost all used this as an opportunity to voice support for the program. One speaker, community elder Dr. Raquel Rubio-Goldsmith, reminded the board of their place in the larger history of the community: "I have been through many superintendents, many administrators, and many boards. And you will be gone, and we will be here."[57] There was a roar from the audience as she returned to her seat and the next speaker approached the podium.

The audio speakers outside were less-than-effective. Unless board members spoke loudly into their microphones, they could not be heard. Board member Miguel Cuevas, largely seen as the swing vote on this issue, could not be heard outside when he spoke. This did not matter for long because as the board came closer to voting on the Stegeman Resolution, the speaker system stopped working entirely.[58] This required a recess for almost 30 minutes to fix the audio in order to comply with open meeting laws. When the meeting re-convened, tensions continued to rise.

Soon the allocated time for the call to the audience came to an end. As there were dozens of additional people wanting to have their voices heard, Dr. "Cintli" Rodríguez requested that the board add more time and even move beyond the allocated three minutes per speaker to allow for more dialogue.[59] Board President Stegeman began by saying, "It has not been board policy to engage in dialogue," to which many in the audience shouted, "EXACTLY!!!"[60] He eventually denied the request, and many in the audience began shouting, "Shame on you!!"[61] There was a certain irony that Board President Stegeman denied the request for extra time when earlier in the meeting, he lectured at length on the meaning of democracy and the need to listen.[62] Again, it was clear that listening for Stegeman meant listening to *him*.

Some did not take kindly to having the board limit their speaking time. So, community members simply began talking. Dr. Katerina Sinclair stood up from her seat in the audience and approached the podium. She began speaking as the mother of a ninth grader about the need to defend MAS.[63] She said her actions were a type of "filibuster," and in response, the mic at the podium was silenced.[64] Pedicone then told her directly, "I am ordering you to leave now." Though his authority to issue such an order remains unclear, several TPD officers carried it out. One officer forced Dr. Sinclair's hands behind her back, and he removed her, surrounded by five other TPD officers.

As the arrest of Dr. Sinclair was occurring, longtime community activist, 69-year-old Lupe Castillo who walked with two canes, approached the podium and began reading from Dr. King's *A Letter from a Birmingham Jail*. She told them, "This is what you need to hear."[65] As she stood at the podium, Dr. Stegeman hit the gavel signaling a recess and he ordered police to clear the room.[66] As with Pedicone, it was unclear what authority Dr. Stegeman had to give such an order to the police, but again, TPD complied. The board members filed into the executive chambers as riot police entered the room from the back. In a moment of extreme irony, six TPD officers, three in riot gear, arrested Castillo as she continued reading from *A Letter from a Birmingham Jail*. As they were taking her out of the meeting, the crowd chanted, "Leave her alone!" The police used the arrest of Castillo to also remove longtime Tucson activists Isabel Garcia and Salomón Baldenegro along with several others.[67] If you remember from Chapter 1, Garcia and Baldenegro were instrumental in the 1960s Tucson walkouts and the formation of MAS at the University of Arizona. History, repeating itself.

One key person thrown out was KOLD cameraperson Edgar Ybarra. There was no explanation for his expulsion, and he was not able to get back in.[68] It was yet another example of the disconnect between the "I value democracy" statements professed by the TUSD Board and TPD, and actions like these that limited the freedom of the press. Dr. Sinclair and six others who spoke out of turn were arrested that evening and charged with misdemeanor criminal trespass.[69] Dr. Sinclair later said, "As a mother of a TUSD student, I have the right to say what I think about my daughter's education.... To arrest a parent for speaking at a public-school board meeting is not viable."[70]

As the arrests continued, audience members could be heard shouting, "WE DEMAND PEDICONE'S RESIGNATION IMMEDIATELY!" This led to several in the crowd chanting, "Pedicone out!" Students in the audience wearing white t-shirts that said, "You can silence my voice but not my spirit," harkening back to the Dugan protest five years earlier, stood on chairs, some with tape over their mouths, raising their fists in opposition to the police repression and board's actions.

After another substantial delay, the board resumed its business and Stegeman went ahead with his resolution despite the strong displays of opposition. He began by reading from his resolution. Chants from outside could be heard at the dais and one audience member stood up and interrupted Dr. Stegeman by stating, "I would like to renew again, that everybody should be allowed the time to speak.... The community wants to speak, so give us the time!"[71] Dr. Pedicone returned to his previous tactic by stating, "Ok, I'm asking you to leave now," and pointed at the Latina speaking. He then said, "Officers, can you please remove this person?" Five TPD officers dressed in riot gear forcibly removed her from the meeting room and later cited her for criminal trespass.[72]

Dr. Stegeman then became visibly upset. He continually pounded his gavel, demanding quiet from the audience but also saying, "We do have freedom of speech here."[73] To this statement, an audience member shouted, "Obviously, we don't!" Dr. Pedicone then intervened and said that the board meeting needed to proceed and that there would be a community forum to further discuss this issue. He then followed up that statement with, "If you cannot control yourselves, we will have to remove you from this room."[74] Stegeman continued to put forth his resolution as unrelenting community members stood up and spoke over him. Pedicone again directed TPD to remove speakers from the room. This pattern continued until seven more community members were arrested.[75]

The chaos inside mirrored the chaos outside as the hundreds of people who could not gain entrance to the meeting formed a human chain around 1010 to prevent TPD from taking those under arrest into holding. This was another tense standoff, and point of full disclosure, Cabrera was part of that human chain after participating in the call to the audience, providing a statistical overview of the MAS student achievement statistics. At one point during the standoff regarding the human chain, a TPD officer standing directly behind him said, "This is bullshit. We should either mace 'em or shoot 'em."[76] This did not sit well with anyone and tensions kept rising as protesters sat, linked arm-in-arm, waiting to see what the police would do.

After about an hour of the standoff, TPD had enough, declared it an unlawful assembly, and began hurling people across the sidewalk breaking up the human chain.[77] It shocked the people in the human chain. As Dr. Andrea Romero, a University of Arizona professor, reported, "We had no warning – nothing from police, like, 'Please move.' … People were being thrown; people were hurt."[78] Meanwhile, negotiations inside of 1010 continued, and eventually the board members opposed to MAS realized that the protesters were not going to go quietly into that good night. They were raging against the potential death of a beloved program. Finally, around 10 p.m., after more arrests and negotiation, Stegeman agreed that the vote on his proposal be delayed.[79]

Protesters were exhausted and some were bloodied due to altercations with the police. Even after the decision to delay vote on the Stegeman Resolution, there was still tension in the air because many thought he wanted the program gone. But it was remarkable how much the community's feelings shifted in a single week. On April 26, there seemed to be an air of inevitability surrounding the elimination of MAS. By May 3, "[r]egardless of the outcome, the actions of UNIDOS serve[d] as continual inspiration throughout the community, as this group of informed, dedicated, insightful, and above all brave students reignited the movement in the fight for ethnic and Mexican American Studies."[80] Their example galvanized the community, and MAS lived, not just another day, but for at least another semester, as the TUSD Board would eventually table the Stegeman Resolution, letting MAS courses continue to count as core credit toward graduation requirements.

But while this was happening in Tucson, back in Phoenix, Huppenthal's independent audit of TUSD's MAS program was wrapping up and would soon release its preliminary findings. We take up the next part of the story in Chapter 5.

5

Was the Fix In?

MAS Goes before an Administrative Law Judge

State Superintendent John Huppenthal was sensitive to the fact that Tom Horne never visited the MAS classes or conducted an audit of the program before finding it out of compliance. Therefore, he and his staff selected Cambium Learning, Inc., to audit the MAS classes to see if violations of A.R.S. §15-112 existed. On May 2, 2011, the external auditor completed its draft report and presented it to staff. The auditor's conclusions, though finding certain curricular shortcomings, found no violations of state law. The final draft was sent to Huppenthal's staff on May 15. This report, as noted by Judge Tashima following the 2017 trial, made three main findings:

(1) The auditors found "no observable evidence was present to indicate that any classroom within Tucson Unified School District is in direct violation of the law" ...;
(2) The auditors found that TUSD's MAS "programs are designed with the intention to improve student achievement," ... [though noting] that "the curriculum auditors did not observe flawless curriculum execution" ...;
(3) The auditors found that "student achievement has occurred" ... and that MAS "is closing the achievement gap."[1]

This is not what Huppenthal expected or wanted. This is not what Huppenthal's staff expected or wanted.

Apparently unwilling to accept these conclusions, Huppenthal then directed his staff and the Arizona Department of Education to undertake their own investigation of TUSD's MAS program. Though it was supposed to be an independent review, just one week after receiving the initial draft report, Huppenthal's leadership team had already concluded, as would be revealed at trial during cross-examination, that the auditor's conclusions were wrong. It ought not to be a surprise, then, that on June 15, 2011, Superintendent Huppenthal issued his findings that TUSD was in violation of A.R.S. §15-112 and ordered TUSD to eliminate the MAS program within 60 days or lose 10 percent of its state funding.

Faced with a loss of up to $15,000,000 in funding, what would the TUSD school board do? Recall that the protests of April 26 and May 3 had reignited community support of MAS and had dramatically altered the political landscape within which the board operated. The community pushback was too much, and the TUSD school board agreed to appeal Huppenthal's ruling through the administrative appeal process. A question arises as to why TUSD chose the administrative appeal route instead of filing a lawsuit in state or federal court.

Administrative proceedings are very different from court proceedings. Typical administrative proceedings involve challenges when a person has been denied benefits or a license or a permit by an administrative agency. For example, if a worker suffers an injury during the course of employment, benefits are determined by the Industrial Commission of Arizona (ICA). If the worker is denied benefits or is dissatisfied with the amount, the worker must seek a hearing through the ICA, and following the hearing, if still dissatisfied, they can then file a special action to get before the superior court. For this kind of dispute, the worker must "exhaust" their administrative remedies before being able to have the matter considered by a court.

While A.R.S. §15-112 provided that if the Superintendent or the State Board of Education found a violation, a school district *could* seek a hearing before an ALJ, it did not provide that this was the only remedy available. Further, though there is a general rule that you must exhaust all administrative avenues for relief "before appealing to the courts,"[2] the Arizona Supreme Court has held that this is not required when the pursuit of administrative remedies would be futile.[3]

Yet this is the pathway TUSD pursued through the law firm it engaged. On June 22, 2011, the law firm of DeConcini McDonald Yetwin & Lacy sent Superintendent Huppenthal a letter giving TUSD's formal "Notice of Appeal of Determination of Non-Compliance with A.R.S. §15-112 and Request for Hearing."[4] This letter set forth four primary reasons as the basis for the appeal. First, the notice of violation was deficient; second, TUSD was not in violation of the statute; third, the law was unconstitutionally vague; and fourth, the notice of violation included provisions other than A.R.S. §15-112. This fourth argument, though perhaps correct as a technical matter, was irrelevant for purposes of determining whether TUSD violated A.R.S. §15-112.

Anyone familiar with the administrative process in Arizona would question, immediately, the inclusion of the third reason. In Arizona, an ALJ cannot declare a law to be unconstitutional. Thus, including this argument as a reason for an administrative appeal was futile. The futility of this argument was readily admitted by the ALJ, who stated in his ruling that because "A.R.S. §15-112 has not been shown to have been declared unconstitutional by any court … the law must be given effect by this Tribunal."[5] Spending time researching and crafting an argument that is known to be futile and then billing your client for this is questionable. The State Bar of Arizona's Rules of Professional Conduct states, "A lawyer shall not make an agreement for, charge, or collect an unreasonable fee."[6] Unless a lawyer is specifically directed by the client to develop what is or should be known to be a futile argument, charging for that work may be "an unreasonable fee."

The fact that the argument was futile, though, should have alerted the lawyers that the administrative relief exhaustion requirement did not apply. In other words, TUSD could have pursued this immediately in state or federal court. TUSD should have been advised of this as an option so that it could make a considered choice about whether to go forward with this administrative appeal on the three other reasons or go directly to state or federal court. To get into federal court, the case has to involve a federal question, or the parties have to be from different states and the amount in controversy has to be more than $75,000. If TUSD thought the statute violated the federal constitution, they could and perhaps should have filed a lawsuit in federal district court.

Two additional reasons call into question the decision to seek administrative review. First, even if TUSD won before the ALJ, Arizona law permits Superintendent Huppenthal to determine if and/or how he would comply with the ruling. By Judge Kowal's own words, his ruling was a "recommendation" to Superintendent Huppenthal.[7] Under Arizona administrative law, Huppenthal was free to accept, reject, or modify Judge Kowal's "recommendation."[8] Essentially, the case held no teeth, because even if Judge Kowal ruled that the classes were *not* in violation of A.R.S. §15-112, Superintendent Huppenthal could disregard the ruling and substitute his own finding as final. This led many in the community to wonder what the point of this administrative appeal was if Huppenthal could do whatever he wanted.

Equally troubling was that Judge Kowal had a very narrow scope in terms of what was relevant in the case. He could only determine whether any of the TUSD MAS classes were out of compliance with A.R.S. §15-112. He did not consider whether the classes were educationally effective, aligned to state educational standards, or increased student achievement.[9] The most central issues from an educational standpoint (e.g., raising student achievement) were deemed irrelevant in this high-profile *educational* case. As we will later see in his ruling, Judge Kowal did not completely abide by this when the state brought in witnesses to claim the MAS classes were educationally unsound.

Further, Judge Kowal refused to consider a key argument advanced by TUSD, that the statute was unconstitutionally vague on its face or as applied against TUSD. If TUSD lost in this administrative proceeding, though it could appeal by filing a special action to review it, the Superior Court could only examine matters that came before and were decided by the ALJ. In other words, the pathway chosen by TUSD, presumably in full consultation with its attorneys, did not really offer a way to challenge the law or its enforcement on constitutional grounds.

As things went, briefs and evidence in the form of exhibits were filed, and hearings were conducted before ALJ Kowal on four dates that summer and fall, August 19, August 23, September 14, and October 17. Twelve witnesses were called. Sometimes, it was difficult to determine which side some of the witnesses supported. Two of the five sitting TUSD board members and the local superintendent testified, and all three made very strong claims *against* the MAS program from their own home district. Though there were some staunch supporters of the program who testified to its educational intentionality and efficacy, it was very telling which witnesses Judge Kowal found credible and which ones he did not. Later, we focus on the testimony that Judge Kowal centered in his decision as well as that which we think should have been given greater weight.

OPENING SALVO: MICHAEL HICKS AND JOHN PEDICONE

Both Hicks and Dr. Pedicone were official representatives of TUSD, the former as an elected board member and the latter as the superintendent of the school district. Both testified in the ALJ hearing, and even though TUSD was appealing the findings of non-compliance, both provided testimony against MAS. Began by, Hicks describing his professional background as being responsible for the traffic signals throughout Tucson and in the surrounding areas, and that he was also an adjunct instructor at the local community college. Despite being on the TUSD Board, his educational background was minimal, and yet he directly testified that he thought the MAS courses were a form of indoctrination and violated state law:

HICKS: Well, it's the same all through the entire process, that there was – I felt there were individuals in the [MAS] course – or in these courses who were teaching to indoctrinate.
[STATE]: And the indoctrination issue involved, did that involve racial issues, to your understanding?
HICKS: Yes.
[STATE]: And did you have concern that a "us versus them" mentality was being created, "us" being the Chicano population and "them" being the Anglo population?
HICKS: Yes.[10]

Some of the evidence that Hicks provided about indoctrination stemmed from his visit to Sally Rusk's class where she was teaching about the Zoot Suit Riots. For those not familiar with this point in history, zoot suits were baggy, oversized, pinstripe suits worn by Mexican American youths in the 1940s called *pachucos*.[11] Zoot suits also found favor among Black youths, leading Ralph Ellison to speculate in 1943 on this cultural phenomenon and that "perhaps the zoot-suit conceals profound political meaning."[12]

On June 3, 1943, eleven White sailors got into a fight with some *pachucos* in downtown LA. Each side claimed the other started it, but the LAPD arrested the Brown youth, letting the White sailors go. The next day, 200 more sailors rode taxis into East LA and targeted *pachucos* indiscriminately, pulling them off street cars, out of movie theaters, beating them, stripping them, and burning their zoot suits.[13] It was not just that anti-Mexican racism ran deep within the 1940s Anglo community – it did. However, there were also restrictions placed on suit sizes to conserve fabric during World War II, and these Mexican American youths (along with some

Filipino and Black youths) were seen as being anti-American, undermining the war effort. This lethal combination of racism and nationalism, fueled by newspaper reporting glamorizing the vigilante sailors, led to over 150 injuries and 500 arrests – almost all of whom were Mexican American youth.[14]

Returning to Hicks' assertion that MAS created an "us versus them" using the Zoot Suit Riots as an historical example from Rusk's class, there does seem to be this dynamic at play. However, "us" in terms of the Zoot Suit Riots was White sailors versus "them" of Brown street youth. Regardless, Hicks stuck to his guns when asked about the program:

[STATE]: I'm going to go pointblank to this question, sir: Is it your belief that Tucson Unified School District is in violation of ARS Section 15-112 today?
HICKS: Yes.[15]

Hicks' limited understanding of history will be further detailed when he was featured in a segment on *The Daily Show* and made reference to the Civil Rights icon "Rosa Clark" (*not* a typo). That, however, is a story for later. Regardless, Hicks' disdain for the MAS program was palpable, and he used his position as a TUSD board member to attack it whenever he could.

Superintendent Pedicone was more measured in his discussion of the MAS controversy. He discussed being contacted by producers from Fox News' *The O'Reilly Factor* because there was an allegation that Chicano Civil Rights icon "Corky" Gonzalez's classic text *Message to Aztlán* was being taught to third graders. He did not find that to be true. He agreed that the deep level of pedagogical engagement MAS teachers gave to their students likely resulted in increased student achievement. Additionally, Superintendent Pedicone addressed a concern raised by his Deputy Superintendent Lupita Garcia that *El Movimiento Estudiantíl Chicanos de Aztlán* (MEChA), through its chapter at Tucson High, might be influencing students in TUSD with its "radical" philosophy. Superintendent Pedicone, to his credit, did not find these allegations to have any merit either.[16]

Given the strange centrality that MEChA played in this controversy, this is an appropriate time to set the record straight about this organization. MEChA was a student organization founded during the Chicano Civil Rights Movement.[17] While primarily rooted in the US Southwest, there are chapters throughout the country and it is largely considered one of the largest and most important Chicano student groups in the country.[18] It has undergone many changes since the late 1960s, such as using Chicanx instead of Chicano to be more gender-inclusive, but the focus has always been the same – the liberation of Chicanx students from systemic racism and any other form of social oppression facing the community.[19] The overall point being this: using MEChA as a racial boogeyman for Tom Horne and his allies was a means of framing those taking account of race and engaging in anti-racist action as the "true racists."

Returning to Superintendent Pedicone's testimony, he doubled down on his belief that students could *not* have acted alone in the April 26 takeover of the TUSD board meeting. He had a number of targets without a lot of specific, articulated evidence:

> [STATE]: Dr. Pedicone, in your e-mail you state, "It is part of my concern about the exploitation of these kids." What kids were you referring to?
> PEDICONE: Both the university students and the high school students that took the action to overtake the dais that night.
> [STATE]: Who were you concerned was or is exploiting those students?
> PEDICONE: In my opinion, there were a number of adults, including some community activists and activists from across the country, that we became aware had encouraged students to take, what I consider to be, inappropriate action. They crossed the line, from my opinion, on appropriate civil discourse and entered into an activity that was inappropriate.[20]

Again, it was beyond Superintendent Pedicone's belief system that current MAS students and recent graduates could have developed and executed the activist disruption of April 26. From that baseline assumption, Pedicone launched numerous accusations against university-affiliated people and community activists as the "adults" who manipulated the "kids" into engaging in civil disobedience, a form of protest he deemed "inappropriate." Returning to some of the questions from Chapter 4, what other options did the students have? The program was going to be eliminated and "civil discourse" was falling on deaf ears because the so-called adults in the room did not actually listen.

Superintendent Pedicone then doubled down on the right-wing conspiracy theory regarding Ward Churchill being the mastermind behind the April 26 takeover. Pedicone was not so brazen as to directly accuse Churchill of orchestrating the takeover, but he came close to implying it:

> There was – one of the individuals in the board room one night was Ward Churchill, a former activist, [who] was known for some of his work following 9/11. There were individuals I believe from the university that encouraged – I don't know them by name – but individuals that I am aware of that have some influence over those students that go into the Mexican American Studies Department at the university.[21]

The presence of activists and University of Arizona MAS-affiliated people meant, in Superintendent Pedicone's mind, that the students were manipulated into taking action on that day. The simple and straightforward interpretation, that the students were critically engaged and dedicated to preserving their studies, fell by the wayside. The amplification of these beliefs became even stronger when another board member, Mark Stegeman, took the stand.

WITH FRIENDS LIKE THESE: STEGEMAN AND "CULT-LIKE BEHAVIOR"

School board member Dr. Stegeman also testified at the ALJ hearing, and as expected, sparks flew soon after he took the stand. While he continually professed support for Ethnic Studies in the abstract, he was one of the fiercest opponents of the TUSD MAS program and was the one to introduce the April 26 motion to demote the program to elective status – the first step toward elimination. At the beginning of Dr. Stegeman's testimony, it is worth noting that he described his expertise as "economics" having graduated with a degree in this field from MIT in 1987. This degree, though, does not make him an authority on all subjects. This should seem like an obvious point, but his testimony and the way Judge Kowal treated this testimony overlooked this foundational issue. Specifically, Dr. Stegeman was not and has never been an expert in curriculum, pedagogy, urban education, psychology, or social movement politics. Most of his initial testimony stuck to issues relevant to his involvement as an elected member of the TUSD Board – an area where his general areas of expertise were not crucial to the discussion because his personal experience was central. His testimony then veered to matters over which he had no formal education, training, or expertise.

First, the state asked him questions to try to establish that the classes were designed for a particular group of students, Mexican Americans, which would violate A.R.S. §15-112 (A)(3). Part of the state's evidence to this point was the following passage from the MAS website about what its courses hoped to accomplish academically and in terms of student identity development: "The end result is an elevated state of Latino academic achievement. For Latino students, the model serves as a mirror. For non-Latino students, the model serves as a window into cultural, historical, and social understanding."[22]

When prompted, Stegeman offered that even though he could not comment on whether from a legal perspective this focus meant a violation of A.R.S. §15-112 (A)(3), he expressed that the classes were designed primarily for Mexican American students. The previous quotation highlights how problematic this state law was because the state's attorneys were trying to argue that this statement meant the MAS program was out of legal compliance. Why? There is little denying that there are persistent gaps in educational achievement along racial/ethnic lines. If helping foster a positive Latino identity, serving as a mirror, leads to increased educational performance, why would the state have a problem with this? How is it possible to address inequality if educators cannot make targeted interventions?

After this line of questioning, Stegeman's testimony took a dramatic and unexpected turn when he described a visit to Curtis Acosta's classroom. Stegeman testified that during his visit, he said he had "an epiphany," realizing that Acosta's class was "pure political proselytizing" and that "[t]his is a cult."[23] Stegeman's charge is extremely serious, and some context is necessary to understand his rationale as it later made headlines.

Acosta's class, like many in the MAS department, began with a unity clap and a recitation of the Luis Valdez poem *In Lak'ech*. The unity clap came out of the United Farm Workers movement where Filipino and Mexican laborers who did not speak the same language could communicate and feel a sense of unity – of common purpose.[24] In addition, *Lak'ech* reads as follows:

> *Tú eres mi otro yo.*
>
> You are my other me.
>
> *Si te hago daño a ti,*
>
> If I do harm to you,
>
> *Me hago daño a mi mismo.*
>
> I do harm to myself.
>
> *Si te amo y respeto,*
>
> If I love and respect you,
>
> *Me amo y respeto yo.*
>
> I love and respect myself.

Not to be too reductive, but *In Lak'ech* is an elaborated version of the Golden Rule, and it was an underlying moral and philosophical orientation of the MAS department.[25] It was a statement about self-respect and love, and it was very telling how Stegeman interpreted this opening to Acosta's class.

Stegeman, by his own admission, did not understand what was happening in the class as he offered, "I had difficulty understanding much of what was said during the ritualized expression. I felt I could understand maybe half of what was being said."[26] Despite this lack of background knowledge or ability to comprehend, Stegeman directly interpreted the opening of class as "something like a prayer," continually characterizing it as "ritualized expression." Even though Stegeman also said that these rituals were somewhat similar to students reciting the Pledge of Allegiance, he nevertheless described what took place in MAS classes as cult-like behavior.

Stegeman made this connection and came to this conclusion, not from his academic training in economics but based on a book he read, Eric Hoffer's 1951 text, *The True Believer: Thoughts on the Nature of Mass Movements*.[27] Hoffer's basic thesis was that there was no discernible difference among mass social movements regardless of their stated goals that "all mass movements are interchangeable."[28] He argued that mass movements prey on mass frustration, especially among the societal poor, and forsake reasoned arguments for emotional and even hate-filled appeals. Stegeman believed that he witnessed more of a religious ceremony occurring in Acosta's class, going so far as to say that there was "no education happening." Instead, Stegeman thought it was more focused on political ideology, ritual expression, and collectivism. He objected to Acosta encouraging his students to attend the Cesar Chavez March and thought the students were losing their individual identities to the collective whole.

Stegeman consistently positioned himself as the "reasoned voice" in the MAS debate. In this posture, it may make sense that he would gravitate toward Hoffer's work and be wary of what he regarded as collective anger surrounding the MAS controversy. Instead of being wary of the anti-MAS forces, he ironically ended up joining that collective. While Hoffer was fiercely critical of groupthink, instead favoring individual reason, there is a major flaw in his thesis. By not paying attention to the grievances being addressed by mass movements and arguing that all mass movements were the same, adherents of Hoffer would lump Hitler's rise to power with Dr. King and the Civil Rights Movement because they both stemmed from collective action predicated upon social critique.

Additionally, not all critiques are equally representative of reality. For example, Hoffer's theorizing homogenizes, making #BlackLivesMatter synonymous with #MakeAmericaGreatAgain, even though the former is a critique of racist police brutality and the former describes a nostalgia for a time that never truly existed. It allows the armchair analyst to frame their discomfort with social activism as an issue of "group think" instead of beginning with the understanding that social activism is *supposed* to make people uncomfortable.[29] It was simpler and more straightforward for Stegeman to focus on the classes, in his view, representing "cult-like behavior."

While there was intense drama during the hearing as Stegeman described his thinking on *True Believer*, it was equally interesting how little drama existed during cross-examination. Not once did the lawyers representing TUSD question what qualified Stegeman to testify about the nature of cult psychology and mass movements, especially since his expertise is in economics. Instead of interrogating Stegeman's lack of qualification to speak credibly on these issues, the TUSD lawyers gave these issues a pass – ceding that ground and giving the opponents of MAS even more reasons to attack the program.[30] Stegeman's invocation of Hoffer and characterization of MAS as fostering collectivism turns out to be consistent with the way Tom Horne and John Huppenthal would smear MAS teachers as negating individual identity for a collective racialized one and teaching hate, akin to Nazis, communists, and even the Ku Klux Klan.[31]

DR. MILEM TAKES THE STAND TO DEFEND MAS

Another University of Arizona professor, Dr. Jeffrey F. Milem, appeared as a witness on behalf of TUSD. He had worked extensively in the field of higher education, specifically examining the relationship between diverse environments and student development broadly speaking. He is a nationally known expert on diversity and has been involved in several amicus briefs in cases regarding affirmative action. In addition, Milem taught a Critical Race Theory (CRT) course at the University of Arizona. Though CRT came out of legal studies, education scholars developed CRT in their field as a means of examining racism in terms of social structures instead of as an individual attribute, seeking to understand how educational outcomes are overdetermined by social forces and entrenched material inequality instead of being produced by individual racist actors.[32] From a social science perspective, this was a profound and important shift in analytical focus.[33] In terms of public discourse, things are more complicated.

CRT has always been the "boogeyman" wherever it shows up. In law, critics were quick to vilify it even as it was emerging.[34] In education, Gloria Ladson-Billings directly addressed this issue in her foundational piece several years before the TUSD controversy when she asked, "Just what is critical race theory and what's it doing in a nice field like education."[35] The word *nice* was central to her analysis because, for too long, education as a field had been too much about *kumbaya* multiculturalism at the expense of critical examinations of structured racial inequities. In her view, CRT centered racism in the analysis, translated that into tangible action, and truly disrupted persistent inequities.[36]

Fast forward to 2012, and Breitbart.com found "damning" evidence that was going to blow the roof off the Obama presidency. That evidence was a video segment where then law student Obama was at a rally where he introduced and hugged Derrick Bell.[37] This was Breitbart.com's smoking gun. Derrick Bell was the first tenured Black professor in the history of Harvard Law School and one of the founders of CRT. He saw racism as a system of oppression instead of an individual characteristic. This may seem like a basic point, but it is critically important to the subject at hand. There are several parallels between this manufactured national controversy and the local Tucson one.

On a national level, Breitbart.com thought it had uncovered the underlying ideological orientation of the Obama administration, and, in a misreading of the facts on the ground, they interpreted Obama hugging Derrick Bell as an indication that he wanted to oppress White people.[38] Though framed as the conspiracy that would bring down the Obama presidency, it turned out to be more heat than light. In a parallel way, the state administrators in Arizona used CRT as a way of framing the program as "anti-American."[39] For the folks in Arizona, CRT was also a "gotcha" moment – albeit with zero understanding of what CRT represents as an academic enterprise.

At the ALJ hearing, Dr. Milem took the stand to defend the use of CRT within TUSD in particular, and to attest to the curricular validity of MAS and its foundation in sound educational theory and practice. In particular, the state came after Dr. Milem about the teaching of "controversial" materials. Specifically, some MAS teachers critically unpacked the following quotation with their students from Sam

Houston, the first governor of Texas, "The Anglo-Saxon race must pervade the whole Southern extremity of this vast continent. The Mexicans are no better than the Indians and I see no reason why we should not take their land." Those representing the state made the argument that quotations like these could only breed hostility and resentment, and specifically, resentment against White people:

[TUSD]: Does teaching students about historical facts, about oppression and racism – does that promote resentment on the basis of race?

MILEM: No, not at all. In fact, I think I'd argue the failure to teach this part of our history is more likely to promote resentment than the teaching of that history.

[TUSD]: Do ethnic – well, why do you say that?

MILEM: It's because, you know, the quote by Houston is the quote by Houston, and it reveals in very real ways the way he thought and the way that other leaders thought at that point in time about Native and Mexican people, you know, in the United States in the Southwest. That was a very real sort of ideology and psychology that existed, affected decisions around public policy in this country. So, to not teach that ignores a really important part of history is oftentimes whitewashed in this country in the sense that we don't have the difficult conversations that we need to have with ourselves about the context, the period of the times, and what shaped those key public policy decisions.[40]

In Milem's evaluation, it was the *failure* to teach historically accurate curricula that led to racial/ethnic divisions. He argued that whitewashing history actually leads to more conflict, not less. Specific to the controversy at hand, the state took the position that teaching MAS created divisions among students. Conversely, Dr. Milem argued that it was the monocultural, inaccurate teaching of historical truths – regardless of how controversial – that was the root of these divisions.

It was curious that the state of Arizona tried to have Milem dismissed on a particular technicality – that he never visited an MAS classroom or conducted a curricular audit of the program, like Tom Horne. Ultimately, this attempt failed. In contrast, the expert witness for the state, Dr. Sandra Stotsky, did review some of the curricular materials of the program. To call it "an audit" would be an overstatement. In addition, it is important to explore the qualifications Dr. Stotsky brought to her work around the TUSD case and whether her areas of expertise qualified her as an "expert" in this case.

THE TROUBLING AND IMPACTFUL TESTIMONY OF DR. SANDRA STOTSKY

The state's expert, Dr. Sandra Stotsky, received her Ed.D. from Harvard and was the 21st Century Chair in Teacher Quality at the University of Arkansas in its Department of Educational Reform (EDRE). This was the same educational department that housed the professor who helped Doug MacEachern launch some of his attacks on the MAS program detailed in Chapter 2. It is rare for departments in colleges of education to have one endowed chair, let alone several. This department, EDRE, was largely established by an approximately $10 million grant from the Walton Family Foundation – as in Walmart.[41] The Walton Family Foundation's educational initiatives have been largely dedicated to market-based reforms of education, in particular pro-school choice initiatives.[42] Of note is that the source of the $10 million donation, previously prominently displayed, has been scrubbed from the department's website, and now simply reads that a "private gift" established it.[43]

A key aspect of Dr. Stotsky's scholarship that brought her to the ALJ hearing was her work in curriculum. She was also the author of *Losing Our Language: How Multiculturalism Undermines Our Children's Ability to Read, Write and Reason*[44] where her controversial thesis argued that the uptake in multicultural education in the 1990s was largely responsible for the decline in student academic performance in English. She additionally asserted that multiculturalism is "a clear race-based political agenda, one that is anti-civic and anti-Western in its orientation."[45] From this orientation, she established her credentials as both an expert in curriculum and multicultural education. The former is a fair assessment. The latter is on much shakier ground. Interestingly, Dr. Stotsky agreed with this assessment as part of her testimony read:

[TUSD]: You consider yourself an expert in K-12 curriculum development?
STOTSKY: I do.
[TUSD]: But you do not consider yourself an expert in ethnic studies?
STOTSKY: No, not an expert.
[TUSD]: Or in Critical Race Theory?
STOTSKY: No.
[TUSD]: Or in critical pedagogy?
STOTSKY: No.[46]

With this as context, the rest of her testimony was self-contradictory. On day four of the ALJ hearings, Dr. Stotsky took the stand, and it was fascinating what she said, what she was not asked during cross-examination, and how Judge Kowal utilized her testimony in his final decision.

Dr. Stotsky was brought in as a witness to rebut Dr. Milem's testimony about the academic/social importance and potential of race-forward curricula. She began by establishing her credentials to speak on the subject, including her academic training and publication record. In particular, she highlighted: "I have published many articles that focus on multicultural education, multicultural literature in particular. I was also – and one of the most recognized ones appeared in the *English Journal* that was about guidelines for incorporating multiethnic and multicultural literature into the reading and English curriculum."[47]

This was a curious way of establishing expertise. Typically, academics establish "impact," or as Dr. Stotsky offered, being "recognized" through academic citations. It is particularly important because it is an indication of how often scholars in the field are using the work. Since the piece's publication in 1994, Dr. Stotsky's earlier-referenced article has been cited *a total* of forty-seven times, which includes the times she cited herself.[48] This was a key piece of scholarship that she offered as an exemplar, establishing her ability to speak credibly to the issue presented before the court. In contrast, Dr. Gloria Ladson-Billings' piece on multicultural education "Toward a Theory of Culturally Relevant Pedagogy"[49] has been cited over 12,000 times.[50] The point is that while no one is debating Dr. Stotsky's qualifications in the area of curriculum, it is a stretch to consider her an expert in *multicultural* education. It was surprising and troubling that the lawyers for TUSD did not really challenge her in this area.

Regardless, the basis of Dr. Stotsky's testimony rested on her critiques of CRT and critical pedagogy – two areas where she admits that she is *not* an expert. While she claimed to be an expert in multicultural education, that claim is spurious at best. For example, she framed CRT – a vein of scholarship dating back to the late 1970s – as not academic and as "designed to arouse emotions." She elaborated: "In my opinion, [CRT is] not academically beneficial, because it is not attempting to develop critical thinking. It is presenting material that is designed to arouse emotions in one direction that a group of students who have been designated as oppressed. That is based on the philosophical background and conceptualization of the program."[51]

Effective cross-examination of Dr. Stotsky by TUSD's lawyers could have brought forth the following: Dr. Stotsky is not an expert in CRT, yet she made the broad claim that this area of study does not promote critical thinking because it "is designed to arouse emotions." Additionally, it is difficult to imagine teaching about the history of oppression in a way that does not arouse emotions.

Consider the following example of what ought to be a non-controversial premise: The Holocaust was a horrific example of attempted genocide. Now consider the film *Schindler's List*. It is difficult to imagine that a person watching that film would not have their emotions aroused as a result of viewing that depiction of history. Teaching about the history of oppression and its ongoing and current effects might naturally provoke intense emotions as part of these lessons. Returning to Dr. Stotsky's testimony, she offered:

> And the material – the content of what was in many of the materials dealt with all the examples of discrimination or violence or unlawful activities that members of this particular group of people, Mexican Americans or Latinos or Chicanos or however they were described... And it would certainly create hostility, resentment in the students that read consistently about what happened to a group of people that they were to see as their ancestors or their community or their parents.[52]

Returning to the Holocaust example, do Jewish people uniformly hate Germans, or is teaching about the Holocaust a means of ensuring that history does not repeat itself? At the ALJ hearing, MAS Director Sean Arce essentially made this point in his testimony: "[A]s students of history, as teachers, we encourage a rehumanization of all people. And by looking at history, we can come to understand that history, and hopefully learn lessons from that history of what dehumanization was in order to prevent that from recurring again."[53]

This perspective, offered by the director of the program about the teaching of accurate history, stands in contrast to Dr. Stotsky's assertion that it inevitably leads to "hostility" or "resentment" – two claims Dr. Stotsky offered but never empirically verified would result from the teaching of MAS.

Returning to the subject of Mexican Americans, we are not arguing that the treatment of Jews in Germany in the 1940s was analogous. However, the historical record shows that the Southwest and Texas were stolen from Indigenous and Mexican peoples by the US. Within these areas, there were lynchings of Brown people, signs that said, "No dogs or Mexicans allowed," and Operation Wetback, the mass deportation of persons of Mexican ancestry, including many who were US citizens.[54] When one specifically examines the treatment of Mexican Americans in Arizona, the historical record is not favorable.

Dr. Maya Angelou, when asked by Dave Chappelle if the multiple assassinations of the 1960s made her angry, responded: "If you're not angry, you're either a stone, or you're too sick to be angry. You should be angry."[55] Dr. Stotsky's criticism of CRT "being designed to arouse emotions" misapprehends what are appropriately emotional responses to historical and current-day oppression. All educators should hope that their students have not become so numb, "stones" or "too sick," and unable to feel the entire range of emotions – including pride, shame, and anger – when learning the history of the United States.

The focus on emotions, however, was a rhetorical device that Dr. Stotsky used to undercut the academic and intellectual legitimacy of the program. That is, if the subject matter aroused emotions, it must *not* be scholarly – as if those two domains are mutually exclusive. She continued, this time taking aim at Paulo Freire who, as detailed in Chapter 1, is widely considered one of the most influential educational theorists in the twentieth century, and his work is taught at the best education schools throughout the country.[56] In contrast, Dr. Stotsky offered: "The material almost consistently showed that students were referencing themselves as members of a so-called oppressed group. This is from Freirean philosophy. I did not find any in which students were either referencing themselves as Americans or as something else, whatever that something else could be, nor did I see them coming up with a different point of view."[57]

That is the nature of Freire's work. One cannot have an oppressed if there is not an oppressor, much like, as previously offered, one cannot have an up without a down or a hot without a cold.[58]

That does not negate the reality of the social analysis, and more to the point, why would Dr. Stotsky require those exploring social oppression to do so without an emotional response? In contrast, Sean Arce's testimony set the record straight about how Freire was applied in the MAS classes:

[STATE]: [Freire's] belief that there was in each society an oppressor class and an oppressed classes [sic]. Is that correct so far?
ARCE: That's much too simplistic in the understanding of Freire. That's just one – that's one aspect of his literature.... Freire also understands that people in the same group, particularly Latinos which he's written about, can oppress each other.
[STATE]: Sure, but –
ARCE: And furthermore, he talks about not wanting to replicate a paradigm of oppression – about rehumanization.[59]

Rehumanization is the core of Freire's life work.[60] Instead, the representatives of the state continually mischaracterized his work to engage in a modern-day red scare due to Freire's orientation in Marxist social analysis,[61] while also framing the use of the "oppressor/oppressed" paradigm as breeding resentment against White people.[62] This battle over accurate representation ran throughout the entire controversy as demonstrated by the misinformation campaigns described in Chapter 2, and it was particularly salient in the ALJ hearing.

JUDGE KOWAL'S RULING

December 27, 2011, was a crisp 64-degree winter day, and many people in the Tucson community were on some form of winter break when Judge Kowal issued his ruling. The ruling circulated quickly through social media. Judge Kowal found the district to be out of compliance with A.R.S. §15-112, in particular for violations of (A)(2) "promoting racial resentment," (A)(3) "being designed primarily for one ethnic group," and (A)(4) "advocating ethnic solidarity instead of treating pupils as individuals." He did not find evidence of any violations of (A)(1), "Promoting the overthrow of the U.S. government," but that was not necessary to find the district out of compliance and a violation of any part of the statute by any course in the district constituted a violation. Judge Kowal then recommended the state Department of Education to withhold 10 percent of TUSD's funding from the date his decision became final until it came into compliance with the statute. It was not just that Judge Kowal found evidence that TUSD was out of compliance with state law, but it was also telling which evidence Judge Kowal used to make this determination in the thirty-seven-page ruling. In summarizing the evidence presented, Judge Kowal stated: "Testimonial evidence presented at the hearing, in conjunction with excerpts from texts, curriculum, assessments, and student work, demonstrates that MAS classes cause students to develop a sense of racial resentment toward the 'white oppressor' or 'dominant' group. The philosophy of 'us against them' is a persistent theme that exists within the MAS program."[63]

There was no disagreement that MAS centered issues of inequality and social oppression in the curriculum and pedagogy. However, the proponents of the program, such as Sean Arce, claimed they taught social oppression out of love for their community and their students, engaging in a process of rehumanization. The opponents claimed that identifying White people as the racially dominant group in the US both historically and contemporarily led to the fostering of "racial resentment." Judge Kowal agreed with the latter point of view relying on "cold" reviews of the classroom materials with no evidence of how those materials were used in the classes, which would have required actual classroom observations to establish.

The importance of this point cannot be overstated. The fact that a certain text is being taught says nothing about how it is being taught. In an extreme example, *Mein Kamf* could be taught to indoctrinate students into antisemitism, or it can be examined as a historical document helping students understand how mass populations can succumb to racist propaganda. The best way to determine use would therefore be classroom observations, but the state focused simplistically on the words in the text instead of *how* it was being taught. There were some substantive, unannounced classroom observations conducted on behalf of the state-commissioned Cambium audit, which found no violations of the state statute in their report.[64] Despite the rigorous nature of the audit, Judge Kowal gave more weight to non-experts such as Dr. Stegeman (cult-like behavior) and Dr. Stotsky (I am not an expert on Critical Race Theory).

In particular, Judge Kowal utilized Dr. Stotsky's testimony when making his ruling despite the obvious contradictions in her testimony. That is, she explicitly said that she was not an expert in CRT or *barrio pedagogy*, while also claiming that these approaches to education did not promote critical thinking. In his ruling, Judge Kowal found her testimony compelling in making his decision. In contrast, Dr. Milem is a nationally recognized expert on racial dynamics in education and has taught CRT classes. To this, Judge Kowal offered, "The Administrative Law Judge finds Dr. Milem's testimony of extremely limited value."[65] Kowal discounted CRT and *barrio pedagogy* as being legitimate forms of education and then credited the interpretations by people like Stotsky and Stegeman, even though neither had expertise in these areas.

Ultimately, Judge Kowal ruled that there were violations of state law within the TUSD MAS program. Jon Justice immediately took to the Tucson airwaves to declare victory as described in Chapter 2. He gleefully said, "We win, you lose!"[66] There was an air of frustration in Tucson, and much of the momentum gained during the April 26 and May 3 school board meetings was waning, with Judge Kowal's decision, it seemed inevitable that TUSD would move to eliminate MAS once and for all.

Returning to the ruling, Judge Kowal's findings were somewhat irrelevant because, as indicated at the beginning of this chapter, State Superintendent Huppenthal was free to accept, reject, or modify the decision. The ruling nevertheless allowed Huppenthal to claim that his finding of violations was vindicated through a legal process where evidence was presented, testimony received, and a decision rendered by a neutral arbiter. He became even more emboldened in his quest to "stop *la raza*."

On January 6, 2012, Huppenthal issued an "Order Accepting Recommended Decision," stating that he "hereby accepts the recommended decision as written without modification."[67] However, Huppenthal, without acknowledging that he had deviated from Kowal's recommendation, made an important modification that would increase the pressure on TUSD. According to Judge Kowal's recommendation, the fine imposed on TUSD would run from the date when his decision became final. If Huppenthal accepted the recommended decision, the noncompliance date would have been January 6, 2012. However, Huppenthal ordered that the 10 percent monthly apportionment would be withheld retroactive to August 15, 2011. When the TUSD Governing Board met on January 10, 2012, the retroactive fine already amounted to several million dollars. An appeal, if pursued by TUSD, would be heard in superior court, but the specter of a fine being retroactively imposed even during the pendency of a permitted legal challenge likely affected TUSD's response, as we detail in Chapter 6.

When TUSD chose to appeal Superintendent Huppenthal's June 2011 Finding of Violation through the administrative process, had it been advised properly about the limits of that process: that an administrative appeal could only examine whether the finding of violation was factually supported and could not examine whether the statute was constitutionally deficient; and that the Superintendent could disregard a ruling by the ALJ if the Superintendent disagreed with it? Properly advised, TUSD should have understood that any victory before the ALJ could, quite possibly, have been an exercise in futility. Was TUSD told that it could forgo the administrative appeal and instead sue directly in state or federal court, where it could challenge the constitutionality of the law? If not, serious questions arise about the legal advice it received.

But if TUSD had been advised properly of its options and yet still chose to go the administrative appeal route, including having its legal counsel go through the motions of making legal arguments it knew an ALJ could never decide, did that indicate that the fix was already in?

6

Caving to Pressure

Intimidation, Repression, and Absurdity at TUSD

Early 2012 was the perfect storm of events that led to the elimination of MAS classes. After the administrative law decision, TUSD declined to appeal the ruling. Superintendent Huppenthal accepted the ALJ's recommendation and found TUSD out of compliance with A.R.S. §12-115, threatening to retroactively withhold 10 percent of the district's state funding if it did not eliminate the program. On a local level, one of the strongest board-member supporters of the MAS program, Judy Burns, passed away suddenly in October of 2011 while the administrative hearings were ongoing. Her appointed replacement, Alex Sugiyama, was an economics lecturer at the University of Arizona, and one of his first votes reappointed Mark Stegeman as the TUSD board president.[1] Some were doubly concerned about whether Sugiyama would be able to function independently as a board member because he worked in the same academic department, the Eller College of Management, as Stegeman at the University of Arizona. As a lecturer, Sugiyama was ineligible for tenure and was subject to an annual review within his department,[2] in which Stegeman was a tenured Associate Professor.

Community members did not have to wait long to see how the new board would address the MAS issue. On January 10, 2012, TUSD board member Michael Hicks introduced a resolution to eliminate the MAS program. It read, in part:

> All MAS courses and teaching activities, regardless of the budget line from which they are funded, shall be suspended immediately.... Students currently enrolled in MAS courses shall be transferred to new or existing sections of other courses, so that they do not lose the opportunity to earn credits and to satisfy requirements because of the suspension of the MAS courses.[3]

The resolution passed 4-1 as many on the board were tired of the controversy and wanted it to be over. Some even said it was time to get back to "real education," implying that MAS did not fit that definition. To them, real education meant the basics of "reading, writing, and arithmetic," and MAS fell outside these bounds. What many critics failed to realize was that MAS was sound educational practice. Engaging students as community-oriented scholars[4] and helping them find a purpose to their education where they saw themselves in the curriculum[5] eventually led to significant increases in educational performance.[6] Despite not having anything to replace the MAS program, four board members (three of whom were non-Latino in a 60+ percent Latino district) eliminated a program dedicated to supporting Mexican American student success.

ELIMINATING THE CLASSES AND BANNING THE BOOKS

While TUSD caved to the pressure, it had to figure out what suspending the program meant in practical terms. As the state tended to find the curricular materials particularly offensive, the district representatives removed all MAS books and materials from the classrooms. For reasons that are not entirely clear, they decided to remove materials while school was in session. Students in these classes described how painful it was to see not just the elimination of these classes that were so central to their academic development and wellbeing but also to witness the forceable removal of this *precious knowledge* from their classrooms.[7]

This led to a contentious debate about whether the books were banned, and this controversy gained national attention.[8] District representatives said that former MAS teachers were not allowed to use the removed texts in their classes, yet they also claimed that this did not amount to a banning. Texts that were listed in an email from TUSD administrators to be removed included the following:

- *Critical Race Theory: An Introduction* by Richard Delgado and Jean Stefancic
- *500 Years of Chicano History in Pictures* edited by Elizabeth Martinez
- *Message to Aztlán* by Rodolfo "Corky" Gonzales
- *Chicano! The History of the Mexican Civil Rights Movement* by Arturo Rosales
- *Pedagogy of the Oppressed* by Paulo Freire
- *Rethinking Columbus: The Next 500 Years* edited by Bill Bigelow and Bob Peterson
- *Occupied America: A History of Chicanos* by Rodolfo Acuña

The official statement from the district, denying that books were banned, read: "NONE of the above books have been banned by TUSD. Each book has been boxed and stored as part of the process of suspending the classes. The books listed above were cited in the ruling that found the classes out of compliance with state law."[9]

Everyone agrees that the books were removed from the classes and stored in boxes. The disagreement arises from whether this amounted to a "banning." Board member Mark Stegeman insisted that there was no book banning,[10] and TUSD's official position included that the titles remained available in district libraries.[11] However, Jeff Biggers in the *Huffington Post* notes that "a partial book ban in classroom teaching is no less egregious than a total ban."[12] His story includes a picture he received the day materials were removed from TUSD classrooms; it shows a box on which "[a]n administrator had reportedly written on the box: Banned books (please remove)."[13]

Board member Stegeman offered an alternative justification for the removal of certain books from MAS classrooms. He stated that, in his understanding, the books were not commonly part of curricula in Arizona and wrote a constituent letter stating, "I am not aware of any other school district in Arizona which has approved these books for use in instruction. If anyone knows of such approvals, then I would be interested to hear about them."[14] He argued that the books were never approved by TUSD, when at least three of the books had been explicitly approved by TUSD.[15]

Removing books and other MAS teaching materials from classrooms garnered national attention.

THE NATIONAL SHAME OF A TUCSON BOOK BANNING

Book bannings frequently conjure images of Nazi Germany, and as previously demonstrated, district representatives vehemently denied that a banning was in place. Many authors were surprised to see themselves on a banned book list, and the national media added to TUSD's collective shame.[16] Bill Bigleow, co-editor of *Rethinking Columbus*, provided an ominous context in an interview with Jeff Biggers for *Salon*: "The only other time a book of mine was banned was in 1986, when the apartheid government in South Africa banned 'Strangers in Their Own Country,' a curriculum I'd written that included a speech by then-imprisoned Nelson Mandela.... We know what the South African regime was afraid of. What is the Tucson school district afraid of?"[17]

While the last question about fear has never been fully assessed, the book banning in Tucson proved to be a controversy that would not die. It was a prominent issue throughout the remainder of the 2011–2012 academic year as it continued to make national headlines.

One group out of Houston, led by Tony Diaz and called the *Librotraficantes* ("book smugglers"), engaged in one of the most high-profile and creative forms of social protest against the book banning in Tucson. Diaz imitated the dress and style of *narcos*, down to the brown leather jacket and the aviator sunglasses (see Figure 6.1).[18] Instead of smuggling drugs or people, the *Librotraficantes* were dedicated to returning "wetbooks" back into Tucson. "Wetbooks" drew a parallel between the manufactured "illegality" of border crossers with a similar manufactured "illegality" of the Tucson banned books. The *Librotraficantes* amassed a collection of the banned books and created a caravan that drove from Houston to Tucson during the spring of 2012.[19] Diaz was able to elaborate on the group's purpose on *Democracy Now!*[20]

The summer break did not give a reprieve to TUSD administrators from the MAS controversy. The momentum of student movements frequently stalls when people disperse in summer. Bucking this trend, student activists continued to apply pressure on TUSD by producing critical and creative forms of social protest. They

FIGURE 6.1 *Librotraficante* by Tony Diaz

created an infomercial around banned books that began with the following disclaimer: "The opinions expressed in the following program are not those of TUSD, since they want nothing to do with educating students to think critically. This is a non-paid advertisement to combat Arizona law HB 2281 and the ban of Mexican American studies in Tucson."[21]

The lead actor in this mock infomercial channeled his inner Billie Mays with an energetic tone reminding the audience, "Do I have a deal for you?" Instead of hawking Oxyclean^{TM} or Shamwows^{TM}, he promoted the banned books, promising that reading them will "rejuvenate, exfoliate, penetrate, and recreate your whole way of thinking!!!" The mock infomercial included testimonials such as, "I used to be socially awkward, but because of banned books I have friends." It told the audience to get banned books before they were locked up in a warehouse. It also implored the audience to read these books now because they are currently banned in Tucson and, soon, might be banned *everywhere*. As with many infomercials, it ended with an 800 number people could call for more information: 1-800-GIMMIE-MY-BOOKS-BACK-FOO!

Viewed well over 250,000 times, the student activists who created this mock infomercial refused to let the issue of banned books die, and the pressure on TUSD continued into the 2012–2013 academic year. September is usually the month when a national Banned Books Week is recognized, and the TUSD controversy was one of the most high-profile book bannings in the country that year.

Author Jeff Biggers continued to highlight the pressing importance of the Tucson banning both locally and nationally.[22] While the book banning was playing out on the local and national stages, students within TUSD refused to accept the elimination of MAS. Within days of the elimination of MAS and the book banning, they staged a walkout.

STUDENTS WALK OUT

In scenes reminiscent of the 1960s Chicano Blowouts, hundreds of students from Cholla, Pueblo, and Tucson High walked out of their classes.[23] If the district was not going to provide them with relevant classes, the district would not have students. Their actions were timed to correspond to the 99th and 100th days of classes, the cutoff used by the state of Arizona to calculate the official average daily attendance, which determines the funding for school districts.[24] Students believed that absences on these days would be the most impactful, a display of student power and a warning of sorts that administrators in the district ignored student demands at their own peril.

When dozens of students from Cholla High School approached TUSD headquarters at 1010, they were met by Assistant Superintendent Dr. Lupita Garcia. She emphatically told the students that she was still concerned with the achievement gap in TUSD and would be redirecting about $80,000 for tutoring, especially in math and science. It should be remembered that TUSD had approximately 60,000 *students* at the time.

When the students said that they were marching for MAS, Dr. Garcia responded, "Unfortunately, this country is called America. Ok? And if you want to live in Mexico like many of our cousins chose to go back, you would study Mexican history."[25] This statement is worth unpacking. First, it was eerily close to "Go back to Mexico" and only exacerbated the situation. Second, one of the student protesters corrected Dr. Garcia, saying that the issue was not one of Mexican vs. American history but rather understanding history and issues pertinent to the Mexican *American* population – especially in the US Southwest.

One student protester said Dr. Garcia was being patronizing and not listening. She took issue with this characterization and ironically shouted, "These are not the facts lady. Young lady, listen to me!"[26] In those two short sentences, Dr. Garcia did exactly what she was being accused of. She demanded the student listen to her, and she dismissed the student statement as factually inaccurate while referring to her as the diminutive "young lady," which indicated that she was being both patronizing and not listening.

The students were hurting. They needed to be heard. They needed space to heal. The leaders of the district were only making things worse. Rather than waiting for administrators to create these needed healing opportunities, which seemed increasingly unlikely, UNIDOS decided to create the School of Ethnic Studies.

UNIDOS PRESENTS THE SCHOOL OF ETHNIC STUDIES

Exactly two weeks after TUSD eliminated the MAS classes, UNIDOS held a day-long, student-centered, community-based school at the El Casino Ballroom. This historic event space held special meaning for Tucson's Chicana/o community, which had since its opening in 1947 hosted weddings, quinceañeras, and other milestone events. More than 100 students participated in the School of Ethnic Studies, which involved keynote speakers, sacred ceremony, round table discussions, an amazing homemade lunch of *pozole*; it was both a learning and a healing space. The organizers described the event and why it was so desperately needed by the community as follows: "Educators from our community, colleges, community organizations and alumni of Mexican American Studies will be presenting their messages and stories about why Ethnic Studies is still alive, active and transforming... By creating our own school, we will have the space to learn our history, culture and contributions. Our education will continue, with or without TUSD approval."[27]

In addition, the organizers engaged in a deliberate media strategy. They were acutely aware that student walkouts and protests are frequently portrayed as nothing more than kids cutting class. Therefore, walking out of school and going to the School of Ethnic Studies reinforced the idea that these students were committed to their studies, and their academic success should be at the center of the MAS debate.

* * *

Describing this event creates another conundrum because some UNIDOS members have expressed that they do not want to be part of this book because of the community divisions deriving from the *Precious Knowledge* controversy. However, one of the authors, Cabrera, was present at this event, consulted on the organizing, gave a lecture, while leading roundtable discussions. In addition, one of the lead organizers has already co-authored a research article on the subject.[28] Therefore, what is told here derives from his firsthand account of the event as well as existing coverage of it, leaving space for others to tell their stories in the future.

* * *

The School of Ethnic Studies was an amazing organizational accomplishment. Two weeks after MAS classes were eliminated, UNIDOS organizers were able to obtain space, food, and speakers, and create an agenda for this impressive event.[29] It is not possible to capture the healing beauty of that day in the written word for those who were not present. However, we will try to paint as vivid a picture as possible.

The night before the School of Ethnic Studies, the organizers went into the program venue – the El Casino Ballroom – and made it a "youth-led" space. This included an art night on January 23. At this event, there was one purpose: Make the space youth-owned. First, it meant transforming the physical space. There were multiple people creating murals to cover the walls of the ballroom.

This was no small feat considering that it was designed to hold 800, and the organizers had one evening to transform the space. It was only through an amazing combination of organizing and volunteerism that the physical space was changed into a youth space. The murals, frequently hip-hop-oriented, represented both the community and the components of the forbidden MAS curriculum. The murals created an educational environment that represented the culture and needs of Mexican American youth – something that was outlawed by the state of Arizona. This rebellious action was not only a metaphorical middle finger to the politicians in Phoenix but also a site of affirmation for those who had lost so much because of racist state policies.

The second part involved transforming the auditory space. It meant both having a DJ booth set up and doing a sound check for the numerous presentations that would occur the next day. While a lot of this work was in preparation for the next day, the DJ's music also served as a backdrop for the art night. The music fueled the visual art and vice versa. Despite exhaustion, the organizers and other volunteers succeeded in making this space reflect the outlawed MAS program. The next day, class was in session.

THE SCHOOL OF ETHNIC STUDIES

The next morning, the School of Ethnic Studies opened its doors to students throughout the district who would have been walking out of school. There was one very important caveat. As media are not allowed in regular school, they were not allowed in the School of Ethnic Studies (see Figure 6.2).

This angered the local media as the MAS controversy was a constant frontpage headline. These restrictions did not sit well with them, although most abided by the rules. The organizers were intentional that they would engage with the media at 3:00 p.m., when school was dismissed.

Everything about the school day was meant to be different from a "usual" school day – to center the culture and the needs of the student participants. For example, instead of starting with the Pledge of Allegiance as mandated by Arizona state law by schools,[30] the organizers had Chucho – a local community activist – lead the participants in the four directions.[31] This brought all participants together, honoring not only a collective cultural heritage but also as a way to honor the "forbidden knowledge."[32] Again, it was a way of orienting the space toward the community as a counter to HB 2281.

The organizers were keenly aware that they not only needed to meet the cultural and academic needs of the participants in the School of Ethnic Studies, but also their basic needs like food. To that end, the organizers worked with a

FIGURE 6.2 School's in Session by George Cabrera

community member to make *pozole* for everyone in attendance, and the smell wafted throughout the entire building during the event.[33] It served as the contradictory reminder that school was in session but also that this was not your traditional school.

The structure of the program reinforced this theme. The day alternated between presentations by people who could speak to different components of the "forbidden curriculum" and then to breakout sessions allowing for deeper, more localized discussions. However, the organizers also knew that a school day – even a school day structured like this – could be a grind. Whenever they felt the room's energy dropping, they told the DJ to drop a beat so there could be an impromptu dance party.[34] Yes, you read that correctly. This school had random dance parties to infuse energy back into the room. For the educators reading this, let us unpack this a little. Let us ask ourselves how many times we have battled declining energy in our classrooms. Let us further consider what we did in response. Was it something like expressing frustration? Maybe anger? How many of us have ever considered having an impromptu dance party for 5 minutes? After a dance party and the subsequent exertion of physical energy, how much more could our students focus?

While class was in session, one member of the local press did not respect the sign on the front door that read "no Media." She sneaked in multiple times, but her professional attire, her impeccably pressed skirt, and blouse gave her away and participants quickly identified her as a member of the press corps. She was asked to leave. She did. Then she sneaked back in, only to be asked to leave – again.

While in session, there was a collective sense that participants in the School of Ethnic Studies were not only learning in a traditional sense but also healing from the trauma of the state-sponsored racism they were trying to combat.[35] While it was only one day, it served as an important reminder of the potential of collective, community-oriented action. It reminded people of the importance of the fight against a repressive state. While this was occurring locally, resistance was receiving national attention and recognition.

ARCE RECEIVES NATIONAL RECOGNITION

While there were many powerful MAS detractors within TUSD and the state of Arizona, nationally, the program continued to gain attention, support, and recognition. On April 2, 2012, the Zinn Educational Project announced Sean Arce as the recipient of the Myles Horton Education Award for Teaching People's History. There are many layers to this, so allow us to unpack. Howard Zinn was a historian, author of the classic *People's History of the United States*,[36] and the namesake for the Zinn Educational Project. The simple yet profound approach Zinn took to his book was that he wondered what history would look like if it was told through the eyes of everyday people as opposed to society's elites. What if we centered unions instead of robber barons? What if we centered activists instead of politicians?

Aligned with this approach, Myles Horton was a co-founder of the Highlander School, a civil rights activist, and considered to be one of the more important critical educators of the twentieth century. Horton and Paulo Freire, through a set of conversations, outlined the underlying principles and purpose of democratic education in their classic book *We Make the Road by Walking*.[37] The Myles Horton Award from the Zinn Educational Project was dedicated to recognizing a person who was embodying these legacies. In 2012, the Project recognized that person as Sean Arce.[38] To support his nomination, 2005 finalist for the Pulitzer Prize in nonfiction, Luis Alberto Urrea, described Arce as "a hero and a viral educator."[39] Howard Zinn's daughter and Representative Raúl Grijalva (D-AZ), among many others, supported Arce for this award, speaking to the critical national importance of the MAS work. While Arce was receiving national accolades, TUSD board member Michael Hicks appeared on *The Daily Show with Jon Stewart*.

TUSD BOARD MEMBER HICKS GOES ON *THE DAILY SHOW*

The same day Arce received the award, April 2, 2012, *The Daily Show* aired a segment entitled "Tucson's Mexican-American Studies Ban."[40] One of the show's correspondents, Al Madrigal, came to Tucson about a month before and interviewed people throughout the community. No one knew how the show would portray the controversy. The segment began with an interview of TUSD board member Michael Hicks – an official staunchly opposed to the MAS program and who introduced the motion to suspend it. Hicks is White but grew up in Tucson's predominantly Mexican American southside. He continually professed that he understood Latino issues, going so far as to say, "I'm probably more Hispanic than some of the others around here."[41]

As his *Daily Show* interview began, Hicks described how he was opposed to the "radical teachings" the MAS courses offered to impressionable students that he believed even called for bloodshed. These are, of course, very serious charges, and Madrigal asked, "When you sat in on these classes, what types of – ." Hicks interrupted and said, "I chose not to go to any of their classes. Why even go? Why even go? I based my thoughts on hearsay from others."[42] While this may seem like a less-than-judicious choice of words, some context is necessary. Superintendent of Public Instruction Horne, as well as his Deputy Superintendent Margaret Garcia Dugan, used a similar explanation to justify why they did not visit the MAS classes.[43] The overall point is that the MAS classes continued to be guilty until proven innocent. That is, the combination of curriculum and the "hearsay of others" was enough to find the classes out of compliance, and almost no amount of evidence to the contrary could dissuade the true believer from their anti-MAS views. The interview went further downhill from there.

Hicks described what he viewed as the "inappropriate" relationship MAS teachers created with their students by buying them burritos once a week.[44] He thought that the gift of food would build a bond and make them loyal to the MAS teachers, which made it more difficult to eliminate the program. MAS teacher Curtis Acosta was brought in as a counter to Hicks in the segment and he asked the simple yet profound question, "Why would giving food to our youths be frowned upon?" He also set the record straight about what the classes offered instead of the "hearsay of others": "We don't teach them to hate White people. What we're trying to do is provide a more complex version of what has happened in our past so that our students are engaged and they can ask themselves critical questions and build their own understanding."[45]

None of this context mattered to Hicks as he strongly believed that the classes were inappropriate and out of compliance with state law. The strong "hearsay of others," for Hicks, was more compelling than firsthand accounts like those of Acosta.

Madrigal asked Hicks, now that TUSD had terminated the MAS program, if they would be moving onto the other programs at TUSD. Hicks responded: "Honestly, this law won't be applied to any other courses. It was strictly written for one course, the Mexican American Studies Program." When asked about TUSD's African American Studies program, Hicks said that that program was not teaching the resentment of a race or class of people.[46]

At this point, Madrigal changed the flow of the interview and asked Hicks how it might be possible, as a "professional educator," to teach about US racial oppression accurately without breeding resentment against White people. To do this, they engaged in a role-playing activity where Madrigal played a Black student and Hicks the teacher trying to explain the history of slavery in the US:

MADRIGAL: How did I end up here?
HICKS: Slavery was ... I gotta' think on that ... Ok. The white man did bring over the, uh, Africans ...
MADRIGAL: What kind of jobs did we do?
HICKS: The jobs that you guys did was basically slavery jobs.
MADRIGAL: So, after we were freed, we got to vote?
HICKS: Yes! Well, you didn't get to vote until later.
MADRIGAL: And we were equal?
HICKS: Almost equal.
MADRIGAL: What? We were sort of like half? Or *three-fifths*?
HICKS: My personal perception of it? I would say you were probably a *quarter*.[47]

Yes, Hicks said that in post-slavery times, Black people were approximately one-fourth of a person. The transcript does not do justice to this exchange, and readers are encouraged to view the entire interview.[48]

Hicks then offered additional insights into Black history. In particular, he found contemporary anti-racists to be promoting violence against White people, and in contrast, he offered this historical lesson, "We now have a Black man as a president. You know, Rosa Clark did not take out a gun and go onto a bus and hold up everybody...."[49] Yes, he referred to civil rights icon Rosa *Parks* as Rosa *Clark*, to which Madrigal sarcastically added the following facetious voiceover, "Sadly, the peaceful lessons of Rosa Clark are lost on the radical reactionaries teaching Mexican American Studies."[50]

Madrigal concluded the interview by probing under what circumstances it would be okay for educators in TUSD to teach MAS. He asked if it would be all right if the district was 100 percent Latino, and Hicks quickly responded, "No!" Madrigal followed up by arguing that at that point, there would be no more White people left. Hicks stated, "Well, if there's no more White people in the world, then, ok, you can do what you want." Madrigal ended the segment with the voiceover response, "Oh, don't worry, Mr. Hicks. We will. We will."[51]

Not surprisingly, there was fallout following the airing of this segment.

THE AFTERMATH OF THE HICKS INTERVIEW

The Hicks interview created outrage given Hicks' central role in eliminating MAS. How could someone so ignorant be entrusted with our children's education, and this became a rallying cry throughout the Tucson community. At the next board meeting, people printed out logos with Hicks' image on it, demanding he resign his position. Outside the board meeting, members of *Las Adelitas* Arizona, Save Ethnic Studies, and *Derechos Humanos* made burritos that were wrapped in the logo, satirizing the "inappropriate relationships" Hicks discussed on *The Daily Show*. The approximately 250 burritos made for this event also called upon community members to become more actively involved in the effort led by David "Abie" Morales to recall Hicks.[52] Prior to *The Daily Show* segment, Morales launched a recall effort against Michael Hicks from the TUSD Board beginning in March. He had to collect 23,542 signatures by July 7 to get the recall on the ballot.[53]

During the call to the audience of the board meeting, University of Arizona professor Dr. Roberto "Cintli" Rodríguez, the alleged ring-leader of the April 26 board takeover, handed Hicks a burrito. Based on *The Daily Show* segment, burritos became a new cultural symbol in Tucson. On the one hand, they represented the way that MAS teachers cared for the basic needs of their students. On the other, they became a way to create public scorn and remind Hicks of the embarrassment he caused the community.

Outside of the school board meeting, people were constantly talking about *The Daily Show* segment. Sometimes, the segment was cathartic as the mask came off the MAS opposition and their true colors shone through on the national stage. For some, it was just a way to laugh to keep from crying about the elimination of the program. One Tucson eatery seized on the moment to create the "Rosa Clark Panini," advertising it on their sandwich board the week after the segment. For opponents of MAS, it was a cringe-worthy moment like fingernails on a blackboard. Many right-wing outlets locally tried to explain the Hicks interview as quotes taken out of context.[54]

The humor was short-lived as not only did the 2012 recall effort fail, but in November of 2014, Hicks was reelected to the TUSD Board. In contrast, eight days after Sean Arce was awarded the Myles Horton Award and *The Daily Show* segment aired, the *Three Sonorans* was kicked off the *Tucson Citizen* and Arce was fired from TUSD.

THE THREE SONORANS AND *TUCSON CITIZEN*

David Morales' version of activist journalism poked the proverbial bear one too many times, and the editors of the *Tucson Citizen* kicked him off the site. The allegations against Morales were that he did not give the public officials he critiqued adequate space to respond and that, according to the *Citizen*, "[Morales demonstrated] a constant reckless disregard for the truth."[55] Some in the community thought the decision was based on political pressure Morales' targets were placing on the *Citizen* and that journalistic integrity was window dressing to mask the actual reason.

Jeff Biggers saw it more as a continuation of the Arizona crackdown on dissident voices, especially considering that the bulk of complaints stemmed from anti-MAS activists and elected officials.[56] Tucson education blogger David Safier – hardly a hardcore leftist or activist – offered a thoughtful commentary on Morales' ouster:

Morales leads with his heart and his passions and goes for the jugular when he writes. Absolute accuracy doesn't seem to be important to him, which, I imagine, gives the journalist in Evans fits.... [Morales] is among the most prominent public voices in the local Hispanic community. No one has posted more video, much of which he or his friends have shot and which can be an invaluable resource to me and others.[57]

Safier opined that the *Three Sonorans* would not "go gently into that good night," and he was correct.[58] Within a few days, the blog was up and running again, this time independently. Regardless of one's feelings about Morales and his coverage, there was little denying that he was at the center of the MAS coverage – keeping both the local community and nation abreast of the developments in the controversy.

In the meantime, TUSD fired the now nationally award-winning director of MAS, Sean Arce.

TUSD FIRES MAS DIRECTOR SEAN ARCE

On a warm mid-spring Tucson night, the TUSD Board voted 3-2 on April 10, 2012, to *not* renew the contract of MAS Director Sean Arce. There were teary-eyed members of the community who spoke during the call to the audience, testifying to the importance of Arce to the students and the community. Board members Stegeman, Hicks, and Cuevas were not moved and voted against renewal, while Grijalva and Sugiyama (who previously voted to ban MAS) voted to renew.[59] The two-and-a-half-hour meeting saw almost four dozen people supporting MAS and Arce, while speakers frequently made sly references to Hicks' appearance on *The Daily Show*.[60] Despite the overwhelming public support of Arce, the vote seemed predetermined, as many did during this time.

The board meeting ended abruptly when a group of students formed a human chain in the middle of the meeting room using plastic zip ties to bind their wrists (see Figure 6.3).[61] They used plastic because people attending these meetings had to pass through metal detectors since the UNIDOS takeover of an earlier meeting.[62]

While these students were chanting "No justice, no peace, no racist TUSD!!!," someone in the audience let off a series of smoke bombs. Multicolored smoke filled the air. Some of the student protesters were prepared, and they put bandanas over their mouths to keep from inhaling the smoke.[63] This led to mass chaos and confusion. TUSD security converged on the protesters and identified one whom they thought was responsible. They tried to apprehend that person, but he escaped into a crowd of MAS supporters, slipping out a side door in 1010.[64] Stegeman would later publicly state that he thought the protests went too far and TUSD had been too lenient up to this point: "We allowed much aggressive free speech, but the smoke bomb went over the line and staff is cooperating with the Tucson police department."[65]

FIGURE 6.3 Students and protesters at TUSD board meeting tied themselves together with plastic ties (© Arizona Public Media (AZPM))

There was a general air of chaos and frustration in the room. In contrast to the tightly orchestrated act of civil disobedience from the year before in April 2011, discussed in Chapter 4, there did not appear to be a clear strategy or goal. An additional layer of tension that same night was that the co-founder of the MAS program, Dr. Augustine Romero, accepted the job of TUSD Director of Student Equity despite a picket line set by the Tucson 11 against being employed by the district – a boycott Romero was not consulted on and did not support.[66] This fostered further division within the community as Romero and the Tucson 11, once strong allies and friends, became adversaries. This reached a boiling point as we will explore in Chapter 8; however, UNIDOS also experienced some repercussions for their activism – unexpectedly from the University of Arizona's Mexican American Studies Department.

UNIDOS GETS BANNED FROM UA MAS

In April 2012, UNIDOS was still organizing around MAS when Dr. Antonio "Tony" Estrada, then the department chair of the University of Arizona's MAS Department, issued a decree that UNIDOS would no longer be allowed to use departmental space.[67] His rationale was simple, UNIDOS was not a registered student group at UA, and therefore should not be accessing departmental space. On the surface, this makes sense, but nonuniversity groups access space on a regular basis. The decision to deny space seemed to be connected to the racial/political climate of early 2012 in Tucson and a response to UNIDOS' activism. That is more of a speculative point, and it will remain an important unanswerable question.

Jon Justice used this incident, UNIDOS losing meeting space at UA, to re-up his attacks on MAS and UNIDOS on his 104.1 *The Truth* talk show. He felt vindicated because of the time he spent "exposing" UNIDOS, which he pronounced OO-nih-dos. By exposing, he meant his unsubstantiated claim that the "adults ended up recruiting a bunch of these kids," including that "a lot of 'em weren't even in TUSD."[68] Continuing to repeat the lie that UNIDOS must have been orchestrated by adult puppet masters, he said the student organizers were "a band of violent misfits"[69] and "a gang, plain and simple."[70] The "violence" Justice referred to was the April 26, 2011, takeover of the board meeting, even though no UNIDOS members physically harmed or even threatened people. With that as context, Justice casually referred to them as a gang with all of the racial implications associated with that term. Using his platform as the most popular right-wing media outlet in Tucson, Justice continued to add gasoline to the fire.

In the meantime, Tom Horne again found himself in the spotlight, although this time it was not for reasons he wanted.

HORNE'S HIT-AND-RUN

Shortly after the Hicks debacle on *The Daily Show*, Tom Horne found some trouble. The then-Arizona Attorney General was involved in a hit and run where the vehicle he was trying to park clipped a parked white Range Rover in a parking garage.[71] The damage to the Range Rover was just over $1,000, and one wonders why Horne did not just leave a note on the car. It turned out that Horne, married at the time, was having an affair with his employee who lived in the condominium complex attached to the parking garage.[72] The woman in the car with Horne previously served under Horne when he was state Superintendent of Public Instruction. She was hired in the criminal division of the Attorney General's office despite having no experience in this area, instead she was a construction and real estate attorney. She had also been suspended by the Arizona state bar and was still on probation when Horne hired her.[73] Horne's spokesperson denied that Horne being in that garage wearing a pulled-down baseball cap and driving someone else's car had anything to do with an affair. Instead, she claimed that he parked there to have lunch at a local Pita Jungle.[74]

The FBI agents who had been following Tom Horne told a different story, including that they observed him and his passenger, after clipping the Range Rover, drive to another level in the garage where they parked and the two "walked to the resident entrance gate, entered a code and entered the resident area of the building."[75] One of the agents offered: "You know, we've heard that Tom is supposed to be honest to a fault ... But he isn't. He's driving someone else's car, crashed, and left the scene of an accident. Having some rendezvous with [his employee] in her apartment. I mean, that's not ethical. That's not honest. That's slimy."[76]

Horne, instead of admitting anything, went on the offensive and asked, "What were they doing surveilling me? ... It seems to me that's something people should raise."[77] The FBI had been following him as part of an investigation of allegations of campaign finance abuse.

As was frequently the norm in the MAS controversy, truth was stranger than fiction. In the midst of this, an important truth emerged with the issuance of "The Cabrera Report."

"THE CABRERA REPORT"

The ALJ hearing commenced. The findings of noncompliance stood. The district caved to the state's political and economic pressure, and the TUSD governing board eliminated the program.

There was a wildcard in this story.

In 2012, TUSD was under a nearly four-decade-long federal desegregation order. Since 2003, it has been overseen by Judge David Bury of the District Court for the Federal District of Arizona. In January 2012, Judge Bury assigned Dr. Willis "Bill" Hawley, professor emeritus at the University of Maryland, as the "special master" on the desegregation case. Judge Bury tasked Special Master Hawley with creating a plan for TUSD that, if properly implemented, would allow them to get out from under federal court scrutiny and move to what is called postunitary status. As part of this designation, Special Master Hawley was guaranteed "access to staff, governing board members, schools and district data."[78] For the unitary status plan Hawley was drafting, he was not only interested in integrating the schools but also addressing race-based academic achievement gaps in the district. He had heard about the academic achievement of students who took MAS courses, but the analyses to this point were descriptive and therefore not sufficient to assess the program's efficacy.[79]

A rigorous analysis that could control for numerous confounding factors had yet to be conducted. Special Master Hawley made his career on empirical analysis, where that which could be observed, tested, and analyzed deserved to be elevated in public policy discourse. He called on a group from the University of Arizona College of Education, led by Dr. Nolan Cabrera, to conduct a rigorous assessment of the MAS program. Along with Dr. Cabrera on the analytical team were Associate Dean Dr. Jeffrey F. Milem and Dean Dr. Ronald W. Marx.

As recounted in Chapter 1, Milem and Marx had previously offered to conduct these analyses for Superintendent Pedicone *pro bono*, but he refused. Now, with Special Master Hawley making a request on behalf of the federal government, Pedicone had no choice but to provide the data. It was, however, a nerve-wracking time for the three scholars involved for a number of reasons. First, the timeline was tight. They had to draft a proposal, work with the human subjects boards of both UA and TUSD, obtain the data, clean the data, conduct the analyses, write up the results, realize they did the results incorrectly, conduct the analyses (again), write them up (again), and submit the final report to Special Master Hawley in six weeks.

The final report was dubbed by the Tucson media and local activists as *The Cabrera Report*.[80] As an aside, Cabrera has always disliked this label because it erases the contribution of his co-authors and makes the report seem more about him than the MAS program. But that is what it was called.

The report, using logistic regression analysis, accounted for confounding issues such as race, gender, socioeconomic status and school services (e.g., being ELL) and came to this conclusion: "These results suggest that there is a consistent, significant, positive relationship between MAS participation and student academic performance."[81] Academic performance in this instance meant passing AIMS (state-standardized tests) after initial failure as well as graduating from high school.

After the release of the report, Special Master Hawley and a number of federal government officials hosted a series of sessions through the district where they heard concerns from community members, and MAS was fresh on many people's minds. At one of the meetings, former MAS teacher Jose Gonzalez referenced *The Cabrera Report* as evidence that the classes should be reinstated.

With this as context, Special Master Hawley's final report was a disappointment for supporters and opponents of MAS alike. He did find the results of the *Cabrera Report* compelling, but he also was not going to challenge the constitutionality of state law. Based upon the strength of the analysis and the community push, the final Unitary Status Plan (USP),[82] in part, read:

> By the beginning of the 2013–2014 school year, the District shall develop and implement culturally relevant courses of instruction designed to reflect the history, experiences, and culture of African American and Mexican American communities. Such courses of instruction for core English and Social Studies credit shall be developed and offered at all feasible grade levels in all high schools across the District....[83]

While this opened up new possibilities, it was incredibly restricted because the district was still bound by state law. That is, they had to offer classes that were similar to the banned ones, also offer ones in African American Studies, *and* still comply with A.R.S. §15-112. This meant that MAS could not truly return.

As the district grappled with how to proceed with the USP, the analysis continued to be refined and was eventually published in the *American Educational Research Journal*, the flagship journal of the American Educational Research Association.[84] The continual refinement of the analysis would be increasingly important in the federal trial regarding the constitutional challenge to A.R.S. §15-112.

FROM CHAOS TO FOCUS: ON TO THE FEDERAL CASE

This chapter canvassed many of the disparate strands of what took place leading up to the federal trial. There were moments of despair brought about by the elimination of MAS, the banning of books, Sean Arce's firing, and UNIDOS being kicked off the UA campus; moments of rebellion such as the walkouts and the School of Ethnic Studies; moments of absurdity like Horne's hit-and-run and Hicks on *The Daily Show*; and moments of celebration with Arce winning the Myles Horton Award and the publication of *The Cabrera Report*. This was the chaos that preceded the federal trial.

While the administrative law hearing with Judge Kowal was perhaps a sham from the get-go, the Tucson 11, joined soon by students, were pursuing what would turn out to be a more fruitful avenue in federal court where they could actually challenge the constitutionality of the anti-MAS law. As time would tell, this would be the most effective strategy at challenging a racist state.

7

The Lawsuit

Losing the First Round

With the loss in the ALJ proceedings and the elimination of the MAS department, the final hopes of overturning HB 2281 lay with the Tucson 11, or simply "the teachers." Even before the law became effective on January 1, 2011, and before the administrative proceedings before Judge Kowal (Chapter 5), Tucson attorney Richard M. Martinez filed a lawsuit on October 18, 2010, challenging HB 2281 in federal district court in Tucson. The plaintiffs were Sean Arce, the Director of MAS, and ten TUSD teachers, Curtis Acosta, Maria Federico Brummer, Dolores Carrion, Alexandro Escamilla, Jose Gonzalez, Norma Gonzalez, Lorenzo Lopez, Rene Martinez, Sally Rusk, and Yolanda Sotelo.

The defendants were Tom Horne, Superintendent of Public Instruction, and the members of the Arizona State Board of Education. Because the plaintiffs were listed in alphabetical order in the complaint, the case came to be known initially as *Acosta v. Horne*. The case was assigned to Judge John M. Roll, chief judge of the United States District Court for the District of Arizona. But a tragic event on January 8, 2011, altered the course of the litigation in unknowable ways.

THE TRAGEDY OF JANUARY 8

On a bright, sunny Sunday morning in Tucson, a local congressional representative Gabrielle Giffords was holding a constituents meeting called "Congress on Your Corner" in a Safeway parking lot in the northwest side of the city. Just after 10 a.m., Jared Lee Loughner opened fire in the middle of the event, killing six people and injuring thirteen others. Representative Giffords was his primary target, and she was shot in the head during the attack suffering permanent brain damage. What does this horrific event have to do with the MAS controversy?

As it was, Judge John Roll was killed in Loughner's hail of bullets.[1] Roll heroically pushed down and shielded one of Representative Giffords' staffers. Following his death, Judge A. Wallace Tashima, a senior judge on the Ninth Circuit Court of Appeals, took over the case.

It is impossible to know if this tragedy affected the ultimate outcome in this case or whether things would have gone differently if Judge Roll had not been slain. Litigants often try to discern, from the judge's biography and previous cases, how they might rule or to what kind of arguments a judge might be receptive. Judge Roll had been nominated to the court by President George H. W. Bush. In a significant civil rights case involving undocumented Latino migrants who had been assaulted by a vigilante rancher, Judge Roll rejected the rancher's motion to dismiss and motion for summary judgment, finding that there was sufficient evidence that a jury could find that the rancher sought to violate the plaintiffs' civil rights.[2] Despite this background, neither who nominated the judge nor previous cases predetermines how a judge will decide.

Similarly, a judge's ancestry does not predetermine how they will decide, although some wondered if Judge Tashima having been confined in a US-run Japanese American incarceration camp during World War II might make him more sensitive to racial issues. We will never know what difference it might have made if Judge Roll had not been slain. Nevertheless, the course of the MAS case was forever altered by the tragedy that occurred on January 8, 2011.

THE LEGAL STRATEGY AND THE PROBLEM OF STANDING

If you believe that a state actor has violated your civil rights, you may bring a lawsuit under 42 U.S.C. §1983 and allege what is known as a constitutional tort. You may seek monetary damages, equitable relief, or both. Equitable relief, the only type pursued in this case, might take the form of declaratory relief, where the court declares that constitutional rights have been violated or declares the law unconstitutional, or injunctive relief, where the court orders the state actor to stop violating your civil rights or orders the state actor to stop enforcing an unconstitutional law. This kind of claim "sounds in equity" and is tried before a judge, and neither party may demand a jury.

The teachers' lawsuit was a §1983 claim against the defendants named only in their official capacity and sought equitable relief (declaratory and injunctive) and no monetary damages. Specifically, the teachers sought a declaration that HB 2281 was unconstitutional; that the enforcement of it by Tom Horne violated the plaintiffs' free speech rights under the First Amendment and violated the equal protection and due process guarantees of the Fourteenth Amendment. They also sought an injunction to forbid Horne and the Arizona State Board of Education from taking any future action to enforce the law. Seeking only equitable relief was strategic – the plaintiffs did not want their claims tried by a jury.

The lawsuit as initially filed was doomed to fail.

The immediate problem was the legal doctrine of standing. In order to bring a legal challenge, you cannot get into court because you claim that a law is unconstitutional. For example, if we (the authors) had wanted to sue the Trump administration to prevent rescission of the Deferred Action for Childhood Arrivals Program (DACA), we would have to demonstrate that we have a legal right that the law infringes. Because neither of us is a participant in the DACA program, we would not have standing to challenge its rescission in court. It would not be enough that we might have DACA recipients as students in our classrooms.

The problem for the teachers and the director is that they teach in public schools, and as government employees, their free speech rights are severely limited by the government speech doctrine. When acting as a public school teacher or administrator, they are considered to be speaking as government employees, and the government may determine what they are permitted to say. In the context of public education, the government is free to determine what is taught, and any limitation the government imposes on what they teach does not infringe any right that they have. This directly knocks out the teachers' First Amendment claim. For a similar reason, because the teachers had no affirmative right to control what they teach and don't teach, their Fourteenth Amendment equal protection and due process claims – that the law restricted in a discriminatory and vague manner what they could and could not teach in the classroom – were also knocked out.

Their attorney Richard Martinez quickly identified these problems, and on April 12, 2011, he filed an amended complaint that added two TUSD students – Maya Arce, who was then a seventh grader, and Korina Eliza Lopez, then a ninth grader. In the amended complaint, Maya was described as a Latina, a seventh grade student attending a school in TUSD, who planned to register for MAS course offerings when she attended high school.[3] Because she was a minor, her father Sean Arce was included as "her next best friend," which is the formal legal status – more commonly "next friend" – that allows him to participate in the legal proceedings to protect his daughter's rights. Korina's "next best friend" was her father, Lorenzo Lopez, Jr. Yes, Sean and Lorenzo, as the MAS director and as an MAS teacher, respectively, were already named plaintiffs in the lawsuit. In addition, another count was added – that the defendants' actions violated the plaintiffs' First Amendment freedom of association. Because there had been an earlier amendment to the original claim, this was the Second Amended Complaint. Also, with Tom Horne becoming Arizona Attorney General and John Huppenthal, Superintendent of Public Instruction, Huppenthal was substituted for Horne as defendant. The case was now *Acosta* v. *Huppenthal*.

Three months later in July, the plaintiffs would seek permission from the court to file their Third Amended Complaint. By then, Superintendent Huppenthal had issued his finding that TUSD was in violation of A.R.S. §15-112. The Third Amended Complaint added those facts and refined its equal protection claims, splitting the equal protection due process claim into three separate counts, alleging that the statute was void for vagueness, facially; void for vagueness, as applied; and that plaintiffs' substantive due process rights had been violated. Though the defendants opposed amending the complaint a third time, the judge granted the motion. The judge also ordered the pending motion for summary judgment dismissed without prejudice, meaning that the plaintiffs could re-file a new motion for summary judgment.[4]

The addition of Maya and Korina may not have been sufficient, at least initially, in terms of standing to sue. Though Maya and Korina have free speech rights as students and thus did not face the same problem that the teachers did, the standing doctrine requires that the harm alleged be actual and not just speculative. The problem for Maya and Korina is that the MAS classes they intended to enroll in were offered only in the junior and senior years. As seventh and ninth graders, though they may have intended to, whether they would actually enroll is speculative. Most of us would not find this to be a problem. Both Maya and Korina and their parents expressed what they intended – to enroll in *all* MAS courses. But federal courts are sticklers about standing, especially it seems when the plaintiffs are racial minorities.

MORE ON THE TRICKY LEGAL NATURE OF STANDING

One of the most infamous standing cases is *Dred Scott* v. *Sandford*. In a tortured opinion written by Chief Justice Roger B. Taney, the Supreme Court refused to reach the merits of whether Mr. Scott, a slave, was free by virtue of having been transported by his owner to a free state. Instead, whether the case was even properly before the Court turned on "a very serious question":

> Can a negro whose ancestors were imported into this country and sold as slaves become a member of the political community formed and brought into existence by the Constitution of the United States, and as such become entitled to all the rights, and privileges, and immunities, guaranteed by that instrument to a citizen, one of which rights is the privilege of suing in a court of the United States in the cases specified in the Constitution.[5]

Taney answered this question in the negative, closing the federal courthouse doors to Mr. Scott.

Of more recent vintage is *City of Los Angeles* v. *Lyons*, which also shows the lengths to which the federal courts sometimes go to determine that a minority plaintiff lacks standing. In 1976, Adolph Lyons was stopped by Los Angeles Police Department officers because one of the taillights of the car he was driving was burned out. Though he complied with all commands, and even as acknowledged by the majority, though there was no provocation or justification, the Los Angeles Police Department (LAPD) officers applied a chokehold. The majority, written by Justice Byron White, says that Lyons was rendered unconscious and suffered damage to his larynx.[6] The dissent, written by Justice Thurgood Marshall, describes it a little differently:

> the officer began to choke Lyons by applying a forearm against his throat. As Lyons struggled for air, the officer handcuffed him, but continued to apply the chokehold until he blacked out. When Lyons regained consciousness, he was lying face down on the ground, choking, gasping for air, and spitting up blood and dirt. He had urinated and defecated. He was issued a traffic citation and released.[7]

Mr. Lyons, in addition to seeking monetary damages against the officers, also sought an injunction to stop the city's policy and practice of authorizing the use of chokeholds "in innumerable situations where [the police] are not threatened by the use of any deadly force whatsoever."[8] Even though, in the period between 1975 and when the decision was rendered in 1983, sixteen persons had died from chokeholds administered by LAPD officers, the majority found that Adolph Lyons did not have standing to challenge this policy and practice because whether he would be subject in the future to a chokehold was speculative. Only Justice Marshall and those who joined his dissent appreciated that Mr. Lyons was a Black man living in Los Angeles. Only Marshall and those who joined his dissent noted that of the sixteen killed by chokeholds during that period, twelve were "Negro males." This fact received no mention in the majority opinion, which found that Mr. Lyons could not prove that he would be stopped in the future by LAPD and, if stopped, be subjected to a chokehold. Because any future harm was speculative, he lacked standing to challenge the policy and practice.

With this as a threshold requirement, it would seem that no one in Los Angeles could have standing to challenge this policy and practice. Instead, this policy and practice can be challenged only indirectly after the fact by those victimized by this policy and practice; the relief available is monetary damages, which the majority in *Lyons* quickly points out as an available avenue. What this means as a practical matter is that Los Angeles remained free to continue its unconstitutional policy and practice so long as the city was willing to answer in damages to chokehold victims to those fortunate enough to get good legal representation necessary to win these difficult police brutality cases. Los Angeles was permitted to maintain this illegal practice because, as a technical matter, no one had standing to challenge it.

Though we know the statistics for Los Angeles during this period, we don't know how many others were killed in the US during that period by similar policies and practices, nor do we know how many have been killed since. One wonders, if the Court had found that Mr. Lyons had standing to challenge this policy and practice, would police departments, including in other cities, continue to have used chokeholds? Would Eric Garner – "I can't breathe" – be alive? Would countless others, including Elijah McClain, the twenty-three-year-old Black man killed by police officers in Aurora, Colorado, or George Floyd, the forty-six-year-old Black man killed by police officers in Minneapolis, Minnesota, still be alive?

What *Lyons* shows is that standing to bring the challenge to HB 2281 was uncertain, even with the addition of Maya and Korina. It may not matter that Maya and Korina intended to enroll. Whether they actually would enroll is speculative; if speculative, a court could deny standing based on *Lyons* and its progeny.

DEFENDANTS MOVE TO DISMISS

On September 19, 2011, the defendants filed a motion to dismiss the complaint based on the government speech doctrine and standing.[9] A motion to dismiss is an efficient way for courts to weed out unmeritorious claims early. This motion to dismiss argued the teachers lacked standing and also asserted that any effect on the teachers' continued employment was speculative as none had been fired, nor was it certain they would be even if the superintendent's finding of violation was made final.

Meanwhile, two months later, on November 16, 2011, the plaintiffs filed a motion seeking a preliminary injunction to prevent the defendants from enforcing HB 2281. A preliminary injunction may be granted at an early stage in litigation if the plaintiffs can prove that they have a strong likelihood of success and if the plaintiffs would suffer irreparable harm before the case can be fully adjudicated.

A hearing on the motion to dismiss and the motion for preliminary injunction was held on December 21, 2011.[10] All the plaintiffs were present in the courtroom. Richard Martinez argued on their behalf. Kevin Ray with the Arizona Attorney General's Office argued on behalf of the defendants. Ray opened by stating that the plaintiffs lacked standing and emphasized that the two student plaintiffs are not eligible to enroll in any MAS classes.

The judge quickly interrupted, saying, "Apparently, one is on the cusp of eligibility, right?" The judge was clearly on top of things. Though there had been a flurry of filings by Martinez on behalf of the plaintiffs totaling hundreds of pages, a key one was a declaration by Korina's father indicating that Korina was now a sophomore and had just registered for her junior year courses, which included American History – Mexican American Perspectives and English – Latino Literature.[11] The registration form was signed on December 14, 2011, and filed with the court the next day.[12] It was fortunate that course registration took place in time for the hearing. Ray though was not willing to concede that registration was sufficient and argued that Korina would only have standing once the classes began in August or September of 2012. The judge seemed skeptical of this argument, but Mr. Ray stuck to it.[13]

When it was the plaintiffs' turn, the judge pushed Richard Martinez on those things that seemed speculative. In particular, Martinez insisted that a consequence of Superintendent Huppenthal's finding of violation, if upheld by the administrative law judge and adopted by Huppenthal, would result in the termination of the MAS Program. The following exchange highlighted the disagreement:

THE COURT: No, but we don't know yet what would be required –
MARTINEZ: Actually, we do, Your Honor.
THE COURT: – as the proposed order says, to bring the program into compliance.
MARTINEZ: We do, Your Honor.
THE COURT: No, we don't.
MARTINEZ: We do.[14]

Martinez then proceeded to discuss why termination of the program was certain, given that John Huppenthal had made a campaign promise to "stop *la raza*," along with other evidence that Martinez argued obviously proved that termination of the program was certain. The judge remained skeptical and directed him to focus on how these points related to standing. The judge then heard the parties on the motion for a preliminary injunction. The judge expressed skepticism about what would happen to the MAS program in the future if the administrative law judge upheld the finding of violation, and this did not bode well for the plaintiffs. At the close of the arguments, the judge took the motions under advisement and promised a quick ruling.

In the meantime, Martinez, recognizing that the judge might be persuaded by the defendants' argument that Maya and Korina didn't have standing and the lawsuit would be dismissed, then filed a complaint in intervention on December 31, 2011, on behalf of Nicholas "Nico" A. Dominguez and his mother, Margarita Elena Dominguez. Nico, a senior at Tucson Magnet High School, was enrolled in MAS classes during the 2011–2012 academic year. If the classes were terminated, he would be directly and immediately impacted. His injury would not be speculative. Also, Nico's mother, Margarita, was not just pursuing the claim as Nico's "next friend," but was also pursuing her own Fourteenth Amendment due process claims as a parent to direct her child's education as part of her rights as a parent.

Intervention, by a party who seeks to bring a claim as a plaintiff, or by a party who seeks to defend against the claim, is permitted under Federal Rule of Civil Procedure 24(b). To succeed, the movant must show that the motion was timely and has a claim or defense that shares with the main action a common question of law or fact. Though the state objected that this motion was filed fourteen months after the initial lawsuit, Judge Tashima found that this delay did not prejudice the defendants, especially because the proposed intervenors "add no new legal arguments to the case, instead entirely embracing the claims presented in Plaintiffs' Third Amended Complaint."[15]

Though no new legal arguments were added by Nico and Margarita, having them participate as plaintiffs-intervenors was important for the case. First, Nico was directly harmed when his MAS classes were terminated, and if the court had any doubts that Maya and Korina had standing, Nico's standing could not be challenged. Second, the complaint in intervention alleged facts that were important for the Fourteenth Amendment political process argument. Nico and Margarita had alleged facts about how they had advocated for the inclusion of MAS courses. At that point in time, before a case decided by the Supreme Court in 2014,[16] courts recognized what is called the political process argument under the equal protection clause. Under this theory, the state may not restructure the political process in such a way that places extra burdens on racial minorities when they seek relief through the political process.

For example, in 1978, Washington state through a voter initiative adopted a constitutional amendment that prohibited desegregative school busing unless there was a court order, which effectively prohibited local school boards from voluntarily adopting busing as a remedy to address de facto segregation. Before the amendment, racial minorities could seek busing to remedy school segregation by advocating directly with local school boards. After the amendment, control over school transportation, normally the province of local school boards, was removed, at least with regard to busing to address segregation. After the amendment, parents and children who sought to address segregation through busing would only be able to do so if they got a court order or if they were able to persuade the statewide electorate to repeal the amendment. The political process had been restructured and placed additional or different burdens on racial minorities. The US Supreme Court endorsed this political process equal protection argument and voided the amendment.[17]

In this instance, because curriculum in Arizona is the province of local school boards, normally, parents and students would need only to persuade the local school board to adopt certain courses. Parents and students who wanted courses on Women's Studies or Holocaust studies need only persuade the local school board to add those courses. After the passage of HB 2281, parents and students who wanted MAS courses would have an additional burden because HB 2281 interfered with local school board autonomy. These facts could have been, but were not, included in the Third Amended Complaint for Sean Arce and Lorenzo Lopez, Jr., who, as the parents of, respectively, Maya and Korina, could have asserted the facts to set up this political process equal protection argument. Nico and Margarita then were crucial in explicitly advancing this claim.

Another practical implication of Nico and Margarita intervening rather than being added directly to the complaint is that it did not interfere with the pending motions filed by the plaintiffs seeking summary judgment and a preliminary injunction. It is likely that intervention was the route chosen because Martinez did not want to reset the clock or further delay the case. As seen earlier, when Martinez sought to amend the complaint for the third time, the defendants opposed this, which required the parties to brief the matter and then for the court to make a decision. Also, as seen earlier, when the court granted the motion to amend the complaint a third time, the judge ordered that the pending motion to dismiss the second amended complaint was now moot and also dismissed without prejudice the pending summary judgment motion. Because the clock is reset each time the complaint is amended, Richard may have sought to avoid that by having Nico and his mother intervene in the lawsuit.

CONTINUED POLITICAL PRESSURE

In the meantime, as recounted previously in Chapter 5, Judge Kowal issued his ruling on December 27, 2011. On January 6, 2012, Superintendent Huppenthal issued his "Order Accepting Recommended Decision." As previously described, Huppenthal, instead of abiding by Judge Kowal's recommendation that the 10 percent withholding of funds begin when the Order was made final, instead made the fine retroactive to August 15, 2011. Huppenthal effectively penalized the district for appealing his June finding of violation. At that point in time, though the program had not yet been terminated, most of the issues Martinez described in the December 21 hearing had come to pass.

Without deciding immediately on Nico and Margarita's motion to intervene, the judge issued an order on January 10, 2012, on the defendants' motion to dismiss and on the plaintiffs' motion for preliminary injunction. As expected, the teachers and the MAS director were dismissed from the lawsuit. Korina, though, was found to have standing because what had arguably been speculative was deemed no longer speculative after Korina submitted her course registration for her junior year and had registered for American History – Mexican American Perspectives and English – Latino Literature. As Korina was found to have standing, the judge was not required to determine if Maya, now an eighth grader, had standing. With the teachers dismissed, the case was now *Arce* v. *Huppenthal*.

In the same order, Judge Tashima dismissed the plaintiffs' free association claim, stating that the plaintiffs had not clearly articulated an argument here and had not countered the defendants' arguments to dismiss this claim. The judge also denied the plaintiffs' motion for preliminary injunction because at that point in time, notwithstanding Huppenthal's finding of violation and Administrative Law Judge Kowal's decision that was adopted by Huppenthal, harm to the plaintiffs remained speculative because TUSD had not yet decided to terminate the program, had not decided whether to appeal the ALJ decision, and if they had appealed, it was uncertain if MAS courses would be permitted to continue while an appeal was pursued. The judge, though, indicated that there might still be a problem for Maya and Korina, at least with regard to the merits of their claim. In a footnote, he stated:

> The Court does note, however, that to the extent that Plaintiff Students' First Amendment Claim rests on their MAS teachers being "willing speakers," the students right to receive information is a corollary to the free speech rights of the teachers ... and, as noted earlier ... public school teachers have no First Amendment rights in the classroom. To this extent, Plaintiffs' likelihood of success on the merits is reduced.[18]

The defendants had not raised this point, but the judge was signaling to the defendants that he was receptive to this argument. Though Judge Tashima did not dismiss the claim brought by Maya and Korina, this footnote signaled that the judge remained skeptical that the students had a viable claim.

THE KOREMATSU CENTER JOINS THE CASE

As we offered in Chapter 3, Robert Chang (author) joined the case as co-counsel in 2012, and he brought with him the resources of the Korematsu Center for Law and Equality that he directs. However, their collective involvement in the case was not certain. In December 2010 and January 2011, shortly after the lawsuit was initiated, and while the case was still before Judge Roll, Vinay Harpalani, a teaching fellow, attempted to contact Richard Martinez to see if the Korematsu Center might assist him. Martinez didn't respond to the emails or phone calls.

A year later, and only after Judge Tashima took over the case, Martinez did respond when Anjana Malhotra, a clinical teaching fellow with the Korematsu Center, renewed the offer of assistance. This time, Martinez responded and accepted the offer. This was puzzling, because why would he accept the assistance from a newly created center in a law school located in the Pacific Northwest when he eschewed offers of assistance by the Mexican American Legal Defense and Educational Fund (MALDEF) and previously ignored the Korematsu Center's offer.

Regardless, the entry of the Korematsu Center proved to be a turning point in the litigation as the Center was able to bring in the resources for what would be the next phases of the litigation.

* * *

Initially, the Korematsu Center provided research support during a chaotic time when Martinez had many irons in the fire. Aside from the demands of his other work, in the MAS case, there was a motion for summary judgment, a cross-motion for summary judgment, a motion for a preliminary injunction, a motion to intervene, and a motion to dismiss. Though he was a solo practitioner, he had assistance then from Jana Happel, a talented lawyer who had practiced for many years in New Mexico.

The Center through its Civil Rights Clinic focused on the concern Judge Tashima had expressed about the students claims. The first important substantive contribution made by the Korematsu Center related to Maya and Korina's right to receive information and ideas that existed independent of whether the teachers had First Amendment rights in the classroom. The key precedent was *Kleindienst v. Mandel*.[19] That case involved a challenge by Ernest Mandel and university professors who invited Mandel to speak at their universities and in other fora but had been thwarted when the state department refused to issue a visa to Mandel for him to enter the United States.[20] The Supreme Court stated, "It is clear that Mandel personally, as an unadmitted and nonresident alien, had no constitutional right of entry to this country as a nonimmigrant or otherwise."[21] It was also clear that Mandel, outside of the bounds of the United States, had no free speech rights. Therefore, any First Amendment theory depended on the standing of the university professors and their right to receive information and ideas. The willing speaker was Mandel, who had no free speech right.

Nevertheless, because the court permitted the university professors to pursue their claim, the court implicitly recognized that the professors' right to receive information and ideas was not dependent on Mandel having free speech rights. In the context of *Arce*, the fact that the teachers as willing speakers had no First Amendment rights did not affect Maya and Korina's claims based on their right to *receive* information and ideas. This point appeared to influence Judge Tashima. During the hearing on the motion for summary judgment, when Martinez referenced *Kleindienst*, the judge's head perked up, and later, in the judge's summary judgment order, no more mention was made that Korina and Maya's standing might depend on the free speech rights of the teachers. Establishing standing was crucial because it doesn't matter how unconstitutional government conduct is – remember *Lyons* – if you do not have a plaintiff who can successfully establish standing.

Another argument the Korematsu Center developed was that even if the teachers could not be the willing speakers for First Amendment purposes, the authors of the books that had been removed from the classrooms were willing speakers. Here, a key case was *Johnson v. Stuart*,[22] a case that Martinez had already identified for the judge in briefing and during the December 21 hearing when the judge asked him what his best case was for the students and standing. The gloss that the Korematsu Center added was to connect Martinez's argument more directly to the judge's concern by identifying the authors of the books, and perhaps even the books themselves, as the willing speakers with regard to the students' right to receive information and ideas. Thinking of the authors as the willing speakers led later to an important part of the amicus strategy before the Ninth Circuit in our appeal after the judge dismissed most of the case on summary judgment. We are getting a little ahead of ourselves.

The broader frame addressed Judge Tashima's second concern about what rights students might have with regard to the curriculum. It was important to concede, pragmatically, that the judge was right – students do not have an affirmative right to receive any particular curricula. Stated differently, the students did not have a right to take MAS courses. The pivot, though, was that this does not mean that the state can do anything it wants. Instead, regardless of the freedom the state has in determining the curriculum, it cannot restrict the curriculum in an unconstitutional manner. Specifically, the state cannot restrict the curriculum if motivated by animus against Mexican Americans or if motivated by narrow political or partisan reasons. This framing was intended to survive the pending cross-motion by the defendants for summary judgment.

This argument relied upon a case that is very familiar to judges, lawyers, and law students, *Meyer v. Nebraska*.[23] In 1919, the Nebraska state legislature enacted a law that made it illegal to teach any subject in any language other than in English.[24] After a teacher was criminally convicted of a misdemeanor because he "taught the subject of reading in the German language to Raymond Parpart, a child of 10 years." At issue was whether this law violated the Fourteenth Amendment, which guaranteed that "No state ... shall deprive any person of life, liberty or property without due process of law."[25] The Court noted that it had not "attempted to define with exactness the liberty thus guaranteed" but that this partially defined "liberty may not be interfered with, under the guise of protecting the public interest, by legislative action which is arbitrary or without reasonable relation to some purpose within the competency of the state to effect."[26] The Court also noted, "Perhaps it would be highly advantageous if all had ready understanding of ordinary speech, but this cannot be coerced by methods which conflict with the Constitution – a desirable end cannot be promoted by prohibited means."[27] This passage was crucial because it permitted us to agree that there was no problem with the *stated* policy of HB 2281, codified as A.R.S. §15-112 (e.g., that public school pupils ought "not to be taught to resent or hate other races or classes of people"). It is a policy that the plaintiffs agreed with. But as the Court in *Meyer* stated, a desirable end cannot be promoted by prohibited means.

ON TO THE SUMMARY JUDGMENT HEARING: THE MAS OPENING SALVO

All of this came before the judge when, on March 19, 2012, Judge Tashima heard arguments on the plaintiffs' motion for summary judgment and the defendants' cross-motion for summary judgment. The day before the hearing, Anjana Malhotra and Robert Chang (author), with two clinic students, Christopher Bhang and Kathryn Kuhlenberg, flew down from Seattle to Tucson to help prepare Martinez for the summary judgment hearing the next day. Even before checking into their hotel, they went to his office. His conference room became the war room. He greeted everyone with pastries and waxed long about the treat. They partook, but they mostly wanted to get down to business, helping Martinez prepare for the next day's summary judgment hearing. He asked for summary documents that presented the best arguments and best cases offensively, on behalf of the plaintiffs' motion for summary judgment, and defensively, to counter the state's cross-motion for summary judgment. Everyone set up their laptops in his conference room, logged in quickly to his WiFi, and got to work. Work commenced and ran long into the night.

The next morning, there was a freak hailstorm, which is unusual for the Sonoran Desert. As far as omens are concerned, it was not apparent at the outset whether this was a bad omen for the plaintiffs or defendants. At the hearing, because it was the plaintiffs' motion for summary judgment and the defendant's cross-motion for summary judgment, Judge Tashima directed: "I'll hear from the plaintiffs first. Plaintiffs can, you know, argue in rebuttal on its motion. Then I'll give defendants the opportunity to argue in rebuttal on the defendants' motion, all right? So both sides will get two shots."[28]

Martinez began by asking the judge if there was anything the judge wanted addressed. This was an unusual gambit. Usually, an attorney will want to control the flow of the presentation. Because this was a motion for summary judgment, Martinez needed to persuade the judge that there were no questions of material fact and that as a matter of law, the plaintiffs prevail on their Fourteenth Amendment due process claims and on their First Amendment overbreadth claims. His thinking, though, as presented to the team from Seattle during the morning's final preparations, was that because Judge Tashima is normally an appellate judge, it was better to hear from Tashima the points he wanted to hear about. That did not make sense to the team because most appellate advocates do not begin by asking the judges what they want to hear. It was too late to change course, so Martinez started this way.

This approach appeared to surprise Judge Tashima, who paused and then stated, "I think the most viable grounds that the plaintiffs assert, and I haven't reached, you know, reached a determination on this yet, are overbreadth and vagueness. I think those are your best grounds, you know."[29] Martinez proceeded to speak for several minutes before the judge interrupted him and said, "Mr. Martinez, you're making a fine argument, but you're really not addressing the issue of vagueness or overbreadth."[30]

When he responded, "I'll narrow into vagueness, Your Honor," the judge said skeptically, "– are you?" This was not a good sign. Martinez then proceeded to speak for several more minutes, a lengthy discussion of facts not closely connected to the vagueness and overbreadth doctrines, before the judge again interrupted him: "But, Mr. Martinez, I think you're getting off the point because, you know, I think you are starting to preach."[31] When he tried to respond, the judge interrupted again and said, "Wait a minute. Let me finish. We're not talking about isolated casual remarks. We're talking about having a program or an instruction of courses.... You are, I think – you're getting off on a tangent. And the question again is now, you know, I asked you to address vagueness, right, and overbreadth."[32]

Martinez then spoke again for several more minutes. The Korematsu Center team saw the lack of interruptions or questions by the judge as a bad sign. It seemed as if the judge was not going to slow things down – he just wanted Martinez to finish.

THE STATE'S RESPONSE: TOM HORNE'S SURPRISING RETURN

It was not a surprise that Tom Horne was present in the courtroom; it was a surprise, though, that he argued the motions himself. Though the case was now *Arce v. Huppenthal*, Horne had been the original defendant. And the statute in question was Horne's most important political accomplishment during his tenure as Superintendent. He had drafted the statute; lobbied for it with the Arizona legislature; tried for three years until it finally became law. Horne had been thwarted from personally enforcing the statute because then-Senator Huppenthal had amended the statute so that it would not go into effect until the next superintendent took office. When he amended the statute, Huppenthal was already running for superintendent. We can only imagine how this must have frustrated Horne. Now at the hearing, Horne appeared determined to see through to completion what he had called for in his 2007 *Open Letter to the Citizens of Tucson* – the death of MAS.

Tom Horne stepped up to the lectern. After making a technical point relating to the state's motion to strike the plaintiffs' statement of facts, which the judge took under advisement, Horne began by equating the MAS Program with the Ku

Klux Klan, stating that it is in the state's interest that courses not teach racist values: "If what we were dealing with was a course designed by the Ku Klux Klan, everybody would see it's obvious the state has that legitimate interest. I think in this case we have shown that this is a course that promotes racist values that the legislature has a valid interest in preventing."[33]

Judge Tashima then nudged him along, saying that he agreed that the legislature has a legitimate interest, and then asked,

> [I]f you take the phrase "promote resentment toward a race or class of people," it's quite a subjective phrase and, you know, it's subject to all kinds of interpretation ... wouldn't you say that the Occupy Movement promotes resentment against a class of people or the Tea Party promotes resentment against a class of people? ... so does that mean a school can't teach ... about the Tea Party or the Occupy Movement because they promote resentment against a class of people? It's an awfully vague command from a legislature, isn't it?[34]

Horne did not have much of a response to these questions from the judge. Given that vagueness was one of the primary theories of the case, plaintiffs took Judge Tashima's questioning as a good sign.

Horne misstepped, though, when he stated, "Tucson Unified School decided not to appeal ... [the administrative law judge's findings] because they thought they couldn't win the appeal." Tashima fired back, "I thought it was because they couldn't afford the attorney's fees." Horne weakly responded, "They cited both reasons, Your Honor."[35] This was a misstep because one of the most important things to safeguard with a court is reputation. One needs to be honest and forthcoming. If a judge thinks that an attorney is not being fully candid, not only does it affect the immediate point, it can color how the judge regards the rest of what you say. In addition, an attorney has a direct ethical obligation based on the Rules of Professional Conduct: "A lawyer shall not knowingly: (1) make a false statement of fact."[36] If Horne knew, as he appeared to admit, that there were two reasons, it is a false statement to present only one reason as if it were the only reason.

As a little foreshadowing, five years later, Judge Tashima in his Order and Opinion stated that "the Court finds Horne ... did not testify credibly regarding their own motivations."[37] Of course, this conclusion came after all the evidence had been presented at trial, including Horne's testimony, but doubts about Horne's candor began with his less than truthful claim here.

Richard Martinez and Tom Horne each had another opportunity to respond to each other and to the court's questions. After the hour-long hearing, everyone walked to Martinez's office to debrief. It can be very difficult to tell from a hearing how a judge is going to rule. Counsel was heartened by the judge's questioning of Horne, especially when he suggested that it was "an awfully vague command from a legislature."[38] The plaintiffs were hopeful.

Then they waited. And waited. And waited.

PLAYING THE WAITING GAME AND
OFFICIALLY JOINING THE MAS TEAM

Not long after the summary judgment hearing, the Korematsu Center team asked Martinez if he would consider the Korematsu Center team joining him as co-counsel. Knowing that the case would be very difficult to win without additional resources, Anjana Malhotra also approached a college friend of hers, Sujal Shah, who was a partner in the San Francisco office of Bingham McCutchen, to see if he and his firm would assist. After Martinez agreed, Malhotra, Shah, and Chang filed their applications in July 2012 to appear pro hac vice in the case. Because they were not admitted to practice in the federal district court for the District of Arizona, they had to seek permission to participate formally in the case. Each filed the required paperwork, paid $50, and attested that they were attorneys in good standing in their respective jurisdictions and had not been subject to disciplinary action. After the judge granted the motions, they were officially counsel to the plaintiffs in this case.

As the months passed, everyone was wondering why it was taking so long for a decision to come out. In the meantime, there were important developments in TUSD's decades-long desegregation case as summarized in Chapter 6. As part of that case, MALDEF, representing the class of Mexican American students, sought to require the inclusion of "culturally relevant curriculum" as part of the desegregation remedy. Specifically, the parties in that case wanted TUSD to "develop and implement culturally relevant courses of instruction designed to reflect the history, experiences, and culture of African American and Latino communities," and for these to be offered as core courses.[39] Not surprisingly, Attorney General Tom Horne sought to intervene in that case. In his filings, he expressed that intervention was required to prevent HB 2281 from being circumvented through the desegregation decree, saying he was concerned that MAS would be reinstated through these culturally relevant courses.

Though the MAS legal team didn't believe that the culturally relevant courses were an adequate replacement for banned classes, they thought the courses would be better than nothing. There was concern that Horne's actions would scuttle even these efforts, and the MAS legal team began taking steps to try to get Judge Tashima's attention. On January 14, 2013, nearly nine months after the summary judgment hearing, they filed a request for an immediate status conference to allow them to address these recent developments to highlight the importance of addressing the summary judgment motions and the plaintiffs' second motion for preliminary injunction that Martinez filed in March 2012. They also requested that the case be placed on an expedited track.[40] On February 1, 2013, they followed up on their earlier filing and asked for a hearing on the pending motion for preliminary injunction.[41] To highlight what was at stake and what proved to be the strongest evidence at the time that MAS courses improved test scores and graduation rates, the MAS legal team included the previously described *Cabrera Report*, discussed in Chapter 6.[42]

In early March 2013, anticipating that something was likely to happen soon in the case, whether a hearing on the preliminary injunction or a decision on summary judgment, Anjana Malhotra and Robert Chang took a new team of students to Tucson to refresh their relationship with the teachers and students and to renew their working relationship with Richard Martinez and with two of the attorneys from Bingham McCutchen. After a series of meetings where they collectively discussed the legal theories underlying the plaintiffs' claims, and still no word from Judge Tashima about a status conference or hearing on the motion for preliminary injunction. The Korematsu Center team returned to the Tucson airport only to find that a windstorm had grounded all flights for at least the next several hours. Learning, though, that flights were still operating out of Phoenix, they rebooked and rented a car to make the 110-mile trek north on the I-10.

About half an hour into the drive, Chang received an email notification that there was a filing in the case. He was driving, so he handed my phone to one of his students. The email notification said that a "Memorandum Order" had been filed by the court.[43] It was eleven days shy of one full year after the summary judgment hearing. Chang told the student to click on the link to access the document. Cell phone service being very spotty between Tucson and Phoenix, the document loaded painfully slowly. The student began reading.

The first paragraph described the suit and what motions were pending before the court. The second paragraph stated, "As discussed below, Plaintiffs' primary motion, with one exception, will be denied." That sounded terrible, but it was possible that the one exception might be enough to void the law or to void the enforcement of the law. But technology being what it was then, the student was unable to skip to the end of the document. Malhotra, as an attorney of record in the case, also received that email notification. She also tried to access the document but also couldn't skip to the end to see what the ultimate ruling was.

The second paragraph did not end on a high note. After noting that certain facts about the statute and its enforcement were concerning, the Order stated: "Nevertheless, these concerns do not meet the high threshold needed to establish a constitutional violation, with one exception. Instead, they are issues that must be left to the State of Arizona and its citizens to address through the democratic process."

Chang listened to every word, trying not to get into an accident as the wind buffeted the large SUV he was driving. What was the one exception on which the plaintiffs won? Was it enough?

As the student kept reading, the atmosphere in the car grew grimmer.

Though Judge Tashima found one provision of HB 2281 to be unconstitutional, whether a course or class had been designed primarily for pupils of a particular ethnicity, he ruled for the defendants in every other regard and held that the statute did not violate the First Amendment. Further, even though neither party had moved for summary judgment on the equal protection claims, the judge, on his own motion, decided that the equal protection claim had been fully and fairly ventilated in the preliminary injunction briefing and that defendants were entitled to prevail as a matter of law. The judge, also on his own motion, denied the plaintiffs' substantive due process claim. Because there were no remaining claims, there was no longer a need for a hearing on the preliminary injunction motion because it was now moot.

Accompanying the Memorandum Order was another document called "Judgment." This two-page document stated:

> In accordance with the Memorandum Order signed and filed concurrently herewith,
>
> IT IS ADJUDGED AND DECLARED that Arizona Revised Statutes, Section 15-112(A)(3) is unconstitutional under the United States Constitution and, therefore, Defendants, the Arizona Superintendent of Education and members of the Arizona Board of Education shall not enforce Section 15-112(A)(3).
>
> IT IS ADJUDGED, except for the above declaratory judgment respecting Section 15-112(A)(3), that Plaintiffs' Third Amended Complaint and Intervenors-Plaintiffs' Complaint-in-Intervention are DISMISSED on the merits.
>
> IT IS FURTHER ADJUDGED AND ORDERED that the Court retains jurisdiction over this case for any future remedial proceedings, should such become necessary.
>
> Each party shall bear his or her own costs.[44]

The plaintiffs lost round one.

8

The Appeal

With a Little Help from Friends
(and a Community Further Divided)

The loss at summary judgment hit hard. The Tucson 11, the student plaintiffs, and their legal team were shocked that the defendants had been granted such a big win. Though there was no question that the plaintiffs would appeal, the MAS legal team had to scramble to plan the strategy for the appeal in addition to doing all the work to research and draft the appellate filings.

The community divisions and fallout stemming from *Precious Knowledge* hit a boiling point. The unresolved divisions festered, much like a cut that is left untreated and eventually becomes infected. This did not just affect people locally in Tucson but also within the national movement to defend MAS. In particular, the National Association for Chicana and Chicano Studies (NACCS), one of the strongest supporters of MAS, became immersed in the controversy.

NACCS STEPS IN

Two weeks after the plaintiffs lost round one of the court proceedings, Dr. Devon Peña, the immediate past chair of NACCS, penned a blistering blog post called "Arizona Update"[1] about the allegations against the *Precious Knowledge* director and what he saw as the silencing of mostly Women of Color who wanted to address gender-based violence in the community. Some context is needed. NACCS is one of the oldest Chicana/o/x-specific academic organizations in existence. It is self-described in its preamble as: "NACCS was founded in 1972 to encourage research to further the political actualization of the Chicana and Chicano community. NACCS calls for committed, critical, rigorous research. NACCS was envisioned not as an academic embellishment, but as a structure rooted in political life."

NACCS is both a scholarly and an overtly political organization dedicated to improving the lives of Chicana/o/xs. In 2012, it supported the plaintiffs in their lawsuit challenging the constitutionality of HB 2281 by filing an amicus brief during the summary judgment proceedings.[2] In addition, it previously sought to draw attention to the struggle in Tucson by screening *Precious Knowledge* at its 2011 meeting.

Once allegations against the director came forth, Peña and his colleague, Dr. Michelle Téllez, co-signed what would later become known as the "NACCS Letter." In it, they called for further investigation into the allegations of rape and three others of sexual harassment, none of which was reported to the police at the time of sending. Peña's post (writing for himself, *not* NACCS) went one step further to offering, "We need a system of restorative justice – one that helps rape victims heal; makes rapists accountable not to the state, but to the victim and the victim's family." But what are the steps necessary to support the healing of the survivor and their family?

There was a quick internal backlash against the letter from local NACCS chapters, as some derided Peña and Téllez as "betraying the movement." These letters and emails went well beyond simple criticism and instead to attack and sometimes threaten both of these community-oriented scholars on deeply personal levels. The biggest challenge came from Ari Palos' legal team, which issued a cease-and-desist order against NACCS. Some argued that potential litigation on this level could do irreparable harm to the organization and there was concern that no formal charges had been filed. Peña and Téllez decided to not pursue their letter any further; however, the legal situation did not prevent Peña from offering his 2013 "Arizona Update."

To that end, he made space for others to contribute their thoughts on the controversy. The post by Dr. Roberto "Cintli" Rodríguez provided an overview of the legal/political struggle around HB 2281, which previewed the internal issues around gender, patriarchy, and gender-based violence within the Tucson community. This then led into a collective statement, also in the blog post, centered on "setting the record straight" regarding the internal community movement. In particular, the anonymous authors made the following statement: "The city of Tucson, Arizona alone stands (as well as with allies in Phoenix) as the only city that will not screen the movie 'Precious Knowledge' out of respect for the once fallen warrior, friend, comrade and ally who suffered a deeply psychological abuse of sexual assault/rape at the hands of film director Ari Palos."

They subsequently offered extremely strong critiques against those they saw as "profiting off the film" (in particular, the Tucson 11), and they also emphasized how continuing to show the film could retraumatize the survivors. From this position, they argued that the film was "a symbol of an internalized tolerance to gender and sexual violence" and was therefore irredeemable. The battle lines were firmly drawn. According to these authors, the film was permanently contaminated with colonized heteropatriarchy, and anyone supporting the film was complicit in this system. This also meant the teachers who had used the film to help fund the legal defense against the state were, according to those penning this part of the blog, actively supporting gender and sexual violence.

With this blog post from the former chair of NACCS, the local politics of Tucson were further placed in the national spotlight. This time, the dividing lines were not as clear-cut as they were when it was *MAS v. the state of Arizona*. Strangely, on a national level, Ethnic Studies in K-12 education was seeing an energy and expansion unseen since the early 1970s.[3] The example of Tucson, in particular the examples portrayed in *Precious Knowledge*, was central to generating the momentum to pass Ethnic Studies requirements throughout the country (see Figure 14.3 to see a map of this expansion). But at what cost?

Regardless, the movement for MAS was suffering greatly. The initial court hearing resulted in a big "L," and the community divisions continued to widen. Meanwhile, the lawyers from the Bingham McCutchen law firm and the Korematsu Center were proceeding with the appeal, unaware of these community dynamics.

THE APPEAL

Here, we take another deep dive into the legal strategy. While it is easy to get lost in the proverbial weeds, we continue to offer these arguments and strategies because they may support future efforts to fight the banning of Critical Race Theory and so-called "divisive concepts".

On April 5, 2013, the plaintiffs filed their notice of appeal.[4] On April 17, 2013, the defendants filed their notice of cross-appeal.[5] Though they had won nearly the entire case, they challenged Judge Tashima's finding that A3 was unconstitutionally overbroad. This provision, addressing classes or courses designed primarily for pupils of a particular ethnic group, was likely of special importance to Arizona Attorney General Tom Horne, who often focused on Ethnic Studies being "racist."

With some amendments to the briefing schedule, the plaintiffs were to file their opening brief on or before November 18, 2013, and the defendants were to file their response and cross-appeal on or before January 31, 2014. Plaintiffs were then to file their reply and response to the cross-appeal on or before April 1, 2014. The defendants then had the option of filing a reply to plaintiffs' response on or before May 1, 2014.

In this complicated legal case, the MAS legal team had its work cut out for them. Some of the difficulty arose because this was Robert Chang's first major case. Though he had been teaching law since 1992, he took his first bar exam and became a member of the bar in 2011. He quickly learned that academia was very different from law practice, and writing law review articles would prove far easier than his primary drafting assignments, writing the Statement of Facts and the section on severability, as well as being the ultimate editor of the brief.

As part of the process, the legal team met in Los Angeles at the end of August. There was not yet a full draft. Martinez may have regretted having deferred the research and drafting to the Bingham and Korematsu Center teams. During the August meeting, junior attorneys from Bingham presented orally on detailed memos they had written on the different legal theories pursued in the appeal. One problem, though, was that Chang had not yet completed the Statement of Facts. It might seem that the Statement of Facts would be the easy part of an appellate brief, that the hard parts must be the legal argument sections. Sometimes that may be the case. But often not. The Statement of Facts is often where a case is won or lost. There is an art to constructing this section that embeds the legal theories into the narrative in such a way that once the judge (or law clerk) has finished reading the statement of facts, if written in a persuasive and compelling way, they will already have a sense of exactly how the outcome should be.

How to embed the legal theories into the narrative for the Statement of Facts also depended on our big picture strategy. What were our specific objectives?

As discussed in Chapter 7, the Third Amended Complaint included six counts (see Figure 8.1).

Because Judge Tashima had sua sponte, on his own motion, granted summary judgment on the plaintiffs' equal protection claim and substantive due process claims, getting those decisions reversed might be thought of as low-hanging fruit. Appellate courts pay very close attention to process, and an immediate question is whether the judge did not give the plaintiffs a fair chance to pursue their claims. A primary role of appellate courts is to correct errors made by the

Count One	Fourteenth Amendment: Equal Protection		sua sponte SJ granted to defendants
Count Two	First Amendment: Free Speech	Overbreadth	SJ granted to plaintiffs on A3; SJ granted to defendants on A1, A2, A4
		Viewpoint Discrimination	SJ granted to defendants even though no party briefed it as part of SJ proceedings
Count Three	First Amendment: Freedom of Association		Dismissed Jan. 10, 2012
Count Four	Fourteenth Amendment: Due Process (Void for Vagueness – Facial)		SJ granted to defendants
Count Five	Fourteenth Amendment: Due Process (Voice for Vagueness – As Applied)		SJ granted to defendants
Count Six	Fourteenth Amendment: Substantive Due Process		sua sponte SJ granted to defendants

FIGURE 8.1 Third Amended Complaint Overview by Robert Chang

court below. They are not to substitute their own judgment about what the correct outcome is. The task for appellants is very clear: identify errors made by the court below.

If the MAS legal team could persuade the appellate court that the plaintiffs did not get a fair chance to present their equal protection and substantive due process claims, then they could get a reversal. A reversal on this basis, however, would typically just reverse the grant of summary judgment and the parties would then return to the trial judge. Winning on these counts would let MAS live to fight another day but would not win the case outright.

Likewise, the fact that viewpoint discrimination was not a basis the plaintiffs moved for summary judgment on, and though defendants in their summary judgment cross-motion reply said that plaintiffs' First Amendment claims should be denied without mentioning or briefing viewpoint discrimination, also made viewpoint discrimination low hanging fruit. One note, though – the MAS legal team did not see this. It was the appellate panel that identified this deficiency in Judge Tashima's summary judgment order without the plaintiffs-appellants specifically bringing that to the attention of the appellate panel.

If the legal team could persuade the appellate panel that not just A_3 was overbroad but that A_2 and A_4 also were, then the entire statute might be found to be unconstitutionally overbroad. A win on this basis would result not just in a reversal of the grant of summary judgment to the defendants but instead would be a complete victory for the plaintiffs, subject of course to a possible appeal by the defendants.

It was also possible to get a complete win based on A_3 and the doctrine of severability. Severability is an arcane legal doctrine that has emerged from the shadows in the legal battle over the Affordable Care Act (ACA) (Obamacare). If one provision of a statute is invalid, an issue arises as to whether that provision can be cut or if the entire statute falls. After Congress reduced the tax penalty to zero for those who do not comply with the individual mandate, a group of states led by Texas claimed that this invalidates the individual mandate and that this is not a severable provision, which means that the entirety of the ACA must fall.[6]

Recall that Judge Tashima found one provision of the statute to be unconstitutional. He had decided, though, that that provision, A_3, *a course or class designed primarily for pupils of a particular ethnicity*, was severable, meaning that it could be excised and the rest of the statute would still stand. If the legal team could persuade the panel that A_3 was not severable, then the whole statute would fall. To win on this, they would have to persuade the panel that the legislature would not have passed HB 2281 if it had not included A_3. This is a tough argument to make, but they thought it important to include because it, too, could provide a total win.

Likewise, if they could persuade the panel that there was a procedural due process problem because the statute was vague on its face or as applied, the plaintiffs would also win outright.

The question for the legal team was whether to go big or go small. Of course, it's not as if they had to choose one or the other. It was more a matter of the emphasis, order, and airtime given to the different theories. And it had to be done in 14,000 words or less.

In Los Angeles in August, Richard Martinez was upset. He wanted things to be further along. Then, toward the end of the Los Angeles meeting, he said he had an announcement. Robert Chang's heart started to race. Martinez said that the team needed to look around the conference table and decide who was going to do the oral argument before the Ninth Circuit. They were all surprised because they assumed Martinez was going to do it. Martinez was not one to shy away from the limelight, including appearances about the case on *Democracy Now!*, in 2012 as well as on the first day of the second week of the trial.[7] He made this media appearance without telling his co-counsel, who only learned of it in real time as it occurred that morning as they were doing final preparation for the day's witness examinations.

Enter Dean Erwin Chemerinsky. The MAS legal team thought of Chemerinsky because he is the author of the leading treatise in constitutional law, a remarkable oral advocate, and is held in high regard by judges throughout the nation. If he became involved in the case, they thought it would serve their clients well. Though the Korematsu Center team had been talking about this possibility since September after the Los Angeles meeting, they decided to wait until they were further along with the opening brief before approaching him.

When Robert Chang finally asked Chemerinsky to join the legal team on October 24, 2013, without hesitation, he said yes, and on a pro bono basis like everyone else. He already knew about the case, thought the law was a terrible one, and thought it was an important civil rights issue. He commented, "I assume that you are fairly far along on the brief that is due on November 18." He noted that he had a Supreme Court argument on December 4 and could read and comment on a draft of the opening brief but would not otherwise be able to assist until the Reply brief.

Chang didn't disabuse Chemerinsky of his assumption that the brief was fairly far along. He was now on the team.

IT'S GOOD TO HAVE FRIENDS (AMICI)

In the meantime, Chang was working with different organizations and law firms that wanted to support this litigation. One way for non-parties to have a say in litigation is to file what are called amicus curiae briefs, literally "friend of the court" briefs. Though the parties in a lawsuit and their attorneys cannot draft or fund the amicus briefs, parties and their attorneys are permitted under the federal rules to coordinate with amici curiae. What this allows is for a party to orchestrate additional support. Amicus briefs can serve a number of important functions. First, they can serve a signaling function. Not many amicus briefs are filed in cases. This changes by the time one gets to the US Supreme Court, where the filing of amicus briefs, and in some cases, numerous amicus briefs, is commonplace. Most cases at the intermediate appellate level have no amicus filings. An even greater percentage of cases at the trial court level have no such filings.

In this case, one amicus brief had already been filed before Judge Tashima during the run-up to the summary judgment hearing. It was filed by Vincent Rabago, a Tucson attorney, on behalf of the NACCS and twenty-six other organizations.[8]

The NACCS amicus brief was beautifully written, and in addition to its legal arguments, the brief provided important contextual information about Chicana/o Studies as an integral part of American education, which had achieved global academic importance, about the importance of Ethnic Studies as a way to improve academic performance by maintaining diverse classrooms, pedagogy, and school curriculum to the benefit of everyone in our multicultural and multiethnic society.

Before the Ninth Circuit, Chang intended to orchestrate the amicus strategy, taking the musical metaphor to heart. Each brief would sound notes from different sections of the orchestra, providing different contextual information and supplementing different aspects of the appellants' arguments.

Amicus briefs are due one week after the party they are supporting files its first brief in the appeal. On November 25, 2013, six amicus briefs were filed supporting the students' appeal from an impressive group of individuals and organizations from across the country, including:

1. Authors of Books Banned from Tucson Unified School District (TUSD)[9]
2. Freedom to Read Foundation, American Library Association, American Booksellers Foundation for Free Expression, Asian/Pacific American Librarians Association, Black Caucus of the American Library Association, Comic Book Legal Defense Fund, National Association for Ethnic Studies, National Coalition against Censorship, National Council of Teachers of English, and REFORMA[10]
3. National Education Association and Arizona Education Association[11]
4. 48 Public School Teachers[12]
5. Chief Justice Earl Warren Institute on Law and Social Policy and the Anti-Defamation League (ADL)[13]
6. LatCrit, Inc.[14]

The amicus brief from the Authors of Books Banned from TUSD had two objectives: first, to highlight that books were in fact removed from classrooms and that this raised the very grave danger of censorship of ideas and different viewpoints; and second, to emphasize that the texts did things very different from what Tom Horne and John Huppenthal claimed they did. The legal team was fortunate to have Brian Matsui of Morrison & Foerster's Supreme Court Practice Group be the lead attorney on this brief.

The amicus brief, filed on behalf of the group led by the Freedom to Read Foundation, supported both the First Amendment viewpoint discrimination and overbreadth arguments. This amazing coalition represented organizations that were especially watchful about the dangers of censorship. As guardians of free expression, they spoke with moral force about the dangers if a lone government official could act on narrow political and partisan reasons to restrict the marketplace of ideas. In addition, the brief supported the overbreadth argument by highlighting how the language in HB 2281 would effectively chill what educators would do in the classroom.

Rhetorically, these first two amicus briefs were intended to remind the court of the horrors of censorship and book banning and the dangers when government officials succumb, as in *Fahrenheit 451*, to the pleasure that comes from burning or banning. Legally, the briefs argued for the critical role courts play and that they were empowered and required under the First Amendment to check this impulse to help ensure an educated citizenry able to participate fully in our democratic institutions.

The amicus brief of the National Education Association and the Arizona Education Association made four crucial points: first, that minority students continue to have persistent educational gaps that current pedagogical approaches are not addressing; second, that research demonstrates that Ethnic Studies programs are pedagogically sound and have been proven to boost minority academic achievement; third, that TUSD's MAS program specifically was pedagogically sound; and fourth, in light of what the MAS program was in fact doing for at-risk[15] minority students, and that the evidence did not support Arizona's claim that its enforcement was motivated by legitimate pedagogical concerns. These points were crucial for our viewpoint discrimination claim, which forbids restricting curriculum if based on narrow partisan or political objectives and not advancing legitimate pedagogical concerns. The brief was largely drafted in-house by attorneys with the National Education Association.

The amicus brief from the 48 Public School Teachers talked about the way teachers use texts to teach reading and critical thinking. The important contribution here is that the brief pointed out that both Superintendent Horne and Huppenthal assumed that public school teachers were incapable of teaching students to read critically. Thus, if students read text that described how a Chicana/o leader, in advocating for excising the colonialist mindset, stated that they must "kill the Gringo," this did not mean that the teachers were advocating or instructing that their students literally "kill the Gringo" as board member Michael Hicks' alluded to in his *Daily Show* interview. This amicus brief said, essentially, that teachers were not stupid, that they were responsible members of society who understood the value of critical thinking and were horrified that HB 2281 and its enforcement would stifle the kind of creative and oppositional thinking upon which this country was founded. This brief was drafted by attorneys at Orrick Herrington, including Mary Kelly Persyn, who would, briefly, join the team representing the plaintiffs.

The fifth amicus brief, actually the first one filed on November 25, was on behalf of the Chief Earl Warren Institute on Law and Social Policy at University of California (UC) Berkeley School of Law and the ADL. This brief supported the equal protection arguments. It was noted that summary judgment on this ground was granted sua sponte, on the judge's own motion. It then quickly ran through the facts that were highly suggestive that the plaintiff students had alleged facts sufficient to reverse the grant of summary judgment. For an amicus brief supporting the equal protection argument, Chang thought the Chief Earl Warren Institute at Berkeley would be the perfect lead amicus party. Here, it was the fact that Earl Warren who, as Chief Justice of the US Supreme Court, championed civil rights and the institution, UC Berkeley, that was intended to add weight based on who spoke. The legal team thought that this brief would help persuade the Ninth Circuit panel that the plaintiffs should at least have a chance to develop and argue equal protection fully before the trial court. This brief was drafted by attorneys at Perkins Coie, including David Perez who had served briefly as the Korematsu Center's first assistant director.

The final amicus brief was submitted by Latina and Latino Critical Legal Theory, Inc., or, as it is known in the legal academy, LatCrit. This brief was authored by a team of attorneys at K & L Gates led by partner Theodore J. Angelis and senior associate Marie Quasius. Chang had worked with Theodore and Marie previously on briefs addressing racial discrimination in the criminal justice system in Washington. The LatCrit brief contributed importantly to the First Amendment Viewpoint Discrimination and Overbreadth arguments, as well as the Fourteenth Amendment due process void for vagueness arguments.

As noted earlier, the amicus briefs collectively were like an orchestra with different sections of instruments. They supported the soloist – here, the appellants. Each amicus brief added musical notes in different registers that supported the plaintiffs' claims. Each brief speaking with force, with authority. All were filed on November 25, 2013.

One additional amicus brief was filed. Cheekily, this brief was filed by the Pacific Legal Foundation in support of neither party and in support of neither affirmance nor reversal. We say cheekily because the Pacific Legal Foundation claimed that it was a neutral brief not supporting either party. In fact, though, it supported the defendants. It argued specifically against the plaintiffs' equal protection political process argument. Claiming that it was a neutral brief was misleading at best, deceptive at worst.

The state then filed its brief in response to our opening brief as well as its opening cross-appeal brief. We then filed our reply to their response and our response to their opening cross-appeal brief. The state then filed its brief in reply to our response to its cross-appeal. The terminology is confusing because this was both an appeal and a cross-appeal. While the legal strategies were being developed, John Huppenthal took to the message boards.

HUPPENTHAL CAUGHT ANONYMOUSLY BLOGGING

While the primary focus at the time was on preparation for the appeal, the racial politics of the state continued to play out. To that end, State Superintendent of Public Instruction John Huppenthal decided to anonymously attack the MAS program in multiple online forums. That anonymity did not last long.

For at least three years under pseudonyms such as Thucydides, Socrates, and Falcon 9, Huppenthal routinely trolled online platforms to trash anything left of center politically, the MAS program in particular. Some of his attacks on the MAS program included, "Just because he won't support the 'we hate Whitey' curriculum of extreme Chicano activists doesn't mean he can't do well among Hispanics."[16] The interesting issue about anonymous blogging is that people will truly show who they are because they do not think that they are being monitored. With no consequences, they tend to "let their hair down," and in this instance, Huppenthal as State Superintendent of Public Instruction thought that MAS meant hating White people. He reiterated this view in another post where he said, "Yes, MAS=KKK in a different color."[17]

Let that sink in for a moment. The KKK is responsible for some of the most egregious domestic terrorism in this country's history against people of color, in particular Black communities. Huppenthal, as one of the most powerful and influential educational leaders in the state, argued that a curriculum dedicated to the educational uplift of Mexican Americans was the equivalent of domestic racial terrorism. That is precisely how twisted the racial politics of Arizona became in the early 2010s.

A liberal blogger named Bob Lord uncovered the charade when he kept linking postings back to IP addresses from the Arizona Department of Education.[18] With a little more digging, he was able to definitively show that it was, in fact, John Huppenthal who was responsible for the comments/blogging/trolling. It was not that difficult because occasionally Huppenthal would accidentally use his real name.[19] This revelation created a firestorm of critiques. Some questioned why he chose to do his trolling anonymously. While many MAS supporters despised Mark Stegeman, at least he would post his own name in the comments section of online articles. Why would Huppenthal hide his identity? Given the inflammatory nature of his comments, the answer seems obvious – it is unlikely that he would never want to publicly state, for example, that, "Obama is rewarding the lazy pigs with food stamps."[20]

Being in the middle of a re-election campaign, Huppenthal called a press conference, during which he cried over his blogging and trolling.[21] Please keep in mind that we are not shaming a man for crying in public. We have enough toxic masculinity in US society as it is. Rather, we are calling into question *why* he was crying. During Huppenthal's public comment, some in the audience said that if he was truly "honorable" as he repeated, he should step down from his office.[22] Was he truly sorry about what he said, or was he only ashamed that he was caught in the act? As his federal trial testimony reveals later in Chapter 12, he was not apologetic for any of the views he expressed; the only remorse he felt was for the distraction he caused. This distraction, unearthed by Bob Lord's investigation of Huppenthal's anonymous online activities, would prove critical at trial.

A COMMUNITY IN PAIN

Losing puts a lot of stress on a movement. By losing, we mean people in the movement losing their jobs, losing their marriages, and of course, losing in Judge Tashima's ruling (see Chapter 7). This creates a great deal of tension, and this social stress was on full display during the summer of 2014 after the briefs were filed in the appeal of Judge Tashima's ruling. A major national conference, the National Association of Multicultural Education (N.A.M.E.) came to Tucson in the fall. As the conference commenced, esteemed scholar and critical educator Dr. Christine Sleeter introduced the MAS panel, which included Curtis Acosta, Sean Arce, Jose Gonzalez, Alexandro "Salo" Escamilla, Sally Rusk, and Norma Gonzalez, moderated by Dr. Anita Fernández, and videotaped by David *"Three Sonorans"* Morales. This part of the session went off without a hitch for an hour. At one point, Jose offered the impassioned mic drop moment when he spoke directly to the political controversy regarding MAS, "What disgusts me is how our children's lives are, like, manipulated, played with, toyed with, and there's no *fucking* accountability."[23] In his wispy, philosophical voice, Jose reminded everyone in attendance what this work was all about: the students.

The panel presentation ended with a unity clap – the clap banned by the state of Arizona and labeled by board member Mark Stegeman as promoting "cult-like behavior." It felt like an act of defiance against a racist state. The presenters retired to a breakout room to host a more in-depth dialogue about MAS. Former MAS teacher Maria Federico Brummer and TUSD board member Adelita Grijalva were also in attendance, as was Auggie Romero.

Auggie posted up in a corner as the discussion commenced, and Jose sat on the ground in front of him – also along the wall. As part of the discussion, Curtis gave an impassioned speech, had to leave early, and told Auggie good-bye on his way out. Curtis put his hand on Auggie's shoulder as he said farewell, and someone yelled out *dale abrazo* – "give him a hug." The plea was both an acknowledgement of deep-seated pain and a call for healing and forgiveness. The hug did not happen.

The conversation shifted then to a difficult question posed by TUSD board member Grijalva, who asked what could or should be moved forward to support the other 49,000 students in the district given the enormous success of the MAS program but the enormous pressure the state was putting on the district. There was a perpetual tension between MAS and the culturally relevant curriculum (CRC) courses that replaced them as mandated in the federal desegregation case.

That was when Auggie interjected with a defense of the CRC courses, "The reality is that the work is back. All bullshit aside, the work is back." Unstated, but understood by many in the room, was Auggie's view that the community needed to support CRC as Auggie had when he returned to lead its development at TUSD. Auggie insisted that MAS is about a curriculum and pedagogy, not specific people, and that MAS, for all intents and purposes, was back in the district under his direction.

This did not sit well with those who thought it critical that MAS, including its name, come back to TUSD with the teachers and administrators who developed, refined, and fought for the program. Salo argued that MAS was not back because the name was not back, to which Auggie quickly retorted, "That's just semantic bullshit!!" Maria tried to interject by saying the district was in transition, and that Salo's classroom continued to represent MAS for his students, but Auggie cut her off, saying to Salo, "Do the work!"

Salo, who was still teaching in the district, said he was doing the work. Auggie thought that actually made his point that MAS was back and yelled, "Exactly! Exactly!!" Salo quickly responded, "Then stop yelling at me *carnal*!" Strangely, though Salo and Auggie were not that far apart in their perspectives, the years of community pain were spilling over into the public sphere.

Maria again tried to make the peace, reminding everyone that the current courses were a work in progress and that the community needed to heal and hold each other accountable. This was when Sean, now standing near Auggie along the back wall, fanned the flames Maria was trying to extinguish by saying, "Accountability? Like this *vato* [pointing to Auggie] selling everybody out."

Before he could finish, Auggie yelled, "Fuck you! You sold everybody out!!! Who'd I sell out? Who'd I sell out?!?!?!"

Sean, a former college football player, and Auggie, a former wrestler, gestured aggressively at each other as their more than 500 pounds of collective mass moved toward each other. Jose, ever the peacemaker, rose from the floor to stand between the two former *compadres*.

The altercation escalated further with four people now standing in between Sean and Auggie and the shouting continued at an even more fevered pitch. Both called each other *vendidos* to the cause, "sellouts," "chumps," and "punk-asses," while Sally, half the size of either individual, was in the middle assertively and repeatedly telling them to just "stop." Finally, Auggie was escorted out of the room.

The entire exchange was captured by David Morales. Several asked him not to post the video on his *Three Sonorans* webpage, in part because it could potentially hurt Sean's reputation. Morales disagreed and thought it important that the public see the character of then-Pueblo High School principal Auggie Romero, a payback of sorts for Auggie breaking the boycott of TUSD on the night that Sean was fired. Some agreed with this sentiment; others thought it was petty. And soon, the world would see these fractures, a community in pain.

Once posted, the video went viral, especially in right-wing spheres. Doug MacEachern continuing to write for the *Arizona Republic* offered the headline, "School principal and fellow Marxist in public brawl."[24] Loretta Hunnicutt, a long-time critic of MAS who long believed the program never left TUSD, used the incident to support her view in a column for the *Arizona Daily Independent* entitled, "Romero claims Mexican American Studies classes never left TUSD."[25] The incident was gleefully covered on right-wing radio, especially 104.1 *The Truth* through Jon Justice's morning show.

This incident and the accompanying 10:36-minute video[26] would be a source of pain, tension, and division for years to come.[27] But strangely, the more internally divided the Tucson community became on the MAS issue, the more national support for the federal lawsuit coalesced.

SAN FRANCISCO, JANUARY 2015: THE LEADUP TO THE 9TH CIRCUIT HEARING

In January 2015, all parties converged on San Francisco. People throughout the country knew the stakes of the hearing. If Arizona was allowed to ban MAS, what would stop other states from following suit? Just before the actual hearing, on January 10, San Francisco's Mission High School hosted an Ethnic Studies Now! Summit. There was a strange historical symmetry with this convening occurring in San Francisco because the San Francisco State University Third World Liberation Front strike of 1968 is largely considered the birthplace of Ethnic Studies.[28]

Just over forty years later, San Francisco was now the site of the greatest legal threat to Ethnic Studies in the country's history. Hundreds of educators, students, and activists came together to learn about the Tucson struggle from Richard Martinez,[29] Lorenzo Lopez,[30] Anita Fernández,[31] Curtis Acosta, Maya Arce,[32] Korina Lopez,[33] and Nolan Cabrera.[34] The presenters spoke to the legal issues at hand in the Ninth Circuit case (Richard Martinez), the core and purpose of Ethnic Studies from the perspective of MAS teachers (Lorenzo Lopez and Curtis Acosta), the educational importance and impacts of Ethnic Studies (Anita Fernández and Nolan Cabrera), and most importantly, the impacts of MAS from the perspective of students (Maya Arce and Korina Lopez). The example of Tucson was at the center of the massive Ethnic Studies expansion during the decade of the 2010s (see Figure 14.3) – an expansion not seen since the late 1960s – and some argue that Ethnic Studies has never seen a greater expansion than during this time period. Activists and educators were searching for guidance, and the Tucson example helped that effort. Like the musical *Hamilton*, it was clear at this point that "History has its eyes on you."

Two days after the Ethnic Studies summit, on the morning of the appellate hearing, there was a line of MAS supporters waiting to enter the courthouse building. A group of *danzantes* dressed in their pre-Columbian ceremonial regalia performed several ceremonial dances on the sidewalk, an action the US Marshals did not appreciate but could not stop. The Marshals kept trying to claim the *danzantes* and the people watching and participating in the ceremony were "blocking foot traffic," but it did not hold. Needless to say, it was unusual, but completely appropriate given the nature of the MAS controversy, that *danzantes* would call upon the spirits of the ancestors to see over and bless the court proceedings while representatives of the state would try to stop them.

THE NINTH CIRCUIT HEARING: THE JUDGES AND THE ADVOCATES

On January 12, 2015, in the James R. Browning Courthouse in San Francisco, the parties found themselves before a three-judge panel. Two, Richard R. Clifton and John T. Noonan, Jr., were Ninth Circuit judges; the third, Jed S. Rakoff, was a US District Court Judge for the Southern District of New York, sitting by designation on this panel. Many appellate courts are overworked, so it is not unusual to have district court judges, including those from other circuits, join panels.

The MAS legal team only learned the composition of the panel a week before the argument, and they were not quite sure what to make of its composition. Judges Noonan and Clifton had both been appointed by Republican presidents. The team knew Judge Noonan was known to frustrate both conservatives and liberals, making it difficult to know how he might lean on this case.

The team did not know much about Judge Clifton. Two years earlier, a student in the Korematsu Center Civil Rights Clinic argued a case before Judge Clifton involving the constitutionality of strip searches of persons who had been civilly committed. Judge Clifton appeared humane in his approach to the issue, and it seemed that he might have ruled in favor of the Korematsu Center's client if the US Supreme Court had not, three months earlier, determined that it was okay to conduct routine strip searches of pretrial detainees. Judge Clifton would later gain some public notoriety as one of the three judges on the Ninth Circuit who ruled, unanimously, against President Trump's travel ban in the first appellate decision on his travel ban. That argument was telecast live on numerous television stations, making Judge Clifton a bit of a household name.

As for Judge Jed Rakoff, the legal team knew even less about him, other than his reputation as a judge who issued rulings that held financial companies liable for their misdeeds. The team thought this was a lucky draw. Another reason they were excited to have Judge Rakoff on this panel is that he was not Judge Tashima's colleague. Some speculated this might be relevant because Judge Noonan had served on the bench with Judge Tashima for twenty years and Judge Clifton for thirteen years. Judge Tashima was well-liked on the court and was widely respected. The legal team understood they were asking these judges to overrule their friend and colleague.

Because of the challenges that the appeal presented, the plaintiffs were fortunate that Erwin Chemerinsky joined the legal team. As noted earlier, Chemerinsky was a leading constitutional scholar in the country. It was likely that most of the law clerks in Noonan, Clifton, and Rakoff's chambers learned from Dean Chemerinsky's constitutional law casebook during law school; it was likely that most of the law clerks kept Dean Chemerinsky's constitutional law treatise handy as they researched and, in some cases, helped to draft opinions.

And he was on the MAS legal team.

Arguing for the defendants was Leslie Cooper. She had only joined the case on behalf of the defendants on January 22, 2013.[35] She came on shortly before the summary judgment order and had participated in the briefing before the Ninth Circuit. The plaintiffs were surprised to see her do the argument because when the defendants filed a notice on December 4, 2014, Robert Ellman, the Arizona Solicitor General, was noted as doing the argument.[36] Instead, he attended the argument, second-chairing for Cooper.

The way most state legal departments are structured, there is an Attorney General's office that is led by an elected attorney general. That person is the top lawyer for the state but is not typically the person who handles arguments or the day-to-day lawyering tasks. The attorney general typically chooses someone to be their solicitor general.

Tom Horne, as Attorney General of Arizona, chose Ellman to be Solicitor General. The MAS appeal was a high-profile case. C-Span had asked for and been granted permission by the Ninth Circuit to broadcast the arguments live. This is the kind of case a solicitor general typically lives for. But Ellman sat out. Among the plaintiffs' lawyers, there was unsubstantiated speculation that he got cold feet when he saw that he was arguing against Erwin Chemerinsky. It turned out, though, that this was not the last we would see of Ellman. Four years later, though he was no longer Solicitor General, Arizona hired him to serve as trial counsel in the case. After seeing him for ten days in the courtroom, the outcome before Judges Noonan, Clifton, and Rakoff would likely not have been any different.

ORAL ARGUMENT

In the packed courtroom, Erwin Chemerinsky stepped up to the lectern. He reached into his pocket and brought forth a small piece of paper on which he had scribbled a few things. Otherwise, he brought nothing else with him. There is a story circulating about one of the solicitor generals in the Department of Justice when Barack Obama was President. This solicitor general had an amazing memory. Usually, when attorneys argue, whether a motion before a trial judge or an appeal before an intermediate appellate court, or before the highest court in a jurisdiction, they bring a notebook or binder. This solicitor general would bring with him a single piece of paper that he would place on the lectern. This piece of paper, though, was blank. He brought it only to dispel the notion that he was egotistically parading his amazing memory before the court and those in the audience.

Though members of the team have not asked him, they would bet that Chemerinsky did not need that small piece of paper. In some ways, he was flexing. It was a very small piece of paper, but as the piece of paper did have some things written upon it, he was not flexing as much as that solicitor general.

At the lectern, MAS supporters tended to agree that Chemerinsky presented a masterful argument, and readers can judge for themselves.[37] Then, as Chemerinsky was prepared to sit down to reserve the rest of his argument time for rebuttal, Judge Noonan, who had largely been silent to this point, said, "I have a couple of questions." Then he said,

> You know that Judge Tashima has been a colleague of mine for a good many years, and I know him as very fair-minded person, and of course, he himself experienced considerable racial discrimination during World War II. I can't believe that he came with any racial animus ... and I tend to look as a starting point, what was the judge like.

This was exactly what we had been fearful of. Judge Noonan, as a longtime colleague of Judge Tashima's, was concerned about what our appeal said about his friend and colleague.

Chemerinsky answered as best he could, "In no way do I attribute any racial animus to Judge Tashima. The racial animus here is about the Arizona Legislature and the Secretaries of Education who implemented the law. However, your honors, although Judge Tashima is your colleague, you have to give de novo review on both the 1st Amendment issue and on the grant of summary judgment...." Chemerinsky then emphasized that Judge Tashima applied the wrong standard when he granted summary judgment. Judge Noonan's questions and concerns highlighted that the MAS legal team was facing an uphill battle.

Leslie Cooper then took her turn at the lectern while Robert Ellman sat at counsel's table behind her to the right. One of her first points was that Dr. Cabrera's study on the impact of MAS courses on student achievement was irrelevant. Judge Clifton asked why this would be irrelevant. Ms. Cooper responded, "The state has plenary authority to set the curriculum for its public school students."

Judge Clifton interrupted and said, "That doesn't make it irrelevant. If it is demonstrated that a given program produces better results in terms of student achievement and that program is outlawed, it would seem to support an inference of discriminatory intent if in fact educational achievement is more successfully attained through the program."

Cooper tried to return to her point that the state has plenary or absolute authority. Clifton wasn't buying it:

> The state has the authority, but if the state rejects a program that is more effective in educating children, doesn't that suggest or strengthen the inference

that the reason the state is acting is not because it wants to produce better educated children? This program does that, according to the evidence. It seems to me that the ... state's regulation is intended with discriminatory intent to hold back a given group of the student population.

In some ways, Cooper's argument made sense. To the extent that the plaintiffs were saying that the superintendents were motivated by animus, if they didn't know about the Cabrera study, then it could not have impacted their decision. Because the Cabrera study came out after MAS was terminated, as a matter of simple logic, the facts established by the Cabrera study could not have impacted their enforcement of the statute. But saying it was *irrelevant* if the program was successful reflected a certain tone deafness. How could it not matter that the program was in fact effective in boosting academic achievement?

The MAS legal team emphasized the effectiveness of the program for an additional pragmatic, extra-legal reason. They did not think the judges would step in and reverse the lower court if the program was not effective. Why waste everybody's time over an ineffective program?

Cooper and Clifton then went around and around about A3 – that prohibited courses designed for a particular ethnic group, with Cooper arguing that the statute, E3, specifically permitted courses that "include the history of any ethnic group and that are open to all students, unless the course or class violates subsection A." Judge Clifton couldn't get his head around the notion that E3 would permit a Mexican American History class because it would run afoul of A3, and as E3 stated, such a course would not be permitted if it violated any provision in A.

Judge Rakoff then interjected. He was gracious in how he interjected, saying, "I am ... maybe not following you, and it may be my fault." He asked, "What's an example of a course that would not violate 1, 2, or 4, but would violate 3 and would therefore be prohibited?"

Cooper offered, "If you had a class that is designed for one ethnicity for the purpose of separating them out, the Irish, the Germans, Jews, Asians, but is not about that group."

Rakoff responded, "I'm not quite sure what you mean by 'purposes of separating them out.'" The judges were having a difficult time disentangling A3 from the other provisions. Judge Clifton in particular appeared perturbed that the state wanted A3 reinstated, suggesting that A3 was evidence of racial animus. "You want that to be in the statute. Why? What would that accomplish? And how would it accomplish something that wouldn't suggest discriminatory animus?"

Judge Rakoff followed up,

Supposing you had a course in the public schools of San Francisco in Chinese history. It was theoretically open to everyone, but lo and behold, in designing it, the designers said with the substantial Chinese population in certain parts of San Francisco, we think this will be especially effective in helping Chinese students to understand their history. If that were in Arizona, would that be forbidden by the statute?

Cooper, "It could be your honor."

There was an audible gasp in the courtroom when she said this. Audience members did not know if she had reflected on the fact that she was arguing in San Francisco, the site of terrible discrimination against Chinese Americans and which had a large number of immigrants from China. How could she admit that such a program, which might better engage students in San Francisco schools, would be forbidden? MAS supporters appreciated, though, her candor.

Clifton jumped in, "And why? How does that not suggest discriminatory animus, we don't want minorities to develop any ethnic pride?"

It was clear that the judges had a problem with A3. That boded well for the MAS legal team on the state's cross-appeal. But would it be enough if Judge Tashima's ruling on A3 would be upheld? The MAS legal team needed either the statute as a whole to fall, or remand to fight another day.

Toward the end of Cooper's presentation, Judge Rakoff pushed Cooper on severability. That portion raised the possibility that the judges might be open to the severability argument and that the time spent developing that argument was not wasted.

Dean Chemerinsky stepped back to the lectern. Though he had intended to reserve four minutes for rebuttal, Judge Noonan's questions had taken away two and a half minutes. He had only ninety seconds. Oral argument is an art. Rebuttal is even more of an art. What could he accomplish during those last moments? Chang scribbled a note to Chemerinsky – "Rakoff seems open to severability."

When Dean Chemerinsky stepped back to the lectern for rebuttal, he made two points. The first was severability. The second was to fall back on the procedural requirements for the grant of summary judgment, a point that Judge Rakoff had emphasized. Rakoff, noting Rule 56 on summary judgment and its official comments, had asked Leslie Cooper about the usual course of things, that if a judge was considering granting summary judgment, sua sponte, why the judge didn't express this to the parties and invite briefing as to whether summary judgment was appropriate. Specifically, if neither party had moved for summary judgment on the equal protection claim, why didn't the judge say he was considering ruling on this and, as a matter of fairness, give the parties the opportunity to brief it and argue it.

After the argument, MAS supporters walked out of the James R. Browning Courthouse, their steps a little lighter. An iconic image printed in the *Huffington Post* shows Tony Diaz, the organizer of *Librotraficante*, discussed in Chapter 3, walking down the courthouse stairs on the phone with a Chicano power fist raised in the air and Sean Arce standing to his left.[38] Defiant hope permeated that cool winter day in San Francisco.

9

A New Hope

A New Legal Team and New Plaintiffs

When it is eleven teachers and three high school students versus an entire state, there are no small victories. Thus, when the US Court of Appeals for the Ninth Circuit ruled on July 7, 2015, it was cause for celebration even though it was a mixed result. The panel found that A3 was overbroad and sustained the ruling of Judge Tashima and denied the cross-appeal. But the panel did not accept the MAS legal team's argument on severability, that the entire statute must fall if A3 was invalid. In addition, the panel did not find that the rest of the statute was invalid because of overbreadth or vagueness. But it remanded to Judge Tashima consideration of plaintiffs' viewpoint discrimination and equal protection claims. Importantly, the panel directed that the equal protection claims merited a trial. This was unusual. Normally, when a trial court is reversed, the appellate court simply states that the matter is returned to the trial court for further determination. Here, the appellate court remanded the equal protection claim for trial. This meant that the defendants would not be able to move for summary judgment on the equal protection claim. The appellate court, though, left it open that the defendants could move for summary judgment on viewpoint discrimination.

Judge Rakoff, a judge from the Southern District of New York sitting by designation on the panel, wrote the opinion. This may have softened the blow for Judge Tashima because the opinion overturning him was written by an outsider and not by his long-time colleagues on the Ninth Circuit. Judge Clifton concurred in part and dissented in part. His dissent didn't believe that a trial was required. Judge Clifton, instead, would have simply remanded both viewpoint discrimination and equal protection for further consideration. In some ways, this made sense because the key error with equal protection was that the parties had not moved for summary judgment on that basis. A simple reversal would have wiped the slate clean and would have permitted either party, at a later point in time, to move for summary judgment. But Judge Rakoff in essence was saying, "You really screwed up. Not only should you not have granted summary judgment without giving the plaintiffs an opportunity to present fully their case, but that even on the facts you had before you, you should have known that there was enough evidence that justified having this claim go to trial." Judge Clifton's dissent reflected that he did not want to join in implying this, but the fact that one of the claims was going to go to trial would become important in securing co-counsel. While the new legal team was being established, the drama of the MAS banning was already turned into a play.

THE SURREAL EXPERIENCE OF MÁS

For more than thirty years, Borderlands Theater Company produced community-oriented theater in the Old Pueblo.[1] It was originally founded as a collective of artists and activists and is a self-described "outgrowth of the early Chicano civil rights movement." By their own admission, the 1990s ushered in an era of more playwright-specific productions that sacrificed a little bit of the community connection. They continued to do community-oriented work, primarily centering issues around the US/Mexico border region.

Productions took an interesting turn in 2013 when the partner team Milta Ortiz and Marc Pinate became the Producing and Artistic Directors of Borderlands Theater. Their approach is called ethnographic-based documentary theater where they spend a great deal of time interviewing and interacting with community members to understand, in great detail, the lived experiences of people whose stories they will dramatize. The approach is one part anthropology and one part dramatic creativity. One of their earlier productions that employed this approach was *Más*, where they dramatized the MAS controversy by talking with and interviewing people directly involved, developing a docudrama play off their narratives. The script, written by Milta, not only explored the racial/educational/political controversy but also brought to light the internal divisions within the community – especially those regarding *Precious Knowledge* and the rape allegations. It was a difficult and necessary form of truth telling for a community grappling with intense trauma.[2]

The play largely takes the narrative arc of the first part of this book, while using pseudonyms for the characters or composite sketches except Adelita Grijalva. Ms. Grijalva is a longtime board member of Tucson Unified, a supporter of MAS, and the daughter of congressperson Raúl Grijalva. It was extremely strange for one of the authors (Cabrera) to be in the audience during a production of *Más* when Ms. Grijalva was in the audience sitting next to him.

It was equally strange and serendipitous for the other author (Chang) to also be in the audience. He was there as a guest of Jana Happel, who had previously assisted Richard Martinez during earlier phases of the case and with her husband, James Anaya, a law professor at the University of Arizona James E. Rogers College of Law. Chang didn't know Ms. Grijalva but was introduced to her. Though he was familiar with Dr. Cabrera's empirical analysis of MAS that had been submitted to the special master in TUSD's desegregation case, the two had not met in person. That would not happen until the next morning when they met for breakfast at Teresa's Mosaic Café to discuss Dr. Cabrera possibly serving as an expert witness in the case.

Returning to the play itself, the story followed the banning and the internal community struggles. The docudrama play explored in painful detail all sides of the controversy (minus Horne and Huppenthal – they were obviously antagonists) and left the community with more questions than answers. Symbolically, the set was a sweat lodge, which is typically a form of purification and healing – something the community desperately needed. Despite the legal case moving through the federal courts, there were deep wounds that continued to fester as we recounted in Chapter 8.

Though we cannot do justice to the nuances of the play, we highlight its closing scene. The protagonists, teachers and students, return to the sweat lodge fire and stand in a circle. They hug each other in turn, two-by-two, going clockwise around the circle. The last two to embrace were "Victor" and "Rudy," obvious stand-ins for Sean and Auggie. The play ended with an aspiration for healing even as emotions in the community were still raw following the altercation at the N.A.M.E. conference.

While the play was instrumental in reigniting interest in the fight for Mexican American Studies (MAS) for people outside of the controversy, it did little to bring the different sides together. This had little to do with the play itself, but instead, it shows how entrenched the different sides were. Nationally, the reception of the play continued to support the reinvigorated interest in Ethnic Studies. Meanwhile, attention and efforts continued to coalesce around the upcoming trial in the United States District Court for the District of Arizona.

RETURNING TO THE LEGAL CASE

Between the submission of the appellate briefs and oral argument, MAS legal team law firm partner, Bingham McCutchen, was going through its death throes. It fell victim to its overly rapid expansion and was in turn absorbed by Morgan, Lewis & Bockius. The MAS legal team was uncertain if Morgan Lewis would be as supportive of this case as Bingham had been. This was compounded by the fact that the Bingham partner working with the MAS legal team was going on parental leave. This did not bode well for continued engagement with the law firm.

After the Ninth Circuit decision, James Anaya contacted Martinez and Chang and offered his assistance. To this point, the University of Arizona College of Law and its professors had largely been silent. One exception was Professor Robert Williams, who showed up at a TUSD board meeting and asked repeatedly, "Why did you ban me?" It turns out that he may have been mistaken. The book removed from TUSD classrooms was *Critical Race Theory: An Introduction*, and not *Critical Race Theory: The Cutting Edge*, an anthology edited by Richard Delgado that included a chapter authored by Williams. Regardless, Robert Williams' point was well taken and appreciated.

Not that it matters, substantively, but the couple, James Anaya and Jana Happel, had children who attended TUSD.

After Anaya came on board, Chang flew to Tucson to meet with them to strategize next steps. One immediate hurdle was that discovery had formally closed. Typically, after a case is filed, a routine pretrial order is issued that sets deadlines. One of the most important deadlines is when discovery closes. During discovery, parties are permitted to submit to each other interrogatories, requests for production, requests for admission, and depose individuals who may have information relevant to the lawsuit. Interrogatories are questions that are posed to the other party. Requests for production are requests for documents. Requests for admission are posed as statements that the other party must admit or deny. Depositions are when you sit down with an individual and pose questions that the individual must answer under oath. There is an art to discovery.

Discovery ended without a formal request that discovery be held open pending the resolution of the summary judgment motions. So, the first thing needed was to move to re-open discovery. The MAS legal team expected that the state would fight them on that.

The other thing they needed to figure out was how they would get all of this done. When the partner at Bingham McCutchen, now a partner at Morgan Lewis, told them that he was taking parental leave from the firm and wouldn't be able to continue on the case, Chang decided that new pro bono counsel was needed, and quickly. One of the first things that happens after a reversal and remand is that the judge orders the parties to appear for a status conference. This was to take place in August 2015. The status conference presents an opportunity to hit the reset button when you find yourself back before the judge.

In retrospect, Chang should have flown down for the status conference held on August 28, 2015. But the Korematsu Center had such limited resources that Chang decided that, rather than fly to Tucson for what would likely be a ten-minute status conference, he would try to appear telephonically. Martinez thought it would be no problem, and two days before the status conference filed a motion for Chang to participate by phone.[3] On the morning of the status conference, the motion had not yet been granted. As the status conference began, Martinez asked the judge about Robert Chang participating by phone. The judge looked at Martinez and said, "You can handle this, right?" Martinez said yes and the judge then denied the motion.

To this day, it is unclear why the judge denied telephonic participation. Maybe he thought it was disrespectful that Chang did not appear in person. Maybe he was annoyed at being reversed. Judges hate being reversed. But the state ended up agreeing to re-open discovery. New deadlines were set. The MAS legal team was on their way, but for the moment, it was just Martinez and Chang.

* * *

James Anaya saved the legal team. He said there was this foundation he had worked with before in New York that matched BigLaw pro bono with worthy causes. He contacted his friend at the Cyrus Vance Foundation, which led to the MAS legal team receiving a call from attorneys from the New York office of Weil, Gotshal & Manges. They were drawn to this case because of its civil rights implications and offered their services pro bono. The two partners on the case were James Quinn and Steven Reiss. They would lead a team of associates, including Luna Barrington and David Fitzmaurice, through the slog of discovery and the trial.

This was a game-changer in the MAS case because, for the first time, the plaintiffs would not be metaphorically outgunned. Even though Weil took the case pro bono, they put a lot of resources behind the effort. This included a budget to hire expert witnesses in addition to the vast amount of legal and trial expertise they brought to the table. Contrast this with the early MAS court proceedings where teachers had to travel throughout the country under the banner "Save Ethnic Studies" to fund-raise for the legal defense fund in a method jokingly described as "one part pass the hat and one part tamales sale." With Weil on board, resources were no longer an issue, allowing laser-like focus on the trial.

In addition to financial resources for litigation costs, it should be noted that both partners were legendary trial lawyers. James Quinn, in addition to his extensive commercial litigation experience, has long been a thorn in the sides of professional sports leagues, representing player Oscar Robertson in his challenge to the National Basketball Association. Specifically, he challenged its rules that in essence tied players to one team for life, though the team was free to part ways with the player. The lawsuit led to a settlement and the creation of the "Oscar Robertson Rule," paving the way for unrestricted free agency for NBA players. He followed this by representing players in *McNeil v. National Football League*, which led to true free agency for NFL players. Quinn recounts these and other legal battles in *Don't Be Afraid to Win: How Free Agency Changed the Business of Pro Sports*.[4]

Steven Reiss, even as a law student at Stanford, was pulled from his studies during his 3L year to work with Anthony Amsterdam, David Kendall, and Peggy Cooper Davis on five death penalty cases pending before the US Supreme Court. He went on to clerk for Justice William J. Brennan Jr. and was one of Justice's former clerks who started the Brennan Center for Justice at New York University School of Law. He left law practice and entered academia, earning tenure at New York University School of Law. He then became only the second tenured professor at New York University Law ever to quit and return to private practice. The two associates from the firm, Luna Ngan Barrington and David Fitzmaurice, were no slouches, either.

*   *   *

In addition to the new team joining as co-counsel, a few changes occurred with the plaintiffs and the defendants. John Huppenthal failed to win re-election and was succeeded by Diane Douglas. Nicholas Dominguez and Korina Lopez graduated from Tucson Magnet High School. They were no longer students in TUSD and therefore no longer had standing to remain plaintiffs because they could not receive the benefit of the equitable remedy sought. By the time the Ninth Circuit decided the case, Maya was about to enter her senior year. The MAS legal team knew that this case would not be resolved while she was still in TUSD, and they needed to add a new plaintiff. Jose Gonzalez had a son, Joseph, who was about to enter ninth grade at Tucson High Magnet School. They agreed that Joseph would join Maya as a plaintiff.

On September 25, 2015, the MAS legal team moved for leave from the court to amend their complaint. They were up to the Fourth Amended Complaint. Because Maya had by then turned 18, Sean Arce was dropped as her next friend; Joseph was added as a plaintiff, with Jose's father serving as his next friend. Some technical changes were made so that the complaint included only the remaining counts – equal protection and viewpoint discrimination. The earlier complaints had described Maya as Hispanic. It now described her as Mexican American.

* * *

Not surprisingly, the state opposed the motion to amend the complaint, specifically opposing the addition of Joseph as a plaintiff. The reason: standing. Their primary argument on standing was based on the idea of redressability, the notion that the court would not be able to provide him any relief. Here, it appeared that they were repeating an argument they had made before the Ninth Circuit, that it was TUSD and not the defendants who had terminated the Mexican American Studies program. Because TUSD determines its curriculum, the court could not order the defendants to order TUSD to reinstate MAS. In the reply, the MAS legal team emphasized that the Ninth Circuit had already rejected this argument.

There is a doctrine called "law of the case," which requires that the decision of an appellate court on a legal issue must be followed in all subsequent proceedings in the same case. The MAS legal team also pointed out that both Maya and Joseph were harmed not just by the earlier enforcement actions, but that enforcement was ongoing, with new evidence we brought before the court in a report issued by Superintendent Diane Douglas. On October 1, 2015, in *Arizona Kids Can't Wait! 2015*, she opened by declaring: "Racism is hard to combat, but academic segregation and the teaching of hate through Critical Race pedagogy must stop now."[5] She also described her continued monitoring of TUSD's culturally relevant courses to ensure they were not violating A.R.S. §15-112.

Her report, issued after the MAS legal team moved to amend the complaint but in time for them to include in their reply, was a godsend. They were able to show the court that even the current superintendent continued to focus on Critical Race pedagogy and that she continued to pay close attention to TUSD's culturally relevant courses to make sure they did not promote resentment or advocate ethnic solidarity. Also of note is the continued construction of Critical Race Theory (CRT) and critical pedagogy as being harmful to students and divisive. CRT came up in the last year of the Trump presidency, when he issued his executive order banning any training that taught it. As we discussed in Chapter 2, the question posed in 1995 by the late Derrick Bell, *Who's Afraid of Critical Race Theory?*, has gained renewed relevance as politicians such as Governors Ron DeSantis (Florida), Sarah Huckabee Sanders (Arkansas), and Glenn Youngkin (Virginia) are tripping over themselves to ban CRT and truthful teaching about the significance of racism in this country's history.

The court granted the MAS legal team's motion for leave to amend. They knew that they would have to voluntarily dismiss Maya as a plaintiff when she graduated, but with Joseph included as a plaintiff, they thought we were good until 2019, by which time the trial should have happened and any appeal, at least at the Ninth Circuit, would be resolved.

The MAS legal team ran into trouble, though, when the state wanted to depose Joseph. Depositions can be rough. Joseph's mother did not want him to go through that. The MAS legal team learned an important lesson, one that Chang makes sure to tell his students. When you are talking to a parent and child about joining a lawsuit, *you need to also talk to the other paren*t, if there is one. This is especially the case if the parents are divorced. Another reason to explore this is that you want to make sure that the child is not placed in the middle if the parents disagree. It is not fair to the child. The family agreed, though, that he would remain a plaintiff until the MAS legal team found substitute plaintiffs.

The MAS legal team was fortunate to have two other families step up. One was Noah González and his father, Jesús, the brother of Jose. The other, Manuel Barcelo and his father, Julian. Noah and Manuel would be entering the ninth grade in TUSD in August 2016. They wouldn't graduate until spring 2020. The MAS legal team then moved to dismiss Joseph as a plaintiff and filed their Fifth Amended Complaint with new plaintiffs on April 29, 2016. This time, recognizing the futility of opposing it, the defendants consented to this filing, and so there was no required court action. Then, in the summer, with Maya having graduated, the MAS legal team stipulated with the defendants to dismissing Maya as a plaintiff. The case would go to trial as *González v. Douglas*.

As the case progressed over the years, the MAS legal team regretted losing Nico, Korina, and Maya as plaintiffs. They could have kept them as plaintiffs if they added a request for nominal monetary damages as part of the "Prayer for Relief." That is actually what it is called at the end of a complaint – Prayer for Relief. Nominal monetary damages are symbolic and are appropriate in instances where there is a constitutional violation but where it may be impossible to quantify the damages in monetary terms. The problem, though, with nominal monetary damages is that that claim sounds in law. The problem was that if the complaint were amended to include a law claim as well as the existing equity claims, the defendants would have had a right to demand a jury trial. Though Judge Tashima had ruled against the plaintiffs at summary judgment, the MAS legal team thought they had a better chance with him than with a jury. Losing the previous plaintiffs was the cost of that strategy.

FINAL PRETRIAL MATTERS

With a new legal team and new plaintiffs, they prepared for trial. Depositions were taken of key witnesses. Discovery requests were made that included interrogatories (targeted questions posed to defendants), requests for admissions, and requests for production. Defendants did what's called a document dump, giving plaintiffs tens of thousands of pages of documents. The new legal team pored over the documents, trying to find needles in haystacks of documents, hoping to find, pardon the phrase, "smoking guns." This work paid off as needles and smoking guns were found, as Chapter 13 reveals.

Notwithstanding what you may have seen in films such as *Erin Brockovich*, discovery resembles more what was depicted in the 2019 film, *Dark Waters*. In that film, based on a true story, Mark Ruffalo plays a law firm attorney whose firm primarily defends corporations who takes on a lawsuit against DuPont. In one scene, DuPont finally complies with discovery requests by "dumping" boxes and boxes of unsorted documents at his office. Though no physical boxes were delivered in the MAS case, the equivalent was provided in electronic form.

The MAS legal team retained three experts: Dr. Nolan Cabrera to provide his opinion on the efficacy of the MAS program; Dr. Stephen Pitti to provide his opinion regarding the use of code words as evidence of discrimination; and Dr. Angela Valenzuela to provide her opinion about the pedagogical basis for MAS. More on the experts is found in Chapter 11 and their role in the trial. Defendants initially retained one expert, Dr. William K. Poston, Jr., and later added Dr. Thomas Haladyna to rebut Dr. Cabrera's report and expert opinion.

As it came closer to the date of the trial, there was one last pretrial conference as well as important final pretrial filings. The final pretrial status conference took place on April 13, 2017. It was Thursday before Easter Sunday. The entire Weil attorney team flew in from New York for this hearing. After the Weil team and Martinez introduced themselves as plaintiffs' counsel, the judge sarcastically asked, "Mr. Martinez, is that all you have? You sure you don't need any more help?" Martinez responded, "Well, unfortunately, Professor Chang couldn't be here today." The judge responded, "But he'll be here for the trial." Martinez responded, "Yes, sir." Things went downhill from there, and the entire trial team was deeply concerned because the judge expressed frustration with Martinez, saying, "You're going to the merits. I am not hearing argument on the motion now. You don't know the difference? ... Ask somebody at your table what the difference is."[6] The judge seemed displeased with Martinez. The rest of the MAS legal team was worried that this dynamic between the two of them might affect the trial.

The final matters, pretrial, related to three important filings. The first was a joint submission that was to be the basis for the final pretrial order that provided the framework for the upcoming trial. It included undisputed and uncontested facts, disputed issues of fact, disputed legal issues, and comprehensive exhibit and witness lists. Each party, five days before trial, submitted their respective Proposed Findings of Fact and Conclusions of Law. The importance of these documents cannot be overstated. One of the Weil associates, David Fitzmaurice, was tasked with drafting the document for Plaintiffs. When Robert Chang arrived in Arizona on Thursday, June 22, 2017, a day after this document was filed, Fitzmaurice looked like he had not slept in days and had a terrible cold. This document was to be the blueprint during trial. If the MAS legal team was able to persuade the judge to agree with their proposed findings of fact, to agree that they had proven their contentions, they thought they stood a strong chance of winning.

THE WAR ROOM AT THE ARIZONA INN

Except for Richard Martinez, the other attorneys were from out of town. For them to run a trial, they needed a war room. The attorneys at Weil Gotshal & Manges were experienced setting up war rooms in far-flung locales. Early on, the Arizona Inn was chosen as the site. It had an outdoor pool large enough to allow lead trial attorney Steven Reiss to do laps each morning to get into the headspace he needed. The restaurant carried Macallan 12, acceptable to the other senior partner on the case, James Quinn; it also had lamb burgers and lamb chops, favored by David Fitzmaurice for lunch or dinner, and avocado toast for breakfast, favored by Weil attorney Luna Barrington. Also, every evening, the Inn hosted, poolside, an ice cream sundae buffet. As for Robert Chang, one thing he came to love was that the Inn set out a huge urn of good coffee placed in its large library reading room promptly at 5 a.m. each day.

One week before trial, Weil sent Steve Mangru to set up the war room at the Arizona Inn in a cottage on the grounds. They shipped enough computers, printers, and legal pads to support a small country. Steve Mangru was also tasked with ensuring that "soft supplies" were there. This included snack foods that included the black licorice favored by Steven Reiss and David Fitzmaurice. This was where the trial strategy would be developed and witnesses prepped. It was also Tucson in the early summer, which meant it was HOT. Despite this, the legal team took breaks by playing tennis … outdoors! The new attorneys fit in well with the motley crew of MAS supporters. It reminded us as authors of the words of Apache in the Chicano underground classic film *Blood in… Blood Out*, "¡Somos pocos, pero locos!"[7]

Unorthodox is sometimes needed to prevail, especially against the power of the state. It is important to remember that the state won consistently in this matter until 2015.

It turned out that it was not just the plaintiffs who had a new legal team. In a surprise, just a month before trial, Leslie Cooper filed a notice with the court of the withdrawal of Assistant Attorney General Jordan Ellel. It is unusual for an attorney who is so heavily involved in preparing for a trial, including having played an active role in the depositions of many who would be witnesses at trial, to leave so soon before trial. Speculation among plaintiffs' counsel was that he looked for and took another job because his heart was not really in it. In looking at the facts and whose conduct he would have to defend, we can't really blame him. This speculation was bolstered when Ellel attended some of the trial in the audience, and he was quite friendly to the plaintiffs' attorneys.

On June 12, 2017, Robert Ellman entered his notice of appearance on behalf of the defendants. Now in private practice, Ellman was the former solicitor general of the state of Arizona, and readers may remember him from Chapter 7 when he filed his acknowledgment of the Ninth Circuit argument, which is usually filed by the person doing the argument. Though he didn't argue, he attended the hearing, and so was certainly familiar with the case. But he did not participate in any of the discovery that followed remand after the appeal. He had a lot of material to absorb in order to be prepared, but that was not the concern of the MAS legal team.

Here we are – at trial!

10

Trial!

Heat rose from the pavement as the Weil team and Robert Chang crossed the street to enter the courthouse on the first day of the trial. The other member of the plaintiffs' legal team, Richard Martinez, was going to meet them in the courtroom. The predicted high was 104 degrees, yet UNIDOS was out in force. On the first day and throughout, they had people on the street corner directly across from the courthouse. They held signs and chanted in support of MAS. While there was still a deep division between UNIDOS and the teachers who were largely driving the court case, the federal trial became a temporary unifying force.

The first week of the bench trial began on June 26, 2017, with a two-week break before resuming on July 17. The court gave the plaintiffs eight trial days to present their case-in-chief; the state was given four days for its defense. The judge, though, strongly encouraged the parties to finish in ten trial days. It seemed that the judge, whose chambers were in Pasadena, California, found Tucson summers to be too hot for his comfort.

Availability, and the parties' agreement to present witnesses out of order, led John Huppenthal to testify on Day 1, all of Day 2, and into Day 3, whereas Tom Horne didn't testify until Day 7. This dynamic also led to the defendants putting on two of their witnesses in the middle of the plaintiffs' presentation of the case. If this had been a jury trial, the MAS legal team likely would not have agreed to mixing up the witnesses because it made it harder to present a cohesive narrative. As this was a bench trial, the team knew that Tashima, with his many years as a trial judge, would have no problem putting together the different pieces of the story.

OPENING STATEMENTS: SETTING THE FOUNDATION

Presenting the trial in this way is similar to the way most films are shot. Though scenes are storyboarded in chronological order, they are almost never shot in said order and instead are sequenced in the end. The legal team expected Judge Tashima to see how the different pieces fit together, yet the out-of-sequence presentation of the case made the closing argument by Steven Reiss even more important than it otherwise might have been (see Chapter 13).

Before things really got underway, the judge granted a defense motion to exclude from the courtroom anyone who was going to testify later in the trial. The judge ordered witnesses out of the courtroom from the start and made it each side's responsibility to police their witnesses. This restriction did not apply to the plaintiffs in the case, and Julian Barcelo and his family attended all three days leading up to Mr. Barcelo's testimony toward the end of Day 3. Nico Dominguez and Sally Rusk were asked to leave because they might be called later as rebuttal witnesses. Jose Gonzalez chose to stay, which foreclosed the MAS legal team from calling him later. As a reminder, Jose was a teacher in the program and was featured, alongside Curtis Acosta, in the film *Precious Knowledge*, and briefly rejoined the case as the next friend of his son, Joseph, who was a student plaintiff for several months. Even after witnesses and potential witnesses left, the courtroom was still packed. The parties then presented their opening statements.

James Quinn delivered the opening for the plaintiffs. It was a workmanlike presentation, just the facts, the legal theories, and how the evidence established them. Having reviewed the transcripts of the earlier proceedings, including the contentious final pretrial status conference on April 13, 2017, the decision was made to be as straightforward as possible, with "no preaching." This decision was based on the negative dynamic that seemed to have developed between the judge and Richard Martinez, including when the judge criticized Richard during the March 2012 summary judgment argument, telling him, "I think you are starting to preach."[1] At this final pretrial status conference, the judge was extremely impatient with the plaintiffs' lawyers but was especially sharp with Richard.[2] There were times when the judge let his frustration with Richard get the better of him. The regard, or seeming lack of it, that the judge had for Richard sometimes led the judge to overreact and make mistakes, as we recount later.

After the plaintiffs, Robert Ellman presented the state's opening. He knew that race discrimination cases based on the equal protection clause are hard to win. It is not enough to show that a state law or policy enforced by a state actor has a racially disparate impact. The US Supreme Court was clear on this issue in *Washington v. Davis*.[3] In that case, the Court declared that, even if a test used for hiring was unrelated to ability to do the job and "excluded disproportionately high numbers of Negro applicants," the use of such a test did not violate the Fourteenth Amendment unless it could be proven that the Police Department was intentionally discriminating against those applicants.[4] Thus, the Court in *Washington v. Davis* made clear that an equal protection claim required *intent*. This boiled down to what Alan David Freeman called the perpetrator perspective, in which a plaintiff had to identify a perpetrator who was a state actor, who had animus, who then acted upon this animus, causing harm to an identifiable victim.[5] This is why equal protection claims are very difficult to win – perpetrators have become very good at masking their racism, not necessarily at being less racist.[6]

Consistent with the state's proposed findings of fact and conclusions of law, Ellman focused primarily on intent, recast as motive: "This case turns on motive. I used to say that a lot as a prosecutor. But in all of those cases, motive was merely evidence of another element. Here it's elevated to the status of an element itself." He then emphasized that the burden was on the plaintiffs to show that the legislature and/or two state superintendents were motivated by racism.[7] Ellman described Tom Horne and John Huppenthal, instead, as being "motivated by a desire to eliminate a Marxist pedagogy of oppression and indoctrinated attitudes of victimization, anger, and resentment" and that they were "motivated to teach students of all background and ethnicities, to value one another as individuals, rather than reducing each other to stereotyped exemplars of their respective races."[8] Ellman also offered that other witnesses who worked with Horne and Huppenthal would testify that they never saw any indication of ethnic or racial bias in the way they conducted themselves.

For causation, they had a simpler argument. Though Horne would gladly take full credit for terminating MAS, because the enforcement was carried out under the Huppenthal administration, the state offered that all Superintendent Huppenthal did was find a violation and impose a penalty. The state's argument here was simply to point their finger at the TUSD Governing Board as the entity that actually pulled the trigger, leading to the result, termination of the program.

Then the defense made what would turn out to be a fatal error. Ellman emphasized that the career educators and administrators responsible for investigating TUSD's MAS program had no prior goal or agenda and that it was only after they conducted a thorough investigation that they came to their own independent conclusions. This could only be true if they had not prejudged the program or not determined in advance that the program violated the statute.

Getting ahead again, the MAS legal team had emails that proved otherwise. Smoking guns, as they were. Or in this case a boat, the S.S. Violation as it was affectionately called in the War Room, that makes its appearance in Chapter 13.

Also, in the opening, Ellman talked about a rap song written by an MAS teacher and decried the lyrics because he "literally called John Huppenthal and Tom Horne *mentirosos*, which is the Spanish for liars."[9] The plaintiffs' attorneys looked at each other, puzzled, when they heard Ellman discuss this rap song that Curtis Acosta wrote for but had not performed at a student-organized community fair. Another surprise was the outrage expressed by Ellman as he tried to use it as a centerpiece in their attempt to undermine Acosta, to characterize MAS teachers as being disrespectful of state and local officials, attitudes they *must* have imparted to their students who *must* have learned their rudeness in MAS classrooms.

After Ellman concluded, a short recess was called, after which the plaintiffs called their first witness, Curtis Acosta. The rhythm of Acosta's testimony was frequently interrupted because he is hard of hearing in his left ear. This tended to occur more when he was being cross-examined by the state.

CURTIS ACOSTA, THE BROWN SCARE, AND "*CACA DE LA VACA*"

James Quinn began by saying, "Good morning, Mr. Acosta," and then asked about his educational background. Acosta provided a brief chronology, including that he earned his Ph.D. at the University of Arizona in Language, Reading, and Culture. Quinn smiled and responded quickly, "I guess I can call you 'doctor.'"

Obviously, Quinn knew that Acosta earned a Ph.D., and maybe it was a little contrived, but this was a way to emphasize Acosta's educational accomplishments. Guided by Quinn's questions, Acosta explained his role in the MAS program, including that he was not formally part of the MAS Department that operated under the supervision of its director, Sean Arce, but instead was a member of the English Department at Tucson High School. This fact was elicited to emphasize that MAS courses were taught in different ways by teachers directly within Arce's department and those who were not.

Dr. Acosta then recounted how he became involved in the MAS Program and explained that it had been "created to address and eliminate the achievement gap," explaining that "historically student outcomes for Mexican-American students and other students of color traditionally have been much lower than European-American students or white students."[10]

As the questioning proceeded, Quinn asked two key questions to undermine some of the state's claims about MAS.

QUINN: In your courses, and to your knowledge, did you teach victimization –
ACOSTA: Never.
QUINN: – of the students?
ACOSTA: No. We were too busy working hard and making up for the skills that had atrophied, like I said earlier, to ever think of ourselves as victims.
QUINN: Did you teach that Mexican-Americans should hate or dislike White students?
ACOSTA: No. That was antithetical to what we did.[11]

This response addressed the charge by the state and some in the district that MAS was racist against White people. In some ways, the defense playbook had a reductive set of equivalences – to talk about racism directed against minorities means that you are talking about racism committed by White people. To say that, one must be saying, then, that White people are racist. This, in turn, necessarily promotes resentment against White people. This same dynamic is playing out today with the bans on CRT and the teaching of racism, in historical or current-day context. Dr. Acosta added:

> [I]t would have been offensive to me personally because I'm bi-racial and I love my mom and she's a pretty Swedish lady, and so I have an affinity for White people. My mom didn't like that term. She liked me to refer to her where she was from, you know, her heritage. But yeah, no, that would have been difficult for me personally.[12]

Ellman moved to strike the response as non-responsive, but even before he could finish his objection, the judge denied it but cautioned the questioner and the witness, saying, "how he feels about his mom obviously is not an issue in this case, right?" The judge's patience was getting tested.

The questions continued and went on to also address the state's assertion that MAS was Marxist. As we explored in Chapter 1, the attacks on MAS were predicated on a reformulation of the 1950s Red Scare coupled with the charges of "reverse racism" or the "Brown Scare." The questions addressed both issues:

QUINN: Did you teach Marxist philosophy in your case [sic]?
ACOSTA: Never.
QUINN: In any of your classes, was there ever any attempt to stir up resentment against Euro American or white people?
ACOSTA: No.
QUINN: In addressing the failing Mexican-American student experience, did that require you to treat other students differently?
ACOSTA: Not at all....[13]

The Marxism question was asked because various state actors engaged in a red-baiting technique, trying to smear MAS teachers as Marxists trying to indoctrinate their students. Then, when asked if he encouraged ethnic solidarity over individuality in his classes, Acosta said emphatically, "No."[14]

But the MAS legal team knew that it was not enough to just say what the courses did *not* do in response to the public and legislative attacks. It was also necessary to explain what did occur within the classrooms. At various points in his testimony, Dr. Acosta described his classroom approach, using the visual metaphor of mirrors and windows. When students are not able to see themselves in the materials they encounter in schools, they frequently shut down. He described how in his own education, he learned "American literature through a European American lens" and that "education traditionally has been Eurocentric."[15] To address this, one of the things he did, along with other MAS teachers, was to include materials "that reflected their lives that reflected their communities. So, if they were reading a story, they could see themselves. So, if they were reading a story, they could see their *abuelita*, their grandma, their *tías*, their aunts and uncles."[16]

He noted that "many of [his] students would say this is the first time not only that they saw themselves or their family or their community in this, but also it was the first time they read a book at all."[17]

When asked by Quinn why this was important, Acosta stressed:

> If we're trying to talk about breaking cycles of poverty, cycles of violence, cycles of incarceration the Mexican-American community has had for generations, then we need some way to engage our students in education, because education is a conduit to, you know, integrating into all the wonderful institutions of our country, and for them to have personal self-worth as well, and to be physically engaged, democratically engaged in this country.[18]

Rather than it being divisive, the MAS teachers saw their program as equipping students for success, allowing them to participate fully in our country's democratic institutions. Instead of sowing division, the classes were meant to foster inclusive excellence.

Dr. Acosta also discussed the way he used his teaching materials to provide windows for his students. It wasn't enough for them to just see themselves; he wanted them to see the broader world, especially in his senior year Latino Literature class, in which he chose materials that provided a "window to other places, other populations,"[19] ultimately leading to increased student performance.[20] The theoretical basis for the pedagogical approach would be supported later during the second week of trial by the expert testimony of Dr. Angela Valenzuela, while the empirical support regarding educational success would be provided by Dr. Nolan Cabrera on Day 4.

Anticipating what Tom Horne was expected to testify about, Quinn asked Dr. Acosta about the student protest of the speaker Horne had chosen to counter Dolores Huerta: "Were the students who were protesting limited to students who were involved in the Mexican-American studies program?" Acosta said that they were not, and that students of all ethnicities appeared to participate. But more importantly, he knew many of the student protestors were not in the program because, from teaching the classes, he knew who was in the program.[21] This last was critical to counter Horne's previous public allegations, and what Horne would assert in his testimony on Day 7, that the protestors were students in the MAS program and that they had learned their rudeness from their MAS teachers.

In additional testimony, Dr. Acosta was able to describe what happened after the administrative law judge ruled and Huppenthal accepted it in January 2012 and issued his 10 percent fine, retroactive to August 2011. He described how he had been advised by his superiors at TUSD that because of the issues of race, class, and oppression in Shakespeare's *The Tempest*, that he "should throw it out."[22] He also described how he was advised to "stay away from terms such as 'race,' 'ethnicity,' 'oppression,' and 'class,'"[23] while also painting a vivid, painful picture of the books and other materials being removed from his class in front of the students.[24]

Quinn concluded the direct examination, and Robert Ellman began his cross. After some initial questions, Ellman asked about an essay prompt Acosta wrote for one of his Latino Literature classes: "The audience encounters Mexicano and Chicano individuals that exploit or abuse people of their own cultural and ethnic heritage. Simultaneously, the immigration laws of this country, which are largely crafted by middle-aged European American men, serve as the framework which creates this environment for exploitation and abuse? In [a] well considered essay, compare the ethical issues along ethnic lines."[25]

The state tried to make it seem as if Acosta was promoting resentment against a particular group of people through this essay prompt, resentment against the White men who "created an environment for exploitation and abuse." The state asked if it promoted resentment toward an ethnic group, which Acosta denied.[26]

A premise at the heart of the challenged statute and the state's questioning appears to be that teaching the truth about racism, historically, and how it may manifest today necessarily results in resentment against White people. Embedded is the notion that students can't handle the truth, a notion we revisit in our discussion of Dr. Angela Valenzuela's expert testimony in Chapter 11 as well as in our Epilogue.

Ellman, in asking these questions, did not get the answers he wanted, but he likely felt that the prompt spoke for itself, that the prompt's "hatefulness" would be obvious to Judge Tashima.

Ellman then called into question Dr. Acosta's knowledge of Shakespeare based on his characterization of *The Tempest*. While this line of questioning did not lead anywhere productive, it allowed Ellman to return to the theme of fostering resentment:

ELLMAN: So you explained to your students, according to your deposition testimony, there are issues in [*The Tempest*] of race, colonization, power, specifically of European power against native new world North Americans, correct?
ACOSTA: Yeah, that was part of the lens of *The Tempest*.

James Quinn objected to Ellman's use of Acosta's deposition testimony, saying that it did not speak to impeaching the witness. The judge overruled the objection, allowing Ellman to proceed.

Ellman then questions Acosta about a speech by Che Guevara used in Latino Literature. Without providing Acosta with a copy, Ellman proceeds to quote portions of the speech, asking each time if Acosta remembered them:

> It is imperative to take political power and get rid of the oppressor classes.
> ...
> If the imperialist enemy, the United States, or any other, carries out its attack against the underdeveloped peoples and the socialist countries, elementary logic determines the need for an alliance between the underdeveloped peoples and the socialist countries.[27]

Ellman then asked, "Don't you agree that that teaches your students class-based resentment and ideology?" Acosta denied this and explained, "[B]ecause we're reading something doesn't put it in the proper context of how we were analyzing it or how the students were asked to analyze it for my classroom."[28]

Interestingly, Ellman did not ask the obvious follow-up question, having Acosta describe the context, including how he asked students to analyze the text. It is likely Ellman did not ask because he did not want the court to have the benefit of this explanation. The insinuation was that the words from the speech could and should be regarded, as later witnesses would testify, literally as that which was being taught to the students. If this were true, it is difficult to square this with statements by witnesses such as Tom Horne and John Huppenthal, that Hitler's

Mein Kampf could be taught in a classroom, that it was not the words, literally, but instead, how the material was taught.

During Ellman's cross-examination of Dr. Acosta, the MAS team was passing notes back and forth, commenting on how much latitude the judge was giving Ellman in his questioning. The oddest example was when Ellman tried to introduce as an impeachment exhibit a 1969 *New Yorker* magazine article by Peter Mathieson called "Profile Cesar Chavez." Quinn immediately objected and was promptly overruled. Ellman continued by quoting a passage in which Chavez attacked the concept of *la raza* during that particular historical moment as potentially harming the United Farm Workers union:

> I hear more and more Mexicans talking about *La Raza* to build up their pride, you know, Chavez told me. Some people don't look at it as racism, but when you say *La Raza*, you are saying an anti-gringo thing, and it won't stop there. Today it's anti-*gringo*, tomorrow it will be anti-negro, and the day after it will be anti-Filipino, anti-Puerto Rican. And then it will be anti-poor Mexican and anti-darker-skinned Mexican. We had a stupid guy who just wanted to play politics with the union, and he began to whip up *La Raza* against the white volunteers, and even had some of the farm workers and the pickets and the organizers hung up on *La Raza*.[29]

Quinn objected again only to be overruled again. This was a head-scratcher, but it seems that Ellman objected to Dr. Acosta defining the term *la raza* as one of inclusivity, arguing that he did not possess the linguistic background and expertise to make said assessment. In contrast, Ellman seemed to be defining *la raza* as "racist" based upon a fifty-year-old narrative. Quinn's objections should have been sustained, but the MAS legal team observed that the judge was being very solicitous of the state's objections but tended to reject the plaintiffs. This difference in treatment was most obvious during Richard Martinez's direct examination of Sean Arce, discussed later.

There was, at the end of Ellman's cross-examination, some much-needed levity. The audience in the courtroom had to try hard not to burst into laughter when Acosta was asked about a spoken word poem written for the 2011 Tucson High Unity Festival. Spoken word poetry is meant to have a cadence, a rhythm that is intimately linked to the creation of meaning in this artform. Performers need both lyrics (substance) and cadence (style) to make it work. In his questioning, Ellman read stanzas written by Dr. Acosta criticizing TUSD Superintendent John Pedicone, Dr. Pedi, in the word poem:

> This place is like a panopticon
> Dr. Pedi in the tower and intercom
> We know whose side that wanksta's on
> It's not a mystery
> I know whose butt they kissing.

When Ellman said "wanksta," the audience laughed, and laughed even harder when Ellman asked Acosta if he was referring to Dr. Pedicone as a "butt-kissing wanksta." Though he agreed that the reference was correct, he denied Ellman's characterization that it was "highly derogatory" or that it "promotes resentment." Ellman's questioning then turned to the next lines where the poem took aim at Stegeman (aka, "Stoogeman"):

> They smile and wave,
> But run the district like a prison
> Stoogeman keeps frontin', but he's an imposter
> Talks a hole in your head but it's just *caca de la vaca*.

When Ellman read the last line about *caca de la vaca*, in his anglicized pronunciation, one audience member let out an audible snort, which only led to more chuckles around them. Ellman then asked Dr. Acosta if *caca de la vaca* "mean[t] cow excrement" and if he was saying that he thought Stegeman "talks cow excrement," to which Acosta succinctly responded, "Yes."

The MAS legal team was surprised that Ellman spent so much time on the poem, making it his final point. It was only as the trial developed that it became clear that the state thought this was critical evidence demonstrating how "disrespectful" Acosta, and by association, other MAS teachers were. It was also critical to support Tom Horne's otherwise unsubstantiated conclusion that the MAS teachers had orchestrated the student protest of Margaret Garcia Dugan and that they had taught them their rudeness.

After a short re-direct by James Quinn and no further re-cross by Ellman, Dr. Acosta was permitted to step down from the witness stand after being on the stand for hours.

MAYA ARCE AND THE PARENTS OF THE CURRENT STUDENT PLAINTIFFS TAKE THE STAND

Earlier, the MAS legal team planned to have the three former student plaintiffs, Nico Dominguez, Korina Lopez, and Maya Arce, take the stand. But in the April 13, 2017, Final Pretrial Status Conference, Judge Tashima made it very clear that he saw little reason or need to hear from the former students and told the team that "at some point, I think you're going to have to think more seriously about striking those people from your witness list."[30] Following the judge's cue, the team decided to call only Maya, leaving Nico and Korina as possible rebuttal witnesses.

Maya took the stand immediately after Dr. Acosta. When she joined the lawsuit in 2012, she was in seventh grade, and now she was 19 and a student at the University of Arizona. For the MAS legal team, Luna Barrington called Maya to the stand. Early in her questions, Barrington asked Maya about her identity. Maya responded by saying that she was Mexican American and that she was "proud to be an American" and proud of her Mexican heritage and culture.³¹ She described how her father was a co-founder of the MAS program at TUSD, and when asked what she knew about the program, Maya responded:

M. ARCE: I know that it was a program that had classes that included Mexican-American history, perspective, literature, and art.
BARRINGTON: What is your understanding as to why the MAS program was created?
M. ARCE: Well, the Mexican-American perspective is not really included in school, and that is why it was created.
BARRINGTON: Why was it important for you to see Mexican-Americans represented in the curriculum?
M. ARCE: I believe that it is important for every student to see themselves in the curriculum, and when you see yourself in the curriculum, it makes it more relatable and easier to learn new concepts.³²

Barrington continued guiding Maya through questions, and Maya told the court about how she had benefited from having MAS teachers visit her elementary school and do weekly mini lessons but that she was not able to take MAS classes in high school because the program had been terminated.³³

Though Leslie Cooper objected when Barrington asked Maya if she took any MAS classes outside of TUSD, the court permitted this line of questioning. Maya then described how, as a freshman in high school, she took a Mexican American literature class from Dr. Acosta at a community center on Sundays. For this class, she received three college credits but no high school credits. She described the challenging curriculum and how it pushed her academically and how she benefited from it. When asked why she only took the class for one year, Maya responded: "It just became more difficult. Realistically, it's not that easy to go outside of school on a Sunday, and I had a really busy schedule."³⁴ Barrington closed the direct examination by asking why Maya decided to become a plaintiff in this case. Maya said: "I decided to become a plaintiff because I believe in standing up for what I think is right, and I believe that I am a voice for those who otherwise may not be heard, for my ancestors, for my community members and for – sorry – generations to come."³⁵

The cold transcript doesn't capture the effect of Maya's words on those in the courtroom. It seemed that, except perhaps the defense attorneys, everyone was captivated by Maya, even the judge. Chang is certain that he saw a warm smile break over Judge Tashima's usually stern demeanor.

Leslie Cooper had the unenviable task of conducting the cross-examination. Cooper first focused on the high educational attainment of Maya's parents, how Maya passed on her first try the state standardized test required to graduate, and that she had taken several Advanced Placement courses, going through them one by one, AP Literature, AP Statistics, AP US History, AP Music Theory.³⁶ In pursuing this line of questioning, Cooper was trying to paint Maya as the sort of student who did not need MAS courses to become engaged in her education. Recall that Curtis Acosta had testified that many of the students who came to his class had never read a book before, and that the materials in his course provided a mirror for them, a way for them to see themselves in the curriculum and became engaged in ways they had not previously been. While Maya may have been atypical in that way, Cooper's questioning did not undercut what Maya had offered about what she had gained in Dr. Acosta's Sunday class.

Cooper closed by asking about TUSD's culturally relevant classes that were implemented as part of the revised consent decree in TUSD's long-running desegregation lawsuit.

COOPER: Have you ever taken any of those classes, Ms. Arce?
M. ARCE: No, I did not.
COOPER: Just a yes or no.[37]

It might seem odd for Cooper to chastise the witness, insisting on "yes" or "no" when all Maya had said was, "No, I did not." Cooper, though, was trying to keep Maya from explaining or expanding on her responses, as becomes evident in the next exchange:

COOPER: Do you know whether it would be possible to see yourself in the curriculum as a competent young Mexican-American woman in these culturally relevant classes taught from a Mexican-American perspective?
M. ARCE: I don't think so. I think that –
COOPER: Yes or no?
M. ARCE: No.[38]

But what's odd is that Cooper then asked Maya to explain the basis for her response:

M. ARCE: I just think that, if they are a replacement to the Mexican-American Studies program, that there would be no reason to ban Mexican-American Studies in the first place. So I just don't think that the material is, I mean, is up to par, in my opinion.[39]

Cooper closed her examination by asking if Maya had attended any of the new culturally relevant curriculum (CRC) classes that TUSD had begun offering, discussed CRC classes with anyone who teaches CRC from a Mexican American perspective, or had any conversations with any friends who took such classes. Maya answered "No" to each of these questions.[40]

Barrington, recognizing that Cooper had done some damage with her closing questions, asked why Maya didn't think she would have seen herself in the CRC curriculum. Maya answered succinctly, "I think that they are, I would say, a filtered version of the Mexican-American Studies classes because – I mean or else under the bill they would be banned as well."[41]

Judge Tashima, again with a warm smile, excused Maya as a witness. Though the state did some damage with the questioning about CRC, it was precluded from doing more with CRC because the judge previously ruled in a pretrial motion that the state could not argue that CRC was an adequate replacement for MAS. Maya effectively conveyed to the judge the benefit that she, as a student, received from the off-site MAS class and put a human face to the student side of things. It did not hurt that the judge seemed captivated by her.

* * *

Because of a quirk of scheduling and witness availability, John Huppenthal was called toward the end of the first day. His testimony consumed all of Day 2 and part of Day 3. Returning to the film metaphor, this "scene" was shot out of sequence; his testimony will be discussed later in Chapter 12.

* * *

The MAS legal team had no intention of calling the current student plaintiffs or their parents. But the team learned that the state was going to put the parents on the stand. The team decided it was better to control the narrative by calling the parents as part of the plaintiffs' case-in-chief.

After the lunch break on Day 3 of the trial, Jesus González took the stand. David Fitzmaurice from Weil conducted his direct examination. After establishing his identity, Mr. González noted that his "three beautiful boys" were present in the courtroom. His son Noah, who was going to be a sophomore in the fall at Tucson High, was one of the student plaintiffs. Mr. González talked about how he and Noah had talked quite often about the terminated MAS classes and that he would "have loved to have [Noah] participate in a course like MAS" and explained:

> It's important to me as a parent that he understand, him being Mexican-American, the heritage, the beautiful – the culture that is to be Mexican. I want him to be proud. And [MAS] has a lot to offer. You know, the music, the dance part, the poetry, all of that, from what I understand, was being taught in the MAS program.[42]

Mr. González also explained that he regretted that he hadn't had the chance to learn Mexican-American Studies until he attended college at Arizona State University. He wished that Noah would have the chance to learn this at an earlier age, that such courses "would have been something special he could have been a part of."[43]

No-nonsense. Beautiful.

And then the state grilled him.

Robert Ellman began by asking about whether he was recruited to be a plaintiff, which Mr. González denied. After a few more questions, Ellman began asking him about the statute at the heart of the case. He put a copy of the statute on the document camera so that Mr. González could see the statute. The image was projected to all the monitors in the courtroom. Ellman then very quickly walked the witness through the different sections, starting with the statute's Declaration of Policy, A.R.S. §15-111: "The legislature finds and declares that public school pupils should be taught to treat and value each other as individuals and not be taught to resent or hate other races or classes of people."[44] Ellman then asked González if he agreed with subsections 2 and 4 of A.R.S. § 15-112, to which he answered in the affirmative.[45] Ellman then asked:

ELLMAN: If you agree with all of these provisions in the statute, why are you challenging the constitutionality of it?
GONZÁLEZ: I am challenging it because my son did not have an opportunity to take part in a MAS program.[46]

Ellman then tried to create additional doubt for the witness by asking if he knew about a study that disputed claims that MAS promoted academic achievement. Mr. González was hesitant when asked if he would still want his son to take MAS classes, saying, "I guess, yes." Ellman then asked if he knew if a Latino Literature class "included a book written by a murderer," referencing *Live from Death Row* by Mumia Abu-Jamal. Mr. González held firm, saying that he wouldn't have a problem with having his son take a course that included that book.[47]

Ellman, though, could see doubt in the hesitance in Mr. González's answers to the last several questions. He pounced. He asked about a speech by Che Guevara, the same one he had asked Curtis Acosta about. Ellman described the speech as advocating that "socialist countries overthrow the United States" and then asked:

ELLMAN: Okay. If I tell you that that is a correct representation, would you still want your son, Noah, to attend this Latino literature course?
GONZÁLEZ: No, I wouldn't.[48]

Ellman then asked if the witness believed teachers should be respectful of the people who run the schools or the people who run the education system. Upon hearing, "Of course," Ellman then put Acosta's rap poem on the document camera. Wanksta! Butt kisser!

ELLMAN: Would you want your sons, either one of them, to take a class from a teacher who would write a poem like that and plan to recite it in front of a large audience that included his own students?
[after an objection by David Fitzmaurice is overruled the question is re-read by the court reporter]
GONZÁLEZ: I would not.
ELLMAN: Knowing what you know now, do you regret becoming a plaintiff in this lawsuit?
GONZÁLEZ: Absolutely not.[49]

Though Ellman didn't get quite the answer he wanted or thought he was going to get, he sat down, appearing quite pleased with himself.

During the cross-examination, David Fitzmaurice and Robert Chang were furiously exchanging notes. They had not anticipated this line of questioning by the state. They decided, though, that less would be more. On re-direct, Fitzmaurice asked only one question, "Do you think the context in which books and teaching materials are used is important to determine whether they're appropriate or not?" to which Mr. González answered, "I do."

With no further questions from either side, Mr. González was excused. People in the courtroom exchanged worried glances. Had the cross-examination hurt the case?

Next was Julian Barcelo, whose direct examination was conducted by Richard Martinez. Afterwards, that evening, Steven Reiss complimented Richard on the masterful job he did in examining Mr. Barcelo. Though Robert Chang did not see it, other members of the MAS legal team insisted that Judge Tashima's law clerk teared up during the examination.

Richard slowly drew out personal information from the witness. The courtroom learned that he was an immigrant who was now a US citizen, that he was a kindergarten teacher in TUSD, that he was married with three boys. The courtroom learned their names and ages, about their education in various schools in TUSD from kindergarten to primary school to middle school and high school, including details about their decision to have their children forego attending their neighborhood schools and instead attend magnet schools that offered bilingual education.[50] Through all of this, Richard spoke slowly; Mr. Barcelo, though animated in his responses, also spoke in measured tones. This introductory phase of the questioning took longer than the entire direct examination of Mr. González. Through much of it, Mr. Ellman was standing up, wanting to object but holding back.

Richard then asked Mr. Barcelo if he knew about MAS being terminated in January 2012. Richard followed this by asking about the testimony Mr. Barcelo had heard in the courtroom about Dr. Acosta's class.

MARTINEZ: Did you hear anything, whether it was a question asked by the plaintiffs' attorneys or by the state, that changed your mind about that, about wanting your son or sons in Mr. Acosta's class? Do you still want them in that class?
BARCELO: Of course.
MARTINEZ: Do you still want Mr. Acosta to teach your sons?
BARCELO: Of course.
MARTINEZ: Even your youngest?
BARCELO: I would be very proud.[51]

Though it took Richard a long time to get there, this line of questioning helped neutralize the harm from the state's questioning of Mr. González.

Toward the close of his examination, Martinez asked what he and his wife's goals were for their sons. Mr. Barcelo said that they had high expectations for their sons' education, including that they would be bilingual and "keep their culture, language, heritage."[52] Then, returning to a point that Curtis Acosta had testified about:

MARTINEZ: Do you want them to be integrated into the larger society?
BARCELO: Of course. Integrated to this beautiful society.
MARTINEZ: Be a part of it?
BARCELO: Of course.[53]

Rather than seeking to be separate, Mr. Barcelo wanted his sons to have the kind of education that would allow them to maintain their identities while integrating fully into US society. Following a discussion of the poem, *In Lak'ech*, Martinez concluded his direct examination.

Robert Ellman conducted the cross-examination. He started by asking, "[Y]ou agreed to be a plaintiff in this case because you were told that the State of Arizona banned Mexican-American Studies, isn't that right?" After receiving an affirmative response, Ellman, as he had with Mr. González, put the text of the statute on the document camera and engaged in the following colloquy:

ELLMAN: Let me put the statute back on the display. Do you believe that this statute bans Mexican-American Studies?
BARCELO: Yeah, I mean –
ELLMAN: Does it actually say that?
BARCELO: Yes.
ELLMAN: Where does it say that?
...
BARCELO: According to this paper, it says right there.
ELLMAN: Can you point out to me where it says that Mexican-American Studies are banned?[54]

Mr. Barcelo looked at the text of the statute on the screen in front of him on the witness stand. This is another instance where a cold transcript fails to capture what transpired. As he continued to look at the screen, the tension in the courtroom rose. He sat and looked. Did not say anything. Sat. Looked at the screen. It probably only went on for a couple minutes, but it felt like forever. Mr. Barcelo later told the MAS legal team that he would have sat silent all afternoon if that's what it took.

Finally, Judge Tashima had enough: "You know, we're wasting a lot of time. Let me say this: I am going to cut this short." Ellman tried to justify this line of questioning, saying that he was trying to establish that the statute by itself does not ban MAS. Judge Tashima cut him off, "No, no, no."[55]

Again, the transcript does not capture what transpired. Tashima continued, "But the point is that [the statute] can be used to ban studies if you apply it a certain way. But whether one is true or not, I mean what difference does it make to what his understanding of that is."[56] Ellman continued to defend this line of questioning, but Judge Tashima cut him off again, asking what difference does it make what Mr. Barcelo understood about the statute. Judge Tashima then asked, "Are you saying it disqualifies him because he read the statute wrongly? To become a plaintiff?"[57] When Ellman said, in essence, yes, the judge cut him off again. Judge Tashima then moves on to criticize the relevance of Martinez's direct examination of Mr. Barcelo and says, "In fact, I don't even know why he was called as a witness."[58]

With that, Mr. Barcelo was excused and the court took a midafternoon break.

A SLOW-MOTION TRAIN WRECK

The direct examination of Sean Arce was a disaster, though not one of his making. The fact that it was a disaster also likely changed the course of the trial. The original plan was for Richard Martinez to conduct the cross-examination of the state's witness, Kathryn Hrabluk. But the interaction between Martinez and Judge Tashima during Martinez's direct examination of Mr. Arce led to the decision made by Steven Reiss, as the lead trial team lawyer, to take on Hrabluk's cross-exam.

Court resumed at 3:13 p.m., and Richard Martinez called Sean Arce to the stand. Similar to Quinn's examination of Curtis Acosta, Martinez began by establishing Mr. Arce's credentials, including that he had a B.A. in Mexican American Studies from the University of Arizona and was completing his doctoral work, also at the University of Arizona, with an Ethnic Studies emphasis. Arce admitted that he was ABD, All But Dissertation, so Martinez was not yet able to address him as "Doctor."

Arce then discussed his previous employment at TUSD as a classroom teacher and advancing to become director of the MAS Program at TUSD. He described his then current position as a high school teacher of Chicano Studies in the Azusa Unified School District in Los Angeles County, California.

Martinez further tried to establish Arce's credentials by asking about his publications on Ethnic Studies, including a recent piece on the implementation of MAS.[59] Martinez then asked about the lectures Arce delivered in the last seven years, to which Leslie Cooper objected as not relevant. It was clear that Judge Tashima was getting impatient at the slow pace of the questioning, several minutes spent on the initial credentialing, much longer than Quinn took with Dr. Acosta.

Martinez then returned to Sean Arce's publication, saying, "Let's start out on the topic of curriculum." The judge, without even an objection from the state, stopped him.

THE COURT: Just a minute. Are you trying to qualify him as an expert?
MARTINEZ: No, sir.
THE COURT: What's the purpose of this questioning then?
MARTINEZ: I'll move right to the question, Your Honor.
THE COURT: All right.

When Martinez asked for Arce's definition of "curriculum," the state objected based on relevance, which the court sustained, explaining that a layperson's understanding of curriculum was not relevant as he was not giving expert testimony.

Martinez tried a different tact, asking, "Is there such a thing as Mexican-American Studies curriculum?" Before Cooper could object, the court shut down this line of questioning. After a back-and-forth, Judge Tashima offered the following direction: "The order is he can't testify on, you know, the meaning of a curriculum or what's a curriculum, what's not a curriculum, what's good enough to be a curriculum, those kinds of questions, you know, because he is not an expert in the area."

The rest of the MAS legal team looked at each other, deeply concerned. This seemed to shut down much of what we expected Martinez to cover with this witness.

Martinez, though, was able to pivot, centering the questions on Arce's personal experiences instead of trying to establish him as an expert. Thus, Martinez elicited that Mr. Arce was director of the Mexican American Studies Department and asked, "In your department, did you develop curriculum specific to the classes that were being offered…"

The judge interrupted and said, "He can testify as to his experience as a director." This interruption, also, was odd. The state had made no objection. Perhaps the judge just saw this as helping limit the questions to permitted areas. Martinez, though, continued to test the judge's patience by working methodically, albeit slowly, through Arce's different roles at TUSD and with the MAS Department. Martinez then returned to the topic of curriculum, asking if Arce and his staff developed curriculum. After an affirmative response, Martinez then asked if the curriculum included units of instruction, and then, what they were.

Arce responded, the state objected, and the court sustained the objection. The direct examination continued in this way, in fits and starts with most objections by the state sustained by the court. Martinez tried his best to elicit testimony from Arce that he and his department engaged in transparency and did not hide what they were doing in the classroom. The judge did not want to hear it.

Martinez then asked Jorge Martorell from the Weil team to project the TUSD high school map onto the courtroom screens, trying to elicit a point that Quinn also tried to elicit from Dr. Acosta on Day 1: that there was a MAS Department with teachers under Arce's direct supervision along with teachers like Acosta who taught MAS courses but were not under Arce's direct supervision. Chang and others on the MAS legal team did not understand the importance of this point. It seemed that little was to be gained. This might show that the principals at these sites approved of the classes, but that had little to do with whether the classes violated the statute or that Horne, Huppenthal, and others acted out of animus.

It seemed that Judge Tashima was of the same mind. The state kept objecting. The judge kept sustaining the objections. The more Martinez protested the judge's rulings, the more the judge dug in, as exemplified in the following exchange:

MARTINEZ: Well, Mr. Huppenthal addressed at length that we were teaching indoctrination and other things in the classroom, and I believe we have – and that somehow that that was driven by the Mexican-American Studies Department. And I believe we have every right to address kind of that kind of salacious labeling by the state to try and say that we're an unpatriotic, un-American curriculum, as opposed to being one that was addressing the most important curriculum issue of the time, which is how do we close the achievement gap for Mexican-American students.

THE COURT: All right. That's a nice speech, but the question hardly goes to that. The objection is still sustained.[60]

Martinez then turned to how MAS sought to close the achievement gap. But even here, the court set up roadblocks. When Martinez asked about drop-out rates at various schools, the state offered the same objection – that Martinez was trying to establish Arce as an expert. When the judge sustained the objection, the following back-and-forth illustrated the increasingly combative nature of the interaction between Martinez and Judge Tashima:

MARTINEZ: You don't have to be an expert, Your Honor, to know when we have a school that is failing its student population and –
THE COURT: Well, you're asking for his opinion. I don't think his opinion as a non-expert is of much relevance, so the objection is sustained. It doesn't matter what kind of picture it paints to him or –
MARTINEZ: I think it does. He's the director, Your Honor. Because I think where you're going to commit your resources for a program that –
THE COURT: Mr. Martinez, I don't know why you keep on arguing. I made a ruling. It would be more productive if you moved on or called another witness.

The rest of the MAS legal team looked at each other, shrugged their shoulders, and sat back in their chairs. They wondered how things could be salvaged.

Martinez tried again to establish that Curtis Acosta did not report directly to Arce. The state objected, and the judge sustained the objection. This is where Martinez's theory of the case differed from that of the others on the MAS legal team. Martinez thought that if teachers not under the direct supervision of Sean Arce were engaging in indoctrination, that this could not be blamed then on the MAS program. Similarly, whatever teachers like Acosta and others not formally in the MAS Department were doing could not be attributable to the MAS Department. The others on the MAS legal team were uncertain how this helped the case, that Martinez seemed to be trying to construct an artificial formalism between the MAS **Department** that did not include Acosta and the MAS **Program**, which it clearly did. Defending the Department while sacrificing those not in the Department but in the Program seemed to be a self-defeating strategy. A violation was a violation.

This was an instance where Martinez, accustomed to working as a sole practitioner and used to working alone, had not reviewed with the rest of the MAS legal team his plan for examining Mr. Arce. Unlike the detailed examination outlines, proceeding question by question that the Weil team created for each of the witnesses its team would be examining, with anticipated impeachment exhibits for cross-examination including precut clips from videotaped depositions, Martinez approached his examinations more intuitively. Though this worked well with Mr. Barcelo, it was a disaster in his direct examination of Sean Arce.

Martinez kept reaching, the state kept objecting, and even when the state did not object, the court shut him down. More and more, Judge Tashima and Martinez argued. Those watching in the courtroom frequently cringed as this continued. The rest of the MAS legal team didn't know how to assist Martinez as the court kept cutting off his questioning, at one point asking, "Are you through now?" Martinez of course answered, "No, sir, I am not through," hoping to run out the clock. The rest of the MAS legal team shared this hope.

Despite the persistent stream of objections from the state sustained by the court, Richard Martinez gamely continued pursuing lines of questioning that occurred to him. The pattern:

MARTINEZ: [question]
COOPER: Objection.
THE COURT: Sustained.
[repeat]

The judge sometimes interjected: "Are you asking a question or having a conversation with counsel?" Often, the judge and Martinez would speak over each other as the court reporter did her best to capture their words, but the pattern described above continued.

As the hands on the clock approached 5 p.m., the judge asked, "How much more time? Take a guess. How much more time do you have on direct?" Martinez said that although he was shortening his direct examination in light of the judge's comments, he had at least another hour. With that, the court called a recess until the next morning.

* * *

Working that evening with his team of students in Seattle, Chang developed an outline of questions that he thought were critical to ask Arce. One claim was that Horne and Huppenthal engaged in selective enforcement of the statute, that some of the evidence they relied upon (i.e., the website for the MAS program) was very similar to what was expressed on the websites for the African American Studies program and the Pan Asian Studies program at TUSD. The state had objected to the plaintiffs' exhibits and screenshots of those websites, and these facts were a critical part of what the plaintiffs submitted as their Proposed Findings of Fact and Conclusions of Law. Arce was identified by Chang as the witness who could testify about these websites, thereby permitting them to be admitted as evidence.

The next morning in the courtroom, when Chang presented the examination outline and asked Richard Martinez to begin with these questions, Martinez initially refused. Apparently, he had a change of heart because he began his re-direct when Sean Arce was recalled to the stand by asking about the websites. He asked Arce about the MAS website. Then he asked whether he had personal knowledge about the websites of the other Ethnic Studies programs. When Arce said that he did, Martinez proceeded to ask questions about them, questions that elicited responses from Arce showing the similarities between what MAS and the African American Studies program and the Pan Asian Studies program and the respective populations they served.

Each, on their face, ought to have drawn the attention and wrath of Horne and Huppenthal if the statute was uniformly and equitably enforced. Yet Horne and Huppenthal only enforced the statute against the MAS program. This was a key selective enforcement fact, and Arce was critical to getting the webpages of the other Ethnic Studies programs admitted. The state kept objecting, and Judge Tashima kept overruling the objections. In his final ruling, Judge Tashima cited TUSD's African American Studies website, stating that Tom Horne and John Huppenthal were aware of it and yet only enforced the statute against MAS.[61]

After this initial success in having this key evidence admitted, the patterns from the previous day resumed. Martinez called up the map of TUSD. He asked Arce if he knew the district's boundaries. The state objected. The court sustained it. Martinez persisted, saying that he was asking in order to determine if TUSD included any Indian reservations. The judge said that was irrelevant. Martinez then asked if materials used in MAS classes were used to promote Marxism, communism, or socialism? Arce answered "No" to each of these questions.[62]

* * *

During her cross-examination, Leslie Cooper pursued a line of questioning that puzzled the MAS legal team. She asked about the name of Arce's department as it changed over the years, going from Hispanic to *La Raza* Studies to MAS. It seemed that she intended to elicit from Arce that the department went from the most expansive or inclusive to a narrower, exclusionary focus.[63]

Cooper's next major line of questioning drew some blood, especially in conjunction with the direct testimony two days later from the state's witness, Kathryn Hrabluk, discussed in Chapter 13. A consistent theme in the plaintiffs' narrative was that the MAS and its courses had been approved and supported by the TUSD governing board. Cooper challenged Arce to identify when the board had approved the MAS curriculum. Arce testified that he brought the MAS Department curriculum before the TUSD Board for its approval multiple times over a thirteen-year period.[64] Cooper asked him if he could provide the dates when this had occurred. When he was unable to, she continued:

COOPER: Would you be able to provide the agenda items which evidenced that you were bringing before the Tucson Unified School District board curriculum for its approval?

S. ARCE: I would have to have access to those and look at those documents.

COOPER: If we gave you access over lunch, could you go on the Tucson Unified School District governing board website and find that information?[65]

When Martinez objected, the court overruled the objection and directed Arce to answer. Arce responded that he was not aware of what was accessible on the website. After some more back and forth between counsel and the court, Cooper moved on, focusing on curriculum approval.

In pursuing this line of questioning, Cooper was setting up the testimony they expected to elicit from their witness, Kathryn Hrabluk. It is quite possible that the TUSD governing board, like many other governing boards in Arizona, did not have the best procedures with regard to approving curricula. Though the state was able to score points regarding TUSD and specific approval of MAS curricula, this line of argument ultimately was not fruitful for two reasons. First, it was uncertain how much attention TUSD's governing board paid to the specific curricula of *any* course or program, including whether they required curricular maps that included the scope and sequence charted over the entire semester or school year. Second, whether MAS (or any other program) had such a curricular map had nothing to do with whether MAS violated the statute in question.

Though Arce testified that he turned over or made available to TUSD's legal counsel all the MAS curricular units, in digital and/or paper form, he was not able to say that these materials were made available to the Cambium auditors. Thus, Cooper's questioning helped the state in its argument that MAS was a rogue program.

Finally, Cooper returned to a persistent theme. She asked about an article Arce had co-written with Auggie Romero, in which the authors "talked about transformative actions being necessary to help students overcome their history of oppression." From this, Cooper asked, "Who are the oppressors in that?" When she did not receive the response she wanted, Judge Tashima interjected: "He's not answering the question. She asked about the person, and he said there are a lot of forces. That's not an answer. Tell us who, Mr. Arce."[66]

This question highlighted an important limitation in the state's theory of the case: if you talk about oppression, one must be able to identify individual oppressors; once one identifies the oppressors, then necessarily the plaintiffs are promoting resentment against the oppressors and violating the statute. This ignores systemic oppression, and it would come to a head during Dr. Cabrera's testimony. The fact that the judge wanted names deeply concerned the rest of the MAS legal team.

With what appeared to be the encouragement of the court, Cooper kept at it. When Arce answered that the oppressor was dominant society, Cooper asked if Horne, Huppenthal, and the Arizona legislators represented dominant society.

Arce answered yes, yes, yes. Arce tried again to argue that context was important, but Cooper followed up by quoting his article title, "The Struggle Against Racism, Fascism, and Intellectual Apartheid in Arizona," and asked, "Are you referring to specific persons as racist there?.... [W]ho are the fascists to whom you refer?"[67]

When Arce responded that he was talking about a system of oppression, Cooper, believing that her work was done, said, "No further questions." Martinez had a short re-direct, followed by a short re-cross by Cooper. With that, Arce was excused, and the court turned to the offer of proof from the plaintiffs.

An offer of proof is a mechanism whereby a party that has been cut off by the court from pursuing a line of questioning is permitted to state to the court what they would have proven given the chance. Quite often, an offer of proof is a formality that allows a party to register their position for purposes of making a record for an appeal, should they lose. Martinez enumerated several areas where plaintiffs felt that objections had been improperly sustained. After listening to Martinez and giving the state a chance to respond, Judge Tashima said:

> Well, I don't think too many cases like this are tried, maybe thankfully, so there isn't much law or much standard of what kind of proof suffices ... but I am not going to review any of my prior rulings.
>
> [B]ut there's one area where I think either I misspoke or you misunderstood what I said, and that has to do with curriculum....
>
> [Mr. Arce] can still testify of his action and his understanding as, say the director, right, of MAS, how he understood the term and how he implemented the term or what he did in terms of curriculum. I really didn't mean to bar that, and if counsel understood it otherwise, it's probably as much my error as his that you had that understanding.[68]

The MAS legal team was surprised to hear this from the judge. This was as close to admitting an error as one is likely to get from a judge. Then Judge Tashima asked if counsel wanted the opportunity to cure the possible error and pursue this line of questioning with the witness or if counsel wanted it just to be reflected as a possible error for an appeal. Of course, Richard Martinez said that he would like to cure.[69]

The judge was pleased to hear this and then permitted Martinez and others on the MAS legal team to prepare for the re-examination of Sean Arce on this narrow topic. In the meantime, the court kept things moving along, and the plaintiffs called their next witness, their first expert, Dr. Nolan Cabrera.

11

Gotcha!

The State Tries (and Fails) to Trip Up the Plaintiffs' Experts

Three Stanford-educated Chicana/os served as expert witnesses for the plaintiffs' case. We highlight "Stanford educated" because the alumni magazine of their alma mater would not cover this issue even after the decision was rendered. Dr. Stephen Pitti, a full professor at Yale University, is an expert on the history of Mexican Americans and anti-Mexican American discrimination.[1] Dr. Angela Valenzuela, a full professor at the University of Texas at Austin, is an expert on curriculum and pedagogy in particular approaches that honor and develop Mexican American students' sense of self through additive instead of subtractive approaches to education.[2] Dr. Nolan Cabrera was then an assistant professor (since promoted to full) in the College of Education at the University of Arizona in Tucson and is an expert in race and education. He led the team that developed the statistical report submitted to the special master in Tucson's never-ending desegregation lawsuit.

The three-pronged strategy using these experts involved Dr. Cabrera testifying as to the educational efficacy of the program. Dr. Pitti would then testify on the historical context leading to the passage of HB 2281, including a close examination of the role that racial animus via "code words" played, including how it was expressed by key actors. Dr. Valenzuela testified about the MAS curriculum and how its pedagogical approach was intended to overcome what she described in her work as the subtractive model of schooling.

THE TECHNICALITIES OF EXPERT WITNESS TESTIMONY

We offer this deep dive into the ins and outs of expert testimony because analogous controversies continue in the present day. Expert witnesses will likely play a key role in combating current bans on books and curricula. Attention to detail is the pathway to eventual victory. Learn from both our successes and our failures.

When a party intends to use experts in litigation, they must identify the expert and typically the expert submits a report that is given to the opposing party. This gives the opposing party the opportunity to know in advance what the expert will testify about so that they can plan how to counter the expert, which might include engaging their own affirmative experts or rebuttal experts. They may also seek to exclude an expert's testimony altogether by filing what is called, in federal court, a *Daubert* motion. The admission of expert testimony is governed by Federal Rule of Evidence 702:

A witness who is qualified as an expert by knowledge, skill, experience, training, or education may testify in the form of an opinion or otherwise if:

(a) the expert's scientific, technical, or other specialized knowledge will help the trier of fact to understand the evidence or to determine a fact in issue;
(b) the testimony is based on sufficient facts or data;
(c) the testimony is the product of reliable principles and methods; and
(d) the expert has reliably applied the principles and methods to the facts of the case.[3]

This rule and the standard developed in *Daubert v. Merrell Dow Pharmaceuticals*[4] empower the trial judge to act as a gatekeeper to prevent unreliable expert testimony that might mislead the factfinder; in a bench trial, the factfinder is the same judge doing the gatekeeping.

September 26, 2016, the day the judge set for certain kinds of motions, saw a flurry of activity. As expected, the state filed *Daubert* motions to exclude each of the plaintiffs' experts. The state also filed a motion for partial summary judgment to dismiss the plaintiffs' viewpoint discrimination claim. The plaintiffs filed their own *Daubert* motion against the state's expert. After further briefing on each motion, the judge ruled.

On February 7, 2017, the judge denied the state's motion for partial summary judgment. This did not come as a surprise to the legal team because the state's filing was, to be blunt, thin. At just over four pages,[5] accompanied by a short document, just over five pages listing seventeen numbered facts,[6] the motion was admittedly longer than their earlier successful cross-motion for summary judgment in 2012, which was only a paragraph long.[7] The state's argument was straightforward: viewpoint discrimination is permissible if there is a legitimate pedagogical objective; and because ALJ Kowal found a violation of the statute, Superintendent Huppenthal's final determination of violation and imposition of penalty was legitimate.

Though the state's motion was thin, the plaintiffs took no chances and filed a much longer response and controverting statement of facts accompanied by hundreds of pages of exhibits. The plaintiffs argued that evidence supporting their equal protection claim likewise supported their First Amendment viewpoint discrimination claim, raising genuine issues of material fact for both claims.[8] Because a trial had already been mandated for the equal protection claim, it made no sense to grant summary judgment to the defendants when many of the same facts went to both claims.

Judge Tashima agreed and held that plaintiffs could still establish Huppenthal was motivated by impermissible motivations (e.g., racial animus), including that his reliance on the ALJ could be found to be pretextual.[9] This allowed plaintiffs' First Amendment claim based on illegal viewpoint discrimination to go forward.

A few days later, on February 10, 2017, Judge Tashima denied the state's motions to exclude Drs. Cabrera, Valenzuela, and Pitti.[10] The judge, however, granted the plaintiffs' motion to exclude Dr. Poston. That the state chose Dr. Poston as their sole expert was a bit of a head-scratcher. His work was limited to reviewing the Cambium Audit and offering his opinion about their audit. The court excluded Dr. Poston as an expert because Superintendent Huppenthal had not (and could not have) relied upon Dr. Poston's opinion when Cambium's conclusions were rejected.[11] But their choice, trying to have an expert undercut the Cambium Audit, may have signaled that they were afraid of Cambium's conclusions on three key points: (1) that there had been no violation of state law; (2) that MAS adhered to state standards; and (3) that it improved education outcomes for its students. Though Dr. Poston was excluded, the state was allowed to have rebuttal experts and they chose Dr. Thomas Haladyna to rebut Dr. Cabrera.

These rulings cleared the decks for the trial to proceed.

* * *

Unlike with other witnesses, the direct testimony of the experts was presented in advance as written declarations. If this was a jury trial, the plaintiffs likely would have objected. With a jury, it's critical to establish the credentials of the expert and to have the expert testify directly their opinions and the bases for them. In a bench trial, because the audience is the judge, and the judge already reviewed the reports as part of the *Daubert* motions, plaintiffs readily agreed to this procedure. In addition, having the direct testimony presented in written form allowed the trial to proceed more efficiently, allowing the trial to finish in ten days instead of the original twelve the court had set aside for the trial.

On Day 4, following most of Sean Arce's examination discussed in Chapter 10, Dr. Cabrera took the stand. Judge Tashima engaged in an introductory colloquy with Dr. Cabrera, reminding him that his direct testimony had already been submitted in writing to the court and that the state will now be cross-examining him. Judge Tashima ordered that the direct testimony of expert witnesses be submitted by May 12, 2017, more than a month before the trial started. While this had the benefit of streamlining the presentation of his testimony, it gave the defense attorneys substantial time to prepare their cross examination. The extra preparation time appears not to have helped.

Their first line of attack was a "Hail Mary." After asking Dr. Cabrera about the dates when he performed his analysis of TUSD student achievement and eliciting that his analysis of the efficacy of MAS was submitted in January 2012 and June 2012 to Special Master Hawley, Cooper stated: "On this basis, plaintiffs [sic] would move to exclude Dr. Cabrera as an expert witness. He doesn't have any information about student achievements that would have been available to the defendants before the program was terminated by TUSD. It thus cannot go to their state of mind."[12] Like the judge's reasoning in excluding Dr. Poston, her point was that by the time Dr. Cabrera's analyses and reports became publicly available in 2012, Superintendent Huppenthal had already made his decision to find TUSD in violation of the statute. When he made his decision, he could not have known of Dr. Cabrera's work.

This attempt to exclude Dr. Cabrera took Plaintiffs' counsel by surprise because the issue had already been decided as previously discussed. While Judge Tashima considered the new motion, Cabrera returned to a conference room the MAS legal team had reserved in the courthouse library. Chang was there helping Richard Martinez and Sean Arce prepare for a special re-direct the judge permitted following the proffer discussed in Chapter 10. Seeing Cabrera, Chang asked, surprised, "What are you doing here?" Cabrera responded, "The state is trying to ban me again."

Months earlier, in denying the *Daubert* motion to exclude Dr. Cabrera, Judge Tashima found that Cabrera's offered testimony was relevant to establish pretext.[13] Because this had been argued and decided already, the plaintiffs' attorneys were surprised by this renewed attempt to exclude Dr. Cabrera. Reiss looked at Fitzmaurice, who shrugged his shoulders. Reiss then stood up and said, exasperatedly, "Your Honor, we've litigated this in motions in limine. Your Honor had briefing, extensive briefing. Your Honor ruled that his expert testimony is admissible. We've resolved this issue, Your Honor."[14]

Judge Tashima closed his eyes, thought for a moment, and then agreed and denied Ms. Cooper's motion to exclude Dr. Cabrera as a witness. One of the MAS legal team members left the courtroom to get Dr. Cabrera, who returned to the stand.

* * *

One line of questioning continued the state's crude understanding of the nature of racism (see the cross-examination of Arce in the previous chapter regarding, "Who are the oppressors?"). The attorneys for the state appeared to believe that for racism to occur, one must identify specific individuals and establish that they are racists, understood as people who harbor explicit views about racial superiority and inferiority and express dislike or hatred of other races. The state thought that the plaintiffs could not prove that the defendants were racists in this sense and would therefore lose.

Cooper questioned Dr. Cabrera about his 2012 article in the *Journal of Curriculum and Pedagogy* entitled, "A State-Mandated Epistemology of Ignorance: Arizona's HB 2281 and Mexican American/Raza Studies."[15]

COOPER: Your article begins with a reference to white supremacy, right?
CABRERA: Yes. It's right there.
COOPER: Who are the white supremacists that you're referring to in this article?
CABRERA: That's not what Charles Mills is talking about.
COOPER: I do not want to know not what Charles Mills is talking about, but whether you are referring – to whom you are referring when you use the phrase "white supremacist."
REISS: Objection. Misstates the article. She's reading.
THE COURT: Overruled. You may answer.[16]

The judge may not have understood why Dr. Cabrera was having difficulty answering the question because the article begins with the following sentence: "Charles Mills argues White Supremacy relies upon a denial that racism exists," or, "*an inverted epistemology, an epistemology of ignorance.*"[17] When Cooper asked about the reference to white supremacy, Dr. Cabrera answered directly – "It's right there." However, when Cooper asked who the white supremacists are, that was not a question Dr. Cabrera could answer because Charles Mills, the philosopher he was quoting, was examining a system of racial oppression – not the actions of individual actors. As Reiss noted, Cooper is in fact misstating the article.

She also misstated the article because the first sentence is not really about white supremacy. Instead, it is about the "epistemology of ignorance" whereby systemic racism is made possible because of a denial of racism. Nevertheless, the judge overruled the objection and directed Dr. Cabrera to answer. He responded:

CABRERA: In this conception, white supremacy does not derive from white supremacists, in the same way that capitalism doesn't derive from capitalists. The ideas that racism is a systemic reality that we are all complicit in maintaining, and the name of that systemic racism, as Charles Mills, who I am citing, argues is named "white supremacy." But that systemic reality does not require to be held up by people with overtly white supremacist viewpoints.
COOPER: Who are the representatives of the white supremacy to which you refer in this article?
CABRERA: Exactly the same response that I just gave. I don't – I am not intent on articulating that one's [sic] individual is a white supremacist. That's not what this does. It's talking about a systemic reality of racial privilege and oppression that he – that – and the relationship between that and this law.
COOPER: And so you see HB 2281 as a furtherance of that systemic oppression?
CABRERA: It continues to enhance it.
COOPER: And you see the persons, Mr. Horne and Mr. Huppenthal, as persons who are responsible for that, correct?
CABRERA: They are key actors in it, but it's a lot bigger than two individuals.[18]

Cooper did not pursue this further, likely believing that she made her point. This "gotcha" was intended to paint Dr. Cabrera as a biased witness who equated HB 2281 with white supremacy but who refused to describe or accuse Mr. Horne and

Mr. Huppenthal of being white supremacists. She likely saw this as a point in their column because, according to the state's theory of the case, you can't have racism unless you have racists. The attorneys for the state appeared unfamiliar with Edward Bonilla-Silva's classic sociological text, *Racism without Racists*.[19]

Cooper's other line of questioning addressed potential methodological flaws, seeking to undercut Dr. Cabrera's conclusions about the dramatic success of the MAS program in improving scores on certain required state tests and on graduation rates. Dr. Cabrera easily defended his methodology and conclusions on the stand, though the state would try again later to undercut Dr. Cabrera's testimony through their rebuttal expert, Dr. Thomas Haladyna.

Reiss followed with a short redirect examination, with no recross by Cooper. Commenting on the fact that there would be no recross, Judge Tashima said, "Good. I have to say Dr. Cabrera, I think you're a lucky guy because you can go home now. You won't have to deal with this mess again. All right? Except in a scholarly manner. Thank you very much, sir, for appearing and you're excused." Later, commenting on Reiss's redirect, Judge Tashima stated: "And I appreciate, appreciate the succinctness of Mr. Reiss's redirect. You know, some people would take that as a sign that the lawyer has confidence in his expert, but, you know, we'll see."[20]

The first part of this comment by the judge was likely given as part of the judge's management of the trial process and intended to encourage all the attorneys to be more succinct. Plaintiffs' lawyers took the second part, including the judge's demeanor, to indicate that he had been impressed by Dr. Cabrera and heartened by the professional presentation by Steven Reiss. Until this point, the MAS legal team thought things were going poorly, especially with the negative dynamic that appeared to exist between the judge and Richard Martinez.

HALADYNA: THE STATE'S LONE EXPERT

The state's lone expert witness at trial was Dr. Thomas Haladyna, an educational psychologist from Arizona State University. He testified on Day 9 after the plaintiffs had concluded their case-in-chief, but as his testimony was offered to rebut Dr. Cabrera's, we include it here.

His primary critique was that the reported results were simply not believable, and he continually walked a fine line suggesting that cheating might have been at play while not making a direct accusation: "Such unusual growth in student achievement warrants investigation as to what, exactly, is the cause. Often, such growth is found to be the result of inappropriate test coaching or cheating. My comment is not intended to accuse the school district of cheating."[21]

It was eerily like the famous scene in the movie *Stand and Deliver* where Chicano students in East LA did "too well" on the AP calculus exam and were accused of cheating. The results were thought to be too good to be true.

Dr. Haladyna also suggested that grade inflation in MAS classes might be at play,[22] even though this could not have been related to passing standardized tests. These are very serious insinuations, and in both his deposition and his trial testimony, Dr. Haladyna called for further investigation regarding cheating and grade inflation, although he himself did not investigate despite having access to all raw data, cleaned data, syntax, and results from Dr. Cabrera's previous analyses. These were provided to him following four subpoenas from Arizona's Attorney General to Dr. Cabrera and the University of Arizona.

At deposition, the continual refinement of the statistical analyses via publication in the *American Educational Research Journal* (*AERJ*) – one of the most prestigious educational journals in the world – was critically important. Dr. Haladyna tended to argue that multivariate analysis of variance (MANOVA) was a better method than logistic regression and that a continuous variable, here test scores, was more appropriate than the binary pass/fail. However, his arguments were primarily theoretical instead of empirical as he did not conduct an independent analysis of the data. He admitted as much when he was cross-examined during the trial:

REISS: And you didn't do your own analysis because it would have taken weeks, even months, to do that analysis, right?
HALADYNA: That's correct.[23]

While statisticians may debate the relative merits of MANOVA versus logistic regression analysis, Dr. Haladyna's contention that the results were "fatally flawed" was hard to maintain against the fact that Dr. Cabrera's analysis passed through the rigorous peer-review process of one of the highest impact journals in the field of education. Even Dr. Haladyna admitted that *AERJ* is a top journal in the field.[24] The academic prestige of the journal in addition to the rigor of the study helped solidify its relevance in the overall case.

Steven Reiss's cross-examination of Dr. Haladyna was a thing of beauty. Repeatedly, Dr. Haladyna would say things not quite consistent with, and sometimes contradictory, to what he said in his deposition. Each time, Steven would ask Jorge to play an impeachment clip. Clip 3 ... clip 6 ... clip 7... clip 11 ... 12 ... 13 ... 14 ... 15. Reiss meticulously prepared these in advance and he would, without missing a beat, call them up to impeach what Dr. Haladyna had just stated in his answers. Reiss had Dr. Haladyna so conditioned by these clips that toward the end of the cross-examination, Steven asked:

REISS: And you would agree, Dr. Haladyna, would you not, that the results, the findings in Dr. Cabrera's report, that these students who had lower mean income, fewer gifted students, more English language learners, lower GPAs in ninth and tenth grade, the fact that they ended up with higher graduation rates and higher passing rates on the AIMS tests than the non-MAS students, that in fact those results are remarkable. Right?
HALADYNA: I think you're quoting me, aren't you?

REISS: I sure am.
(Laughter in the courtroom.)
REISS: You would agree, right?
HALADYNA: It is remarkable.²⁵

At the end of the cross-examination, Steven asked Dr. Haladyna to confirm what was part of his direct trial testimony submitted in written format: "If Dr. Cabrera's claims are true, then we have an incredibly important intervention in education that will help millions of students, including Mexican-American and other ethnic/racial groups." Steven asked, "You said that, right?" Dr. Haladyna said, "Yes," ending the cross-examination.²⁶

After a long break for lunch, there was a short redirect by Leslie Cooper followed by a shorter re-cross by Steven Reiss, after which Dr. Haladyna was excused.

YES, ANTI-MEXICAN RACISM EXISTS: DR. PITTI TAKES THE STAND

The plaintiffs' next expert, Dr. Stephen Pitti, testified on Day 7. The MAS legal team did not expect Dr. Pitti to testify until Day 8, but the examination of Tom Horne took an unexpected turn and went more quickly than expected. Partway through the morning's examination of Horne, Steven Reiss turned to Robert Chang and said, "Go prep Dr. Pitti. We're going to need him here after lunch. He's likely to go on this afternoon." Until this point, the team had not decided whether Dr. Valenzuela or Dr. Pitti would go first. Initially, the team leaned toward Dr. Valenzuela because Dr. Pitti's testimony was more directly connected to the *Arlington Heights* factors for the plaintiffs' equal protection claim. But Reiss saw something about how the day was going that led him to reverse the order. This meant that Chang missed the rest of Horne's testimony. Here again, having six attorneys on the team at trial made a difference because Chang could leave to finish preparing Dr. Pitti.

Back at the Arizona Inn, Chang found Dr. Pitti as he was finishing a late breakfast. Chang explained that he was likely to testify that afternoon. Dr. Pitti took it in stride. He had been prepped the evening before, and as he finished his breakfast, he reviewed an additional list of potential questions or topics that might come up in cross-examination. The list was Chang's best attempt to get into Leslie Cooper's and Robert Ellman's heads to guess where they would probe for weaknesses, the gotchas. The list turned out to be only partially helpful because Ellman ended up asking about things that none of the MAS legal team would ever have guessed.

As with Dr. Cabrera, Dr. Pitti's written declaration was submitted as his direct testimony. After Pitti was sworn in as a witness, Robert Ellman proceeded with his cross-examination. His initial line of questioning tried to discredit Dr. Pitti based on his area of expertise, US history:

ELLMAN: You don't hold a degree in political science, do you?
PITTI: I hold a degree in U.S. history.
ELLMAN: So the answer is "no"?
PITTI: "No."[27]

After establishing, firmly and emphatically, that Dr. Pitti did not have a degree in political science, which was never claimed or in dispute, Ellman asked if he held degrees in psychology ("No"), linguistics ("No"), law ("No"), and education ("I do not"). Ellman then asked if Dr. Pitti ever lived in Arizona ("No"), ever spent an extended period of time in Arizona (paraphrase – not really), or visited Arizona to do research to prepare his expert report ("No"). At one point, the usually reserved and humble Dr. Pitti offered: "I've been working as a historian for 20 years. I have degrees in the field. I'm a full professor in the field in perhaps the top department in the country."[28]

From here, Ellman asked a series of questions about "code words." Dr. Pitti's Declaration, submitted as his direct testimony, stated that he developed an expertise in "the use of code words that disguise animus and are used to advance political objectives."[29] Ellman noted that Dr. Pitti's curriculum vitae didn't include a single reference to "code words." Chang took this line of questioning to be an attempt to undercut the possibility that Dr. Pitti had expertise on "the use of code words that disguise animus and are used to advance political objectives." Further, the line of questioning about other disciplines seemed suggestive that those disciplines but not history might have something meaningful to offer the Court on "code words." Ellman then tried to score points by asking if a person can get a degree in code word usage, to which Dr. Pitti responded, "Not to my knowledge."[30]

From here, Ellman's questioning took another odd turn, asking Dr. Pitti to agree "that history is not considered a hard science based on its epistemological limitations." After some additional exchange, Ellman asked what he may have thought was his knock-out question: "You can't apply the scientific method to historical research, can you?"[31]

Dr. Pitti, not missing a beat, said, "That's not true, actually. One of the most famous and important books in the historical profession actually did exactly that." Dr. Pitti then proceeded to briefly describe Thomas S. Kuhn's classic text, *The Structure of Scientific Revolutions*.[32] Ellman, though, was not having any of it and proceeded to the point he was hoping to make: "Can you employ the scientific method to determine whether someone is or is not using a code word?" Ellman also directed Dr. Pitti's attention to a sentence in his declaration, "Politicians and activists working on behalf of ballot initiatives and legislative acts created a political atmosphere that encouraged opposition to Mexicans and Mexican-Americans by white voters in twenty-first century Arizona," and asked, "Can you prove that's true?"[33]

In the ensuing colloquy, Dr. Pitti explained that code word analysis was an accepted method of historical interpretation. This line of questioning seemed to ignore the fact that much of this had already been litigated when the defendants filed a motion in limine seeking to exclude Dr. Pitti as an expert. In that motion, they devoted a whole section: "IV. Dr. Pitti's 'Code Words' Analysis Should Be Excluded as Irrelevant and Unreliable."[34] Judge Tashima, in rejecting the motion to exclude Dr. Pitti, expressly rejected that argument, finding that code word analysis is both relevant and reliable, with the Ninth Circuit having "repeatedly held that 'the use of "code words" may demonstrate discriminatory intent.'"[35] Judge Tashima already concluded that "as a professor and historian who studies the political history of Arizona, Dr. Pitti has 'extensive experience … analyz[ing] the meaning of [the relevant] conversations.'"[36] As with Dr. Cabrera, the state repeated a failed argument hoping for a different result.

It is hard to fault the defendants for trying to discredit Dr. Pitti's report, declaration, and testimony, but it seemed to be a poorly directed trial strategy. Rather than discrediting Dr. Pitti, the questioning appeared to have the opposite effect. Though Judge Tashima decided independently based on the evidence and testimony that key actors used code words to accomplish specific political objectives and that the use of code words disguised racial animus, he devoted a long paragraph citing Dr. Pitti's direct testimony as corroborating the judge's conclusion.[37]

Ellman's next line of questioning tried to discredit his expert report because of bias. One of the questions Dr. Pitti's report was to address was "Have Mexican-Americans been subject to racial discrimination and racial animus?" Ellman asked, "In 2015, before you began your research [for your expert report], didn't you already firmly believe that Mexican-Americans had been subject to racial discrimination and racial animus?"[38]

Dr. Pitti admitted that based on his previous study of the subject, he firmly believed that Mexican Americans were subjected to racial discrimination and then added, "It would have been hard to find an American historian who does not know something about the history of racial animus and racial discrimination directed at Mexican-Americans in the United States. I think that I brought to this a deeper understanding than most, given my expertise."

Not satisfied with the response, Ellman repeated his question. Then Robert Chang popped out of his chair and said, "Objection. Asked and answered." Ellman grumbled, "If I could get an answer, I would rest." Unfortunately, the transcript does not capture the courtroom dynamics. The transcript simply states: "Objection sustained. He's answered about as much of an answer as you're going to get." What the transcript missed was the amusement animating Judge Tashima's face. It was clear he was enjoying the cat-and-mouse game being played. Normally, when an attorney is questioning a witness, the attorney is the cat; but here, Dr. Pitti was clearly the cat. Judge Tashima observed the interaction with a wry smile, and Chang was pleased because his first-ever objection was sustained.

An important colloquy occurred that afternoon before a recess was called with questioning to continue the next morning. Ellman directed Dr. Pitti's attention to page 23, paragraph 54 of his declaration: "Horne appears to have assumed that the Mexican-American Studies Program used primary materials (speeches, works of poetry and fiction, and visual materials) to endorse political positions, rather than to illustrate the development of American history, politics, and culture." After asking Dr. Pitti if Ellman read it correctly, Ellman continued: "And it also says: 'Horne's criticism completely misunderstands the role that primary materials play in teaching and makes the critical error of assuming that the inclusion of primary source material equates with endorsement of what is stated in the primary material.' Is that correct?"[39] Pitti answered in the affirmative. Pitti's testimony criticized the assumption the state made about the materials, that having students read primary historical materials meant that the teacher endorsed the views contained in them.

Ellman then shifted to a Hitler analogy, demanding as the colloquy progressed, "So you will not say categorically that it's always inappropriate to put a poster of Adolf Hitler up on the wall of a classroom?"[40] Pitti did not take the bait, saying that it would be important to know a teacher's pedagogical reason for putting up such a poster.[41] In a nutshell, Ellman was looking for a blanket condemnation of a hypothetical Hitler poster being placed on a classroom wall in order to set up his gotcha – that this would require a similar condemnation of a "Che" Guevara poster. This goes back to the unforgiveable sin Huppenthal thought Curtis Acosta committed because his classroom had a poster of Che Guevara but not Benjamin Franklin. Ellman apparently thought this was a checkmate move. As the judge would make clear in his written opinion issued one month later, he did not find this line of argumentation persuasive.

After excusing Dr. Pitti and asking him to return the next day to resume questioning at 9 a.m., Judge Tashima asked counsel their plan for the next day. In a surprise to the MAS legal team, Ellman said he thought he had at least two more hours of cross-examination of Dr. Pitti. The judge turned to Chang, who said that the length of the re-direct would depend on the scope of Mr. Ellman's cross-examination the next day but that he did not expect the re-direct to take more than half an hour.

* * *

The next day, Robert Ellman, acting as if he was the cat but forgetting the previous day when Pitti made him the mouse, tried to pounce by asking, "Are you generally familiar with the great works of Latino literature? ... How about *100 Years of Solitude* by Gabriel García Márquez?"[42] This led to a Q&A that showed the state grasping at straws.

Dr. Pitti quickly corrected Ellman and tried to educate him about the difference between Latino and Latin American literature: "Gabriel García Márquez, as I'm sure you know, is a South American author, who is more consistently identified as a Latin American author, and that's certainly a topic and a book of great interest to Latino writers, to Latino communities ... but it's not commonly treated in most settings as a ... work of Latino fiction."[43]

Ellman persisted: "So the fact that it's written in Spanish by a native Colombian author and it's fiction doesn't qualify it as Latino literature?"[44] After Dr. Pitti again explained the difference between Latino and Latin American literature, Ellman asked, "Wouldn't you agree that this course is an exception because it includes Indigenous literature from Central and South America? They're not Americans."[45] It took Dr. Pitti a moment to understand where Ellman was headed. It seems that because García Márquez was a native Colombian, Ellman thought García Márquez's work qualified as Indigenous literature from Central and South America. Dr. Pitti explained patiently that "Indigenous" does not mean to literally be from there and that García Márquez, though a native Colombian, was not a voice of Indigenous literature from South America.

One of the most difficult things to teach a law student or young attorney is when to sit down. But rather than sitting down, Ellman doubled down. He asked if Dr. Pitti was familiar with the giants of what Ellman called *Latino* literature. He expressed incredulity that Gabriel García Márquez, Mario Vargas Llosa, Jorge Luis Borges, Julio Cortazar, Carlos Fuentes, Juan Rulfo, Ernesto Sabato, and Octavio Paz were not included in the MAS Latino Literature class and asked: "Isn't the omission of works by these authors like leaving Mark Twain and John Steinbeck out of an American literature course?"[46] This raises a dynamic that operates for Latinas/os as well as for Asian Americans, the notion that Latino is synonymous with Latin American in the same way that Asian American gets confused or conflated with Asian. Ellman's question appears to reflect his own notion of Latinos as perpetual foreigners, associated forever and inseparably from their countries of origin. Dr. Pitti summed up this point:

> [T]here was a strong tendency among policy members and members of the media to equate people of Latino descent with non-citizens.
>
> And that's been a persistent pattern ... [a] problem that people of – Mexican Americans and other people of Latino descent faced despite whatever their citizenship status might be.... There's a kind of lumping together, what scholars have often called racialization, the kind of creation of an imagination of a common set of racial characteristics by which people are defined as similar, regardless of how different they might have been.[47]

Chang thought that Judge Tashima might be sensitive to these points because he may have experienced the same as a Japanese American during World War II who found himself incarcerated as a child with his family in Poston, Arizona. General DeWitt who ordered the removal and incarceration of Japanese Americans infamously expressed, "A Jap is a Jap." Mr. Ellman's line of questioning was based on a deeply flawed premise that Pitti's responses made clear.

Ellman then turned to the theme of red-baiting that began with the questioning of Dr. Acosta on Day 1 of the trial.

ELLMAN: Will you agree with me that Che Guevara is a communist?
PITTI: I would – I believe that's true.
…
ELLMAN: Would you also agree with me that Paulo Freire is a Marxist?
PITTI: It's my understanding that Paulo Freire, at least for part of his life, was a Marxist.
ELLMAN: So there was a factual basis for believing that the Mexican-American courses at least contained politically radical material, correct?
PITTI: Yes. [then turning to the judge] And may I qualify that, Your Honor?
THE COURT: Yes, certainly.[48]

Dr. Pitti then explained that the focus of Mr. Ellman's questions on Che Guevara and Paulo Freire actually made Dr. Pitti's point, that Ellman in his cross-examination was himself using code words:

> Again, that's an example of the kind of code words in the use of the Mexican-American Studies Program to reiterate a connection between radicalism and Mexican-American Studies, and, by extension, Mexican-American educators and perhaps the broader community at a time in which concerns about Latin American radicals, about un-American immigrants coming into Arizona, were very much, were very critical to public debate surrounding these bills. So I thank you for raising the issue because it does drive to a central point of what I've shown, I think, and demonstrated the importance of code words and the importance of the depiction – the focus in depicting Mexican-American Studies on people like Che Guevara, people like Paulo Freire, and pulling out the fact that they were Marxist or communists to be critical in describing what that program was.[49]

It is a shame that there is no courtroom video. Words cannot describe fully the way Ellman was glaring at Dr. Pitti. A small smile on Dr. Pitti's face seemed to indicate that he knew he had gotten under Ellman's skin, using Ellman's own words as illustrations of the racist code words he described in his expert report.

Undeterred, Ellman took up a discussion of "*Raza*" and "*Aztlán.*" When asked by Ellman if he had read correctly a paragraph from Dr. Pitti's declaration, Dr. Pitti corrected Ellman's pronunciation.

PITTI: Aztlán. Not Azatlán. It's two syllables, not three.
ELLMAN: Aztlán?
PITTI: Exactly.
ELLMAN: Thank you.
PITTI: Thank you.[50]

The MAS legal team did their best not to laugh; they didn't want Ellman's death glare to turn on them.

Ellman then turned to MEChA, one of the state's favorite bogeymen. Ellman: "You say … 'Horne used code words when he associated Raza studies or the MAS program with Aztlán and MEChA….' Then … you say that: 'Horne's characterization of MEChA is simply incorrect…. Horne's ahistorical statements about MEChA show how contemporary politicians have conflated twenty-first century education concerns with those of the founders of MEChA more than 45 years ago.'" Then, finally, he got to a question. Ellman asked, "When you say, 'ahistorical,' do you mean that it's an outdated perception?"[51]

Ellman then asked about one of MEChA's founding documents, *El Plan Espiritual de Aztlán* and represented to Dr. Pitti and to the Court that this document was on the front page of the webpage of the University of Arizona MEChA chapter.[52] This emphasis on "front page" was to contradict Dr. Pitti's earlier statement that MEChA had evolved and was a very different organization nearly fifty years later.

Dr. Pitti surprised Ellman by saying,

> I sort of thought that the *El Plan Espiritual de Aztlán* was located under the history tab on this web page online. Can you tell me if that's true? It was the last time I looked. It would suggest that this was understood as a historical document by the MEChA chapter of the University of Arizona. Is that in fact the case?[53]

This statement and questions from Dr. Pitti provoked another long glare from Ellman before he responded somewhat sheepishly, "I believe it was the front page, but I don't require you to accept that for purposes of your answer.... But you will accept that it's part of the website, is that fair?"[54]

What Ellman didn't know and couldn't have known was that the evening before, Dr. Pitti and Robert Chang spent some time on the University of Arizona and national MEChA webpages. Though Chang had to leave Horne's examination earlier that day, he saw from the transcript that Ellman tried to connect the dots, asking Horne about *El Plan Espiritual de Aztlán* and about the national and University of Arizona MEChA webpages. What Chang hadn't expected, though, was that Ellman would misrepresent where the document was on the webpage. Out of an abundance of caution, Chang asked Jorge Martorell to take screenshots of the University of Arizona MEChA webpage – first the homepage, and then screenshots that followed each click that would lead to the document. Jorge had, at the ready, screenshots Chang could show the court as well as color printouts of the same.

In his questioning of Horne, Ellman referred only to the materials being available on the national and UA MEChA websites. With Dr. Pitti, Ellman represented that the specific document is on the front page of the UA MEChA website. But when asked about it, Dr. Pitti responded with his devastating statement and questions, worth repeating: "I sort of thought ... [the document] was located under the history tab on this web page online. Can you tell me if that's true? It was the last time I looked."[55]

It was astounding to see Dr. Pitti, trained in history and not in law, turn the tables. Witnesses are supposed to answer questions, not ask them. "Can you tell me if that's true?" This question is a trap. Dr. Pitti knew that if Ellman said it was true, the MAS legal team had the documentary evidence to pounce.

Another death glare from Ellman.

After equivocating, Ellman quoted passages from *El Plan Espiritual de Aztlán*, and the following colloquy ensued:

ELLMAN: Do you think it's reasonable for a person reading this, who is not a Mechista, to be – for that to cause resentment in that person reading these statements?
PITTI: I think I – I'm sorry. I think I need to know who this reasonable person is. Are we talking about a Mexican-American student? Are we talking – Sorry ... I said I would need to know who this reasonable person is.
ELLMAN: A reasonable person is a white person who's not a member of MEChA. Do you think this is likely to cause resentment in such a person?[56]

The attorney representing the state of Arizona, when asked for a clarification of who was a reasonable person, equated "[a] reasonable person" as "a white person."

Ellman, rather than discrediting Dr. Pitti, actually made the case for the plaintiffs, giving concrete examples of the very things Dr. Pitti indicated were manifestations of animus. In addition, Ellman clearly misrepresented the prominence of *El Plan Espiritual de Aztlán* on the University of Arizona MEChA chapter website. Chang hammered this point home in his re-direct examination of Dr. Pitti, when Chang walked him through a series of questions that showed precisely where the document was, with screenshots projected onto the monitors in the courtroom, for all to see.

Chang's re-direct also addressed a point Ellman scored when he asked Dr. Pitti who Raul Hector Castro was and why there were no references to Castro in Dr. Pitti's report. Ellman enjoyed turning the tables, lecturing:

> I am going to tell you that Raul Hector Castro was the first Mexican-American governor of Arizona who was elected in 1974. ...
>
> If you're attempting to establish that there was a history of anti-Mexican sentiment in Arizona, don't you think it's significant to let the reader of your report know that over 40 years ago the state elected its first Mexican-American governor?[57]

Once reminded of who Castro was, Dr. Pitti placed Castro's electoral success into context and stated "that the fact that Castro was governor in the 1970s does not provide evidence" that Arizona in the ensuing decades was welcoming of Mexican Americans.[58]

In Chang's re-direct, he addressed the point the state was trying to make about Castro, asking: "Do you believe that the election of Barack Obama as president means that antiblack racism is over?" Dr. Pitti answered, "No."

In his final set of questions, Chang asked if historians studied discrimination and why. Dr. Pitti stated that historians have studied it extensively and that understanding discrimination is critical to "understanding the history of human society."[59] Chang then asked about code word analysis as an accepted methodology in the field of history and whether there was anything he had heard in this courtroom that would lead him to change any conclusions or opinions expressed in his expert report or in his direct testimony that he had submitted by declaration. He answered no, meaning that he was sticking with his report and declaration.

Chang wanted to end with Dr. Pitti's powerful words from his declaration. He was concerned, though, that if he asked Dr. Pitti to read it, the state would object because this was simply repeating his previous testimony submitted by declaration, though unaired in court. Chang asked Jorge to project page 9 of Dr. Pitti's declaration onto the courtroom monitors. He then asked Dr. Pitti to read to himself each sentence of paragraph 25. Chang did not have him read it aloud, but by projecting it onto the courtroom monitors, he wanted everyone to read and absorb, in the silence, Dr. Pitti's powerful conclusion:

> When properly understood within the context of the history and contemporary discrimination directed against Mexicans and Mexican Americans in Arizona, it is my expert opinion that government officials, politicians, and private citizens have used code words and have mischaracterized Ethnic Studies, Mexican American Studies, and TUSD's Mexican American Studies Program in order to advance their political objectives.... [M]any of the reasons offered to justify enactment and enforcement of HB 2281 were not legitimate and instead were based on mischaracterizations of Mexican American Studies, Mexican American Studies program educators and students, and Mexican American Studies curricula and pedagogical approaches.[60]

Perhaps gimmicky, but in the silence, everyone in the courtroom was reading from the monitors that were all around the courtroom. Judge Tashima placed his face up close to the monitor, reading.

After a short re-cross, Dr. Pitti was excused and court recessed for lunch.

SUBTRACTIVE SCHOOLING V. THE MAS WAY

Dr. Angela Valenzuela then took the stand. She wrote the book, literally. As Curtis Acosta testified on Day 1, Dr. Angela Valenzuela's *Subtractive Schooling* provided an important frame in developing the MAS Program. This makes perfect sense when one considers the thesis of her book, as she provided in her direct testimony, that the education of Mexican American students is "predicated on a curriculum, pedagogy, and policy framework that is 'subtractive.' ...[S]chools take away resources from Mexican American students by requiring that those students give up certain aspects of their culture, like the Spanish language and their cultural identities, in order to force assimilation. This results in Mexican American students losing interest in learning."[61]

She highlighted how subtractive models of schooling "deprive Mexican American students of culturally relevant resources."[62] Here, the teachings of Paolo Freire meet up with Ethnic Studies. Freire criticized what he called the "banking model of education," the practice of educators who sought only to "deposit" information into the brains of students. This traditional model of education, which disregarded and discounted students' rich cultural knowledge, was what Dr. Valenzuela critiqued as "subtractive schooling." The flip side of Dr. Valenzuela's subtractive schooling was the affirmative version that recognized and built upon students' cultural orientations and traditions, recognizing that students come to school with a rich repository of cultural knowledge.

Dr. Valenzuela offered that Ethnic Studies and MAS countered subtractive schooling. She detailed the positive impact that Ethnic Studies had on students.[63] She then described the curriculum map for TUSD's American History – Mexican American Perspectives she reviewed, along with a curriculum unit written by an MAS teacher. Through no fault of her own, this was the extent of the direct MAS curriculum provided to her to make her assessment. The state would seize upon this to challenge her overall conclusion that MAS courses were aligned to state standards and were consistent with best practices in Ethnic Studies and that there was "no evidence that the MAS curriculum in TUSD conveyed any intention of teaching victimization or resentment against whites" and that "TUSD's MAS program is a sound program that was properly implemented."[64]

Leslie Cooper conducted the cross-examination for the state. During this questioning, Cooper relied heavily upon Kathryn Hrabluk's testimony that took place during the first week on Day 5. Cooper knew that Hrabluk's testimony, discussed later in detail in Chapter 13, had been impactful. Over the objections of the plaintiffs, Hrabluk had, in effect, testified as an expert on curriculum; she described an ideal version of a curricular guide that included scope and sequence, with curricular units composed of discrete lesson plans, again mapped onto the guide. After constructing this ideal, Hrabluk effectively testified that TUSD's MAS program had nothing that approached this kind of curriculum map.

Dr. Valenzuela countered that the MAS program was sound and properly implemented.[65] First, Cooper nibbled around the edges. She asked about particular materials and curricular units. She then asked about nearly a thousand pages the state produced, which were only made available to Dr. Valenzuela shortly before she was called to the stand.

Cooper found an additional way to challenge Dr. Valenzuela's direct testimony. One problem for the MAS legal team was that the MAS program, though it gave to the legal department at TUSD over 200 curriculum units, did not turn over a curriculum map with scope and sequence, at least as defined by Arizona Department of Education (ADE) official Kathryn Hrabluk. Dr. Valenzuela based her expert report and direct testimony on what had been provided to her: Sean Arce's 2011–2012 curriculum map for 11th grade history and a single curriculum unit developed by former MAS teacher Norma Ballesteros. Though Arce's curriculum map might pass muster, it only covered 11th grade history. And this had not been provided to the Cambium auditors or to Kathryn Hrabluk and the ADE investigators.

A careful reader will wonder, even if Arce's curriculum map passes muster, what about the other courses? Cooper pushed effectively on this point, highlighting that, other than Sean Arce's draft 2011–2012 curriculum map, no other comprehensive map had been provided for any other courses. Without this, what would the basis be for any opinion expressed about other MAS courses? Yet Dr. Valenzuela made a broader pronouncement in her written direct testimony: "TUSD's MAS curriculum met widely recognized requirements for curriculum design, including alignment with state and Common Core standards. It includes higher-order thinking, socio-emotional learning, and the cultivation of an academic identity."[66]

The state made the most of this overclaim by Dr. Valenzuela. Building off Kathryn Hrabluk's testimony on Days 5 and 6, Cooper got Dr. Valenzuela to agree that curriculum included three parts: "[w]hat the students are going to learn"; "[h]ow it's going to be taught to them"; and determining "whether they've learned the material" or assessment.[67] After working through definitions for "curriculum unit" and "lesson plan," Cooper then challenged the basis for Valenzuela's assessment of the entire MAS program, and got her to admit that she made an inference about the program based on the provided curricular map of 11th grade history.[68] Cooper grilled Dr. Valenzuela about how she could draw an inference about the entire program based only on the two items. It did not help that the curriculum map provided by Sean Arce and submitted to the court with Dr. Valenzuela's expert report and declaration had a "draft" watermark on every page. Cooper kept emphasizing "draft" and "a single course" in her questions.[69] Cooper also challenged Dr. Valenzuela about the other supplied item, specific lessons designed for K-5.[70]

Cooper then returned to the state's major attack point: "So you drew your conclusions about the TUSD MAS curriculum on the basis of a draft pacing guide for an American history class. Right? ... And a curriculum unit with seven lessons for K-5, right?" Dr. Valenzuela then discussed other information that she used that allowed her to draw broader conclusions, including interviews with Sean Arce and other MAS teachers. She included what she had learned about the MAS program and its curriculum in the film *Precious Knowledge* and from published scholarly articles written about the MAS program. Dr. Valenzuela had discussed this earlier as "triangulating information from various sources in order to render a judgment."[71]

When pushed by Cooper on the apparent lack of curricular maps for other MAS courses, Dr. Valenzuela offered that courses can have an "implicit roadmap." Cooper then quoted from the Cambium Audit: "The auditors did not find a well-defined solitary document that provided the integrated, comprehensive guidance needed to direct, monitor, and assess effective curriculum implementation.... There was no observable evidence provided to the auditors to indicate a well-defined curriculum detailing clear long- and short-term goals within each course, along with pacing guides and use of formative and summative assessments."[72]

When asked questions about why Cambium did not find a well-drafted curriculum, Dr. Valenzuela offered that they had not allowed for an implicit curriculum. Cooper then asked: "Is that an understood term in educational pedagogy, 'implicit curriculum'?" to which Dr. Valenzuela answered, "I'm not sure."[73]

It was the end of the day, and Dr. Valenzuela was on the stand the entire afternoon, but Cooper wasn't done. The cross-examination resumed the next morning. After laying the foundation with the witness, the state moved for the admission of hundreds of pages of curricular units that it had turned over to the plaintiffs shortly before trial, which Dr. Valenzuela reviewed when she arrived in Tucson at the beginning of the week.

Leslie Cooper's questions began with one of those units. She placed Exhibit 561B before the witness. Luna Barrington and Robert Chang looked at each other. At breakfast that morning, Chang told Barrington and Dr. Valenzuela that Cooper was going to ask about the lynching photos and to be ready with a response. After representing to the witness that this was a curriculum unit available for fourth through seventh graders, Cooper stated:

COOPER: This is a series of pictures, and I am going to show you that the pictures that I am going to use are this, Chicanos lynched in Santa Cruz, California, May 3rd, 1877, by 40 vigilantes. And then we have this picture as well, but we can't – there's no caption... Now ... – you understand that these pictures were used in curriculum units for fourth graders, right?
...
Do you think it's appropriate to use with elementary school students?
VALENZUELA: I think it could be, yes. I think we have to rely on the teachers' professional judgment in so much of this, if not all of it.[74]

When Cooper appeared incredulous that photos such as these could be shown to nine-year-olds in a public-school setting by a teacher, Dr. Valenzuela deftly explained that assessing the appropriateness of using material like this was not simply yes or no, that the use of pictures such as this for younger students would require scaffolding, including placing it in the context of what the teacher was trying to accomplish, the lesson plans that preceded and followed it. Cooper, though, kept pushing for a yes or no answer: were the pictures appropriate or not? She was not satisfied with "it depends" and was not willing to acknowledge the role and importance of a teacher's professional judgment in making that decision for their class.

Cooper's examination that morning was relatively brief. Luna Barrington then conducted the re-direct. One of the first things she did was to address a point Cooper challenged Dr. Valenzuela on, a statement made in her report/declaration about how MAS courses aligned with Common Core standards for social studies. The previous day, Cooper represented to Dr. Valenzuela and the court that there were no Common Core standards for social studies. Dr. Valenzuela was surprised by the challenge and wasn't quite sure how to answer.

It turned out that there were common core standards, which the MAS legal team confirmed after Dr. Valenzuela's first day of testimony. The next day, after asking Jorge to put the website onto the courtroom monitors, the following colloquy ensued:

VARRINGTON: Is this the Common Core website that you looked at?
VALENZUELA: Yes.
…
BARRINGTON: You see here that there are, in fact, Common Core standards for history social studies, correct?
VALENZUELA: That is correct.
BARRINGTON: So Ms. Cooper was incorrect when she said that there were no Common Core studies for social studies, is that correct?
VALENZUELA: Yeah, she was incorrect, and we were correct at the time.

This was the second time that attorneys for the state misrepresented or were mistaken about the websites they used to challenge the expert witnesses. Luna Barrington did a fantastic job showing this to the court. Chang and Barrington were able to show that the defendants' attorneys appeared to be taking things out of context and may have mischaracterized them.

Then, returning to the importance of context and to show differences between what Dr. Valenzuela and the ADE team did to determine if materials were improper, Barrington asked, "If you were trying to understand the context in which these materials were being taught, what would you have done?" Dr. Valenzuela answered:

> What I would have done is I would have done what the state did not do. I would have talked to the teachers. I would have observed their classrooms. I would have asked for lesson plans. I would have asked for unit plans. And even if they didn't have a curriculum map, they had a structure, and it was sequential, and even the materials that were supplied to me this week used that word … "sequentially," that the materials should be used sequentially, which suggested they had an implicit curriculum map.[75]

She added that the fact that the MAS teachers met regularly to discuss what they were doing in their courses and classrooms also indicated that there was "not only coherence, but profound philosophical underpinnings to" the program. And she would know about those profound philosophical underpinnings. Dr. Valenzuela, after all, wrote the book.

Barrington wrapped up her re-direct by asking if there was anything Dr. Valenzuela heard in the courtroom that would lead her to change any of the opinions she expressed in her report or in her written direct testimony. Dr. Valenzuela said no and added that the new material she reviewed and the courtroom conversation "deepened my … strengthened my conclusion. I was very, very pleased to read [the new materials provided by the state] and to go through them, because it actually underscored or reinforced what I had already presumed and assumed and analyzed and synthesized to be true."[76] Though Barrington's re-direct was able to limit some of the damage, the state had been able to neutralize important aspects of Dr. Valenzuela's expert testimony, mostly because she had been given an incomplete set of materials on which to evaluate the entire program.

After a short re-cross by Leslie Cooper, Dr. Valenzuela was excused. She was the last witness for the plaintiffs, leading Steven Reiss to stand and say, "Your Honor, the plaintiffs rest."

While in this chapter, we explored the nuances of the expert testimony, the tenor of the court was dramatically different when Horne and Huppenthal took the stand on Days 7 and 1, respectively. Their testimony is recounted in Chapter 12.

12

Doubling Down on Racism

Horne and Huppenthal Take the Stand

FIGURE 12.1 John Huppenthal Outside of the Courtroom by Bryan Parras

While it took a dedicated collective and a massive disinformation campaign to attack and eliminate MAS as demonstrated in Chapter 2, Tom Horne and John Huppenthal (see Figure 12.1) were the centers of power leading this effort. They both played critical roles that led to the passage of the law, which, by design, gave a great deal of unilateral authority to the State Superintendent of Public Instruction to make determinations of noncompliance as well as to impose severe penalties. In addition, they used the bully pulpit of their offices and their election campaigns to condemn MAS while proclaiming themselves as the ones who would ultimately eliminate the program.

Thus, it is not surprising that during their testimony, both were unrepentant about their decade-long assault on MAS. Instead, they were proud of what they had done. They both believed they were on righteous missions even when faced with an incredible amount of evidence to the contrary. Their collective testimony showed their strong opposition to the program, but bubbling just beneath the surface was the anti-Brown racial animus at the center of the Arizona education cultural wars of the early 2010s. Inadvertently, their targeting of this program, disregard of countervailing evidence, and willingness to bend (or break) the rules or procedures to eliminate MAS would eventually be used to demonstrate their biases. It was a classic case of being one's own worst enemy.

TOM HORNE: A CANADIAN IMMIGRANT TELLS CHICANOS THEY'RE "UN-AMERICAN"

I went on a crusade against [Mexican American Studies] and destroyed the entire program.
– Tom Horne court testimony[1]

On Day 7 of the trial, plaintiffs' attorney James Quinn called Tom Horne to the stand. Normally, on direct examination, attorneys are not supposed to ask witnesses leading questions, except as it might be necessary to develop the witness's testimony. But under Federal Rule of Evidence 611 and with the court's permission, Mr. Quinn was permitted to treat Horne as an adverse or hostile witness and ask leading questions in his direct examination.

The plaintiffs' strategy was straightforward – to let Mr. Horne's actions and words speak for themselves. He was happy to oblige; in some ways, he was too happy. The plaintiffs' attorneys thought he might try, as John Huppenthal did during the first week of the trial, to claim that he had not sought to eliminate the program and that instead, it was the TUSD governing board that took that action. Nope.

Horne was happy to report that he had sought the elimination of the program since his 2007 *Open Letter*, that he drafted a bill that would allow him as State Superintendent, to eliminate MAS, and that as Attorney General, he offered his assistance to the Department of Education to put a stop to MAS. He proudly volunteered that he previously argued summary judgment in 2012 before Judge Tashima.

Somewhat like Michael Hicks' embarrassing appearance on *The Daily Show with Jon Stewart*, Tom Horne kept returning to the twice-ruled unconstitutional component of the statute that classes were not allowed to be offered if they are designed primarily for students of a particular ethnic group. He seemed to have forgotten, or did not care, that Judge Tashima had found this provision unconstitutional and the Ninth Circuit had affirmed this part of the ruling. Horne, though, kept defending this provision as necessary to prevent the type of education that had existed in the Jim Crow South. Plaintiffs' attorney James Quinn asked if this meant like slavery, and Horne responded:

HORNE: No. I was referring to segregation. That's what they did in the South before Civil Rights. They put African-American kids in one class, and they put the white kids in another class.
QUINN: You just agreed with me that, in fact, anybody could take any one of the classes, so they weren't being divided by race.
HORNE: I did, but I also told you that it was designed for them, the curriculum said it was for them, their leader testified in a nationally televised debate with me that he wanted to appeal to the DNA inside them, which could only be the kids that were of that background. And it was a division of kids by race, and I thought that was wrong. And the white kids who took the course, because they didn't know any better, ended up regretting it because they got dissed for being white. And they had to sit there while they were told not to fall for the white man's traps.[2]

Prior to this exchange, Quinn went to great lengths to establish that students took the MAS courses of their own volition. Despite this, Horne believed that the MAS pattern of racial clustering harkened back to the forced segregation and racial violence of Jim Crow. It was extremely telling that Horne only found MAS students in a largely Mexican American district as "segregating," but he never found anything wrong with White students on the northside of Tucson taking AP European history class as segregating. Horne ultimately saw MAS as harmful to White students, although he was rarely as publicly overt in his beliefs as he was in his testimony.

Horne was then asked about his reaction to Dolores Huerta's commentary that began bringing this issue to a head where she said, based on their legislative agenda (in particular the anti-migrant/anti-Brown Sensenbrenner Bill of 2006), that "Republicans hate Latinos." While we have already detailed the event and the subsequent controversy, what was very telling was how Horne saw and interpreted this Civil Rights icon's words. He was explicit in labeling her words "hate speech," but he initially denied that he used those words. It was only when Quinn presented Horne with his office's press release from April 14, 2006, where Horne said, "I can personally testify to the inaccuracy of Mrs. Huerta's hate speech,"[3] that he said he stood by those words. It was also a continuation of the attacks on MAS whereby those calling out racism – in this instance, a Civil Rights icon against repressive legislation – were accused of inciting hate. It was the same way Huppenthal called MAS the KKK of a different color and Horne could accuse the MAS of promoting segregation akin to Jim Crow.

This was not the only area where Tom Horne used his testimony to rewrite history. There was a famous picture of MAS students and local Tucson Brown Berets protesting the attacks on the program. Horne and Margaret Garcia Dugan held a press conference documented extensively in *Precious Knowledge* where they both attacked the program as being revolutionary and anti-American. During Horne's testimony, he particularly focused on the use of a raised fist:

HORNE: You put your fist in the air as a – I mean, I've seen a lot of movies about the 1930s in Germany where people put their fists in the air.
QUINN: Well, when those two African-American athletes raised their fists in the air in 1968 in the Olympics in Mexico City, do you think that was rude, or were they simply having a protest?
HORNE: I thought it was rude as heck. They were representing this country, and they did that. I was – I was not pleased with that.
QUINN: One last question. Isn't it true that –
HORNE: They had benefited in this country. They had been – they had the honor of being Olympic athletes, and they were – they were downgrading their country in an international forum. You think that's good?[4]

This was emblematic of Horne's approach. First, he used inapt comparisons that distorted history. The raised fist was not a symbol in Germany in the 1930s. Rather, it was the raised arm with the palm down accompanied by chanting or shouting "Heil Hitler" or "Sieg Heil."[5] But Horne's inaccurate comparison equating Nazis and their raised fists with protesting TUSD students with their raised fists allowed him to argue that the students were the real racists.

Horne, though claiming to be a student of history, ignored history when convenient. When Quinn sought to correct Horne's error by providing the historical record about the raised Black Power fist used by Tommy Smith and John Carlos during a medal ceremony at the 1968 Olympics to protest the horrific conditions Black Americans faced back home, Horne brushed this away and called them unpatriotic, insufficiently grateful to the country that had given them so much. Indeed, the athletes were ungrateful and downright rude, which was exactly how Horne viewed the protesting TUSD students.

Horne also rejected that the First Amendment protected the students who protested Dugan's rebuttal speech:

HORNE: Raised their fists in the air, which is a pretty extremist thing to do.
QUINN: It's part of their – it's part of their First Amendment precious right, isn't it, sir?
HORNE: Not in that context, no.[6]

Horne explained, "It's not appropriate to create a negative environment when a guest speaker comes. You can ask hard questions, but that kind of rude behavior I think is inappropriate for students in a school."[7] It was at this point that Quinn had him. Quinn reminded him that the students were not allowed to ask any questions, let alone any hard questions, Horne had to admit this was true.[8]

There was a biting irony in Horne's testimony. When he testified, he was the Arizona Attorney General; to take office, he had to swear to support the Constitution of the United States.[9] He had previously stated that the right to protest is "precious" and protected by the First Amendment.[10] Yet he would not afford this protection to the Tucson High School students who protested silently. In his eyes, they were rude, rude, rude. In case there was any doubt about how Horne felt about them, he used the words "rude," "rudely," and "rudeness" at least fifteen times during his testimony to describe the students.[11]

A favorite tactic throughout Horne's testimony was to establish guilt by association. One of his favorite talking points throughout his several-year campaign against MAS was to associate it with MEChA – one of the oldest Chicana/o student groups in the country. Horne claimed that MEChistas advocated revolution against the US government.[12]

And though he admitted to being shocked by Huppenthal's blog posts and that Huppenthal equating MAS to the KKK was hate speech,[13] Horne saw no irony when he turned around and used a similar tactic. Instead of Klansmen, Horne used Nazis. No one was surprised when he did this. When he argued the March 2012 summary judgment proceeding before Judge Tashima, he opened his argument by saying that "[i]f what we were dealing with was a course designed by the Ku Klux Klan, everybody would see it's obvious the state has that legitimate interest."[14] In his next sentence, he described MAS as "a course that promotes racist values that the legislature has a valid interest in preventing."[15] Horne had long been comfortable comparing MAS with Nazis and Klansmen, even as he condemned others who drew such comparisons.

Another contradiction revealed in Horne's testimony was his selective colorblindness. As previously described, Horne kept recycling his story that he was at the March on Washington, where his takeaway was that a colorblind approach to education was the only type he supported. He thought anything race-conscious, like MAS, was itself racist. Then, with no indication of cognitive dissonance, Horne recognized the political advantage in having his bill, HB 2281, introduced in the legislature by Steve Montenegro, described by Horne as "a Central American immigrant."[16] He admitted that Montenegro being Hispanic was a plus in trying to get the bill passed.[17] On the one hand, MAS teachers were condemned for being race-conscious because only colorblindness was acceptable; on the other hand, Horne did not hesitate to exploit Montenegro's ethnic background.[18] Similarly, Horne emphasized that three of the five teachers whom he cited in his finding of violation were either from Mexico or had Mexican heritage.[19] Race did not matter to Horne, except when it did.

Horne's inclusion of persons of Mexican and Central American ancestry in his campaign against MAS likely included another dimension, that he himself could not be engaging in racism against Latinx people because Latinx people supported him. Early in his testimony, he proclaimed proudly that he had a plaque on his wall thanking Horne from a group called "Hispanics [sic] for the Children."[20] On cross/re-direct by the state, he described the group as "English for the Children" and that the award included a picture "of a bunch of Hispanic students and their parents."[21]

Returning to the findings of noncompliance with state law, a key point of contention in Horne's testimony was the fact that he never visited an MAS classroom or conducted an audit of the classes. His approach was summed up in the following exchange:

QUINN: It never really crossed your mind that there might have been ways to improve the MAS program. Correct?
HORNE: I did not think so. I thought that – I mean, I studied it very closely, and I thought we're dealing with the Potemkin Village problem again.[22]

Horne was particularly smitten with the metaphor of the Potemkin Village as he used it throughout his testimony. He explained that Grigory Potemkin deceived Catherine the Great about the extent of rebuilding taking place in the Crimea by building movable villages that appeared prosperous: "So the raft [carrying Catherine the Great] would come to a village, and ... it would look like a prosperous village.... And as soon as the raft went on down the river, they would rush the movable village to the next village. And behind these movable villages was utter devastation and poverty and misery."[23]

In Horne's mind, any inspection of MAS would not reveal the truth because he believed that MAS teachers would put up a façade, a "Potemkin Village" that did not represent the true – in his mind, insidious – nature of the program.

Equipped already with a "tremendous amount of evidence" that the MAS program was in violation of state law[24] – that evidence being from largely anonymous sources and disgruntled former employees talking about issues that occurred in 2007 and before – he felt comfortable as he was leaving office as Superintendent at the end of 2010 to conclude that the program violated state law despite not conducting an audit.[25]

Based on his prior-gathered evidence, Horne characterized MAS as "propaganda."[26] When Quinn framed Horne's beliefs about the program as "assumptions," Horne was upset and shot back that he had been a lawyer for forty years and that he knew how to conduct an investigation,[27] despite admitting earlier that he never conducted an investigation. Horne was convinced that the MAS program was in violation of state law, and nothing would change his mind.

Horne's circular logic was on full display when challenged about his rejection of the Cambium Audit's findings of no violations of state law:

QUINN: You are just arguing that, Mr. Horne. You weren't there. You have no idea what, in fact, the observers from Cambium saw during the period of their examination.
HORNE: I know what they reported. They didn't report any of the things that were reported by the teachers who were actually there, when people weren't being studied and were showing what was actually going on.
QUINN: Maybe they didn't report it because it wasn't happening. That's possible, isn't it?
HORNE: It wasn't happening at the moment they were there, but it was happening in general in the courses because – for which I had overwhelming evidence both

from the teachers and from the written literature. And they were subjected to a Potemkin Village, and they were shown a show, and they believed it.[28]

In his view, anything painting MAS in a positive light must be the result of deception. There must have been something wrong with the way the audit was conducted instead of something wrong with his own personal evidence collection and analysis.

Horne was also asked how he could have found MAS out of compliance *before* the statute went into effect.

QUINN: Isn't it fair to say that the statute itself couldn't be applied to behavior that occurred before it went into effect? You're a lawyer. You know that, don't you?
HORNE: Well, my view was that it was a continuing situation and that it needed to stop.
QUINN: Could you read back the question. (Reporter read back the last question and answer.)
HORNE: I stand by that answer.[29]

A few minutes later, Quinn allowed Horne one more chance to rethink his response, and Horne defiantly reiterated, "I stand by my answer."[30]

A final important line of questioning by the plaintiffs probed why Horne only went after MAS and no other race-conscious program at TUSD. In discussing an email written by Mark Anderson lobbying for passage of HB 2281 that said, "We need to satisfy Tom Horne, who wants to be able to get rid of the La Raza program in Tucson," Horne testified, "I would have said I want to get rid of all of the ethnic studies programs, but the one that first attracted my attention, the one I have evidence for, is the MAS program."[31]

While Horne said he wanted to eliminate all forms of race-conscious education, his actions told a different story. Additional evidence of his selective prosecution comes from his treatment of Tucson's Paulo Freire Freedom School. As we previously explored, the Brazilian educator and his book *Pedagogy of the Oppressed* that cited some Marxist theorists were central reasons Horne offered for attacking the MAS program. However, the school in Tucson bearing Freire's name was *never* investigated. One key difference: students taking MAS classes were predominantly Mexican American; the students in the Paulo Freire Freedom School, predominantly White.[32] Similarly, the TUSD African American, Native American, or Pan Asian Studies programs were never investigated for violations of state law. Horne's singular focus on MAS was critical evidence to support the plaintiffs' First and Fourteenth Amendment claims.

Finally, Quinn did a masterful job of running down Horne's legislative history that was riddled with anti-Brown pieces of legislation and political rhetoric. For example, when running for Attorney General in 2010, part of Horne's campaign platform was "build the wall," several years before Trump made it a national slogan. Horne also actively fought bilingual education and pushed for English-only,[33] attacked resident instate tuition for DACA (Deferred Action for Childhood Arrivals) students,[34] accepted political support from anti-Mexican Sheriff Joe Arpaio,[35] tried to prevent TUSD from implementing Culturally Relevant Courses even though they were mandated by a federal unitary status plan,[36] trying to remove teachers from classrooms with "heavy accents,"[37] among many others. Each of these Horne explained as either a "crusade against racism"[38] or a "concern about illegal immigration,"[39] but his long record of supporting anti-Brown policies was clear and the attacks on MAS were an extension of this history.

Before concluding his questioning, Quinn drove home Horne's radical anti-MAS campaign by highlighting his campaign materials. While Horne used his crusade against MAS on his website, he tried to frame it as not as relevant because it did not make his twelve major accomplishments section. However, when pressed, Quinn made Horne admit that, in fact, attacking MAS was core to Horne's work:

QUINN: [Attacking MAS] was an issue?
HORNE: Yeah.
QUINN: To stop *La Raza*?
HORNE: Absolutely.[40]

* * *

Robert Ellman began his cross-examination by giving Mr. Horne a chance to recover from his direct examination and present a self-serving narrative to refute any charge that he harbored racial animus. In this story, Mr. Horne was the heroic anti-racist, the antithesis of what he was accused of. He began with a deeply personal family history that informed his personal philosophy:

> Well, I regard racism as the biggest evil in human history and in contemporary human life, and my very strongly felt philosophy, which I believe is the philosophy of this country, is that we're all individuals and what matters is what we know, what we can do and what is our character and not what race we've happen to have been born into. That's as deep a belief as one can have. And you asked me what lay behind it. I suppose a lot of things. Part of it I will say is personal. My parents were Polish-Jewish refugees from Hitler. All of their considerable extended families were killed in the Holocaust. So, I know on an almost firsthand basis how evil racism can be.[41]

He described how he "didn't grow up with an atmosphere of racism" because his parents regarded people expressing racial prejudice as being vulgar. He then pivoted to invoke John F. Kennedy's famous 1963 address to Congress, paraphrasing him to say "Race plays no proper role in American life or law."[42] After declaring that his "whole life has been a crusade against racism," Horne went on to trot out his participation in the 1963 March on Washington and to declare fealty to the portion of Dr. King's speech when he dreamt of the day when his children would be judged by the content of their character instead of the color of their skin.[43]

He also emphasized that during the 1963 March, he saw none of the rudeness that he experienced in the protests by students at TUSD. Horne's selective memory of history allowed him to remember a whitewashed version of Dr. King, ignoring the "rudeness" Dr. King exhibited when he protested and was jailed repeatedly.

The state had a playbook when questioning Horne, asking variations of the question, "Are you a racist?" to which Horne would reply, "No." For those who think this is an oversimplification, here is a direct quotation:

ELLMAN: Finally, was racial animus or viewpoint discrimination any part of your motivation in drafting, lobbying for, or enforcing HB 2281?
HORNE: No, racial animus is that which I fought against my whole life.[44]

This was a strange line of questioning because of an obvious point – no one in contemporary life wants to be labeled "racist." Even modern-day KKK members maintain that they are not white supremacists.[45] While this may seem like an apples-to-oranges comparison, the point is that a denial of racism by itself does not establish it as a fact. Yet this was the state's strategy. In their Preliminary Proposed Findings of Fact and Conclusions of Law, a conclusion they hoped Judge Tashima would adopt verbatim was: "Horne stated squarely that he harbors no racial animus toward Latino students, and this Court found that statement credible. Moreover, it was corroborated by other witnesses who knew and worked with Horne, and nothing in Horne's background suggests he dislikes or holds disdain for Latinos."[46]

The defense continued, seeking to establish Horne's nonracist bona fides. Horne talked about visiting Mexico, learning Spanish, reading Mexican history, and the support he received from Hispanic people in his political and legislative work.[47] Later on redirect, James Quinn revisited Horne's testimony about how he hosted people from Mexico at his home and that he played piano for them, and asked point blank, "Is that some form of some of my best friends are Mexicans?"[48] Horne was not amused.

Ellman went through Horne's legislative agenda where the line of questioning was almost identical although it was interesting to see a generally long-winded man like Horne be so succinct in this space. Ellman directly asked Horne if anti-Mexican bias was driving the legislative support for HB 2281, and Horne simply replied, "No."[49] Ellman asked further if there was a hidden agenda about the passage of HB 2281 related to race, and Horne again replied simply, "No."[50] Ellman also tried to reframe Horne's anti-immigration stances by asking if people were conflating "anti-illegal immigrant" with "anti-Mexican" to which Horne responded, "Well clearly."[51] In response to Dr. Pitti's expert report, Ellman asked Horne specifically about code words and *Dog Whistle Politics*[52] in terms of his public statements regarding MAS:

ELLMAN: Were you using racial code words?
HORNE: I never used a racial code word in my entire life.[53]

Again, it was yet another form of the question – "Are you a racist?" – expecting that Horne's denial would be taken at face value.

Tom Horne, anti-racist hero.

Because Horne had been examined as an adverse witness as part of the plaintiffs' case-in-chief, Ellman's examination was a hybrid cross-examination as well as a direct examination. After Ellman concluded, following a short recess, the judge asked, "This is redirect, right?" to which James Quinn responded, "I guess it's redirect. Recross. I'm not even sure what we've determined it. But it's 're.'"[54] We were getting toward the end of a long day of testimony.

On redirect/cross, Quinn focused his questions to strengthen the plaintiffs' claims regarding code words. This is when additional discussion of raised fists took place. As he had before on direct examination, Horne admitted to everything he had done. It is quite possible that he may have been surprised that he was not awarded a medal for his antiracism stance and his antiracism work.

As the day came to a close and Horne was dismissed from the witness stand, people in the courtroom were exhausted. Hearing Horne's continued self-righteous crusade against MAS triggered many painful memories for several MAS supporters in the courtroom that day. It was also a persistent reminder of the stakes involved in the proceedings. In addition, kid reporter Amaru continued to report in his *All Power to the Kids News and* centered his reporting that day on a schism between Horne and Huppenthal that frequently went unnoticed in the MAS debate but would be critically important in the trial: "Today we heard from Superintendent Tom Horne [who] admitted that his coworker compared the KKK with Mexican American Studies, and Mr. Tom Horne admitted that was racist. That was a pretty big victory because we're trying to tell the judge that it was racism that got rid of Mexican American Studies. Stay tuned, stay woke."[55] It was telling that Horne would admit that Huppenthal's framing of MAS was racist even though, as noted earlier, he frequently used similar approaches. Judge Tashima saw through Horne's self-serving claim of being an antiracist crusader and found Horne's testimony about his motivations not credible. In other words, borrowing from the prose poem Ellman tried to bludgeon Curtis Acosta with on the trial's first day, Horne was a *mentiroso*.

HUPPENTHAL: A WHITE GUY FROM SOUTH TUCSON FINISHED WHAT HORNE STARTED[56]

Will the real John Huppenthal please stand up?

According to John Huppenthal, he is a person who is "the reverse of biased [against Latinos]. If I could help these kids, I would lay down in the mud and let them walk over my back." Yet, when asked about his apology when his anonymous racist blogging became public, Huppenthal walked it back: "I don't know if 'apology' is the right description…. I viewed it more as apologizing for the distraction…. I've had a chance to sort of get rested …, and I don't – I don't apologize for any of it."[57] With that, Huppenthal doubled down on his racism. He went on to describe a struggle between good and evil:

REISS: But in fact, Mr. Huppenthal, you said your war with MAS was a battle that never ends, right? Right?

HUPPENTHAL: It's eternal. It goes back to the plains of the Serengeti, you know, when we were evolving as a human race, the battle between the forces of collectivism and individualism. It defines us as a human race.[58]

Much like Tom Horne, Huppenthal saw this as a crusade, a war. In an interview with the Western Free Press on February 29, 2012, Huppenthal compared himself to Hannibal, who vanquished the Romans despite being vastly outnumbered by them. Like "Hannibal did to the Romans," Huppenthal said he stretched MAS and its supporters out over the course of a year, "and then when we finally encountered them in court [before the ALJ] it was a knockout punch."[59] His words showed a deep personal investment in a foregone conclusion instead of simply fielding evidence and objectively enforcing law.

In addition, Huppenthal, rather than answering the questions, vacillated between offering extensive editorials on events and issues he thought damning to the program and retreating to some version of "I do not remember" when he did not want to divulge something that would hurt the attack on MAS. Huppenthal's testimony continually stood out as both centrally important in the case as well as bizarre at times, like his invocation of the Serengeti.

Similar to Horne, Huppenthal presented his version of Mexican Americans being his best friends and that therefore he could not harbor any racial animus. He was a White guy from the very Brown southside of Tucson, a biographical fact that is part of his narrative that he is not racist.[60] For example, in court, he described Marcelino Lucero as someone who taught him long division in third grade and realizing, "geez, he knows English as well as I do."[61] In an op-ed following the trial, Huppenthal described Lucero as having taught him fractions in the third grade. Huppenthal added details that he did not include in his trial testimony, such as "Hispanics" came to his sleepovers and birthday parties and that he went to their quinceañeras.[62] Coming from a large, poor family, he found refuge in wrestling and stated repeatedly how hard work is the ticket to success. He came out of poverty to become an Arizona State Senator, House Representative, and Superintendent of Public Instruction. In Huppenthal's view, why can't everyone else?

Huppenthal was the last witness called on Day 1 of the trial. Though he was no longer formally a defendant in this case, his close association with the defense led the court to grant permission for Steven Reiss to treat him as an adverse or hostile witness. Reiss began his examination by reviewing Huppenthal's legislative record and his instrumental role in securing the passage of HB 2281. Though Huppenthal claimed he initially opposed the legislation because he believed in local control over educational issues, he ended up being pivotal in the bill's passage as he used his visit to Curtis Acosta's classroom, captured in *Precious Knowledge*, to justify his opposition to the program.

The questioning of Huppenthal by Reiss quickly became tense because Huppenthal appeared to have predetermined information he wanted in the record even if it was not responsive to Reiss's questions. At one point, Reiss bluntly stated, "I am sorry, I really do hate to be rude, but the way this works is I have to ask a question, and you get to answer it. Okay?"[63] This dynamic recurred throughout Huppenthal's testimony.

Later, Huppenthal became testy when Reiss asked about why he changed his mind about how he perceived MAS as a dangerous program. *"I didn't change my mind. Public policy is always a balancing of conflicting principles that you can hold at the same time and you have to balance them."*[64] The questioning turned to *Precious Knowledge* and Huppenthal's stated reasons for attacking MAS. Specifically, Reiss asked if Huppenthal's concern stemmed from the program "planting evil ideas in the students' minds."[65] Huppenthal said, "I would not characterize it that way."[66] Like an NFL replay official, Reiss went to the tape. The tape, in this instance, was a clip from *Precious Knowledge* played in court where Huppenthal asserted: "Well, the idea that – the idea that you have oppression taking place in society and that's a dominant theme of the class, I thought that was an unhealthy idea, at least."[67] Much like Horne's testimony, Huppenthal continually tried to backtrack on things that he had already said. Fortunately for the plaintiffs, and unfortunately for the state, much of it was on tape, including from Huppenthal's previously videotaped deposition, and the Weil team was ready to play clips as needed to refresh Huppenthal's memory or to impeach his testimony.

Huppenthal tried to reframe issues as Tom Horne did – focusing on the investigations into the program as the basis for creating his opinion. This rhetorical strategy allowed him to frame his opposition as being based on something inherently wrong with the program as opposed to his personal distaste for it:

> Well, again, the – we went through an extensive investigation of what was going on in the class. I went down there and sat in the class myself and witnessed what I felt were a number of inappropriate things. So, there was quite a collection of evidence to come to a conclusion. I don't know that I would phrase it as evil ideas, but ideas that would be of great concern.[68]

At the center of this response was the issue of whether Huppenthal had prejudged the program. That is, could any amount of countervailing evidence persuade him that the program was in compliance with state law? He already disregarded the findings of a third-party neutral audit and campaigned on "I will stop *la raza*," so the answer appeared to be "no."

When Huppenthal was directly questioned about the Cambium audit, his first line of defense was to place responsibility on his leadership team at the Arizona Department of Education. Instead of taking responsibility for the audit, he framed it as other people's work, "I didn't personally decide to hire an auditor or an outside auditor. I turned the entire investigation over to my senior staff."[69] When that did not work, he instead claimed that it was not truly an audit, "It's more proper to think of it as an inspection, and when people are being inspected, their behavior changes."⁷⁰ This response echoed Horne's Potemkin Village line. When Huppenthal was finally faced with the fact that his own commissioned audit found no violations of state law and actually found evidence of increased student achievement, he resorted to repeating, "I do not recall."⁷¹ He even denied knowing the basic scope of the work.⁷²

This lack of memory stood in stark contrast to Huppenthal's testimony from earlier in the day when he discussed the care he took to read and analyze the works of Paulo Freire, "The Brazilian Boogey Man," from Chapter 2. Huppenthal recalled, "I took the time to pull all of Paulo Freire's works and actually read his books."⁷³ For anyone who is familiar with Freire, this statement is likely false. Paulo Freire wrote twenty books, and most of them are extremely dense and difficult to get through. This, again, was Huppenthal portraying himself as scholarly when it is unclear if he understood the concepts in *Pedagogy of the Oppressed*. This is reminiscent of when Horne was asked about Rodolfo Acuña's *Occupied America* and said, "The mere title is – I think shows what kind of propaganda it is."⁷⁴ Horne and Huppenthal appear to believe that Freire's *Pedagogy of the Oppressed* was used to teach Mexican American students that they were oppressed and to hate White people. Both intentionally ignored or failed to appreciate Freire's lessons, which are so mainstream that they play foundational roles in university education departments and teacher education programs. This is standard fare in university education departments, but apparently it was too subversive for MAS, though it was okay for the Paulo Freire Freedom School in Tucson with its majority White student body.

Finally for the day, Reiss allowed Huppenthal, like Horne, to describe his use of the term *La Raza* as it was a continual issue throughout the controversy. His response very strongly mirrored Horne's in being a dramatic misrepresentation of the actual meaning, which in and of itself was telling:

REISS: And by "*La Raza*," what did you mean?
HUPPENTHAL: *La Raza*, the specific meaning of the words, means "the race." But its meaning in the context of a Republican primary campaign, it became shorthand for stop the slandering of the founding fathers, stop the unbalanced examination of the founding fathers, stop indoctrination of students into a Marxist oppressed/oppressor framework. So, it just became shorthand for a – it was a way of communicating with Republican primary voters.⁷⁵

Again, it would be humorous if the consequences were not so tragic of having another White man defining what *La Raza* meant. It was a somber reminder of how easy it was for Huppenthal and those attacking MAS to not only use racial *dog whistle politics*⁷⁶ but also the red scare to rally their base. In a strange, unintentional way, Huppenthal directly corroborated everything that Dr. Pitti would subsequently testify about the use of code words by public officials to trigger unconscious racism in the masses.

The energy in the courtroom mirrored the 104-degree Tucson heat outside. As people went to their cars, it was almost impossible to make it across the street without sweating through one's shirt.

* * *

Day 2 began with another testy exchange about amending a pretrial order. At the center of the issue was Huppenthal's online trolling. David Fitzmaurice on behalf of the plaintiffs argued again that Huppenthal should be compelled to produce his blogging activities as they spoke to his prejudiced views about Mexican Americans and the program. Huppenthal continually refused under the guise that the posts were publicly available even though he was subpoenaed to do so two years before the trial began. Judge Tashima eventually denied the pretrial order, but the plaintiffs still had a number of his blog posts they uncovered in their pretrial research.

When Huppenthal took the stand again, he continued to not answer direct questions and insisted on editorializing when there was not even a question on the floor. Steven Reiss was about to ask another question about the Cambium audit, and Huppenthal interrupted him to provide his personal philosophy about what constituted an audit. Before he could finish, the usually mild-mannered Reiss interjected forcefully, "Again, Mr. Huppenthal, I don't want to be discourteous or interrupt you, but you've got to answer my questions."[77] It reached a head in a subsequent exchange when Huppenthal tried to answer a question that was not being asked.

REISS: Well, more importantly –
HUPPENTHAL: More importantly than that –
REISS: There's no question pending. Mr. Huppenthal, there's no question –
HUPPENTHAL: I need to –
REISS: Your lawyers can ask you to explain or expand on any answer when they examine you.[78]

Again, Huppenthal had trouble following the rules – attorneys ask questions and witnesses answer.

As the direct examination continued, Huppenthal continued to squirm as his assertion that loads of "additional materials"[79] were the basis for him finding the program out of compliance while also downplaying the results of the Cambium audit. He had to admit that aside from the audit and his own personal visit to Curtis Acosta's class, there were no other classroom observations in creating the basis for his findings. That was critically important[80] because it is not simply about curricular materials, but *how* those materials are taught. Huppenthal himself later agreed with this premise when he offered, "I mean, in the last year we put in place Bible studies standards. I mean, really, just about any publication should be allowed to be in a school, but it's how you use it that is the key." The more he talked, the deeper the hole he dug.

The idea of selective prosecution – in particular against Mexican Americans and MAS – took center stage as the examination turned to the other racial/ethnic programs in TUSD and, again, the Paulo Freire Freedom School. Huppenthal testified that his office did not receive complaints against this school as was the case with TUSD MAS and that his lack of attention of this had absolutely nothing to do with the students at the Freedom School being predominantly White. Unexplained was why it might be a problem for MAS students to be taught according to Freire's pedagogy but the same did not hold at the Paulo Freire Freedom School. Why did Huppenthal think MAS students were being taught to hate America and indoctrinated into Marxism but did not fear the same for the predominantly White students at the Freedom School?[81]

Ultimately, Huppenthal attempted to portray himself as a rational, thoughtful person. He continually said that he had no intention of terminating the MAS program,[82] and that his office "offered, as a department, to be an agent of assistance in helping them do that; but for a variety of reasons, we couldn't get there."[83] However, he tripped himself up again because his rationale did not hold up under scrutiny – actually it did not hold up to his own words.

For example, as mentioned earlier, Huppenthal gave an interview in 2012 to the conservative *Western Free Press* in which he described his anti-MAS strategy as "stretching them out" as a means to end the program.[84] Central to his approach was implementing the 10-percent sanction that could financially cripple the already financially hurting district.[85] When he did issue his formal findings of noncompliance, he made the sanctions retroactive to increase financial pressure on the district.[86] Every one of his policy-related actions showed a man keenly focused on eliminating the program even when there was countervailing evidence like the Cambium audit. His own findings of noncompliance against the district collapsed under scrutiny.

For example, quotations attributed to *Critical Race Theory: An Introduction* never appeared in the text,[87] as well as using ellipses to misrepresent a quotation from *500 Years of Chicano History in Pictures*.[88] He was so unrelenting in his attacks on MAS that one of Huppenthal's last acts in office – as previously discussed – was to find TUSD again out of compliance even though the MAS program was already eliminated.[89] He again tried to backtrack by saying he was "uncomfortable" with issuing a finding so late in his term and that it was spearheaded by his staff, but the evidence of his persistent attacks on MAS seemed to undermine this assertion. Huppenthal maintained that he was a neutral observer of the evidence provided and that "my objective was to advance the ball down the court academically."[90]

Huppenthal was asked to explain his findings of noncompliance for KRS-One's *Introduction to Hip-Hop* based on the reason cited by his office, Section (A)(4) where classes cannot promote ethnic solidarity:

REISS: Do you know what ethnic group the material promoted ethnic solidarity for?
HUPPENTHAL: No.
REISS: Do you know if hip-hoppers is an ethnic group?
HUPPENTHAL: No, I don't.[91]

Finally, Reiss' questioning turned to Huppenthal's blogging as Falcon 9. While Huppenthal was nervous during the previous questioning, his demeanor turned to almost defiant. When asked about his post, "No Spanish radio stations, no Spanish billboards, no Spanish TV stations, no Spanish newspapers. This is America, speak English," he admitted that he posted those words but claimed they were "out of context."[92] Surprisingly, the usually verbose Huppenthal did not expand on how his words were taken out of context. That was probably for the best because he then had to face more of his own blog posts.

Remember, Huppenthal earlier argued that the evidence against MAS compelled him to find the district out of compliance with state law? Remember when Huppenthal continually claimed that he was simply a neutral arbiter without a horse in the race? Remember when he continually framed himself as an intellectual and a scholar objectively analyzing the evidence provided to him? Well, on his first day in office, he blogged: "*La Raza* means 'The Race.' It doesn't mean the Mexican race, unless you use it as a shorthand for that. But it's also shorthand for classroom studies that depict America's founding fathers as racists, poisoning students' attitudes towards America."[93]

Later that year, Huppenthal's tirades grew bolder using an age-old technique of critiquing the anti-racists as being the true racists. However, he went one step further by throwing Hitler into the mix, much like Horne did: "The Mexican American Studies classes use the exact same technique that Hitler used in his rise to power. In Hitler's case it was the Sudetenland. In the Mexican-American Studies case, it's Aztlán."[94]

Blogging anonymously, Huppenthal compared the teaching of MAS to the rise of Hitler. Reiss asked him if he actually wrote the blog posts, such as "The infected teachers are the problem."[95] But instead of answering questions about the blog posts, he went on a tirade about the teaching of history. Huppenthal was upset that a TUSD administrator said that Benjamin Franklin harbored racist views, and he wanted to correct that view. He also wanted to "correct" the picture that Reiss was painting by adding the following context: "When you get into the blogs, it gets pretty snarky, and I look at these and I wish I had spent a little more time editing and persuading, but it's sort of a bare-knuckled brawl out on the blocks."[96]

Huppenthal became his own worst enemy on the stand. The subsequent questions were more of the same. Reiss would ask a direct Yes/No question, and Huppenthal would go on another diatribe. While Reiss could have asked the judge, as he had before, to direct the witness to answer the questions, he allowed Huppenthal to offer his unsolicited explanations. The more Huppenthal spoke, the more he contradicted his earlier testimony.

Finally, Reiss turned to Huppenthal's public apology for the blogging where he cried at the press conference. Huppenthal said he was dealing with another controversy at the time, working long hours, and was physically exhausted when he made his public statements. He did not like the distraction that he caused, but in terms of apologizing for his blogging, he offered, "I've had a chance to sort of get rested and look back at it, and I don't – I don't apologize for any of it."[97] Sorry, not sorry.

Even after his tearful public apology covered by national media in 2014, Huppenthal continued to blog, including during the week before he took the stand, where he commented, "This has to qualify as one of the most meaningless trials in history."[98] When the state objected, Reiss offered that this went directly to animus. Judge Tashima overruled the objection allowing additional questions that elicited from Huppenthal an extended answer concluding his direct testimony, insisting that the MAS controversy was something very threatening to TUSD.[99]

* * *

The cross-examination of Huppenthal followed almost the exact same format as Horne's (i.e., Q: *Are you a racist?* A: No). Leslie Cooper began by asking Huppenthal what he had been doing since leaving (i.e., voted out) the State Superintendent's office. He became a math teacher in South Phoenix, but Cooper made it a point to both stress that his students were "at-risk" and about 50/50 Black and Latino and coming from the "highest crime rate zip code in the state."[100] Cooper asked why he did this work, allowing Huppenthal to return to his personal narrative of coming from South Tucson, living in the house his dad built for $500, and how the neighborhood had the highest crime and poverty rates in Tucson.[101] Huppenthal kept saying the goal was to make it for students from South Phoenix and South Tucson to make it to "Harvard, Stanford, and Yale."[102] This goes back to the state's foundational argument in this case: Would a racist do this type of work?

The questioning then turned to Huppenthal's time as State Superintendent of Public Instruction. He testified that he wanted to make the largest improvements in academic performance of any state in the nation, and he argued that he accomplished that during his time in office. Then Cooper had him break down achievement by race to which Huppenthal responded, "African-American eighth graders in Arizona placed number one in the nation. They defeated all other 49 states in math."[103] He also mentioned that Hispanic students were 11th in the nation in these rankings, up from 35th.[104] Cooper then asked Huppenthal the following:

COOPER: Was it your goal to increase the student achievement of Arizona's Hispanic student population?
HUPPENTHAL: Absolutely.[105]

She also asked if his goal was to improve the outcomes for African American and Native American students, to which he also responded in the affirmative.[106] He talked about his work with the Navajo Nation and his race/ethnicity-specific advisory groups,[107] which was very similar to Horne's testimony. These two state-level leaders were colorblind and attacked anything that was racially conscious – until they did not.

The focus then shifted to Huppenthal's visit to Curtis Acosta's class. He repeated his assertion from *Precious Knowledge* that Acosta was well dressed in a clean white shirt as if that had something to do with his teaching abilities. Huppenthal then turned to his specific objections to the class. He tried to say that he believed that all of Curtis' students could go to college, but that the MAS curriculum was destructive.[108] Cooper asked Huppenthal what he found objectionable in Acosta's class, and he returned to the picture of Che Guevara in the classroom. Huppenthal, again the self-proclaimed scholar, offered, "I have studied his history in Cuba,"[109] leading him to the conclusion that it was like having "a poster of a mass murderer up on the wall."[110]

The questioning took a banal turn when Cooper started asking about the reasons for changing the statute's enforcement date to the time that Huppenthal would be in office. He continually made reference to it not being about working through tricky political situations and *in no way* about him wanting to be able to take credit for eliminating MAS.[111] Huppenthal described the way his team conducted the MAS investigation, noting their educational credentials and making note that he did not direct them to find MAS out of compliance.[112] Huppenthal described his team's assessment of the MAS program as there being "very little evidence of organized curriculum,"[113] something Dr. Valenzuela tried to refute later in the trial. Finally, Huppenthal used his testimony to explain why he thought that the Cambium audit was fatally flawed.[114] This component of the cross-examination concluded in almost an identical way that Horne's did – with a form of "Q: Are you a racist? A: No.":

COOPER: Did you intend to express any discriminatory animus to Mexican-Americans by the words that you used in those blogs?
HUPPENTHAL: No.
COOPER: Did racism play any part in your decision to find TUSD in violation of A.R.S. 15-112?
HUPPENTHAL: No.
COOPER: Did ethnic bias have any part of your decision to issue that finding?
HUPPENTHAL: No.
COOPER: Are you biased against Latinos?
HUPPENTHAL: No.[115]

Cooper just asked Huppenthal directly if he was a racist, and he said no. Somehow, the state thought this would be compelling evidence.

Two very different versions of John Huppenthal were presented in the courtroom. One version would lay down in the mud and let Mexican American kids walk over his back; the other delivered the knockout punch that eliminated a program that had improved educational outcomes for at-risk students, most of whom were Mexican American. Judge Tashima decided that the first version was not the real John Huppenthal. Tashima repeatedly found Huppenthal's stated motivations for his actions as superintendent to not be credible.[116] Huppenthal, like Horne, was found to be a *mentiroso*.

13

The S.S. Violation and the Close of Trial

Before getting to the S.S. Violation and closing arguments on the last day of trial, we will review the bit players associated with the defense as well as the missing witnesses – people whose planned testimony was described in Defendants' Preliminary Proposed Findings of Fact and Conclusions of Law[1] – who were not called at trial.

THE "BIT" PLAYERS

The first is Mark Anderson, who was called at the beginning of Day 3. The plaintiffs called him as their witness to elicit details about his assistance to Tom Horne in shepherding HB 2281 through the Arizona legislature. Anderson had served for fourteen years in the legislature and was the chair of the House Education Committee from 2004 to 2008. A seasoned politician, he had deep familiarity with the legislative process. After he left the legislature, Anderson worked from 2009 to 2010 for Tom Horne in the Arizona Department of Education (ADE), assisting Horne to lobby legislators on certain bills, including HB 2281. The plaintiffs sought testimony that Anderson helped Horne pass a law that would allow Horne to terminate the MAS program.

James Quinn conducted the direct examination of Mr. Anderson as an adverse witness. Quinn asked:

> QUINN: Now, in 2010, you lobbied to pass legislation that was aimed at eliminating the MAS program in Tucson, correct?
> ANDERSON: I think that would have been one of the effects of the legislation, yes.[2]

After Quinn repeated Anderson's answer, seeking confirmation, Anderson qualified his answer, saying that the bill would not necessarily have eliminated the MAS program, that "[i]t would have given the district an opportunity to alter the program a bit, adjust it, so that it didn't violate the statutes."[3] Quinn then asked, "Well, wasn't it Mr. Horne's objective to get rid of the program?" When Anderson denied that getting rid of the program was Horne's objective, Quinn confronted Anderson with his own February 3, 2010, email, in which he wrote to legislative counsel: "We need to satisfy Tom Horne who wants to be able to get rid of the *La Raza* program in Tucson."[4]

Quinn then asked Anderson about what happened to the bill as it went through the legislative process, including how the bill was altered to replace Horne's original prohibitions, A1 (designed primarily for a particular group) and A2 (advocate ethnic solidarity), with two different provisions. When Anderson did not recall whether the new provisions would reach the *La Raza* program, Quinn "refreshed" Anderson's memory with an impeachment exhibit. This email, sent by Anderson on February 25, 2010, to Representative Reagan, asked her to support an amendment that would restore Horne's original prohibitions. Anderson told her that without Horne's original language, "the bill will not effectively reach the *La Raza* program at TUSD."[5] As questioning continued, Quinn was able to get Anderson to admit to other communications that showed that his lobbying efforts on behalf of Tom Horne had a singular focus: the MAS program at TUSD.

Robert Ellman conducted the hybrid cross-examination and direct examination of Anderson. For the cross, Ellman focused on the legislative process, demonstrating effectively through Anderson that nothing unusual happened in terms of the process itself. HB 2281 was proposed; it went through various committees; amendments were proposed and voted on; a version of the bill was ultimately approved by the House and the Senate. Nothing to see here.[6]

Ellman then tried to address the singular focus on TUSD's MAS program. Ellman was able to elicit from Mr. Anderson that he became aware that the problem with the program was indoctrination, that "[i]t was trying to influence young impressionable students to have certain political views and to actually foster kind of a resentment."[7] Anderson further testified that these were Tom Horne's concerns. Then, despite Anderson stating that he had not read Horne's last-days-in-office finding of violation, Ellman proceeded to read large chunks of the complaints of the former teachers, in effect testifying through hearsay, though confirming each time that these were the types of complaints Anderson had heard.[8]

In addition, returning to what Ellman identified in his opening on Day 1 as the importance of motive, he asked Mr. Anderson if, in his twenty-some years of knowing Horne, he had "ever heard [Horne] express any racial or ethnic prejudice against any group"[9]; if he had "any reason to think that [Horne] harbors any racial or ethnic bias"[10]; and if he had "any reason to believe that Tom Horne supported HB 2281 out of a racial or ethnic bias against Latino or Hispanic students."[11] To these questions, Anderson answered, respectively, "Absolutely not"; "Not at all"; and "No." These questions were directed toward the racial animus needed for the Fourteenth Amendment Equal Protection claim. Ellman, addressing the First Amendment viewpoint discrimination claim, asked if Horne wanted the bill "so that a superintendent could impose his or her own narrowly partisan or political beliefs upon a school district." Anderson said, "No."

Whether called by the defense or the plaintiffs, the state asked this same series of questions of those who had worked with or for Tom Horne or John Huppenthal.

* * *

Like Mark Anderson, Stacey Morley was a witness associated with the defense that the plaintiffs called as part of their case-in-chief. From 2008 to 2011, Morley was a research analyst for the Arizona Senate Education Committee, chaired by then-senator Huppenthal, and worked closely with Huppenthal because he was the chair. From 2011 to 2015, Ms. Morley worked for the ADE, hired by Huppenthal after he became superintendent.[12]

Barrington, like Reiss had been with his witnesses, especially Dr. Haladyna, was ready with her impeachment clips. In questions about the amendment Huppenthal proposed, drafted by Morley, that delayed the effective date of the statute, Morley denied that Huppenthal was concerned about TUSD being treated fairly, only to be confronted by her 2015 deposition testimony "that Mr. Huppenthal was concerned that Mr. Horne wouldn't treat TUSD fairly."[13]

Luna Barrington then asked what Huppenthal thought of Horne. Morley denied hearing that "Mr. Huppenthal thought that Mr. Horne was very much a politician and not so much a public servant." Barrington played video that showed Ms. Morley saying exactly what she had denied. When asked if she stood by her deposition testimony, Morley had no choice but to say yes. Another impeachment clip reminded Ms. Morley that in her 2015 deposition, she said that there were no concerns expressed during the weekly senior staff ADE meetings during the time of the Cambium Audit of the ability of Cambium to conduct its audit.[14]

Morley then testified about her role in investigating MAS, saying that she reviewed curricular materials, but admitting that she had no background in teaching or familiarity with any of the materials or textbooks. Morley at first dodged the question about what she knew about *how* these materials and textbooks were taught, but Barrington persisted: "But you're not a career educator, so you're not familiar with how lessons are being taught in a classroom, correct?" Morley had no choice but to say, "Correct," and that she never observed the materials being used in the classroom and had never visited an MAS classroom.[15]

The final point Luna Barrington was able to elicit from Stacey Morley was that there was already a law on the books, A.R.S. §15-341, that the superintendent could have used to remove inappropriate curricular material. Morley agreed that HB 2281 was unnecessary if the problem was just inappropriate curricular material. She admitted, though, that the existing statute, 15-341, did not include the ability to impose a fine or withhold funding, and that it did not give the superintendent the ability to terminate a program.

Leslie Cooper reminded the court that Ms. Morley was being called by both the plaintiffs and the defendants and then began her hybrid cross and direct examination. Cooper's questions elicited that Ms. Morley knew John Huppenthal at least a decade longer than when she served as the research analyst for his committee, going back to when she was a legislative intern in 1997, when John Huppenthal was the Senate Education Committee chair. Then, the stock questions: whether she had "ever see[n] him display discriminatory intent against any group"; whether she had "ever see[n] him display discriminatory animus against Mexican-Americans"; and because of Huppenthal's anonymous blogging, whether she "believe[d] that those blogging activities and the statements that he made there indicate a discriminatory animus against Mexican-Americans." To each of these questions, Morley answered, "No," "No," "No."[16]

* * *

Robert Franciosi was called on Day 6 as a defense witness in the middle of the plaintiffs' case-in-chief. Again, this shuffling of witnesses was made necessary because of witness availability. After establishing that Franciosi was hired by and worked for Tom Horne between 2003 and 2011 as Deputy Associate Superintendent for Research and Evaluation at the ADE, the animus questions for Franciosi followed the state's script: whether he "ever hear[d] Tom Horne say anything that would you to believe he might be a racist"; whether he "ever hear[d] him say anything that indicated he was biased or prejudiced against Hispanic people generally or against Mexicans or Mexican-Americans specifically." Franciosi answered "No" and "No."[17]

Ellman then asked whether Franciosi had any investigative or policymaking role regarding the *Raza Studies*/MAS controversy, to which he responded: "I was requested to do a study on the academic impact of participation in the Raza program." After establishing that this was completed in the fall of 2009, Ellman asked, "What conclusion did you reach in your research?"

Richard Martinez stood up quickly and objected, arguing that opposing counsel was seeking to elicit expert testimony. This went to the pretrial skirmishing about what evidence would be admitted and excluded. Though Dr. Franciosi conducted a statistical analysis of student achievement in the MAS program, the state had not disclosed him as an expert witness. Though the plaintiffs filed a motion to exclude his testimony, the judge accepted the state's representation that they would not ask Dr. Franciosi to "give any opinion or other testimony that requires specialized knowledge, and will be asked only to recount what Horne instructed him to do."[18] Ellman, by asking him what his conclusions were, was skating close to the edge, but this was a bench trial without a jury and Judge Tashima gave himself "an admonitory instruction that I should not consider this for the truth but only for the fact that it was communicated to Superintendent Horne and what effect it had on him. So, on that basis, the objection's overruled."[19] Franciosi was then free to testify that he had communicated the results of his analysis to Tom Horne. Thus, he was allowed to offer a statistical analysis of the MAS program without having to be established as an expert in this area. It was a slick maneuver by the defense.

Franciosi also testified that Elliott Hibbs had asked him to look at Cambium's analysis of the academic impact of the MAS program. Again, in theory, not testifying as an expert, he said that Cambium or TUSD's statistical department "made a curious choice with regards to the sample of students they looked at, and I just – they didn't explain it to my satisfaction, so I just pointed that out to them."[20]

Richard Martinez conducted the cross-examination. First, he sought to establish that Franciosi was biased based on his work for several years with the Goldwater Institute and based on a book he had written about public education and school choice. These questions did not land or were cut off by sustained objections. Then, Martinez asked why Franciosi only examined scores on the state AIMS (Arizona Instrument to Measure Standards) test and not also graduation rates as Dr. Cabrera had. Franciosi responded, "I considered using graduation rates, but my thinking was that they wouldn't provide a very good evidence if the classes weren't rigorous. So if the students were graduating because they were taking classes that were easy, I didn't – "[21] Martinez became visibly angry and interrupted the witness, only to have the court tell him to let the witness finish his answer. Franciosi continued, "So if these classes were less rigorous than, say, a regular curriculum, then matriculation rates would not tell you anything. It would just be picking up easy credits."[22]

Martinez asked loudly, "Sir, why would you assume that these classes ... are less rigorous.... Why would you assume that?" When Franciosi said that he did not assume that but had no way of comparing rigor. Martinez, still visibly agitated, engaged in the following heated exchange:

MARTINEZ: Wasn't the truth of the matter, sir, that, because it was a program dealing specifically with Mexican-Americans, that you assumed that this was probably some easy class and that a group of educators in Tucson got together to make an easy class so that they could pass Mexican-American students along?
FRANCIOSI: No.
MARTINEZ: That's what you assumed, isn't it?
FRANCIOSI: No, it's not.
MARTINEZ: You assumed that, because there's Mexican-American teachers in the classroom and Mexican-American students in that classroom, that there couldn't be a rigorous program in that classroom because neither one is capable of presenting that curriculum or successfully passing that curriculum, didn't you?
FRANCIOSI: I had no information on who was teaching the class, and I did not assume anything about who was teaching the classes or what the curriculum was.
MARTINEZ: Sir, but the suspicion came into your mind, and the suspicion comes into your mind –[23]

At this point, even though Ellman had not objected, Judge Tashima stepped in and told Martinez to stop badgering the witness. There was certainly something to Franciosi's decision not to look at graduation rates as this was a key outcome in Cabrera's statistical analysis, but Martinez may have overplayed his hand. Martinez's questions, which were stated loudly in an aggrieved tone, were intended to draw from Franciosi an admission that he made a racist assumption. But the witness was never going to admit that. Members of the MAS legal team could see that Franciosi remained composed during this exchange but had a bloom of red on his cheeks.

Martinez may have read it as Franciosi being embarrassed about having his racism exposed and tried to get him to admit it. The court, though, seemed to see it as a human response to being badgered by counsel. The court was not going to put up with it.

Dr. Franciosi's testimony on direct was exactly what the state was looking for. Even though his findings could not be used directly to refute Dr. Cabrera's analysis or Cambium's analysis of the academic impact of MAS classes, the fact that he provided his conclusions, that there was no evidence of positive impact, bolstered both Horne's and Huppenthal's decisions to find a violation. Whether his methodologies and conclusions were valid – which they were not – was irrelevant from the defense perspective because they provided a race-neutral reason to disregard the MAS program's claims of positive impact. His conclusions, regardless of their validity, were very relevant as to Horne and Huppenthal's state of mind when they made their decisions.

THE MISSING WITNESSES

John Stollar had decades of experience as a teacher and school principal. He joined Superintendent Huppenthal's administration in spring 2011 as Deputy Superintendent, in time to participate in the ADE review of the MAS program. In a court filing less than a week before trial, his name was included on a short list of the state's significant witnesses.[24] This filing indicated that Stollar and Kathryn Hrabluk played key roles in deciding that the Cambium Audit was deficient and in conducting their own independent review of the MAS program. Stollar testified at the administrative proceedings discussed in Chapter 5. The MAS legal team was surprised that the state ended up not calling Stollar. The team, though, was pleased because, based on the 2016 videotaped deposition, they expected that Stollar would have been an effective witness for the state.

The other significant witness not called but named in the pretrial court filing and discussed by Ellman in his opening remarks on Day 1 was Margaret Garcia Dugan. As Horne's Deputy Superintendent, Dugan played a critical role in this story, especially as the speaker, the "proud Latina Republican," who prompted the silent student protest characterized as rude by Tom Horne. Ellman represented in his opening remarks that she worked closely with Tom Horne for over a decade, during which "[s]he never observed a hint of racial or ethnic bias in any of his actions, including actions related to HB 2281."[25] The MAS legal team could only speculate as to why she was not called.

* * *

We turn next to two of the state's witnesses, Kathryn Hrabluk and Elliott Hibbs, who would provide pivotal testimony.

SCOPE AND SEQUENCE! THE EMAILS! FACE VALUE!

On Day 5, the defendants called their first witness, Kathryn Hrabluk. Leslie Cooper conducted the direct examination. Her first question asking her to describe her background as a teacher and an administrator prompted a long response, spanning several court transcript pages as she detailed her twenty-seven years as an educator.[26] As a witness, she appeared measured, thoughtful, and confident. Steven Reiss leaned over during the direct and whispered to Robert Chang, "Wow. She's a really good witness for them." He tried to interrupt the flow or cut off avenues of questioning through objections that Judge Tashima mostly rejected.

Cooper established that Hrabluk worked approximately eight years at ADE while Horne was superintendent, leading to the stock animus question: "Did you ever see Mr. Horne display any racial animus toward any group while you were employed by the Department of Education." Hrabluk responded, "No, I did not." Cooper followed up eliciting that Hrabluk "believed he was committed to the success of all students" and that this "included Arizona's minority and low socioeconomic status students."[27]

Cooper established that Hrabluk worked with Superintendent Huppenthal for four years. Hrabluk testified that she never saw Huppenthal display any discriminatory animus toward any group and that he was committed to the success of all of Arizona's students.[28] Cooper asked if Hrabluk had ever witnessed Horne or Huppenthal impose their own partisan or political beliefs on others, to which Hrabluk responded, "No, I did not."

Cooper then moved to state standards, curriculum maps, and curricular units. At this point, Steven Reiss objected, arguing this was straying into expert testimony. Judge Tashima rejected the objection, saying that all Hrabluk was testifying to was based on her experience as a teacher and an administrator. The MAS legal team did not understand why the judge was permitting Hrabluk to testify on matters that were largely closed off during Sean Arce's testimony, when Arce would likewise have been testifying based on his experience as a teacher and administrator. If Arce had been able to explain during his direct examination about the MAS curriculum, including how the teachers developed and implemented the scope and sequence for their classes, Dr. Valenzuela may have had an easier time on the witness stand. Though this appeared to be a double standard, there was little the MAS team could do about it.

Hrabluk testified on the importance of having a curriculum map with curricular units that might include a series of lessons, all mapped through a defined scope and sequence, along with planned assessments to determine student progress and attainment.[29] Then, despite another objection from Reiss that this was an expert opinion, Hrabluk offered that an auditor would have no way to understand what was going on in a program, no way of evaluating it, if there was no curriculum map.[30]

Hrabluk's testimony then turned to her role in the ADE investigation of MAS. She described Elliott Hibbs as her superior, who was responsible more for the administrative side of things, whereas Hrabluk was the educator. Hrabluk then described how John Stollar was added to the team.[31] Hrabluk explained that she and her ADE colleagues became concerned about the Cambium Audit. She criticized what Cambium portrayed as a positive, saying that it was dangerous for MAS educators to build rapport with students because it could allow the educators to impose their biases.[32] This sentiment is reminiscent of what was recounted in Chapter 6 when TUSD board member Michael Hicks described to *The Daily Show* the inappropriate relationship MAS teachers created by buying burritos for their students once a week.[33] Hrabluk's opinion, while speculative, supported the notion that students in the thrall of their teachers were susceptible to indoctrination. Steven Reiss objected and moved to strike. The court overruled the objection and rejected the motion.

Cooper returned to the Cambium Audit and asked if the auditors were provided with a cohesive curriculum map with scope and sequencing. Hrabluk said no and that without such a map, there was no way to know what was really being taught in the MAS classes.[34] Hrabluk then testified that the deficiencies in the Cambium Audit meant that Cambium's conclusion that there was no violation of the statute could not be relied upon and that ADE needed to conduct its own supplemental, independent investigation of MAS.[35]

When asked how ADE conducted its investigation, Hrabluk described how she and others in ADE examined curricular materials from the MAS program and that they unanimously agreed that the MAS program violated A2 and A4 of the statute. Cooper then opened the door to what would prove fatal to Hrabluk's review of the MAS materials. Cooper asked: "Did you see materials ... that on their face appeared to be biased and inappropriate as measured against A.R.S. 15-112?" Though Hrabluk gave the answer Cooper was seeking, "Yes," the phrasing "on their face" would come back to haunt the state.

* * *

Steven Reiss then began his cross-examination. Because of the upcoming July 4 holiday, and because of witness availability, Day 5 was scheduled to conclude at lunchtime. Reiss knew that he had just an hour. He also knew that he did not want to complete his cross-examination that day. Those in the courtroom audience may not have appreciated the artistry that Reiss showed in timing his questions to end with the emails. The emails!

Reiss began by asking about the process ADE used to solicit bids and select the contractor to perform the audit of MAS. Reiss also established that any shortcomings of the curriculum did not, itself, violate the statute.[36] Reiss further established that Hrabluk and others accepted Cambium's plans for conducting the audit and that Hrabluk remained in regular contact with the lead Cambium investigator.[37] When

Reiss asked if, at any time during the audit, whether she or others at ADE thought there were deficiencies, Hrabluk demurred from saying there were "deficiencies," but instead that she and others in ADE had "concerns."[38] Hrabluk, though, admitted that no internal ADE communications or communications with Cambium indicated deficiencies during Cambium's investigation.[39]

Then Reiss started in on the emails. The first question established that ADE officials made sure that the Cambium auditors were provided materials supplied by Laura Leighton, a private citizen who had advocated against MAS for several years. Prompted by Reiss's questioning, Hrabluk agreed that Leighton had an extreme point of view.[40]

Reiss then asked Hrabluk about *the* email. Plaintiffs' Exhibit 84. Though plaintiffs included this exhibit in their pretrial filings, a review of the depositions of witnesses associated with the defense indicates that none were asked about this email chain. Reiss was watching the clock and knew he was getting near the end of the short trial day. This email chain would irrefutably rebut a statement made by Robert Ellman in his opening. As discussed in Chapter 10, Ellman committed a fatal error when he stated that the career educators and administrators who investigated MAS had no prior goal or agenda and that it was only after they conducted a thorough investigation that they came to their own independent conclusions.

This email, a needle in the haystack of thousands of pages provided by the state as part of a discovery dump, would prove to be a smoking gun. One email in this string was dated May 9, 2011. Elliott Hibbs asked Hrabluk "how [Cambium] missed the boat."[41] Reiss then asked about the next smoking gun email chain, Plaintiffs' Exhibit 86. This email chain among ADE officials including Hibbs, Stollar, and Hrabluk included the following:

> Conclusion: The existing TUSD's MASD program of study must be terminated, suspended immediately and will not be permitted to operate until the Tucson Unified School District's governing board complies with the required and necessary action of establishing a process outline provided earlier for appropriate curriculum development that includes full alignment to state standards and along with full and complete transparency with the process and the instructional model.

The date of the email was May 12, 2011 – after ADE officials were given the draft Cambium Audit but before they received Cambium's final report on May 15.

Reiss emphasized "Conclusion." Reiss asked, "So on May 12th, 2011, before receiving the final Cambium Audit, and before even starting to conduct your own investigation, you and Mr. Hibbs and Mr. Stollar had already concluded that the MAS program was in violation of 15-112, right?" Leslie Cooper objected, but the judge overruled it and directed the witness to answer. Though Hrabluk refused to answer directly, the damage had been done. The email showed that ADE officials were already drafting their own "Conclusion" that the MAS program must be terminated even before beginning their independent investigation.

Reiss stopped here, leaving the judge to think about this during the two-week recess before Hrabluk's cross-examination resumed on July 17.

* * *

During the two-week break, a new line of questioning became apparent to the MAS legal team. To prepare for possible rebuttal witnesses, Robert Chang interviewed two former MAS teachers. Sally Rusk gave Chang a ride to the airport on the Saturday after the first week of trial. During the drive, Rusk revealed that she used the district-approved textbooks in her history and government classes.[42] This included the textbook *The American Vision*. A phone interview with Rene Martinez revealed that he had used that book in his MAS history class, including that he would encourage students to think critically by having them compare the way *The American Vision* described certain historical events with the way supplemental MAS materials did.[43] Then Chang remembered that the Cambium Audit included that their auditors saw *The American Vision* in use in some of the classrooms they visited.

He then ordered a copy of *The American Vision* and had it delivered to the Arizona Inn so it would be there when he returned to Tucson on Wednesday, July 12, to meet the rest of the MAS legal team to prepare for the final week of the trial. Chang would later tell anyone who would listen that this was the best $105 he had ever spent.

* * *

The genius of Steven Reiss's cross-examination on Day 5 was that he ended on a high note for the plaintiffs, having undercut a critical argument of the defense. This was the last impression that the judge took into the two-week break. When trial resumed on July 17, Reiss hit those same points again on the morning of Day 6. He provided to Ms. Hrabluk portions of the trial transcript of her Day 5 testimony. Reiss went through the chronology again and repeated his questions about the emails. He reminded the witness that ADE had not started its investigation as of May 9, when Hibbs wondered how Cambium "missed the boat," or by May 12, which included ADE's "Conclusion." Hrabluk confirmed that ADE had not yet begun its investigation as of those dates.[44] Hrabluk tried to recover by saying that they had enough information at that point in time to make this conclusion.

Steven Reiss then drew her attention to her testimony from Day 5 during the state's direct examination:

> Question: At the conclusion of your review of the Cambium audit, did you feel that the department had enough information to determine whether the MAS classes violated A.R.S. 15-112? Answer: No. We concluded we did not have enough information. Question: When you say "we," to whom are you referring? Answer: That was really a final decision by Superintendent John Huppenthal, but it was

a joint decision and joint discussions between myself, John Stollar, Elliott Hibbs, and the superintendent.[45]

On May 12, they had enough information to conclude there was a violation. On May 12, they did not have enough information. Reiss, using her previous testimony as impeachment, was able to undermine her credibility. Like Horne and Huppenthal, her own words became her worst enemy.

Next, Reiss moved on to ask how she and other ADE officials conducted their investigation. Hrabluk admitted that they just read the MAS curricular materials. Reiss asked if Hrabluk or others knew how these materials were used or taught in the MAS classrooms.

REISS: I'll ask the same question I just asked, which is: You wrote that even though you had no idea how the materials were used, right?
HRABLUK: Well, we had no idea because there was no written plan. So, when we looked at the materials, we looked at them really from a literal standpoint.
REISS: But you'll agree with me that you had no idea how the materials were used, right?
HRABLUK: That's correct, because there was no plan.
REISS: Okay. And you just took the materials at face value, right?[46]

Hrabluk had no choice but to admit that that's what they did, though she again tried to justify this approach because of the lack of a curriculum map with scope and sequence. But Hrabluk had to admit that she and the other ADE officials did not know if any of the offending materials was in fact used in classes or, if so, how they were used.[47]

Reiss then pivoted to *The American Vision*. He called Ms. Hrabluk's attention to the portion of the Cambium Audit where the auditors identified the book as "Seen in use." When asked if she had examined this book as part of her review of MAS curricular materials, she said that it was possible but that she didn't have a memory of doing so. Then Reiss testified, though phrasing it as a question:

REISS: And do you have any memory that in that book, which is over a thousand pages, no more than 30, but probably, more accurately, 18 pages deal with Mexican-Americans in the United States?
HRABLUK: Six years later, I have no memory whatsoever.

Based on her previous response, Reiss knew that she would have no memory of this. He also suspected, though, that we were not likely to put on a rebuttal witness to testify that the 1,000+ page book had only eighteen pages on Mexican Americans. Reiss only knew this because Chang had, upon his return to the Arizona Inn, spent an afternoon going over every page of the book.

Reiss then had Jorge project short excerpts from the book onto the courtroom monitors. The first is on page 490: "The Imperialist Vision. The Main Idea. A desire for world markets and belief in the superiority of Anglo-Saxon culture led the United States to assert itself as a world power."[48]

Then from the next page:

> Anglo-Saxonism: The work which the English race began when it colonized North America is destined to go on until every land that is not already the seat of an old civilization shall become English in its language, in its religion, in political habits, and traditions to a predominant extent in the blood of its people. John Fiske, quoted in The Expansionists.[49]

Upon being asked by Reiss, Hrabluk stated that she would have no objection to these excerpts being taught. With the second excerpt, Hrabluk added that she would have no objection to it being "presented as the thinking in 1898 by John Fiske."[50] Reiss followed up by saying, with no question, "Right. It would depend on how it's being taught," to which Hrabluk emphatically agreed, "Exactly."

Reiss then asked if the earlier excerpts violated the statute. When Hrabluk declared, "As a stand-alone quote, all by itself, regardless of what else was taught in the 180 days of instruction, I wouldn't expect so." Reiss then had Jorge project the press release about Huppenthal's June 15, 2011, Finding of Violation, and asked about the examples cited as violations: "Ever since the birth of the U.S., its rulers had dreamed of expanding across the continent. So, the Anglo expansionists first took over Texas by deception and force. They deliberately provoked the war on Mexico in 1846–1848. The invasion ended with the Treaty of Guadalupe Hidalgo. U.S. forces treated the Mexicans living there as a conquered inferior race."[51]

Hrabluk admitted that this excerpt, found to violate the statute, was comparable to the excerpts from *The American Vision*.[52] Reiss did not ask a follow up asking her to explain why she thought one violated the statute while the other did not. He felt that he did not have to. Sometimes, less is more, and he knew that he would return to this point in the closing argument.

Reiss then closed his cross-examination by asking if, as a career educator who cares deeply about education and improving education, she would support a program that had valid, reliable consistent data over years that the program was effective in improving education outcomes. Hrabluk answered that any such program "needs to be supported by their district."[53]

Leslie Cooper did her best on re-direct to recuperate Hrabluk's testimony. Much of it revisited what had already been elicited during the direct examination on Day 5, but unlike Day 5, it was scattershot, making it less effective than it might have been.

On re-cross, Steven Reiss offered the entire book, *The American Vision*, as an exhibit. With no objection by the state, the court accepted it. Reiss reminded Hrabluk that the book had been adopted by TUSD and asked if the use of the book could provide balance against the other materials that were potentially problematic. Hrabluk answered, "Potentially."

When counsel for both parties expressed that they had nothing further with this witness, Judge Tashima surprised everyone in the courtroom by saying that he had a couple questions for the witness. It is not unusual for a judge in a bench trial to ask questions of a witness, but Judge Tashima's colloquy went nearly ten minutes. As Tashima asked his questions, in addition to the audience, both legal teams paid close attention. When a judge asks questions, it signals what the judge thinks is important to get right for their decision.

* * *

Judge Tashima's first set of questions explored what Hrabluk found defective about the Cambium Audit. Hrabluk emphasized the limited nature of the classroom visits, which meant that she and other ADE staff could not conclude much based on those visits. Tashima then raised Hrabluk's criticism that MAS courses lacked curricular maps that included scope and sequence, asking her to confirm that not having these would make classroom visits less effective because an auditor would not be able to determine the educational purpose or value of the program. Hrabluk said that the judge understood her criticism.

Tashima followed up by asking what ADE did that Cambium did not. Hrabluk answered that "the auditors of Cambium had not done a complete review of all the materials that … had been submitted to them because they ran out of time. So we did a more thorough or complete review of the materials that had been submitted."[54]

At the end of this portion of the judge's questions, several on the MAS legal team were worried. It seemed that he was giving credence to Hrabluk's reasons for disregarding the conclusions of the Cambium Audit. But then things took a turn.

Judge Tashima asked how she and the ADE team determined that the materials specifically referenced as violations were found to be violations. Tashima acknowledged that a lot of materials, including *The American Vision* textbook as well as the MAS materials "obviously have passages that could, I think, from an educator's point of view, be misused, almost like you could use propaganda, you know – " Hrabluk interrupted the judge to say, "That's correct." The judge continued, "– to inculcate an immature mind with certain, you know, beliefs. Right? It's possible." Hrabluk agreed.

Then Tashima shifted to confirm that she "had no – almost no evidence of how it was taught in the classroom. Now how did you … come to the conclusion that these materials were being misused in the MAS program?" After he repeated his question, Hrabluk said that they "took those materials, as they had been submitted, at face value."[55] Tashima asked further about "face value," and referenced *The American Vision* quotes Mr. Reiss offered.

HRABLUK: Well, you don't – without an explanation of how it was used, how did teachers –
THE COURT: That's what I say, there was no explanation at all?
HRABLUK: Right. No.

THE COURT: So, you accepted that as being taught as literally true?
HRABLUK: Well, we accepted those materials as the materials that were used in instruction, yes.

It was hard to discern how Tashima was taking this, but some on the MAS legal team thought that he was incredulous that the words would be taken literally. The reader may recall some of the examples found to be violations by Horne and which were discussed in detail in the 48 Public School Teachers Amicus Brief in Chapter 8. The teachers pointed out the absurdity that assigning a speech that includes "Kill the Gringo" somehow indicates that the teacher is using it to teach students that they ought to literally kill the Gringo.

After one final question by each side, Ms. Hrabluk was excused.

THE S.S. VIOLATION

On Day 9, the state put on its final defense witness, Elliott Hibbs. Robert Ellman conducted the direct examination. He quickly elicited the fact that Hibbs had been in government service for thirty-nine years. Though he did not say it explicitly, the names of the Arizona governors who appointed him to government positions indicated that he had received appointments from Democrats and Republicans. Hibbs came to work for Superintendent Huppenthal as his chief operating officer from 2011 to 2015. Hibbs had known Huppenthal, though, since the 1990s when they worked together to create an incentive program for state government. After determining that Hibbs interacted frequently with Huppenthal, Ellman asked the animus questions: "… [whether] he held racist views"; "… biased or prejudiced against Hispanic people generally"; "… biased or prejudiced against Mexicans or Mexican-Americans in particular?" Hibbs responded, "No," "No," and "No."[56]

Ellman then asked about Huppenthal's blogs that became public in 2014. Hibbs said that he was flabbergasted because this did not seem like the person he had come to know over twenty-or-so years, and that he asked Huppenthal "if it was true … [and] asked him what in the world he was doing."[57] Hibbs then reported that Huppenthal admitted it was and described how "he liked to go on the liberal blogs and … create controversy, put digs in, try to get the other liberal side to be upset about things."[58] Huppenthal also claimed that what was reported in the press did not include the full blog posts or the complete context.[59]

What followed then was a walk-through of the events early in Huppenthal's term as superintendent relating to the premature Horne Finding of Violation up to the May 2, 2011, draft report from Cambium. Hibbs described how concerned his staff members, John Stollar and Kathryn Hrabluk, were when they received the draft, that they, including Stacey Morley, did a concentrated review of the draft.[60]

Ellman then used an effective trial presentation technique to cast doubt on the Cambium findings. He selected portions in the report that discussed negative aspects of MAS materials or other problems they identified. Ellman read each negative item, followed by a question about whether this raised any concerns. After running through the negative points raised in the draft report, Ellman contrasted that with the draft's conclusions that there was no observable evidence of violations of the statute. Ellman elicited from Hibbs that these conclusions did not appear to match up to all the negative points the draft had described.[61]

Ellman then asked about the May 9, 2011, email, in which Mr. Hibbs asked his staff members how Cambium "missed the boat." Hibbs then inadvertently undercut the defense strategy. Remember, Ellman in his opening on Day 1 stated that career educators and administrators conducted a thorough investigation and came to their own independent conclusions. Hrabluk had testified on Day 5 that after ADE finished its review of the Cambium Audit, it did not have enough information to make any determination with regard to the statute. Hrabluk had also testified that ADE didn't begin its independent investigation until after the final Cambium Audit issued on May 15. Hibbs, though, gave a different story.

ELLMAN: Now, at that point in time, May 9th, 2011, had the team reached a final decision about whether TUSD was in violation of the statute?
HIBBS: Well, yeah, I would say that the team had, based on the information provided, reached a conclusion that there was a violation of the statute.

The MAS legal team does not know if this was the answer Ellman expected. He tried to salvage things by asking: "Was the process still ongoing though?" Though Hibbs said, "Yes," he continued and repeated: "But the team itself, based on what they had seen in the draft report, felt that there was a violation of the statute."[62]

Ellman then tried to salvage the damage from the May 12 email chain, which included the conclusion that TUSD was in violation of the statute and that its MASD program must be terminated. Ellman asked, "[W]as that a final determination or was it still tentative as of May 13, 2011?" Hibbs responds that it was tentative because the ADE staff did not actually make the final decision, which was to be made by the superintendent. Hibbs repeated, though, that "based on the review of the materials in the draft report, the staff had come to the conclusion that there was enough information there to validate a termination or suspension of the program."[63] Again, Hibbs contradicted Hrabluk.

* * *

When the direct examination of Hibbs ended, the court took its mid-afternoon break, resuming at 3:51 p.m. Steven Reiss got up to do the cross. He began by asking about Huppenthal's blogs. Unlike Tom Horne who emphatically called Huppenthal's blogs racist, Hibbs denied that the blogs expressed racist views.[64] Reiss was surprised by this response, so he moved on to questions about the role Hibbs played leading to Superintendent Huppenthal's June 15, 2011, Finding of Violation. Because it was cross-examination, Reiss asked leading questions such as, "And you never concluded that the MAS program at TUSD violated 15-112, did you?" Hibbs denied this, saying that he thought he did conclude there was a violation. Reiss then played a video impeachment clip. In his 2016 deposition, Hibbs stated that he had not come to a conclusion that the statute had been violated and that it was not his role to determine if there was or was not a violation.[65]

Reiss continued his highly effective strategy of using Hibbs' words against him. When asked if Huppenthal characterized MAS as having a Marxist-based curriculum, if he had described Freire's *Pedagogy of the Oppressed* as Marxist, Hibbs said he did not recall. Reiss asked for impeachment video clips 20 and 21 to be played. The courtroom, including the judge, saw and heard Hibbs testify affirmatively to each. Then Reiss asked about Hibbs' May 9, 2011, email to Kathryn Hrabluk directing her to contact Cambium "to get a better understanding of how they missed the boat." Then:

REISS: And the boat they missed is the SS Violation, right? That is that there was a violation of 15-112.
HIBBS: I'm going to say yes...[66]

Immediately after this exchange, Luna Barrington emailed Robert Chang and David Fitzmaurice who had returned to the war room to help prepare the closing. Barrington wrote, "Steve asked him if the boat he was referring to in the email was the SS Violation and he said 'yes.' Incredible."[67]

The MAS legal team had been referring to the "missed boat" in the email as the SS Violation. On the evening after Day 5 of the trial, James Quinn had sent a congratulatory email to everyone on the outstanding effort and reminded everyone, "Don't forget the good ship SS Violation for Hibbs."[68] The MAS legal team never thought their inside joke would become part of the trial. Thus was christened, officially, the SS Violation.

Reiss followed up by asking if, "on May 9th, before even receiving the final Cambium report, you reached a conclusion totally contrary to that in the Cambium report, the independent Cambium report, that there was, in fact, a violation of 15-112, right?" Hibbs responded, "Yes, based on the discussions, yes."[69] In his closing the next day, Reiss would use Hrabluk's and Hibbs's testimony to destroy the state's contention that the ADE staff had not prejudged the MAS program.

After Hibbs was excused, the court asked the MAS legal team what their plans were for the next day with regard to rebuttal witnesses. Reiss said the plaintiffs had not made their final decision, that there may be one, possibly two. Reiss then said something about closings taking place on Monday, and the judge said loudly, "No. No. No. No." The judge insisted that closings take place the next day.

Plaintiff and defense counsel had no choice but to agree. Each team knew it was going to be a long night.

THE LAST MORNING IN COURT

On Day 10, after addressing admission of trial exhibits, the judge asked if plaintiffs had decided how many witnesses they were going to call for their rebuttal case. Steven Reiss said, "Yes, we have, Your Honor. And I think you'll be pleased with the number. It's zero."[70] The judge was indeed pleased.

* * *

How the plaintiffs got to zero involved much drama the previous night. There was deep disagreement among the MAS legal team members. One idea was to have only one rebuttal witness, teacher Dolores Carrion, who taught Chicano Art at Pueblo High School as part of the MAS program at TUSD. Most of the team, though, thought that while her testimony would reveal the absurdity of terminating creative art classes, it did not advance the plaintiffs' case.

Richard Martinez wanted the rebuttal witness to be Rene Martinez, a former history teacher in the MAS program who was now an assistant principal in a school in the Phoenix area. Rene was Richard's son. Richard also insisted that he conduct the examination. Every other MAS legal team member opposed this, saying that it was a terrible idea for a father to conduct the examination of his son. Those in opposition also did not think that Rene's testimony would provide anything needed to advance the plaintiffs' case.

Robert Chang was concerned that an examination by Richard of his son Rene would end up not focusing on the plaintiffs' First and Fourteenth Amendment claims but instead would become a full-throated defense of the MAS program to respond to the attacks on it that had been made over the years by people like John Ward, Hector Ayala, Doug MacEachern, Tom Horne, and John Huppenthal. Chang thought it would be a disaster.

In the end, Steven Reiss as the lead trial attorney made the call. No rebuttal witnesses. The team could focus then on getting everything ready for closing arguments.

* * *

The lawyers for the plaintiffs went step-by-step through a stack of seventy meticulously created PowerPoint slides encapsulating their entire argument. In an hour, Reiss marched quickly through the slides, first outlining the legal theories: equal protection under the Fourteenth Amendment and viewpoint discrimination under the First Amendment; the levels of scrutiny; and the *Arlington Heights* framework:

1. The impact of the official action and whether it bears more heavily on one race than another;
2. The historical background of the decision;
3. The specific sequence of events leading to the challenged decision;

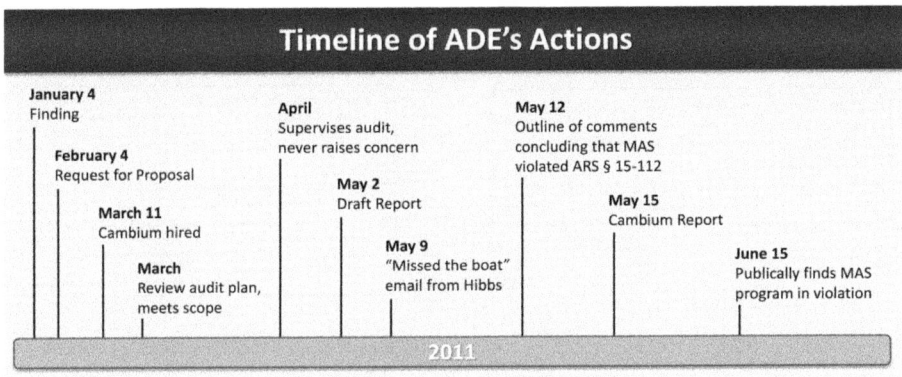

FIGURE 13.1 Timeline of ADE's Actions courtesy of Robert Chang

4. The defendants' departures from normal procedures or substantive conclusions; and
5. The relevant legislative or administrative history.

Reiss walked the court through each of these, highlighting the evidence produced at trial that related to each. He presented a "greatest hits" version of what was presented at trial. The slides also had page citations to transcript testimony, deposition testimony, and exhibits. As Reiss went through the slides, the MAS legal team could see Judge Tashima's clerk furiously writing down the citations. The team took this as a positive sign.

Three of the most effective slides provided detailed timelines of the actions of Horne, Huppenthal, and the ADE. The timeline for Huppenthal was especially devastating because it included Huppenthal's blog posts, which frequently occurred around the same time as his public actions or decisions. The ADE timeline was so important that the presentation of this timeline included ten slides. The first includes the overall timeline (see Figure 13.1).

The next slides focused on a particular date and then had callouts of the key testimony, including the following focused on May 9, 2011, and the S.S. Violation (see Figure 13.2).

Reiss emphasized again Huppenthal's blog posts (see Figure 13.3).

Devastating.

And throughout, Tashima's law clerk continued to note the citations.

Then, recognizing the importance of Judge Tashima's questioning of Kathryn Hrabluk, the three slides right before the final slide presented these visuals followed by text from the court's questioning of Hrabluk (see Figures 13.4 and 13.5).

In contrast, the attorneys for the state had no visuals.

Leslie Cooper delivered the state's closing arguments. She focused on the lack of curricular maps with scope and sequence, including that the plaintiffs' expert, Dr. Valenzuela, admitted that the MAS program did not have an explicit curriculum.

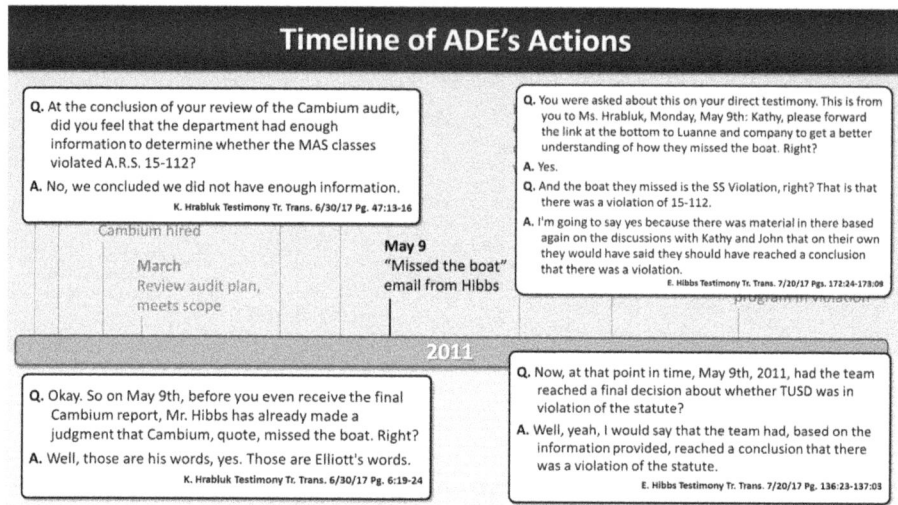

FIGURE 13.2 ADE Timeline with Key Testimony courtesy of Robert Chang

She lambasted Curtis Acosta, repeating words from his rap poem. She raised again the pictures of lynchings. She defended Tom Horne's actions and the evidence he put forward to the public that highlighted problems with the MAS program. She denied that Horne was motivated by racial animus: "Why would a goal-oriented racist, bent on eliminating the MAS program, include a right of appeal to an independent agency in the statute that he wrote?"[71]

Huppenthal's blogging activities made it more difficult for Cooper to disclaim animus on his part. Instead, she chose to say that Huppenthal's actions were inconsistent with being what she described as "goal-oriented racist":

> A goal-oriented person ... who is motivated by racial animus, would have stood on the Horne finding. A goal-oriented person would not delegate the investigation to ... non-partisan unbiased persons [ADE staff]. A goal-oriented person would not have left them to their professional skill to find a result. He would have dictated it. He didn't interfere or even participate in their investigation. A goal-oriented person motivated by racial animus would not have retained the services of an independent auditor or perhaps one that might even have been too liberal or too conservative...
>
> ...
>
> A goal-oriented racist wouldn't hold out a helping hand. In fact, he passed on several opportunities to shut down the MAS program.[72]

Posing what a hypothetical goal-oriented racist would or would not do seemed like a desperate attempt to defend against charges of racism, especially because a smart, goal-oriented racist might do exactly all those things in order to insulate himself from charges of racism.

Cooper went after the plaintiffs' experts. Dr. Valenzuela's opinions could not be trusted because she brought "her firmly held opinions about" the efficacy of

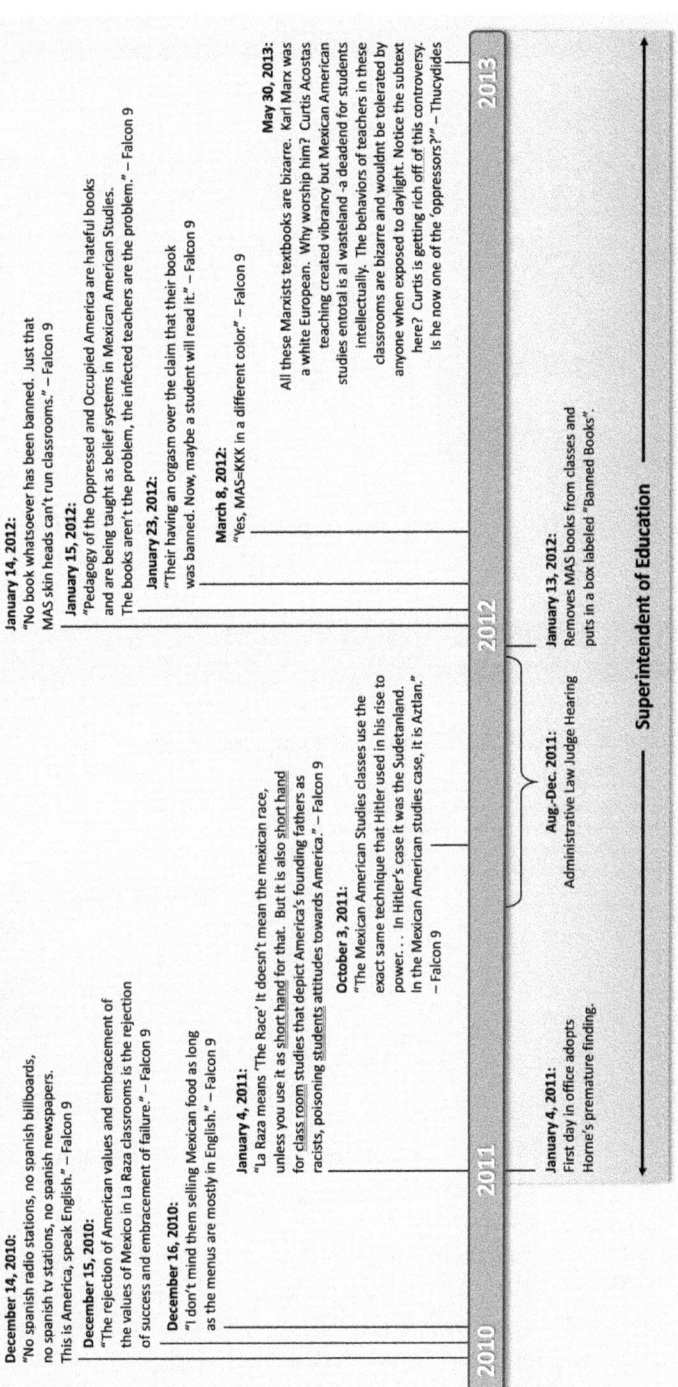

FIGURE 13.3 Huppenthal Blog Posts courtesy of Robert Chang

FIGURE 13.4 *The American Vision*: "Seen in Use" courtesy of Robert Chang

FIGURE 13.5 "I'd say it's comparable" courtesy of Robert Chang

Ethnic Studies. Dr. Cabrera's opinions could not be trusted because he was biased, being an MAS supporter and writing articles like "A State-Mandated Epistemology of Ignorance: Arizona's HB2281 and Mexican-American Raza Studies," saying, "you don't need to know anything else about that article except the title."[73] And Dr. Pitti? Cooper described him as being biased and as having "come down from his ivory tower to visit us."[74]

Cooper returned to the state's overarching defense: "They have no direct evidence of discriminatory animus, and their indirect evidence isn't persuasive."[75] After a final point about viewpoint discrimination, she sat down.

After a brief recess, Steven Reiss gave a ten-minute rebuttal. Much of it highlighted points already made in his first hour of closing arguments. He made it a point, though, to address the lynching pictures:

> You just heard it: Let's take an example of a picture. Do you think it's right to show this picture of lynchings to … it may well be right to show that to 10-year-olds. They are not naïve. They know what's going on. They live in a society where they see this kind of violence on their video games, in movies, on the internet....
>
> There are many legitimate reasons why you would show that picture to 10-year-old students. But they just say that … these materials … show[ ] these courses violated the statute.
>
> That's just nonsense.[76]

Children can handle the truth.

Reiss emphasized the benefits for at-risk students who took MAS classes. In doing so, Reiss told the court that when children are taught the truth, through materials in which they can see themselves, they become engaged learners. It is no wonder, then, that the MAS program produced these improved academic outcomes. It followed then that "[t]he notion that we would kill or squash these programs in their infancy, it's just a shame. Worse than a shame."[77]

After Steven Reiss concluded, Judge Tashima took the case under submission. Then, in a surprising moment of self-deprecating humor, in denying the need for post-trial briefing, the judge said:

> So I think I have a fair grasp of the law and I can, you know, go back and look at the [trial] file.
>
> On the other hand, you know, when it first went on appeal, I thought I had a pretty good grasp of the law, too, see.[78]

Everyone in the courtroom laughed.

POST TRIAL

The trial ended at noon, and as folks exited the building, the sun blazed down but there was electricity in the air from the thunder storms the night before. A crew of about 17 decided to get lunch on the patio of Taco Giro on Grande. There was a collective sigh of relief as the trial was over, but there was also a palpable nervous energy as no one could read Judge Tashima's poker face. As the *micheladas* and *margaritas* were served, the mixture of Tucson locals and the legal team reflected about what this trial meant to the students and the community. Steven Reiss commented about what an honor it was to be part of such an important case, and how the outcome of the verdict would affect the lives of so many youth – not just in

Tucson but throughout the country. His voice cracked as he and several others at the table were choked up, thinking about the ramifications of the case. After more than seven years of protracted struggle, the highest profile Ethnic Studies trial in the country's history had concluded.

* * *

That evening, one of the former MAS teachers Sally Rusk opened up her house to the people involved for a potluck dinner to mark the end of this part of the fight. Some of the lawyers, teachers, and experts were able to make it on the overcast, muggy evening in Tucson. The monsoons had not yet hit the Old Pueblo, but they were coming soon, and the slightly overcast sky reminded them of the upcoming seasonal change. Folks kept trying to predict how Judge Tashima would rule, worried because he favored the state at summary judgment. Everyone knew that the legal team, experts, and witnesses gave everything to this trial. No one, however, was interested in "moral victories." The eyes of the nation were on Tucson, and with the expansion of K-12 Ethnic Studies programs, a legal defeat in this trial could have massive ripple effects throughout this larger movement. Conversely, a legal victory would help validate Ethnic Studies as educationally sound. Also, it might discourage other states from enacting legislation like HB 2281.

Dinner at Sally's was a special evening. One of the attendees was a local Chinese herbalist who brought Milagro's tequila with a beautiful glass agave as part of the bottle. She suggested we do a toast to mark the end of the trial. Cabrera quietly approached her and inquired, "That is a really expensive bottle. Are you sure you want us to use it for a toast?" She responded that it was not a big deal because a local importer who was sweet on her would occasionally leave a bottle of tequila on her front porch as a reminder of his romantic interest. She said, "I probably shouldn't say this in this crowd, but the guy's name is Mark Huppenthal – John's brother!"

It was a perfect way to toast the end of the trial – with Huppenthal tequila.

The party faded quickly as people were exhausted. One small group meandered down 4th Avenue and into Che's Lounge[79] to grab a last drink before calling it a night. One member of the Weil team asked the group, "Do you know what we would play in the war room as we prepped for this trial?" A couple of people in the group in unison replied, "What?" He said with a little grin on his face, "Kid Frost's *La Raza*!!!!" The table erupted with laughter.

In the late 1990s, Kid Frost, now just Frost, was one of the few Chicano hip-hop artists to gain notoriety. Kid Frost's *La Raza* was an unabashedly Chicano pride anthem.

> *Vatos, cholos, you call us what you will*
> *You say we are assassins an' we are sent to kill*
> *It's in my blood to be an Aztec Warrior*
> *Go to any extreme and hold no barriers*
> *Chicano and I'm Brown and I'm proud.*

The song talks about the stereotypes Chicanos face on the daily (*vatos/cholos* – aka Mexican "gangsters") but then flips that sentiment to take pride in being "an Aztec Warrior" who is brown and proud. In every verse, Kid Frost repeated the refrain, "This is for *La Raza*" For downtrodden Brown folk, Kid Frost's anthem has served as a source of cultural strength for more than two decades.

Weil, Gotshal & Magnes LLP is a New York-based, international firm with more than 1,100 lawyers across three continents. As one of the lawyers on the case, David Fitzmaurice proclaimed in his thick Irish accent, "Weil doesn't fuck around!" To use the vernacular of the youth, they're ballers. They are not just ballers, but they are international ballers in Manhattan headquartered two blocks away from Trump Tower. The image of this crew bobbing their heads to *"La Raza"* while developing a legal strategy for the highest profile Ethnic Studies case in U.S. history is strange, hilarious, and totally appropriate.

Finally, as the MAS crew was reminiscing about the trial, Priscila Rodriguez, one of the students featured in *Precious Knowledge* walked in to also grab a drink. She was in Tucson briefly as she was leaving to pursue her PhD in Ethnic Studies at UC San Diego, and it was a reminder of how small the Old Pueblo truly is. It was a perfect reminder of why the work was so important. It is not some theoretical exercise. It has tangible effects on communities throughout the country. It was easy to get lost in legal arguments or beta coefficients, and this was a wonderful reminder of the true importance of the work.

On that note, the MAS crew called it a night.

14

Victory and National Renaissance Amidst Backlash

> When you expect nothing and get everything, that's destiny.
>
> Milko Velka, *Blood In, Blood Out*

When the trial began, no one knew how it would go. Some thought that because Judge Tashima had been incarcerated during World War II because he was Japanese American, he might appreciate how racial scapegoating operates. However, if he had this racial sensitivity, it did not seem evident in his first ruling when he granted summary judgment to the state on nearly every claim. During the trial, people in the courtroom were looking for signs of whether Judge Tashima was favoring one side or the other in his demeanor but consistently came up with nothing. What did it mean that he threatened to hold the plaintiffs' attorney, Steven Reiss, in contempt of court for the first time in his career – a career that included three arguments at the US Supreme Court? Were there patterns evident in Judge Tashima's rulings on objections? Based on this, the MAS legal team felt that the judge appeared for much of the trial to favor the state. The team, though, thought a shift occurred during the second trial week. His gruffness during Week 1 seemed to give way to him appearing to enjoy himself at times during Week 2. Did Judge Tashima give deference to one side more than another? There were no clear-cut answers to any of these questions, but they were ones that kept people in Tucson and around the country wondering. The uncertainty made time move at a snail's pace in anticipation of the ruling.

August 22, 2017, seemed like an average Tuesday in the Old Pueblo. It was hot in the desert, and the cicadas were humming, telling of impending rain. Rain in the desert is cleansing, and Arizonans especially needed it because that same day, President Trump held a rally in Phoenix where he lent support to Sheriff Joe Arpaio who was under fire for racially profiling Latinos and violating court orders. Trump at his rally said, "So was Sheriff Joe convicted for doing his job?" hinting at the potential of a pardon that would later come.[1] With all of the attention on Phoenix, the news of a trial verdict caught many off guard.

On this average Tucson summer day, Judge Tashima issued his ruling, a blistering forty-two-page opinion that declared that the state violated both the First and Fourteenth Amendment protections of TUSD Mexican American students when enacting and enforcing the law.[2] It concluded that HB 2281 was developed and enacted for partisan political gain by fostering racial animus.[3] During a quick call between the Weil team and Robert Chang, Steven Reiss commented that the opinion with its detailed findings of fact and citations to the trial transcript and exhibits made it bullet-proof, meaning it was extremely unlikely that the Ninth Circuit would overturn it. Chang commented his surprise that Judge Tashima found for the plaintiffs on enactment. Others from Weil agreed. If the judge ruled for plaintiffs only on enforcement, the statute would still be valid, except for A.R.S. § 15-112(A3), and future state superintendents or the Arizona Board of Education could enforce the statute against school districts. TUSD and its culturally relevant courses would remain subject to scrutiny and vulnerable. But because Tashima found that the statute had been enacted in violation of the First Amendment, no one would be able to enforce it. Chang, though, expressed concern that the ruling on enactment was more vulnerable to challenge on appeal, including if it got to the US Supreme Court.

Judge Tashima's ruling stood in stark contrast to Judge Kowal's. As discussed in Chapter 5, despite the TUSD-paid law firm arguing for the law's unconstitutionality, the administrative law judge had a narrow task – to consider whether TUSD had any courses or classes that ran afoul of any of HB 2281's four prohibitions. Whether the law was unconstitutional was not something Judge Kowal could decide. This again begs the question of why TUSD chose to pursue administrative proceedings with the limited relief it would get if it prevailed.

In finding racial animus, Judge Tashima found the evidence presented by the MAS legal team to be compelling, including within the theoretical framework provided in the testimony of Dr. Stephen Pitti and his counter to the "dog whistle politics" of elected Arizona officials. Ian Haney López wrote in *Dog Whistle Politics* that it is not enough to identify racist politics that prey upon subconscious racism among the White masses.[4] Rather, it is important to call them out, move them from the unconscious to the conscious. He elaborated: "Rather, dog whistle appeals remain inaudible to most, instead resonating with their unconscious racial anxieties and eliciting support only so long as they remain hidden. It seems that dog whistle politicians manipulate these background views and emotions, but succeed with most whites only so long as the racial appeals stay below conscious recognition."[5]

In many respects, this is what the trial accomplished. Especially through Dr. Pitti's testimony, the plaintiffs were able to establish how racism was at the root of both enacting and enforcing A.R.S. § 15-112.

Judge Tashima was very clear on this point in his final ruling as he specifically cited the use of "code words" in making his ruling. He was particularly critical of the way representatives of the state used specific terminologies that were not well understood by the general populace and/or had no basis in facts to generate opposition and hostility to the program. He offered:

> Certain frequently invoked terms and concepts, including "Raza," "un-American," "radical," "communist," "Aztlán," and "M.E.Ch.a," [sic] operated as derogatory code words for Mexican Americans in the MAS debate. These terms functioned as code words by standing for a racial group, see, e.g., (Horne using "Raza" to mean Mexican American in referring to "Raza studies for the Raza kids"), and by drawing on negative mischaracterizations that had little to no basis in fact.[6]

While many of these terms do not have an inherently negative connotation – *la raza* for example – both Horne and Huppenthal continued to use them in a pejorative manner. One might ask why casting a negative light on specific terminology could have such a devastating impact. Judge Tashima continued in his ruling that context was extremely important: "These particular words were effective codewords with Arizona voters because they drew on '[p]eople['s] … concern[s] about illegal immigration' and the 'Mexicanization' of Arizona that were prominent during 'the 2006 to 2011 time frame.'"[7]

Within this context, Horne and Huppenthal became their own worst enemies because their testimony provided the most compelling evidence that demonstrated racial animus. Judge Tashima noted Huppenthal's campaign to "stop *la raza*" and the $40,000 behind the radio spots, the lack of any Arizona Department of Education staff audit of the MAS program, the limited nature of Huppenthal's commissioned audit, and Huppenthal's "anonymous" blogging against MAS.[8]

Judge Tashima went further, citing Dr. Cabrera's statistics demonstrating the program's efficacy to rule that removing the program created educational harm to students in the district, especially Mexican American students.[9] Many in Tucson's MAS community were surprised by the force with which Judge Tashima wrote. There was no ambiguity in his words. Those banning MAS acted out of racial animus and for partisan political gain, limiting the educational opportunities of Mexican American students as a result. Many following the controversy closely already knew this, but it was incredibly important to have a federal judge affirm this position. It put the state and its representatives on the defense instead of offense. The tables finally turned.

LOCAL TUCSON RESPONSE

Back in the Old Pueblo, there was a boisterous celebration that echoed throughout the country. Immediately, community members took to Facebook and Twitter to announce the victory. Despite the remaining divisions in the community, everyone celebrated the dismantling of the racist and politically driven banning of MAS. Cabrera called Auggie and said, "*Mano*, the ruling came down and we won!" There was silence on the phone, and Auggie started to tear up, struggling to form a sentence. Cabrera summarized Judge Tashima's argument, punctuating it with, "We won *mano*." Auggie responded, "¡*Gracias mano!*" In some way, all were vindicated in this fight by the ruling.

David Morales was one of the first to break the news, writing a quick piece for the *Three Sonorans*. He began by outlining Judge Tashima's ruling focusing on the constitutional violations of Horne and Huppenthal. The second part of his post then shifted to a point he had been pushing in TUSD for years: "Mexican American Studies may return to TUSD." The "may" has always been the sticking point because even with the lifting of the ban, there is nothing mandating MAS *must* return. It just opens the door, and there remains the ongoing debate about to what degree the Culturally Relevant Classes are sufficiently close to MAS or if they are completely different.

But there was a collective sigh of relief, one heard throughout the country, because a loss at trial for the plaintiffs in Tucson could have led to bans of Ethnic Studies throughout the country. UNIDOS emphasized this point in their public statement on the ruling:

> Since 2010 the community of Tucson has fought tirelessly to keep and reimplement the Mexican American Studies program. Today was a major victory in our struggle, and we hope that it leads to many more .... As a community we celebrate this victory with all those who have supported and pursued the dismantling of this racist act against the Mexican-American community.
>
> With this accomplishment we must remember that the fight is not over. UNIDOS and the community of Tucson will continue to resist any injustice that plagues our community. We would like to thank all our allies and those who never lost hope in the fight.
> *Esta victoria es para el pueblo.*
> *In Lak'ech.*
>
> U.N.I.D.O.S. Youth Coalition[10]

UNIDOS was elated but also well aware that injustices remained unredressed in the local community and nationally.

The local papers tended to center on criticisms of Tom Horne, John Huppenthal, and the banning. Now that it was officially decreed by a federal judge that the MAS banning was racist, they were more willing to fall in line and frame HB 2281 as a racist social policy. One of the more visible statements was by political cartoonist David Fitzsimmons of the *Arizona Daily Star* (see Figure 14.1).

"Fitz," as he is locally known, went directly after the two unrepentant political opportunists, putting them in the corner wearing dunce caps for their officially racist behaviors.

Not all of Tucson response was positive. Loretta Hunnicutt offered some of her last words on the subject, stating that "Arizona schools [are] now free to 'promote

FIGURE 14.1 The Ethnic Studies Ban Was Racist (© *Arizona Daily Star*)

resentment toward a race or class of people.'"[11] Her sour grapes report misrepresented the ruling. Jon Justice at this point moved to Minneapolis and did not comment on the outcome. Doug MacEachern had stopped writing for the *Arizona Republic* in 2014, and he was silent on social media regarding the ruling. Another op-ed columnist for the *Republic* critiqued the ruling with a strange headline: "If a bigot bans ethnic studies, the law is unconstitutional?"[12] Though not fully articulated, the author of this op-ed raised the question between enforcement and enactment, and suggested that the US Supreme Court might overturn the ruling, as it had when it put a stop to lower federal courts that had found that President Trump's travel ban was motivated by animus. It was a desperate, last-gasp attempt to support the MAS banning that ultimately fell flat.

In contrast, the victory was celebrated nationally in ways that dwarfed the local elation.

NATIONAL VICTORY LAP

The importance of this legal victory cannot be overstated. Those are not just the words of us as authors, but those on a national level who continually followed the controversy. Returning to Ulises Bella, the multiple-horn player for the renowned group Ozomatli philosophically commented:

Stuff that happens in Arizona, people are talking about it here in LA., and I'm sure vice-versa. Now, in the current climate, the environment with families being torn apart – the attacks on education was just one of the many consistent attacks on us as a culture and as a people …. Especially when it does work out, it's very inspiring …. It's like, "Oh shit, we're not always losing! We're taking baby steps, but we're rockin'!"[13]

He understood that the overturning of the MAS ban reverberated far beyond Tucson. Ulises understood that *raza* were constantly under attack, whether through anti-immigrant legislation, kids in cages, or the banning of MAS. From this context, there were no small victories. A win for one was a win for all. To reiterate, it was critically important to be reminded that "we're not always losing!"

From this perspective, Tony Diaz of *Librotraficante* fame, reporting from Houston, argued that the ruling "gives nation some hope for future."[14] The BBC in the segment *PRI's The World* ran an in-depth analysis where they not only covered the ruling but also interviewed an MAS graduate, Dr. Luis Valdez (not the playwright), about the impact of the program on students who took it.[15] The ruling was covered by almost every national outlet such as the *New York Times*,[16] *Washington Post*,[17] *Los Angeles Times*,[18] *NPR*,[19] *NBC*,[20] *ABC*,[21] and the *Huffington Post*.[22] The rest of the country fell in line with what many in Tucson had known for years: the MAS ban was both racist and political. Its implications ran well beyond the Tucson locale, as Ulises offered one more time, "It definitely felt like a victory for all of us. Even in these small battles, it inspires people to keep the train moving. Anyone involved in activism will tell you it's a marathon."[23] Now, with the ruling, others beyond the activist communities were on board with the MAS and Ethnic Studies cause nationally.

The joy felt by some in Arizona was punctured three days after the MAS ruling when President Trump pardoned Sheriff Joe Arpaio. It brought many back to reality – the reality that the racism that was so endemic to Arizona in 2010 when HB 2281 and SB 1070 were enacted and gave the state a black eye had become, nationally, the new normal. Lalo captured the moment with another political cartoon (see Figure 14.2).

Regardless, on that one night of August 22, the desert rains flowed, marking the beginning of the end of this instance of state-sponsored racism. In 2010, the odds seemed insurmountable. Now, nearly eight years later, MAS supporters were vindicated in federal court and the importance of the legal victory could not be overstated. But a question loomed: Would the state appeal?

* * *

Before an appeal could even be considered, additional court proceedings were necessary to determine the remedy; the August 22 decision only established liability. The state fielded a new legal team for this litigation stage. After the trial, Leslie

FIGURE 14.2 *Welcome to Arizona* by Lalo Alcaraz/Go Comics

Cooper left the attorney general's office to work with the Maricopa Community College system, and Robert Ellman, in private practice, was not retained to continue on the case after the trial concluded.

The new lawyers on the case were ready for a protracted fight. We learned this accidentally after the October 30, 2017, remedies hearing. One of the authors of this book, Cabrera, happened to be in the elevator of the federal courthouse when he was joined by the state's new lawyers. They did not recognize Cabrera because they were not part of the previous trial and he was dressed in his usual garb – khaki Dickies™ shorts, *huaraches*, and a lavender *guayabera*. This was a far cry from the pressed black suit, spit-polished shoes, and double Windsor tie Cabrera wore in court.

The state's lawyers began the elevator ride whispering to each other about how weak they thought the plaintiffs' case was. With each floor, they became more agitated. By the end of the short ride, the state's lawyers were whisper yelling about the "injustice" of the current case. Cabrera stood in the corner pretending to look at his phone. As the doors opened, profanities were spewed as they made their way across the lobby. As they left the building, the conversation was punctuated with, "And we will take this case all the way to the goddamn Supreme Court!!!"

When Cabrera relayed this to the MAS legal team, the usually unassuming Steven Reiss said with a little swagger, "Bring it on. I'm 3-0 before the Supreme Court!"

In the briefs and at the October hearing, the plaintiffs and defendants disagreed on the appropriate remedy. The new lawyers for the state argued that Horne and

Huppenthal were simply bad actors, that declaratory relief was appropriate without an injunction. They argued: "[A]n injunction is simply not necessary. If the final judgment of this Court includes declaratory relief and Defendants take future action to violate that declaratory judgment, Plaintiffs may initiate post-judgment proceedings to enforce this Court's order. Unless and until that occurs, declaratory judgment is sufficient."[24]

Conversely, the plaintiffs argued that declaratory relief holding that the law was enacted and enforced in violation of the constitution and a permanent injunction against enforcing this state law were both necessary. Plaintiffs pointed to Superintendent Diane Douglas's ongoing enforcement of A.R.S. §15-112 against TUSD, including that ADE classroom observers used a form that included space for them to log violations of HB 2281's A3 prohibition, even though A3 was found unconstitutionally overbroad by Judge Tashima in 2013, affirmed by the Ninth Circuit in 2015.[25] The fact that Superintendent Douglas was still trying to enforce even the unconstitutional provision indicated the need for an injunction. Plaintiffs noted: "Defendants' efforts to shield Superintendent Douglas from the Court's ruling by any means necessary – no matter how meritless – cast serious doubt on their intention to comply with a declaratory judgment alone. The Court should therefore, permanently enjoin all Defendants … as well as the Board of Education from taking any action pursuant to A.R.S. §15-112."[26]

Judge Tashima agreed with the plaintiffs and issued his final judgment on December 27, 2017, and ordered a permanent injunction against the state.[27] This forbid the state from enforcing the law. It took away the superintendent's ability to withhold funds from any school in Arizona if the superintendent thought a district was in violation of A.R.S. § 15-112.

On top of that, the state was required to pay plaintiffs' legal fees.

But would the state appeal? Remember, the new lawyers for the state were eager to take this all the way to the Supreme Court. The state had thirty days after this final judgment to decide. The MAS legal team and MAS community waited as the days passed. When the clock hit midnight, Mountain Standard Time, on January 26, 2018, with no alert through the federal court's electronic filing system, the MAS legal team knew that the state decided not to appeal. Apparently, the sentiment in the AG's office appeared to change after Judge Tashima's final remedies order.

We can only speculate about why the state did not appeal. Perhaps state officials considered how badly they lost at trial and how the state was already on the hook for potentially millions of dollars in legal fees owed to the plaintiffs' attorneys, which would only grow if they appealed and lost again. But the point is that they chose not to appeal.

Regardless, they did not appeal. The case was over. And borrowing from the musical *Hamilton*, "We won! We won! We won! We won!!!!"[28] UNIDOS echoed this sentiment on their public Facebook page:

BIG NEWS CONTINUES TO FLOW FROM HB2281 BATTLE
AZ PERMANENTLY FORBIDDEN FROM USING HB2281 TO BAN THE
MEXICAN AMERICAN STUDIES PROGRAM.[29]

This celebration did not stop their continued critiques of the MAS movement, but they saw the court case as a win for themselves as well. This victory left many questions unresolved because the law only addressed whether districts in Arizona *could* have the classes. It did not mandate that they had to have them, and this became a source of tension in post-trial Tucson.

MAS AND A STILL HOSTILE BOARD: AN INTEREST CONVERGENCE STORY

In Critical Race Theorist Derrick Bell's conception of interest convergence theory, he posited that the interests of communities of color will only be advanced if they also converge with the interests of White people.[30] He noted: "Racial justice – or its appearance – may, from time to time be counted among the interests deemed important by the court and by society's policymakers."[31] This insight, applied to *Brown v. Board of Education*, led him to posit that in addition to concerns about an abstract notion "about the immorality of racial inequality," it was critical to appreciate that "those whites in policymaking positions [were] able to see the economic and political advances at home and abroad that would follow abandonment of segregation."[32] But *Brown* and its decision on remedy in *Brown II* did not end the practice of segregated education.[33] This does not negate the importance of those decisions but highlights the limits of a pronouncement about the unconstitutionality of segregation without a truly effective remedy.

In a similar way, Judge Tashima as the decision-maker at trial accepted the plaintiffs' claims that the law had been enacted and enforced in a discriminatory manner and that it disproportionately harmed Mexican American students. It is important to remember the limited constitutional right of the students, the right to receive information and ideas, which does not include an *affirmative* right to have MAS in the TUSD curriculum. Though Judge Tashima told the state of Arizona and its officials what they could not do, ordering the return of MAS to TUSD was beyond his authority. Only the TUSD Governing Board could bring MAS back.

Despite the victory for MAS in federal court, the board by this time was openly hostile to this form of education. There was a period of time, 2012–2016, when MAS supporters had a slim 3-2 majority on the governing board (Grijalva, Foster, and Juarez). But any vote then to bring back the program would likely have resulted in another finding of violation and loss of funds because A.R.S. §15-112 was still on the books. By 2017 when the law banning MAS was overturned, Rachael Sedgwick had been elected as a new TUSD board member. One of Sedgwick's papers as a UA law student showed her opposition to the program;[34] her entry on the board tipped the scales against MAS, 3-2. This meant that despite the court ruling, the program was not coming back.

In the wake of Judge Tashima's ruling, Grijalva and Foster introduced a motion in early 2018 that would have allowed, but not required, teachers in the district to teach the MAS curriculum. Foster called it an "olive branch" meant to alleviate some of the pressure teachers experienced from the state banning of MAS.[35] Grijalva added, "To not acknowledge the fact that [the law] was unconstitutional is irresponsible of this board."[36] Sedgwick, in contrast, claimed the resolution was "repetitive" because the federal court already ruled the law to be unconstitutional and that reintroducing MAS would turn Tucson back into a "warzone."[37] Given Sedgwick's previous and public opposition to the MAS program, these rationales seemed more like window dressing. She used the 3-2 board majority to quash Grijalva and Foster's resolution by making a verbal resolution that the Culturally Relevant Classes were to do "what is necessary" to close achievement gaps in the district.[38] It was a way to sidestep the MAS issue without directly opposing the former program.

To justify her opposition, Sedgwick – a White woman – said that coming from the US/Mexico border city of Nogales, she understood "how culturally relevant courses can improve academic outcomes for Latinos."[39] Additionally, board member Michael Hicks of *The Daily Show* infamy offered that he – a White man – grew up on Tucson's Southside and, as previously noted, was "probably more Hispanic than some of the others around here."[40] Sedgwick and Hicks "attempted to tout their Latino bona fides" as giving them insight and authority on the issue.[41] Stegeman joined them, consistent with his earlier musing during the administrative law hearing that MAS fostered dangerous groupthink as recounted in Chapter 5.

In response to Sedgwick, Hicks, and Stegeman's obstruction, Grijalva penned an op-ed arguing that the MAS program, now that the banning was lifted, should be recognized for its incredible accomplishments.[42] While it may not have been as powerful as an actual board resolution, it was still important in terms of the public discourse regarding MAS, and solidified Grijalva as one of the most consistent public officials in support of MAS. Remember, she was only one of two board members to come out and engage the UNIDOS students when they took over the school board meeting on April 26, 2011. Her term concluded on December 31, 2022, ending an eighteen-year run on the TUSD school board.

In 2018, Michael Hicks lost his bid for reelection and was replaced by Leila Counts.[43] Given his central role in eliminating the MAS program and the national embarrassment that he brought on the community from his appearance on *The Daily Show*, many in Tucson wondered how he was able to hold on to his seat for so long.

The next year in 2019, the other anti-MAS stalwart, Mark Stegeman, now in the 3-2 minority, resigned from the board.[44] He said it was because he no longer believed that TUSD could make the necessary reforms to be successful.

With these changes, one might wonder why the board has not brought MAS back. The simple answer may be that MAS is still a political hot potato and Arizona is still a red (sometimes purple) state. There is fear and trepidation about reigniting old fights as Sedgwick alluded to earlier. Structurally, it is also not possible to recreate the magic that was MAS circa 2008 because the key players are no longer there. Sean Arce completed his PhD at the University of Arizona, and he currently works in Southern California developing and implementing Ethnic Studies curricula. Auggie Romero was the principal of Pueblo High School until the board fired him in what one board member referred to as a "witch hunt."[45] It was a highly unusual move and seemed to be retribution for Romero's years-long involvement in developing and advocating for MAS. Similar to when Arce was fired by the board, there was an outpouring of community support that fell on the deaf ears of three board members who were not to be moved.[46]

The current composition of the TUSD Board, however, does not have any holdovers to the MAS controversy, so it is uncertain in which direction the district will move. Regardless, it will not be possible to recapture the training, dedication, and development of the original program as most of the people have either moved on, retired, or moved up. Further, whether this board will act will likely turn on whether they see bringing MAS back as converging with the interests of White elites – policymakers, media, and others – who remain in positions of power in Tucson. Bell might have predicted that despite the successful coalition building among communities of color that supported the court victory, an affirmative remedy, real change, always requires more.

THE TUCSON 11 ET AL.: WHERE ARE THEY NOW?

As the dust settled from the MAS battle, only a few remained. Sally Rusk was recognized as the 2013–2014 Pueblo High School Outstanding Teacher of the year,[47] and she earned a well-deserved retirement shortly thereafter, concluding an illustrious educational career. Curtis Acosta left TUSD as well and formed his own consulting company, Acosta Educational Partnership.[48] Additionally, he assumed a role at the University of Arizona, directing the College of Education's Language and Cultural Studies program.[49]

Maria Federico Brummer moved into an administrative role within TUSD becoming the director of Mexican American Student Services for the district,[50] and Lorenzo Lopez Jr. also joined the administrative ranks becoming the director of Culturally Relevant Pedagogy and Instruction, currently serving more than 5,500 students annually.[51] Predictably, during Lopez's approval process, Michael Hicks voted against his appointment.[52]

Alexandro "Salo" Escamilla still works as a teacher within TUSD, as do Norma and Jose Gonzalez, both of whom are also now known as "Dr." after completing their graduate studies at the University of Arizona. Norma and Jose also co-created the Xicanx Institute for Teaching and Organizing (XITO)[53] along with former Prescott College professor Dr. Anita Fernández, Dr. Arce, and Dr. Acosta. XITO offers professional development, working with educators to rehumanize educational spaces, offering many of the lessons learned from the development of the MAS program. Through XITO and Acosta Educational Partnerships, the lessons of MAS are being systematically passed on to the next generation of educators.

Rene Martinez left Tucson and became an assistant principal in a Phoenix school district. Dolores Carrion continues to teach fine arts in TUSD at Pueblo High School, and Yolanda Sotelo substitute taught at Pueblo as well and found herself in the middle of another controversy – this time regarding alleged grade changing and again involving Auggie Romero.[54]

David Morales is still occasionally blogging for the *Three Sonorans*, but now on *Medium* instead of his personal website. On the other side of the political aisle, 104.1 *The Truth* no longer exists as it became "Family Life Radio" and, as previously mentioned, "Jon Justice" relocated to Minnesota. John Huppenthal has faded into political irrelevance. As for Tom Horne, he somehow resurrected his political career as we will offer in the Epilogue.

Some of the seeds planted by the MAS program have blossomed into incredible examples of what now retired Dr. Roberto "Cintli" Rodríguez calls "creation resistance."[55] That is, one can disrupt the system by tearing down parts of it, or one can build alternative structures.

Alternative opportunities.

Alternative visions of the future.

Additionally, the University of Arizona continues to grapple with the complexities of the issue. For example, as late as February of 2019, the university's MAS Department passed a resolution to ban the screening of *Precious Knowledge*[56] and the mere mention of the movie in the community can easily start a fight. Additionally, mentioning MAS, Auggie, Sean, or the *Three Sonorans* can also lead to fights. The collective memory and associated emotional trauma are still bubbling just beneath the surface. People who have been friends for years no longer speak. For many involved in the trial, their physical, mental, and emotional health has declined.

While the MAS controversy seems to have moved on from the community, the community does not seem to have moved on from the controversy. Maybe labeling it a "controversy" is too flippant because these wounds run deep for many who are still grappling with them. It was not simply a cute political game that Horne and Huppenthal were using to gain higher office. Real people's lives hung in the balance, and they were treated as expendable – causalities of a racist culture war that should never have been fought in the first place.

One tragedy of the banning of MAS is that it took experienced teachers out of classrooms and stifled the education of Brown youth. Consider how much time, effort, and resources it is taking to build and provide the Culturally Relevant

Courses mandated by the court in the federal desegregation case. All of this could have been avoided if a few opportunistic politicians in Phoenix had not used the MAS program to leverage political gain by stoking xenophobia and racism in the Arizona electorate.

How many students experienced harm because Horne and Huppenthal decided to play their racist games with the MAS program? How many more students would have graduated if TUSD had meaningfully defended the program instead of caving to political pressure? How many precious lives were lost because they were denied this precious knowledge? We offer these questions that are almost impossible to answer for the following reason: these are not simply political games because they have material consequences for the very children these elected officials purportedly serve.

CONCLUSION: TO NEW BEGINNINGS

Long range goals deal with: the philosophy of self-determination and total liberation, the building of confidence and independent action, the right to make decisions that affect our children and their future, the right to select our allies, the choice to pick our friends and determine our own political direction, to control our economic resources and human values.

Rodolfo "Corky" Gonzales, *The Past-Present-Future of the Chicano Movement*[57]

Spoken more than four decades ago, in many respects, the struggle of MAS is still grappling with the long-term goals outlined in "Corky" Gonzales' classic statement. So much of this movement and the state repression centered around issues of community self-determination or that right being stripped away. In a red state that continually emphasized "local control" over educational issues, a racist state law was passed when said local control was being exercised by Brown folks. It took a decade of educational, grassroots, and legal struggle just so that Chicanas/os could exercise the same educational autonomy that more affluent and White sections of town are able to do as a matter of practice.

To riff on a favorite phrase of James Baldwin, this is our collective challenge to *Begin Again*.[58] The metaphor of the phoenix seems appropriate at this juncture. It is appropriate because the example of the banned MAS program has been a central figure in the creation of a nationwide movement where Ethnic Studies is a central component for addressing systemic educational inequities. Rising from the ashes, new forms are taking shape as another generation of students are able to access, engage, and explore this beautiful, community-oriented, critically conscious, precious knowledge.

The metaphor is bittersweet, however, because MAS has not risen from the ashes in TUSD. However, inspiration from the program and the fight for MAS in Arizona has been part of the rationale for Ethnic Studies mandates that have been passed in Washington, Oregon, California, Nevada, Texas, Indiana, Vermont, and

FIGURE 14.3 Map of State-Based Ethnic Studies Bills and Requirements by Wayne Au

Rhode Island, in addition to such legislation having been considered in twelve others (see Figure 14.3).[59] The value of this legal victory will be judged by the Ethnic Studies programs that continue to grow and develop throughout the country.

Make no mistake. Despite the attacks occurring in certain states such as Florida with its 2022 Stop W.O.K.E. Act, Ethnic Studies is undergoing a renaissance, and this is a unique opportunity to both use the struggles of the past, learn and grow from their mistakes, and ultimately to give Ethnic Studies to the next generation.

The stakes are still incredibly high because the center of this issue and every Ethnic Studies development over the last fifty years has been about community-based self-determination.[60] That is the power of Ethnic Studies – that it does not require our beautiful Chicana/o, Black, Asian American, and Native American students to lose their cultural heritage and assimilate into Whiteness. Instead, they are able to exist and to learn on their own terms, in their own culture, in an environment of social validation. They are encouraged to be politically active, applying their studies to improve the community, something that should be encouraged in any participatory democracy.

Many want to replicate the success of the Tucson MAS program in their locale, and to those, we offer the following advice. First, remember that MAS efficacy was documented when the program had been able to reach maturation. Please do not overpromise Ethnic Studies as a miracle panacea for race-based educational inequities. Second, please make sure that your Ethnic Studies is actually Ethnic Studies. Having students stand up and read Dr. King's "I Have a Dream" speech in January is not Ethnic Studies. The "heroes and holiday" or "foods and fiestas" versions of this work have never been effective. Instead, return to the roots of Ethnic Studies and let the following questions guide your work: "What is Ethnic Studies at its core? How does it differ from traditional (White) forms of education? What will be required to *collectively* reimagine education in a way that actually supports and centers the cultural histories of minoritized students? What will be required to make this creative reimagination a reality?"

While these questions have been posed in the K-12 Ethnic Studies context, they are equally important and compelling for those doing higher education Ethnic Studies.

When Ethnic Studies is done well, it is frequently seen as subversive and even threatening, as evidenced by the MAS controversy. Therefore, those building and developing Ethnic Studies programs additionally need to be prepared to defend it.

Yes, this is a discipline that is outside of the Western canon, and it centers the cultural products of communities of color.

Yes, it tells the truth about the atrocities experienced historically and contemporarily by communities of color, and it does not gloss over the violence and racism of many people considered national heroes.

Yes, it is an overtly political form of education that centers structured inequities in analyses, and it is one that encourages students to not only critique oppression but also to do something about it.

Yes, it intentionally blurs the lines between the community and the school.

Yes, it does *not* require students of color to assimilate into White societal norms to succeed academically. Why is any of this a problem?

A huge proportion of the time spent defending MAS was spent simply countering mass misinformation and disinformation in the public spewed by critics such as Horne, Huppenthal, the Hunnicutts, Glenn Beck, Jon Justice, MacEachern, and even some TUSD representatives such as Stegeman, Hicks, Cuevas, and Pedicone. As set forth in Chapter 1, a program like MAS is a different form of education, and that is precisely the point. It does not, therefore, make it hateful or un-American. As consistent MAS defender and retired UA professor Dr. "Cintli" Rodríguez offered, the critics of MAS were actually the ones taking a radical position by framing MAS as un-American.[61]

Ultimately, this work comes back to the adage, "Insanity is doing the same thing over and over again and expecting different results."[62] What was offered before MAS was not working, and reforms continually retread failed approaches (e.g., tutoring, remedial education, charter schools, vouchers, Teach for America, etc.).[63] Jeff Duncan-Andrade and Ernest Morell reframed this issue arguing that the educational system is, in fact, working precisely as it was designed.[64] That is, structured racial inequities and White supremacy are foundational to the US, and the educational system was created to support and recreate this form of social oppression. Perhaps this is part of what was so threatening about the MAS program to its critics – that it represented the incredible threat of a good example, a good example of non-Eurocentric, community-oriented, critical education.

The creative reimagining of education, led by the MAS teachers but including students, parents, certain TUSD administrators, community activists, artists, bloggers, and lawyers, offered a bold new vision of what public education could be – embodying Immortal Technique's words recounted in Chapter 3 regarding "no one person can do everything, but everyone can do something." They developed a form of community-engaged, self-determined education, and that was a key threat to the powers that be. They were not asking permission for the educational system to be more inclusive of Chicana/o students, but rather, they were demanding and creating space to do this critically important work. The word "demand" might seem too aggressive, but recall the prophetic words of Frederick Douglass where he offered, "Power concedes nothing without a demand. It never has and it never will."[65] The power structures of education were pushing students of color more into the prison-industrial complex than into college,[66] in what Michelle Alexander refers to as the *New Jim Crow*.[67] Applied to Brown folks, Nancy Acevedo calls this system the *New Juan Crow*.[68] Therefore, a *demand* was necessary to disrupt this structured racial/educational inequity because polite requests either fell on unhearing ears or were talked to death with little tangible action taken. Demands were, thus, an exercise in political power.

The power of the collective that lodged these demands for Mexican American educational equity also served to be a community liability as different factions began turning on each other as the legal case developed. This development was not unexpected from a historical perspective as there were massive internal divisions within the original Chicana/o Rights Movement.[69] This was not just specific to Chicanas/os as many other movements of the 1960s experienced similar divisions, the most high-profile being the splintering of the Black Civil Rights struggle between the Martin and Malcolm camps. While we as both authors and people deeply embedded in the MAS struggle offer thoughts about how to support and defend Ethnic Studies against a repressive state, we struggle to see how to navigate these internal divisions. While we were both more closely aligned in our work with the teachers and the court case, we also see validity in those calling for a boycott of *Precious Knowledge*. Perhaps that is the lesson from both the Civil Rights Movement and the struggle for MAS – that there will be inevitable internal divisions as committed, principled people collectively dedicate themselves to struggle and therefore, it is necessary to be prepared for this to occur. For us, this is an unsatisfactory answer, but it is the best we have right now because, even with 20/20 hindsight, we do not see how this schism could have been avoided. Even calling it a "schism" upsets some in the movement because they think it is dismissive of what they see as the underlying social harms that occurred within the MAS movement.

Regardless of the orientation of any MAS supporter, they were all loud and assertive, using their voices to call out the racism of the state and the district in banning the program. A less known phrase from Douglass' aforementioned speech continued: "Find out just what a people will quietly submit to, and you have found out the exact amount of injustice and wrong which will be imposed upon them."[70] What was so powerful about the MAS struggle was that supporters of the program identified a massive, persistent injustice – structured, race-based educational inequity – and refused to quietly submit to that as a given reality. They further refused to acquiesce to the racist and partisan attacks on the program even as many of the leaders in the district capitulated.[71] Instead, they raged against it by organizing, speaking, litigating, and creating a collective, counter-hegemonic display of community power.

Their work serves as a beautiful reminder of the incredible potential of a dedicated collective to transform public education. Their inspiration has led to a national Ethnic Studies renaissance. We hope that you will likewise be inspired to help realize the potential following the highest-profile Ethnic Studies case in US history.

In 1974, Chicano historian, activist, and co-editor of *El Plan de Santa Bárbara* Juan Gomez-Quiñones argued, "The future of Chicano Studies is yet to be built."[72] We extend this argument to Ethnic Studies in contemporary times, and with the newfound momentum behind this effort, the time is now to realize the potential of Gomez-Quiñones' charge.

We conclude with a question only you can answer: where is your place in the Ethnic Studies Renaissance?

Epilogue

Children Can Handle the Truth – Children Need the Truth

In April 2023, C.R.T. Forward, a project housed in the UCLA School of Law's Critical Race Studies Program, issued a report, *Tracking the Attack on Critical Race Theory*.[1] It detailed President Trump's attempt toward the end of his presidency to quash the teaching of so-called "divisive concepts."[2] Though President Biden quickly rescinded it, politicians around the country recognized that they could use "divisive concepts," including Critical Race Theory and Ethnic Studies, to gain political support and, in some cases, to help them gain political office. Politicians were able to scare people about how these divisive concepts were being used to "indoctrinate" children – dog whistle politics at its best or worst.

In our Prologue, we discussed politicians with national aspirations: Governor Ron DeSantis, Governor Sarah Huckabee Sanders, and former governor and former US Ambassador to the UN Nikki Haley, who have jumped on the banning bandwagon. There are, to be sure, variations on what is forbidden. Much of it, though, seems to be motivated by the notion that the concept of "race" itself is dangerous, rooted in a version of radical colorblindness, including that schools ought *not* to be teaching children the truth about racism in US history.

In a proposed version of a Florida first-grade textbook, the story of Rosa Parks was scrubbed of any reference to race or skin color: "Rosa Parks showed courage. One day, she rode the bus. She was told to move to a different seat. She did not. She did what she believed was right."[3] Likewise, the story of Fred Korematsu was scrubbed: "Fred Korematsu grew up in California. He wanted to be treated with respect. Some people treated him differently. He worked hard for everyone to be treated with respect."[4] His race, Japanese American incarceration, and his challenging of this state-sanctioned racism were noticeably absent.

This proposed version of the Florida first-grade textbook is in line with what the Florida State Board of Education has issued with regard to a new history standard, requiring that students be taught that "slaves developed skills which, in some instances, could be applied for their personal benefit."[5]

At the center of these attempts to remove race from classrooms is a certain racist benevolent paternalism, the notion that children can't handle the truth.

But the struggle over Mexican American Studies in Arizona teaches us that the opposite is true. If children are old enough to be targets of racism, children can handle learning the racial truth. Maybe more importantly, children need to be told the truth.

The evidence presented at the final trial revealed that the district-approved textbook for American History for juniors in high school included *only* eighteen pages about Mexican Americans in a book that ran over 1,000 pages. Imagine year after year of this, from kindergarten through high school. When students do not see themselves in the materials, they disengage. When schools engage in subtractive schooling, sending overt and covert signals that deny or denigrate certain cultures and backgrounds, students disengage.

As the evidence presented at trial demonstrated, when students see themselves in the material, they become engaged in their education and academic outcomes improve.

Children can handle the truth. Children *need* the truth.

Yet we find ourselves in the midst of a political frenzy in many states. Politicians are stirring up their constituencies for political gain, taking pleasure in banning, burning. Ironically, they call themselves "freedom fighters" while censoring educational topics – necessarily limiting freedom.

Even Arizona, which ought to know better from the decade-long battle over Mexican American Studies in the streets and courtrooms, seems to have succumbed to a new collective amnesia. After almost a decade of protracted grassroots and legal struggle, both authors of this text are exhausted and want to turn the metaphorical page on this chapter in civil rights history. Instead, and to quote Michael Corleone from *The Godfather, Part III*, "Just when I thought I was out, they pulled me back in."[6]

During the 2022 election cycle, Tom Horne once again threw his hat into the ring to be the Arizona State Superintendent of Public Instruction. His campaign read like Mad Libs™ from his runs in the early 2010s. This time, instead of "Mexican American Studies," his campaign signs and website read, "Stop Critical Race Theory."[7] During the 2022 election cycle in Arizona where the voting populace elected a Democrat for Governor, Senator, and Attorney General, the state electorate appears to have forgotten Horne's history.

They forgot that a federal judge said the law Horne was central to in passing and implementing violated the constitutional rights of Brown kids and was, in both intent and effect, racist.

They forgot about the millions in legal fees that his failed war on Mexican American Studies cost the state.

They forgot about Horne's hit-and-run, affair with a member of his staff, and FBI investigation.

Most importantly, they forgot how he was central to the elimination of the most robust and effective Ethnic Studies program in the country.

On November 17, 2022, when Horne was declared the victor over incumbent Kathy Hoffman, he was granted power by the electorate to begin his new crusade against another imagined enemy – Critical Race Theory. But this new crusade was just a continuation of his previous one. His campaign website reveals that he cannot wait to return to office so he can enforce the law he wrote, referring to A.R.S. §15-112. He even misread Judge Tashima's Final Order, claiming that all Tashima did was rule that the particular enforcement of the law against TUSD was unconstitutional, even though Tashima "adjudged" that the "State of Arizona, acting through its Legislature and Governor, acted contrary to the First and Fourteenth Amendments to the Constitution of the United States in enacting §15-112."[8] You cannot be any clearer than that.

We close by returning to a slogan from the Chicana/o Civil Rights Movement that spawned Mexican American Studies, ¡La Lucha Sigue!

The struggle continues.

The struggle over censorship.

The struggle over educational self-determination.

The struggle over truth.

We offer this book because we need children to be offered the truth.

Notes

NOTE ON CITATION TO COURT DOCUMENTS AND TRANSCRIPTS

Court documents from *González v. Douglas*, No. 4:10-cv-623-AWT will be referenced by an ECF number, assigned automatically by the Electronic Court Filing system. Testimony from the 2017 trial in that case will be on trial day and page. Testimony from the 2012 administrative hearings In the Matter of the Hearing of an Appeal By: Tucson Unified School District No. 1, No. 11F-002-ADE, will reference the date, morning/afternoon session, and page.

PROLOGUE

1. Eddie S. Glaude Jr, *Begin Again: James Baldwin's America and Its Urgent Lessons for Our Own* (New York: Crown, 2020).
2. Lucy Tompkins, "Here's What You Need to Know about Elijah McClain's Death," *New York Times*, October 19, 2021, www.nytimes.com/article/who-was-elijah-mcclain.html.
3. Information about each can be found here: Alia Chugtai, "Know Their Names: Black People Killed by the Police in the US," *Al Jazeera*, accessed March 1, 2024, https://interactive.aljazeera.com/aje/2020/know-their-names/index.html.
4. Katie Rogers, Lara Jakes, and Ana Swanson, "Trump Defends Using 'Chinese Virus' Label, Ignoring Growing Criticism," *New York Times*, March 18, 2021, www.nytimes.com/2020/03/18/us/politics/china-virus.html.
5. Sarah Schwartz, "Map: Where Critical Race Theory Is Under Attack," *Education Week*, last updated June 13, 2023, accessed March 1, 2024, www.edweek.org/policy-politics/map-where-critical-race-theory-is-under-attack/2021/06.
6. Nikki Haley (@NikkiHaley), "CRT Is Un-American," Twitter, January 30, 2023, https://twitter.com/NikkiHaley/status/1620062018832302080.
7. See, for example, Hannah Natanson, Clara Ence Morse, Anu Narayanswamy, and Christina Brause, "An Explosion of Culture War Laws Is Changing Schools. Here's How," *Washington Post*, October 18, 2022, www.washingtonpost.com/education/2022/10/18/education-laws-culture-war/.
8. Ray Bradbury, *Fahrenheit 451* (New York: Simon & Schuster ed., 2018).
9. *Arizona School Bds. Ass'n, Inc. v. State*, 501 P.3d 731, 734-35 (Ariz. 2022) (listing the challenged provisions: HB 2898, SB 1824, SB 1825, and SB 1819, combined and passed through a set of budget reconciliation bills).

10. Ibid, 741–742 (striking down all challenged statutes for violating the so-called "title" requirement and one, SB 1819 for violating the so-called "single subject rule").
11. Caitlin Sievers, "Hobbs Vetoes Bill That Banned 'Critical Race Theory' in Arizona Schools," *Arizona Mirror*, March 9, 2023, www.azmirror.com/blog/hobbs-vetoes-bill-that-banned-critical-race-theory-in-arizona-schools/.

1 OF COURSE, IT'S A DIFFERENT EDUCATION, THAT'S THE POINT

1. Trial Day 1 (Acosta testimony), 52.
2. Ibid, 52–54.
3. Ibid, 55–56.
4. Felipe A. Coronel, "Young Lords" [recorded by Immortal Technique]. On *The Martyr*. Viper Records, 2011.
5. Roberto "Cintli" Rodríguez, *Our Sacred Maíz Is Our Mother: Indigeneity and Belonging in the Americas* (Tucson, AZ: The University of Arizona Press, 2014).
6. Rodolfo "Corky" Gonzales, *Message to Aztlán: Selected Writings of Rodolfo "Corky" Gonzales* (Houston, TX: Arte Público Press, 2001); Otto Santa Ana, *Brown Tide Rising: Metaphors of Latinos in Contemporary American Political Discourse* (Austin, TX: University of Texas Press, 2002); Otto Santa Ana and Celeste González de Bustamante, eds., *Arizona Firestorm: Global Realities, National Media and Provincial Politics* (New York: Rowman & Littlefield, 2012).
7. Nolan L. Cabrera, Jeffrey F. Milem, Ozan Jaquette, and Ronald W. Marx. "Missing the (Student Achievement) Forest for All the (Political) Trees: Empiricism and the Mexican American Studies Controversy in Tucson," *American Educational Research Journal* 51, no. 6 (2014): 1084–1118.
8. See, for example, Julio Cammarota and Augustine F. Romero, eds., *Raza Studies: The Public Option for Educational Revolution* (Tucson, AZ: The University of Arizona Press, 2015).
9. Rodolfo A. Acuña, *The Making of Chicana/o Studies: In the Trenches of Academe* (New Brunswick, NJ: Rutgers University Press, 2011); Carlos Muñoz, *Youth, Identity, Power: The Chicano Movement* (New York: Verso, 1989); Fabio Rojas, *From Black Power to Black Studies: How a Radical Social Movement Became an Academic Discipline* (Baltimore, MD: Johns Hopkins University Press, 2007).
10. Gonzales, *Message to Aztlán*, 78.
11. Acuña, *Making of Chicana/o Studies*.
12. Juan Gomez-Quiñones, "To Leave to Hope or Chance: Propositions on Chicano Studies," *Parameters of Institutional Change: Chicano Experiences in Education* (Hayward, CA: Southwest Network, 1974): 153–166.
13. For the full text of *El Plan de Santa Bárbara*, please see http://mechadeucdavis.weebly.com/uploads/9/7/0/4/9704129/el_plan_de_santa_barbara.pdf
14. Ibid, 9–10.
15. Gomez-Quiñones, "To Leave to Hope or Chance."
16. Ronald Takaki, *A Different Mirror: A History of Multicultural America* (New York: Little, Brown and Company, 1993), 16–17.
17. Michael W. Apple, *Official Knowledge: Democratic Education in a Conservative Age*, 3rd ed. (New York: Routledge, 2014).
18. Takaki, *A Different Mirror*.
19. Rodolfo Acuña, *Assault on Mexican American Collective Memory, 2010–2015: Swimming with Sharks* (Lanham, MD: Lexington Books, 2017), 210.

20. Ibid.
21. Christine E. Sleeter, *The Academic and Social Value of Ethnic Studies: A Research Review* (Washington, DC: National Education Association, 2011); Richard R. Valencia, *The Evolution of Deficit Thinking: Educational Thought and Practice* (New York: Routledge, 2012).
22. Evelyn Hu-DeHart, "The History, Development, and Future of Ethnic Studies," *Phi Delta Kappan* 75, no. 1 (1993): 50–54, at 52.
23. Rojas, *Black Power*; Sleeter, *Value of Ethnic Studies*.
24. Ibid.
25. Tom Horne, "An Open Letter to the Citizens of Tucson, June 11, 2007," ECF 64-2, at 2.
26. See, for example, Eduardo Bonilla-Silva, *Racism without Racists: Color-Blind Racism and the Persistence of Racial Inequality in America* (New York: Rowman & Littlefield, 2016); Michael Omi and Howard Winant, *Racial Formation in the United States*, 3rd ed. (New York: Routledge, 2015).
27. Nolan L. Cabrera, *White Guys on Campus: Racism, White Immunity, and the Myth of "Post-Racial" Higher Education* (New Brunswick, NJ: Rutgers University Press, 2019).
28. Yoohyun Jung, "Ex-Schools Chief Huppenthal Unapologetic over TUSD's Ethnic Studies Program," *Arizona Daily Star*, June 27, 2017, https://tucson.com/news/local/education/ex-schools-chief-huppenthal-unapologetic-over-criticism-of-tusd-s/article_3c083457-04ba-583c-836a-193ea53621ae.html.
29. Cabrera, *White Guys*, 10.
30. Acuña, *Swimming with Sharks*; Rojas, *Black Power*; Sleeter, *Value of Ethnic Studies*.
31. *Brown v. Board of Education*, 347 U.S. 483 (1954).
32. Gary Orfield, Erica D. Frankenberg, and Chungmei Lee, "The Resurgence of School Segregation," *Educational Leadership* 60, no. 4 (2003): 16–20.
33. Darius V. Echeverría, *Aztlán Arizona: Mexican American Educational Empowerment, 1968–1978* (Tucson, AZ: The University of Arizona Press, 2014).
34. Martin Luther King Jr., *Why We Can't Wait* (New York: Signet Classics, 2000).
35. Echeverría, *Aztlán Arizona*, 19.
36. Ibid, 23.
37. Ibid, 43.
38. Acuña, *Making of Chicana/o Studies*.
39. Echeverría, *Aztlán Arizona*, 42.
40. Ibid.
41. See Trial Day 7 (Horne testimony), 28.
42. For an extended exploration student organizing, see Echeverría, *Aztlán Arizona*, chapters 3–5; Acuña, *Making of Chicana/o Studies*.
43. Curtis Acosta, "The Impact of Humanizing Pedagogies and Curriculum Upon the Identities, Civic Engagement, and Political Activism of Chican@ Youth" (doctoral dissertation, University of Arizona, 2015); Cammarota and Romero, *Raza Studies*.
44. Martín Sean Arce, "'They Tried to Bury Us, But They Didn't Know We Were Seeds'/'Trataron de Enterrarnos, Pero no Sabían Que Éramos Semillas' – The Mexican American/Raza Studies Political and Legal Struggle: A Content Analysis" (doctoral dissertation, University of Arizona, 2019); Conrado Gómez and Margarita Jiménez-Silva, "Mexican American Studies: The Historical Legitimacy of an Educational Program," *Association of Mexican American Educators Journal* 6, no. 1 (2012): 15–32.
45. Arce, "They Tried to Bury Us"; Gómez and Jiménez-Silva, "Mexican American Studies."
46. Gómez and Jiménez-Silva, "Mexican American Studies," 18.

47. Arce, "They Tried to Bury Us"; Gómez and Jiménez-Silva, "Mexican American Studies"; José Angel Gutiérrez, "The Chicano Movement: Paths to Power," *The Social Studies* 102, no. 1 (2012): 25–32.
48. Acosta, "Humanizing Pedagogy"; Arce, "They Tried to Bury Us"; Gómez and Jiménez-Silva, "Mexican American Studies"; Cammarota and Romero, *Raza Studies*.
49. Diane Ravitch, *The Death and Life of the Great American School System: How Testing and Choice Are Undermining Education* (New York: Basic Books, 2016).
50. Acosta, "Humanizing Pedagogy"; Cammarota and Romero, *Raza Studies*.
51. Cammarota and Romero, *Raza Studies*; Augustine Romero, Sean Arce, and Julio Cammarota, "A *Barrio* Pedagogy: Identity, Intellectualism, Activism, and Academic Achievement through the Evolution of Critically Compassionate Intellectualism," *Race Ethnicity and Education* 12, no. 2 (2009): 217–233; Acosta, "Humanizing Pedagogy"; Martín Sean Arce, "Xicana/o Indigenous Epistemologies: Towards a Decolonizing and Liberatory Education for Xicana/o Youth." In *"White" Washing American Education: The New Culture Wars in Ethnic Studies*, Denise M. Sandoval, Anthony J. Ratcliff, Tracy L. Buenavista, and James R. Marín, eds. (Santa Barbara, CA: Praeger, 2016), Vol. 1: 11–40; Arce, "They Tried to Bury Us"; Ravitch, *The Death and Life*.
52. Arce, "They Tried to Bury Us"; Cammarota and Romero, *Raza Studies*.
53. One of the most prominent examples of this rhetoric was Tom Horne's, "Open Letter."
54. Acuña, *Making of Chicana/o Studies*.
55. Ibid; Rojas, *Black Power*.
56. Acosta, "Humanizing Pedagogy"; Acuña, *Making of Chicana/o Studies*; Arce, "Xicana/o Indigenous Epistemologies"; Arce, "They Tried to Bury Us"; Cammarota and Romero, *Raza Studies*.
57. Gomez-Quiñones, "To Leave to Hope or Chance," 155.
58. Dee Hill Zuganelli, "Chicano Studies: Proliferation of the Discipline and the Formal Institutionalization of Community Engagement, 1965 to Present" (doctoral dissertation, University of Arizona, 2016).
59. Acuña, *Making of Chicana/o Studies*.
60. Muñoz, *Youth, Identity, Power*; Sleeter, *Value of Ethnic Studies*.
61. Gomez-Quiñones, "To Leave to Hope or Chance," 156.
62. Cammarota and Romero, *Raza Studies*; Muñoz, *Youth, Identity, Power*.
63. Zuganelli, "Chicano Studies."
64. Curtis Acosta and Asiya Mir, "Empowering Young People to Be Critical Thinkers: The Mexican American Studies Program in Tucson," *Voices in Urban Education* 34, no. Summer (2012): 15–26; Arce, "Xicana/o Indigenous Epistemologies"; Romero, Arce, and Cammarota, "A *Barrio* Pedagogy"; Romero and Cammarota, *Raza Studies*.
65. Romero, Arce, and Cammarota, "A *Barrio* Pedagogy."
66. Richard Delgado and Jean Stefancic, *Critical Race Theory: An Introduction*, 2nd ed. (New York: New York University Press, 2012).
67. Executive Order 13950 of September 22, 2020, Combating Race and Sex Stereotyping, www.federalregister.gov/documents/2020/09/28/2020-21534/combating-race-and-sex-stereotyping.
68. Executive Order 13985 of January 20, 2021, Advancing Racial Equity and Support for Underserved Communities Through the Federal Government, www.federalregister.gov/documents/2021/01/25/2021-01753/advancing-racial-equity-and-support-for-underserved-communities-through-the-federal-government.
69. Map: Where Critical Race Theory Is under Attack (June 11, 2021, updated November 9, 2021), www.edweek.org/policy-politics/map-where-critical-race-theory-is-under-attack/2021/06.

70. Cabrera, Milem, Jaquette, and Marx, "Missing the (Student Achievement) Forest."
71. ALJ Hearing Transcript, October 17, 2011, Morning Session, 11–15; Tom Horne, "Finding by the State Superintendent of Public Instruction of Violation by Tucson Unified School District Pursuant to A.R.S. 15-112(B)" (Phoenix, AZ: State of Arizona Department of Education, December 30, 2010).
72. Paulo Freire, *Pedagogy of the Oppressed*, 30th anniversary edition (New York: Herder and Herder, 2000); Paulo Freire, *Education for a Critical Consciousness* (New York: Continuum, 2008); Paulo Freire, *Pedagogy of Hope* (New York: Continuum, 2008); Paulo Freire and Donaldo Macedo, *Literacy: Reading the Word and the World* (Westport, CT: Bergin & Garvey, 1987).
73. Freire, *Pedagogy of the Oppressed*.
74. Horne, "Open Letter," 2.
75. See, for example, Liam Julian, "'Raza Studies' Defy American Values," *CBS News*, July 2, 2008, www.cbsnews.com/news/raza-studies-defy-american-values/.
76. Horne, "Open Letter."
77. Peter McLaren, *Che Guevara, Paulo Freire, and the Pedagogy of Revolution* (Lanham, MD: Rowman & Littlefield, 2000).
78. Freire, *Pedagogy of the Oppressed*.
79. McLaren, *Pedagogy of Revolution*.
80. Cammarota and Romero, *Raza Studies*.
81. Lemons, "White Lies," *Phoenix New Times*, May 12, 2011, www.phoenixnewtimes.com/news/ethnic-studies-equals-politically-conscious-latino-students-which-is-exactly-why-its-enemies-want-to-kill-it-6448734.
82. Cammarota and Romero, *Raza Studies*; McLaren, *Pedagogy of Revolution*.
83. Nolan L. Cabrera, Elisa L. Meza, and Roberto "Cintli" Rodríguez, "The Fight for Ethnic Studies in Tucson," *North American Congress on Latin America's Report on the Americas* 44, no. 6 (2011): 20–24; Anita Fernández and Zoe Hammer, "Red Scare in the Red State: The Attack on Mexican-American Studies in Arizona and Opportunities for Building National Solidarity," *Association of Mexican American Educators Journal* 6, no. 1 (2012): 65–70; Lemons, "White Lies."
84. R. Tolteka Cuautin, Miguel Zavala, Christine Sleeter, and Wayne Au, eds., *Rethinking Ethnic Studies* (Milwaukee, WI: Rethinking Schools, 2019); Muñoz, *Youth, Identity, Power*; Rojas, *Black Power*.
85. Three Sonorans, "MAS Trial Week 2: Tom Horne Still Hates Ethnic Studies, Scholars Destroy State Attorney's Attempt to Defend MAS Ban," *Medium*, July 19, 2017, https://medium.com/tson-news-by-three-sonorans/mas-trial-week-2-tom-horne-still-hates-ethnic-studies-scholars-destroy-state-attorneys-attempt-31ac618c5225.
86. Sleeter, *Value of Ethnic Studies*.
87. The different assessments prior to Cabrera's included: David F. Cappellucci, Christina Williams, Jeffrey J. Hernandez, Luanne P. Nelson, Teri Casteel, Glenton Gilzean, and Gershon Faulkner, "Curriculum Audit of the Mexican American Studies Department, Tucson Unified School District" (Miami Lakes, FL: Cambium Learning, 2011); Department of Accountability and Research, "AIMS Achievement Comparison for Students Taking One or More Ethnic Studies Classes: Initial Passing Rate Versus Cumulative Passing Rate by AIMS Subject and Cohort Year" (Tucson, AZ: Tucson Unified School District, January 6, 2011); Department of Accountability and Research, "Selected Statistics – 2010 (Four Year) Graduation Cohort" (Tucson, AZ: Tucson Unified School District, January 6, 2011); Augustine F. Romero, "Towards a Critically Compassionate Intellectualism Model of Transformative Education: Love, Hope, Identity,

and Organic Intellectualism Through the Convergence of Critical Race Theory, Critical Pedagogy, and Authentic Caring" (doctoral dissertation, University of Arizona, 2008); Romero, Arce, and Cammarota, "A *Barrio* Pedagogy"; Save Ethnic Studies, "Analysis and Evaluation of Mexican American Studies Student AIMS & Graduation Outcome Data That Was Produced by TUSD Director of Accountability & Research – David Scott and Misrepresented by Alexis Huicochea in Her March 13, 2011 *Arizona Daily Star Report* 'Ethnic Studies Claim in Question'," (2011) (on file with Cabrera).
88. For a sample of the studies that were critiqued, see Cappellucci et al., "Cambium Audit"; Nolan L. Cabrera, "Lies, Damn Lies, and Statistics: The Impact of Mexican American Studies Classes." In Cammarota and Romero, *Raza Studies*: 40–51; Department of Accountability and Research, "AIMS Achievement Comparison; Department of Accountability and Research, Selected Statistics – 2010."
89. *Precious Knowledge*, directed by Ari Palos (United States: Dos Vatos Films, 2011): 24:00.
90. Ibid, 55:45.
91. Robert Franciosi, "The Effect of Tucson Unified Ethnic ('Raza') Studies on Student Achievement" (Phoenix, AZ: Arizona Department of Education, October 22, 2009).
92. David Scott of TUSD's Department of Accountability and Research were reported in news outlets such as Alexis Huicochea, "Ethnic Studies Claims in Question," *Arizona Daily Star*, March 15, 2011, http://azstarnet.com/news/local/education/ethnic-studies-claim-in-question/article_c316a3d0-7ff5-5f87-874e-6b7cf3b515f3.html. However, the full results were not as publicly available as the previous analyses.
93. Curtis Acosta, "Huitzilopochtli: The Will and Resiliency of Tucson Youth to Keep Mexican American Studies Alive," *Multicultural Perspectives* 16, no. 1 (2014): 3–7.
94. Acuña, *Swimming with Sharks*; Nolan L. Cabrera, "A State-Mandated Epistemology of Ignorance: Arizona's HB2281 and Mexican American/Raza Studies," *Journal of Curriculum and Pedagogy* 9, no. 2 (2012): 132–135.
95. Mario T. García and Sal Castro, *Blowout!: Sal Castro and the Chicano Struggle for Educational Justice* (Chapel Hill, NC: University of North Carolina Press, 2011).
96. Acuña, *The Making of Chicano Studies*; Cammarota and Romero, *Raza Studies*.
97. Cyrus E. Zirakzadeh, *Social Movements in Politics: A Comparative Study*, expanded ed. (Berlin, Germany: Springer, 2006).

2 THE BROWN SCARE

1. Derrick A. Bell, "Who's Afraid of Critical Race Theory?" *University of Illinois Law Review* 1995, no. 4 (1995): 893–910.
2. Ibid, 895.
3. Ibid, 908 (discussing Randall L. Kennedy, "Racial Critiques of Legal Academia," *Harvard Law Review* 102, no. 8 (1989): 1745–1819).
4. Hannah Natanson, "'Slavery Was Wrong' and 5 Other Things Some Educators Won't Teach Anymore," *Washington Post*, March 6, 2023, www.washingtonpost.com/education/2023/03/06/slavery-was-wrong-5-other-things-educators-wont-teach-anymore/.
5. Otto Santa Ana and Celeste González de Bustamante, eds., *Arizona Firestorm*.
6. Other states which passed laws like SB 1070 included: Utah, Georgia, Indiana, Alabama, and South Carolina, www.nilc.org/issues/immigration-enforcement/sb-1070-lessons-learned/
7. Prohibited Courses and Classes, Enforcement, A.R.S. §15-112. (2010).
8. Anna O'Leary, Andrea J. Romero, Nolan L. Cabrera, and Michelle Rascon, "Assault on Ethnic Studies," in Santa Ana and González de Bustamante, *Arizona Firestorm*: 97–120.
9. Bell, "Who's Afraid," 1995: 893.

10. Edward S. Herman and Noam Chomsky, *Manufacturing Consent: The Political Economy of the Mass Media* (New York: Random House, 2010).
11. Ibram X. Kendi, *Stamped From the Beginning: The Definitive History of Racist Ideas in America* (New York: Nation Books, 2016).
12. Ibid.
13. Alfonso Gonzales, *Reform Without Justice: Latino Migrant Politics and the Homeland Security State* (Oxford: Oxford University Press, 2013).
14. Ibid.
15. O'Leary, Romero, Cabrera, and Rascon, "Assault on Ethnic Studies."
16. See, for example, Eric Sagara, "'Hate-speak' at School Draws Scrutiny," *Tucson Citizen*, April 13, 2006, http://tucsoncitizen.com/morgue/2006/04/13/9256-hate-speak-at-school-draws-scrutiny/.
17. Jeff Commings, "Silent Protest By Students Greets State Official's Speech," *Arizona Daily Star*, May 13, 2006, http://tucson.com/news/local/education/precollegiate/silent-protest-by-students-greets-state-official-s-speech/article_0132cca7-c8a3-53f6-b001-883faoca86ao.html.
18. Horne, "Open Letter."
19. Ernesto Portillo, Jr., "Neto's Tucson: The Vindication of Dolores Huerta," *Arizona Daily Star*, September 30, 2017, http://tucson.com/news/local/neto-s-tucson-the-vindication-of-dolores-huerta/article_feb39962-9157-57cc-8a27-941e0130fe57.html.
20. Trial Day 7, 32–33.
21. Trial Day 7, 162.
22. Lindsay Perez-Huber, Corina B. Lopez, Maria C. Malagon, Veronica Velez, and Daniel G. Solórzano, "Getting Beyond the 'Symptom,' Acknowledging the 'Disease': Theorizing Racist Nativism," *Contemporary Justice Review* 11, no. 1 (2008): 39–51.
23. Ian Haney López, *Dog Whistle Politics: How Coded Racial Appeals Have Reinvented Racism and Wrecked the Middle Class* (Oxford: Oxford University Press, 2015).
24. Tom Horne, "Open Letter," 1.
25. Michael E. Dyson, *I May Not Get There with You: The True Martin Luther King, Jr.* (New York: Simon and Schuster, 2000).
26. Cornel West, ed., *The Radical King* (Boston: Beacon, 2015).
27. Ibid, 3.
28. Coleman Hughes, *The End of Race Politics: Arguments for a Colorblind America* (New York: Thesis, 2024).
29. Dinesh D'Souza, *The End of Racism: Finding Values in An Age of Technoaffluence* (New York: Free Press, 1996).
30. Anderson Cooper, "Ethnic Studies Ban Racist?," *CNN*, May 13, 2010, video, www.youtube.com/watch?v=TgvOdD5bVsg.
31. Three Sonorans, "Tom Horne-Richard Martinez – Ethnic Studies Debate Part 1/5," March 22, 2011 video, www.youtube.com/watch?v=Itomw_bAhXg.
32. Ibid, 10:20.
33. Three Sonorans, "Tom Horne-Richard Martinez – Ethnic Studies Debate Part 2/5," March 22, 2011, video, www.youtube.com/watch?v=1LimMi3yZ94: 5:49.
34. Trial Day 3, 218.
35. Ibid.
36. Trial Day 7, 5–6.
37. John Ward, "Raza Studies Gives Rise to Racial Hostility," *Tucson Citizen*, May 21, 2008, www.amren.com/news/2008/05/raza_studies_gi/.
38. Ibid.

39. Rodolfo F. Acuña, *Occupied America: A History of Chicanos*, 3rd ed. (New York: Harper & Row, 1988); Vilma Ortiz and Eddie Telles, "Racial Identity and Racial Treatment of Mexican Americans," *Race and Social Problems* 4, no. 1 (2012): 41–56; Richard R. Valencia, *The Evolution of Deficit Thinking: Educational Thought and Practice* (New York: Routledge, 2012).
40. Kathryn Neckerman, ed., *Social Inequality* (New York: Russell Sage Foundation, 2004).
41. Valencia, *Evolution of Deficit Thinking*, 133.
42. Alexis Huicochea, "Former TUSD Teacher's Mexican American Studies Suit Dismissed," *Arizona Daily Star*, February 13, 2013, https://tucson.com/news/local/education/precollegiate/former-tusd-teacher-s-mexican-american-studies-suit-dismissed/article_d1d2dd2d-9e73-503a-b3af-54cbacc7e253.html.
43. Ward, "Raza Studies."
44. Cabrera, "State-Mandated Epistemology."
45. Huicochea, "Former TUSD."
46. Mari Herreras, "Bring Knives to TUSD Board Meetings, Leave Civil Disobedience at Home," *Tucson Weekly*, August 11, 2011, www.tucsonweekly.com/TheRange/archives/2011/08/11/bring-knives-to-tusd-board-meetings-leave-civil-disobedience-at-home.
47. Horne, "Open Letter," 3.
48. Doug MacEachern, "Smoke and Mirrors Obscure Raza Studies," *Arizona Republic*, August 17, 2008, V.3.
49. Doug MacEachern, "Secretive *Raza* Studies in Tucson Needs a Close Look," *Arizona Republic*, January 20, 2008, V.1.
50. Doug MacEachern, "Ethnic Studies in Tucson Schools Make Latinos See Themselves as Victims," *Arizona Republic*, June 6, 2010, B.11.
51. MacEachern, "Smoke and Mirrors."
52. See, for example: Doug MacEachern, "Bogus Arguments for Tucson Ethnic Studies Finally Debunked," *Arizona Republic*, March 6, 2011, B.11; Doug MacEachern, "Judge's Ruling on Ethnic Studies in Tucson Validates All Criticism," *Arizona Republic*, January 8, 2012, B.10; Doug MacEachern, "A Bit of Leftist Engineering in Tucson Expensive," *Arizona Republic*, February 10, 2013, B.10.
53. Tusconans United for Sound Districts, *Facebook*, www.facebook.com/TU4SD/.
54. M. Perez, "Loretta Hunnicutt, Glenn Beck Explore Indoctrination in TUSD Schools," *Arizona Daily Independent*, May 13, 2011, https://arizonadailyindependent.com/2011/05/13/loretta-hunnicutt-glenn-beck-explore-indoctrination-in-tusd-schools/.
55. Dan Gibson, "Jon Justice, Our Own Mini-Rush Limbaugh," *Tucson Weekly*, March 6, 2012, www.tucsonweekly.com/TheRange/archives/2012/03/06/jon-justice-our-own-mini-rush-limbaugh.
56. Steve Lemons, "White Lies," *Phoenix News Times*, May 12, 2011, www.phoenixnewtimes.com/news/ethnic-studies-equals-politically-conscious-latino-students-which-is-exactly-why-its-enemies-want-to-kill-it-6448734.
57. Jon Justice, "Welcome to the New Year," *My Nerd World with Jon Justice*, January 1, 2012, video (4:10) www.youtube.com/watch?v=_YPl8vhOZkc.
58. Ibid, 4:45.
59. Ibid, 3:40.
60. José Vasconcelos, *The Cosmic Race/La Raza Cósmica*, trans. Didier T. Jaén (Baltimore, MD: Johns Hopkins University Press, 1997).
61. Gonzales, *Message to Aztlán*.
62. Horne, "Open Letter," 1–3.
63. Haney López, *Dog Whistle Politics*.

Notes to Pages 27–34

64. Christina G. López, "No, Conservative Media, That's Not What 'La Raza' Means in Spanish." *Media Matters*, June 7, 2016, www.mediamatters.org/sean-hannity/no-conservative-media-thats-not-what-la-raza-means-spanish.
65. López, "No, Conservative Media."
66. Michael W. Apple, *Official Knowledge: Democratic Education in a Conservative Age* (New York: Routledge, 2014); Nolan L. Cabrera and Chris Corces-Zimmerman, "Beyond Privilege: Whiteness as the Center of Racial Marginalization." In *Marginality in the Urban Center: Costs and Challenges of Continued Whiteness in the Americas (and Beyond)*, eds. Peary Brug, Zachary S. Ritter, and Kenneth R. Roth (New York: Palgrave Macmillan, 2019): 13–29.
67. *New State Ice Co. v. Liebmann*, 285 US 262 (1932).
68. Otto Santa Ana, *Brown Tide Rising*, 69.
69. James King, "Jon Stewart Calls Arizona 'The Meth Lab of Democracy' in Response to Trifecta of Wild West Legislation," *Phoenix News Times*, April 27, 2010, www.phoenixnewtimes.com/news/jon-stewart-calls-arizona-the-meth-lab-of-democracy-in-response-to-trifecta-of-wild-west-legislation-6635528.
70. Cabrera, Meza, and Rodríguez, "The Fight for Ethnic Studies."
71. Kendi, *Stamped*, 505.
72. Santa Ana, *Brown Tide Rising*, 69.

3 THEY TRIED TO BURY US, BUT THEY FORGOT WE WERE SEEDS

1. Immortal Technique, One (Remix), Revolutionary Vol. 2 (2003).
2. Acuña, *Making of Chicana/o Studies*; Martha Biondi, *The Black Revolution on Campus* (Berkeley, CA: University of California Press, 2012); Gomez-Quiñones, "To Leave to Hope or Chance"; Muñoz, *Youth, Identity, Power*.
3. Complaint, *Acosta et al. v. Horne*, No. 4:10-623-TUC-JMR, October 18, 2010, ECF 1 (D. Ariz., 2010).
4. Three Sonorans, "HB2281 Lawsuit–Lawyer Richard Martinez," *Three Sonoran News*, October 18, 2010, video (0:30), www.youtube.com/watch?v=lbRHZr5kjF8.
5. Alexis Huicochea, "Educators Sue Over Ethnic-Studies Law," *Arizona Daily Star*, October 19, 2010, https://tucson.com/news/local/education/educators-sue-over-ethnic-studies-law/article_30117283-166a-5257-b199-3884edde947c.html.
6. Three Sonorans, "HB2281 Lawsuit," 2:00.
7. Ibid, 5:15.
8. Ibid, 6:15.
9. Three Sonorans, "HB2281 Lawsuit – Students," *Three Sonoran News*, October 18, 2010, video (0:33), www.youtube.com/watch?v=-1sIOwLDZ84.
10. Ibid, 0:54.
11. Ibid, 1:20.
12. Three Sonorans, "Acuña Reception," *Three Sonoran News*, June 7, 2010, video, www.youtube.com/watch?v=JQ9zv1edRRQ.
13. "American Educational Research Association Responds to Suspension of Mexican American Studies in Tucson," *American Educational Research Association*, February 23, 2012, www.aera.net/Newsroom/AERA-Highlights-E-newsletter/AERA-Highlights-Archival-Issues/AERA-Highlights-February-2012/AERA-Responds-to-Suspension/Suspension-of-Mexican-American-Studies.

14. Ibid.
15. "Statement on Tucson Mexican American Studies Program," *Modern Language Association*, February 2012, www.mla.org/About-Us/Governance/Executive-Council/Executive-Council-Actions/2012/Statement-on-Tucson-Mexican-American-Studies-Program.
16. Proposed Amici Curiae Brief of the National Association of Chicana and Chicano Studies et al., at 2, CV 10-623-TUC-AWT (D. Ariz. March 8, 2013), ECF 181-1.
17. Lalo Alcaraz, interview with Nolan Cabrera, January 22, 2020 (on file with Cabrera): 7:23.
18. Ibid, 8:44.
19. Ibid, 8:40.
20. Santa Ana and González de Bustamante, eds., *Arizona Firestorm*.
21. Lalo Alcaraz interview, 14:12.
22. Ibid, 14:49.
23. Bill Moyers, "Between Two Worlds – Life on the Border," *Moyers & Company*, May 4, 2012, video, https://vimeo.com/41540037.
24. Ibid, 28:05.
25. Ibid, 28:25.
26. Ibid, 28:33.
27. Acuña, *Swimming With Sharks*; Jeff Biggers, *State Out of the Union: Arizona and the Final Showdown Over the American Dream* (New York: Nation Books, 2012).
28. Moyers, "Between Two Worlds," 29:25.
29. Ibid, 30:09.
30. Ibid, 30:30.
31. For an elaboration of this argument, see, for example, R. Tolteka Cuautin, Miguel Zavala, Christine Sleeter, and Wayne Au, eds. *Rethinking Ethnic Studies* (Milwaukee, WI: Rethinking Schools, 2019).
32. Marisa Bernal, "Ozomatli Performs for a Cause at Save Ethnic Studies Concert," *Arizona Daily Star*, February 16, 2012, https://tucson.com/entertainment/music/ozomatli-performs-for-a-cause-at-save-ethnic-studies-concert/article_2164c281-9295-5893-89f5-ad5e79fdda27.html.
33. Ulises Bella, interview with Nolan Cabrera, January 28, 2020 (on file with Cabrera), 7:29.
34. Bernal, February 16, 2012.
35. Bella interview, 5:29.
36. Ibid, 9:30.
37. Mari Herreras, "A Documentary on TUSD Ethnic-Studies Program Gets Its Tucson Premiere," *Tucson Weekly*, March 24, 2011, www.tucsonweekly.com/tucson/classroom-battle/Content?oid=2620701.
38. MalintZINE, "Girl Code, Responsibility, Accountability and In Lak Ech," *MalintZINE*, March 22, 2013, https://malintzine.wordpress.com/2013/03/22/girl-code-responsibility-accountability-and-in-lak-ech/.
39. Devin Boone, "My Other Me: A Community Saves Mexican American Studies. Can Mexican American Studies Save a Community?" *Medium*, November 16, 2018, https://medium.com/@devinelizabeth/my-other-me-f9a128281116; originally published as Devin Browne, Boone is now Browne's married name.
40. Boone, "My Other Me."
41. Ibid.
42. Ibid.
43. MalintZINE, "Girl Code."

44. Devon G. Peña, "Arizona Update: HB2281 and Beyond – Four Documents," *mexmigration* (blog), http://mexmigration.blogspot.com/2013/03/arizona-update-hb2281-and-beyond-four.html.
45. Maylei Blackwell, *¡Chicana power!: Contested Histories of Feminism in the Chicano Movement* (Austin, TX: University of Texas Press, 2011).
46. Boone, "My Other Me."

4 UNIDOS, THE STUDENT MOVEMENT, CONSPIRACY THEORIES, AND MILITARIZED SCHOOL BOARD MEETINGS

1. Alexis Huicochea, "TUSD Argues for Appeal of Horne Finding," *Arizona Daily Star*, January 22, 2011, https://tucson.com/news/local/education/tusd-argues-for-appeal-of-horne-finding/article_6efc75fe-5ff3-59e8-908f-a1217db8ab5a.html.
2. Ibid.
3. September 30, 2011 draft of Nolan L. Cabrera, Elisa L. Meza, and Roberto "Cintli" Rodríguez, "The Fight for Ethnic Studies in Tucson," *North American Congress on Latin America's Report on the Americas* 44, no. 6 (2011): 20–24.
4. Cabrera, Meza, and Rodríguez, "Fight for Ethnic Studies."
5. Curtis Acosta and Asiya Mir, "Empowering Young People to be Critical Thinkers: The Mexican American Studies Program in Tucson," *Voices in Urban Education* 34, no. Summer (2012): 15–26.
6. Cabrera, Meza, and Rodríguez, "Fight for Ethnic Studies."
7. Ibid.
8. Ibid, 24.
9. Mari Herreras, "Expect Empty Seats at Tonight's TUSD Governing Board Meeting," *Tucson Weekly*, April 12, 2011, www.tucsonweekly.com/TheRange/archives/2011/04/12/expect-empty-seats-at-tonights-tusd-governing-board-meeting.
10. Mark Stegeman, *Resolution Concerning the Scope and Structure of TUSD's Ethnic Studies Programs and Maintaining Political Balance in the Classrooms* (Tucson, AZ: Tucson Unified School District, April 26, 2011).
11. Devin Boone, "My Other Me: A Community Saves Mexican American Studies. Can Mexican American Studies Save a Community?" *Medium*, November 16, 2018, https://medium.com/@devinelizabeth/my-other-me-f9a128281116.
12. See, for example, Tom Horne's statement on this component of the issue here: Tom Horne, *Finding by the State Superintendent of Public Instruction of Violation by Tucson Unified School District Pursuant to A.R.S. 15–112(B)* (Phoenix, AZ: State of Arizona Department of Education, 2010).
13. Mark Stegeman, "TUSD President Stegeman Offers Perspective on Mexican American Studies Debate," *Tucson Citizen*, June 15, 2011.
14. Mari Herreras, "Ethnic Studies Resolution Hardly a Solution," *Tucson Weekly*, April 23, 2011, www.tucsonweekly.com/TheRange/archives/2011/04/23/ethnic-studies-resolution-hardly-a-solution.
15. The recounting of this action stems from Cabrera being present at the time of the takeover. We write in the third person because it is confusing given both of our firsthand knowledge to shift between first and third person narrative throughout this book.
16. Cabrera, Meza, and Rodríguez, "Fight for Ethnic Studies."
17. Ibid.
18. Alexis Huicochea, "Ethnic Studies Supporters Overtake TUSD Meeting: Youths Protest Changes to Mexican American Studies Courses," *Arizona Daily Star*, April 27, 2011,

https://tucson.com/news/local/education/ethnic-studies-supporters-overtake-tusd-meeting/article_176f8aed-4b95-53fc-9b49-0959cd5a26e5.html.
19. Arizona Republic, "Who's in Charge at Tucson Unified?" *Arizona Republic*, April 28, 2011, www.azcentral.com/arizonarepublic/opinions/articles/2011/04/28/20110428thur1-28.html
20. Media Matters Staff, "Beck Fearmongers Again about Arizona School's Ethnic Studies Program," *Media Matters for America*, May 5, 2011, www.mediamatters.org/video/2011/05/05/beck-fearmongers-again-about-arizona-schools-et/179379.
21. Cabrera, Meza, and Rodríguez, "Fight for Ethnic Studies."
22. John Pedicone, "Adults Used Students as Pawns in the TUSD Ethnic Studies Protest," *Arizona Daily Star*, May 1, 2011, https://tucson.com/news/opinion/adults-used-students-as-pawns-in-tusd-ethnic-studies-protest/article_26542dfa-7d79-5682-85d5-7aaed9947ac8.html.
23. Ibid.
24. Ibid.
25. Mari Herreras, "Violent Messages: A Professor at the UA Is Threatened after People Opposed to TUSD's Ethnic Studies Names Him on a Video," *Tucson Weekly*, July 7, 2011, www.tucsonweekly.com/tucson/violent-messages/Content?oid=3081080.
26. Mari Herreras, "Violent Messages."
27. Ibid.
28. Nolan L. Cabrera, Jeffrey F. Milem, Ozan Jaquette, and Ronald W. Marx. "Missing the (Student Achievement) Forest for All the (Political) Trees: Empiricism and the Mexican American Studies Controversy in Tucson," *American Educational Research Journal* 51, no. 6 (2014): 1084–1118.
29. Ibid.
30. Ibid.
31. Stephen Lemons, "Doug MacEachern Goes Off Deep End in Ward Churchill Email Exchange," *Phoenix New Times*, May 18, 2011, www.phoenixnewtimes.com/news/doug-maceachern-goes-off-deep-end-in-ward-churchill-email-exchange-6503034.
32. Ward Churchill, "'Some People Push Back': On the Justice of Roosting Chickens," September 12, 2001, https://theanarchistlibrary.org/library/ward-churchill-some-people-push-back-on-the-justice-of-roosting-chickens.
33. Jonathan Shikes, "Glen Beck Calls Out Ward Churchill Who Appears at an Arizona Protest (Video)," *Westword*, May 13, 2011, www.westword.com/news/glenn-beck-calls-out-ward-churchill-who-appears-at-an-arizona-protest-video-5908390.
34. Peter Dreier, "Community Organizers: Thank you, Sarah Palin," *Huffington Post*, September 26, 2008, www.huffingtonpost.com/peter-dreier/palin-attacks-on-communit_b_129568.html.
35. Shikes, "Glen Beck Calls Out Ward Churchill."
36. Ibid.
37. Ibid.
38. Lemons, "MacEachern Goes Off Deep End."
39. See, for example, ibid.
40. Richard Delgado, "Storytelling for Oppositionists and Others: A Plea for Narrative," *Michigan Law Review* 87, no. 8 (1989): 2411–2441.
41. Nolan L. Cabrera, Elisa L. Meza, Andrea J. Romero, and Roberto "Cintli" Rodríguez, "'If There Is No Struggle, There Is No Progress': Transformative Youth Resistance and the School of Ethnic Studies," *Urban Review* 45, no. 1 (2013): 7–22; Daniel Solorzano and Tara Yosso, "Critical Race and LatCrit Theory and Method: Counter Storytelling Chicana and Chicano Graduate School Experiences," *International Journal of*

Qualitative Studies in Education 14, no. 4 (2001): 471–495; Octavio Villalpando, "Self-Segregation or Self-Preservation? A Critical Race Theory and Latina/o Critical Theory Analysis of a Study of Chicana/o College Students," *Qualitative Studies in Education* 16, no. 5 (2003): 619–646.
42. Cabrera, Meza, and Rodríguez, "Fight for Ethnic Studies."
43. Cabrera, Milem, Jaquette, and Marx, "Missing the (Student Achievement) Forest."
44. Cabrera, Meza, and Rodríguez, "Fight for Ethnic Studies."
45. *Three Sonorans*, "Mark Stegeman vs MAS Student Angelica Peñaran," *Three Sonoran News*, April 26, 2011, video (0:15), www.youtube.com/watch?v=5X0HYpDun2w.
46. Cabrera, Meza, and Rodríguez, "Fight for Ethnic Studies," 24.
47. Ibid.
48. Ibid.
49. Carmen Duarte, "Problems Must Be Talked Out, 300 Youths Told," *Arizona Daily Star*, April 29, 2011, https://tucson.com/news/local/education/teen-town-hall-focuses-on-tusd-protest/article_03bda998-46da-500b-993d-c9346cb0069c.html.
50. Ibid.
51. Ibid.
52. Mari Herreras, "Open Letter from Mark Stegeman," *Tucson Weekly*, April 29, 2011, www.tucsonweekly.com/TheRange/archives/2011/04/29/open-letter-from-mark-stegeman.
53. Duarte, "Problems Must Be Talked Out."
54. Miguel Cuevas, "Proposed Changes Won't Harm Program: Guest Opinion By TUSD Board Member Miguel Cuevas," *Arizona Daily Star*, May 3, 2011, https://tucson.com/news/opinion/proposed-changes-won-t-harm-program/article_19b4f1db-da4f-5293-925f-81880e3e2ee0.html; Alexis Huicochea, "TUSD Meets for 4 Hours Amid Big Crowd, 100 Police," *Arizona Daily Star*, May 4, 2011, https://tucson.com/news/local/education/precollegiate/article_280abcc6-c923-5da4-9700-4eced2e105be.html?mode=video; Stephen Lemons, "Tucson Unified School District's Tuesday Night Debacle," *Phoenix New Times*, May 4, 2011, www.phoenixnewtimes.com/news/tucson-unified-school-districts-tuesday-night-debacle-6502625.
55. Huicochea, "TUSD Meets for 4 Hours"; Lemons, "Tuesday Night Debacle." The sheer magnitude of the police presence at this meeting and the chaos that ensued are very difficult to capture via the written word. For readers who would like a detailed, first-hand account of how these events unfolded, please visit: *Three Sonorans*, "The TUSD Tragedy – Save Ethnic Studies," video, https://vimeo.com/23516724.
56. Mari Herreras, "Tucsonans Prepare for John Huppenthal's Ethnic-Studies Decision," *Tucson Weekly*, June 9, 2011, www.tucsonweekly.com/tucson/talking-it-over/Content?oid=2983845.
57. Gabe M. Schivone, "Tucson's High-Profile Battle Over Censorship in Its Largest School District Didn't Begin with the Now-Infamous AZ Ban on Mexican-American Studies (MAS)," *The Nation*, May 8, 2012, www.thenation.com/article/tucsons-history-school-censorship/.
58. Mari Herreras, "Last Night's TUSD Ethnic Studies Resolution Meeting Gets an F," *Tucson Weekly*, May 4, 2011, www.tucsonweekly.com/TheRange/archives/2011/05/04/last-nights-tusd-ethnic-studies-resolution-meeting-gets-an-f.
59. Ibid.
60. *Three Sonorans*, "The TUSD Tragedy–Save Ethnic Studies," *Vimeo*, May 9, 2011, video (23:08), https://vimeo.com/23516724.
61. KOLD, "TUSD Board Postpones Vote on Ethnic Studies Issue," *Tucson News Now*, May 3, 2011, www.tucsonnewsnow.com/story/14566801/overflow-crowd-shows-up-for-tusd-ethnic-studies-meeting.

62. Herreras, "Tucsonans Prepare."
63. Huicochea, "TUSD Meets for 4 Hours."
64. *Three Sonorans,* "TUSD Tragedy," 24:18.
65. Ibid, 25:35.
66. Herreras, "Meeting Gets an F."
67. Ibid.
68. Ibid.
69. Huicochea, "TUSD Meets for 4 Hours."
70. Ibid.
71. *Three Sonorans,* "TUSD Tragedy," 31:50.
72. Huicochea, "TUSD Meets for 4 Hours."
73. *Three Sonorans,* "TUSD Tragedy," 34:45.
74. Ibid, 36:21.
75. Huicochea, "TUSD Meets for 4 Hours."
76. This was a quotation heard from the author Cabrera while he was in a human chain around 1010. It was heard by others in the chain and documented in his notes about the night.
77. *Three Sonorans,* "TUSD Tragedy," 42:30.
78. Herreras, "Tusconans Prepare."
79. Huicochea, "TUSD Meets for 4 Hours."
80. Cabrera, Meza, and Rodríguez, "Fight for Ethnic Studies," 24.

5 WAS THE FIX IN?

1. *González v. Douglas,* 269 F. Supp. 3d 948, 960 (D. Ariz. 2017).
2. *Minor v. Cochise County,* 125 Ariz. 170, 172, 608 P.2d 309, 311 (1980).
3. Ibid; See also *Estate of Bohn v. Waddell,* 174 Ariz. 239, 248, 848 P.2d 324, 333 (Ct. App. Ariz. 1992) (citing Minor).
4. Letter from Deconcini law firm to Huppenthal, 6 ER at 1085–1091.
5. In the Matter of the Hearing of an Appeal By: Tucson Unified School District No. 1, No. 11F-002-ADE, December 27, 2011, 35, 19 [ALJ Decision].
6. Arizona R. Sup. Ct. ER 1.5(a).
7. Stephen Ceasar, "Tucson Ethnic-Studies Program Violates Arizona Law, Judge Says," *Los Angeles Times,* December 27, 2011, https://latimesblogs.latimes.com/nationnow/2011/12/arizona-tucson-ethnic-studies-.html.
8. A.R.S. §41-1092.08(B).
9. ALJ Decision.
10. ALJ Hearing Transcript, *González v. Douglas,* ECF 192, August 19, 2011, Morning Session (March 15, 2012), 110.
11. Gustavo Licón, "'¡La Unión Hace la Fuerza!'(Unity Creates strength!): M.E.Ch.A. and Chicana/o Student Activism in California, 1967–1999" (PhD dissertation, University of Southern California, 2009); Luis Valdez, *Zoot Suit and Other Plays* (Houston, TX: Arte Publico Press, 1992).
12. Larry Neal, "Ellison's Zoot Suit." In *Ralph Ellison: A Collection of Critical Essays,* John F. Callahan, ed. (New York: Oxford University Press, 2004): 81–108, 67 (quoting Ralph Ellison).
13. Acuña, *Occupied America*; Gustavo Licón, "¡La Unión."
14. Acuña, *Occupied America,* 238; Gerardo Licón, *Pachucas, Pachucos, and Their Culture: Mexican American Youth Culture of the Southwest, 1910–1955* (doctoral dissertation, University of Southern California, 2011).

15. ALJ Hearing Transcript, August 19, Afternoon Session, 121.
16. Ibid, 126–127.
17. Gustavo Licón, "¡La Unión," 21–68.
18. Acuña, *Occupied America*, 249; Gustavo Licón, "¡La Unión," 21–68.
19. Gustavo Licón, "¡La Unión," 155–204.
20. ALJ Hearing Transcript, August 19, Afternoon Session, 96–97.
21. Ibid, 97.
22. Ibid, 70–71.
23. Ibid, 77–78.
24. Kim H. Owens, "In Lak'Ech, the Chicano Clap, and Fear: A Partial Rhetorical Autopsy of Tucson's Now-Illegal Ethnic Studies Classes," *College English* 80, no. 3, (2018): 247–270.
25. Julio Cammarota and Augustine F. Romero, eds., *Raza Studies: The Public Option for Educational Revolution* (Tucson, AZ: The University of Arizona Press, 2015).
26. ALJ Hearing Transcript, August 19, Afternoon Session, 56.
27. Eric Hoffer, *The True Believer: Thoughts on the Nature of Mass Movements*, reprint ed. (New York: Harper Perennial, 2019).
28. Ibid, 17.
29. Nolan L. Cabrera, Cheryl E. Matias, and Roberto Montoya, "Slacktivism or Activism?: The Potential and Pitfalls of Social Media in Contemporary Student Activism," *Journal of Diversity in Higher Education* 10, no. 4 (2017): 400–415.
30. See, for example, Loretta Hunnicutt, "TUSD Appeal to Save 'Ethnic Studies' Reveals 'Cult,'" *Arizona Daily Independent*, August, 21, 2011, https://arizonadailyindependent.com/2011/08/21/tusd-appeal-to-save-ethnic-studies-reveals-cult/.
31. See Chapter 12 (discussing in detail trial testimony of Tom Horne and John Huppenthal).
32. Richard Delgado and Jean Stefancic, *Critical Race Theory: An Introduction*, 2nd ed. (New York: New York University Press, 2012); Daniel G. Solórazano and Tara Yosso, "Critical Race and LatCrit Theory and Method: Counter Storytelling Chicana and Chicano Graduate School Experiences," *International Journal of Qualitative Studies in Education* 14, no. 4 (2001): 471–495.
33. Nolan L. Cabrera, "Where Is the Racial Theory in Critical Race Theory?: A Constructive Criticism of the Crits," *Review of Higher Education* 42, no. 1 (2018): 209–233.
34. See, for example, Randall L. Kennedy, "Racial Critiques of Legal Academia," *Harvard Law Review*, 102, no. 8 (1989): 1745–1819; Daniel A. Farber and Suzanna Sherry, "Beyond All Criticism?" *Minnesota Law Review* 83, no. 6 (1999): 1735–1766.
35. Gloria Ladson-Billings, "Just What Is Critical Race Theory and What's It Doing in a Nice Field Like Education?" *International Journal of Qualitative Studies in Education* 11, no. 1, (1998): 7–24.
36. Ladson-Billings, "What Is Critical Race Theory."
37. David A. Graham, "Breitbart.com's Massive Barack Obama-Derrick Bell Fail," *The Atlantic*, March 8, 2012, www.theatlantic.com/politics/archive/2012/03/breitbartcoms-massive-barack-obama-derrick-bell-video-fail/254213/.
38. Ibid.
39. See, for example, Tom Horne, "An Open Letter to the Citizens of Tucson, June 11, 2007," ECF 64-2, at 2.
40. ALJ Hearing Transcript, December 14, 2011, Afternoon Proceedings, 12.
41. Gene V. Glass, "The strangest academic department in the world," *Education in Two Worlds* (blog), May 12, 2014, http://ed2worlds.blogspot.com/2014/05/the-strangest-academic-

department-in.html; George N. Schmidt, "Wal-Mart 'Scholars' at the University of Arkansas Prove, Once Again (Again!), That the Walton Family's Voucher and Pro-'Choice' Ideologies Are Beautiful Good and True...," *Substance News*, June 2, 2011, www.substancenews.net/articles.php?page=2305.

42. Diane Ravitch, *The Death and Life of the Great American School System: How Testing and Choice Are Undermining Education* (New York: Basic Books, 2016).
43. Department of Educational Reform, University of Arkansas, https://edre.uark.edu.
44. Sandra Stotsky, *Losing Our Language: How Multiculturalism Undermines Our Children's Ability to Read, Write, and Reason* (New York: The Free Press, 1999).
45. Ibid, 7.
46. ALJ Hearing Transcript, October 17, 2011, Morning Session, 33.
47. Ibid, 13.
48. This number was retrieved from Google Scholar on February 27, 2024: https://scholar.google.com/scholar?hl=en&as_sdt=0%2C3&q=Academic+guidelines+for+selecting+multiethnic+and+multicultural+literature&btnG=.
49. Gloria Ladson-Billings, "Toward a Theory of Culturally Relevant Pedagogy," *American Educational Research Journal* 32, no. 3 (1995): 465–491.
50. This number was retrieved from Google Scholar on February 27, 2024: https://scholar.google.com/scholar?hl=en&as_sdt=0%2C3&q=Toward+a+Theory+of+Culturally+Relevant+Pedagogy&btnG=.
51. ALJ Hearing Transcript, October 17, 2011, Morning Session, 20.
52. Ibid, 28–29.
53. ALJ Hearing Transcript, September 14, 2011, Morning Session, 42.
54. Acuña, *Occupied America*, 244–257.
55. Joe Berlinger, "Dave Chappelle and Maya Angelou," *Iconoclasts* (New York, NY: SundanceTV, 2006): 19:58.
56. Peter McLaren, *Che Guevara, Paulo Freire, and the Pedagogy of Revolution* (Lanham, MD: Rowman & Littlefield, 2000).
57. ALJ Hearing Transcript, October 17, 2011, Morning Session, 51–52.
58. Nolan L. Cabrera, *White Guys on Campus: Racism, White Immunity, and the Myth of "Post-Racial" Higher Education* (New Brunswick, NJ: Rutgers University Press, 2019).
59. ALJ Hearing Transcript, September 14, 2011, Morning Session, 58.
60. McLaren, *Pedagogy of Revolution*, 92.
61. Rodolfo Acuña, *Assault on Mexican American Collective Memory, 2010–2015: Swimming with Sharks* (Lanham, MD: Lexington Books, 2017), 210; Jeff Biggers, *State Out of the Union: Arizona and the Final Showdown Over the American Dream* (New York: Nation Books, 2012).
62. Acuña, *Assault on Mexican American Collective Memory*, 135–145; Anna O'Leary, Andrea J. Romero, Nolan L. Cabrera, and Michelle Rascon, "Assault on Ethnic Studies," in Santa Ana and González de Bustamante, *Arizona Firestorm*: 97–120.
63. ALJ Decision, 14.
64. David F. Cappellucci, Christina Williams, Jeffrey J. Hernandez, Luanne P. Nelson, Teri Casteel, Glenton Gilzean, and Gershon Faulkner, *Curriculum Audit of the Mexican American Studies Department, Tucson Unified School District* (Miami Lakes, FL: Cambium Learning, 2011).
65. ALJ Decision, 17.
66. Justice, January 1, 2012: 3:40.
67. *González v. Douglas*, 269 F. Supp. 3d 948 (D. Ariz. 2017).

6 CAVING TO PRESSURE

1. Dylan Smith, "TUSD Ousts MAS Director in Chaotic Meeting," *Tucson Sentinel*, January 4, 2012, www.tucsonsentinel.com/local/report/041112_tusd_arce/tusd-ousts-mas-director-chaotic-meeting/.
2. Dean's Task Force, "Guidelines for Appointment, Evaluation, and Promotion for Career-Track Lecturers, Senior Lecturers, and Professors of Practice," *Eller College of Management*, June 29, 2018, https://facultyaffairs.arizona.edu/sites/default/files/Eller%20Career_Track_Guidelines%20approved.pdf.
3. Tucson Unified School District No. 1 Governing Board Regular Meeting, *Tucson Unified School District*, January 10, 2012, http://govboard.tusd1.org/Portals/TUSD1/GovBoard/docs/gbminutes/01-10-12Regular.pdf.
4. Augustine Romero, Sean Arce, and Julio Cammarota, "A *Barrio* Pedagogy: Identity, Intellectualism, Activism, and Academic Achievement through the Evolution of Critically Compassionate Intellectualism," *Race Ethnicity and Education* 12, no. 2 (2009): 217–233.
5. Curtis Acosta and Asiya Mir, "Empowering Young People to Be Critical Thinkers: The Mexican American Studies Program in Tucson," *Voices in Urban Education* 34, no. Summer (2012): 15–26.
6. Nolan L. Cabrera, Jeffrey F. Milem, Ozan Jaquette, and Ronald W. Marx. "Missing the (Student Achievement) Forest for All the (Political) Trees: Empiricism and the Mexican American Studies Controversy in Tucson," *American Educational Research Journal* 51, no. 6 (2014): 1084–1118.
7. Curtis Acosta, "Huitzilopochtli: The Will and Resiliency of Tucson Youth to Keep Mexican American Studies Alive," *Multicultural Perspectives* 16, no. 1 (2014): 3–7. To view some of the students' firsthand accounts of the book removal, please see: *Three Sonorans*, MAS Students Speak Out About Their Classes and Books Being Banned in Tucson, January 15, 2012, *Three Sonorans*, video, www.youtube.com/watch?v=-OUSbELFpX8; *Three Sonorans*, Pedicone's TUSD Perpetuates Historical Trauma Against Latinos, January 16, 2012, *Three Sonorans*, video, www.youtube.com/watch?v=MJW4q2QMZ0s.
8. Rodolfo F. Acuña, "Censorship in Tucson," *Counter Punch*, February 7, 2012, www.counterpunch.org/2012/02/07/censorship-in-tucson/; Jeff Biggers, "Who's Afraid of 'The Tempest'?" *Salon*, January 14, 2012, www.salon.com/test/2012/01/13/whos_afraid_of_the_tempest/; Mari Herreras, "TUSD Banning Books? Well, Yes, and No, and Yes," *Tucson Weekly*, January 17, 2012, www.tucsonweekly.com/TheRange/archives/2012/01/17/tusd-banning-book-well-yes-and-no-and-yes; Roque Planas, "Why 'Book Ban' Is the Right Term of What Tucson Did to Mexican American Studies," *Huffington Post*, September 26, 2014, www.huffpost.com/entry/arizona-book-ban_n_5887926.
9. John Ames, "TUSD: No Books Have Been Banned," *KOLD*, January 17, 2012, www.kold.com/story/16538459/tusd-no-books-have-been-banned/.
10. Ibid.
11. Emily J. M. Knox, "Indoctrination and Common Sense Interpretation of Texts: The Tucson Unified School District Book Banning," *Journal of Intellectual Freedom & Privacy* 2, no. 2 (2017).
12. Jeff Biggers, "Yes, Virginia, They Still Ban Books in Tucson, Arizona," *Huffington Post*, September 28, 2012, www.huffingtonpost.com/jeff-biggers/yes-virginia-they-still-b_b_1923928.html.
13. The image of the box labeled, Banned Books, is powerful and, as Jeff Biggers notes, haunting; it can be viewed in Jeff Biggers, "Yes, Virginia, They Still Ban Books in Tucson, Arizona," *Huffington Post*, September 28, 2012, www.huffingtonpost.com/jeff-biggers/yes-virginia-they-still-b_b_1923928.html.

14. Mari Herreras, "Yes, Virginia, the TUSD Board Did Approve Three of the Banned Books," *Tucson Weekly*, January 25, 2012, www.tucsonweekly.com/TheRange/archives/2012/01/25/yes-virginia-the-tusd-board-did-approve-three-of-the-banned-books.
15. David A. Morales, "2007 TUSD Book Approval List," *SCRIBD*, June 12, 2007, www.scribd.com/document/78885886/2007-TUSD-Book-Approval-List.
16. Biggers, "Yes, Virginia"; Richard Delgado and Jean Stefancic, "Book Banning in Arizona," *Academe Blog*, January 2, 2012, https://academeblog.org/2012/01/24/book-banning-in-arizona/.
17. Biggers, "Who's Afraid of 'The Tempest'?"
18. Bryan Parras, "Wet Books: Smuggling Banned Literature Back into Arizona," *YouTube*, January 17, 2012, video, www.youtube.com/watch?v=l-n3tvPz5ak.
19. *Nuestra Palabra*, "Librotraficante Caravan Route: Arizona Banned Our History. We Decided to Make More," *Librotraficante*, www.librotraficante.com/Caravan-Sked.html.
20. Amy Goodman, "'El Librotraficante' Tony Diaz Defies Ethnic Studies Book Ban with Caravan to Arizona," *Democracy Now!*, March 9, 2012, video, www.youtube.com/watch?v=fFdE_-0a2ss.
21. UNIDOS, "Banned Books Commercial," *unidostucson*, July 14, 2012, video, www.youtube.com/watch?v=_Su3YU9KDs4.
22. Biggers, "Yes, Virginia."
23. *Three Sonorans*, WALKOUT – Cholla and Pueblo Meet up with Tucson High School, *YouTube*, January 23, 2012, video, www.youtube.com/watch?v=EERvGq9vLsg.
24. State of Arizona Department of Education, "The Equalization Formula for Funding School Districts and Charters in the State of Arizona" (Phoenix, AZ; AZDE, December 20, 2010), https://ade.az.gov/schoolfinance/faqs/funding/equalization%20formula%20funding.pdf.
25. *Three Sonorans*, "TUSD Walkout and Dr. Garcia Takes Questions About MAS Ban Under Supervision," *YouTube*, January 13, 2012, video, www.youtube.com/watch?v=w4wUyoKzsgs, 13:10.
26. Ibid, 15:08.
27. Mari Herreras, "UNIDOS' School of Ethnic Studies," *Tucson Weekly*, January 24, 2012, www.tucsonweekly.com/TheRange/archives/2012/01/24/unidos-school-of-ethnic-studies.
28. Nolan L. Cabrera, Elisa L. Meza, Andrea J. Romero, and Roberto "Cintli" Rodríguez, "'If There Is No Struggle, There Is No Progress': Transformative Youth Resistance and the School of Ethnic Studies," *Urban Review* 45 no. 1 (2013): 7–22.
29. Ibid.
30. Nolan L. Cabrera, *White Guys on Campus: Racism, White Immunity, and the Myth of "Post-Racial" Higher Education* (New Brunswick, NJ: Rutgers University Press, 2019).
31. For a description of the Four Directions, please see: https://tucson.com/news/local/runs-bring-healing-to-barrio-chicano/article_14e4e25e-2c78-5d04-9eae-202fbc2f2d46.html.
32. Cabrera et al., "School of Ethnic Studies."
33. Ibid.
34. Ibid.
35. Ibid.
36. Howard Zinn, *A People's History of the United States: 1492-Present* (New York: Routledge, 2015).
37. Myles Horton and Paulo Freire, *We Make the Road by Walking: Conversations on Education and Social Change* (Philadelphia, PA: Temple University Press, 1990).
38. Debbie Reese, "Sean Arce, Director of Mexican American Studies Department in Tucson Unified School District, Receives Prestigious Award," *American Indians in*

Children's Literature, April 3, 2012, https://americanindiansinchildrensliterature.blogspot.com/2012/04/sean-arce-director-of-mexican-american.html.
39. Ibid.
40. Al Madrigal, "Tucson's Mexican-American Studies Ban," *The Daily Show with Jon Stewart*, April 2, 2012, video, www.cc.com/video-clips/ovmy09/the-daily-show-with-jon-stewart-tucson-s-mexican-american-studies-ban.
41. Hank Stephenson, "TUSD Board Majority Sidesteps Effort to Resurrect Aspects of Mexican American Studies," *Arizona Daily Star*, January 31, 2018, https://tucson.com/news/local/tusd-board-majority-sidesteps-effort-to-resurrect-aspects-of-mexican/article_620f0e1b-6b09-57c3-ae4c-342130d3b612.html.
42. *Daily Show*, 1:15.
43. *Precious Knowledge*.
44. *Daily Show*, 2:02.
45. Ibid, 1:40.
46. Ibid, 2:40.
47. Ibid, 3:15.
48. Ibid. To see the full segment, please go to: www.cc.com/video-clips/ovmy09/the-daily-show-with-jon-stewart-tucson-s-mexican-american-studies-ban.
49. Ibid, 4:18.
50. Ibid, 4:22.
51. Ibid, 5:04.
52. Alexis Huicochea, "Effort Under Way to Recall TUSD Board's Hicks," *Arizona Daily Star*, March 13, 2012, https://tucson.com/news/local/education/precollegiate/effort-under-way-to-recall-tusd-board-s-hicks/article_cea6b8b3-e19f-59a0-b8d7-0b92f55849c3.html.
53. Ibid.
54. Loretta Hunnicutt, "TUSD's Hicks Appears on The Daily Show," *Arizona Daily Independent*, April 3, 2012, https://arizonadailyindependent.com/2012/04/03/tusds-hicks-appears-on-the-daily-show/.
55. Dylan Smith, "Citizen Pulls Plug on Three Sonorans Blog," *Tucson Sentinel*, April 4, 2012, www.tucsonsentinel.com/local/report/040412_three_sonorans/citizen-pulls-plug-three-sonorans-blog/.
56. Biggers, *State Out of the Union*.
57. David Safier, "'Three Sonorans' Blog Pulled from the Tucson Citizen," *Blog for Arizona*, April 4, 2012, https://blogforarizona.net/three-sonorans-blog-pulled-from-the-tucson-citizen/.
58. Ibid.
59. Alexis Huicochea, "TUSD's Arce Voted Out Amid Protest," *Arizona Daily Star*, April 11, 2012, https://tucson.com/news/local/education/precollegiate/tusd-s-arce-voted-out-amid-protest/article_0c151184-f523-540f-8f94-ad95f48777ca.html.
60. Dylan Smith, "TUSD Ousts MAS Director in Chaotic Meeting," *Tucson Sentinel*, April 10, 2012, www.tucsonsentinel.com/local/report/041112_tusd_arce/tusd-ousts-mas-director-chaotic-meeting/.
61. Ibid.
62. Fernanda Echavarri, "TUSD Fires Mexican American Studies Program Director," *AZPM*, April 12, 2012, www.azpm.org/p/headlines/2012/4/11/712-tusd-fires-mexican-american-studies-program-director/.
63. Alexis Huicochea, "Cops Seek TUSD Smoke Bomb Culprit," *Arizona Daily Star*, April 11, 2012, https://tucson.com/news/local/education/precollegiate/cops-seek-tusd-smoke-bomb-culprit/article_2752a49b-d93b-583c-a406-b3ba702e7865.html.
64. Ibid.

65. Arizona Daily Independent, "TUSD Board Member Says Protesters Crossed the Line," *Arizona Daily Independent*, April 20, 2012, https://arizonadailyindependent.com/2012/04/20/tusd-board-member-says-protesters-crossed-the-line/?amp.
66. Devin Boone, "My Other Me: A Community Saves Mexican American Studies. Can Mexican American Studies Save a Community?" *Medium*, November 16, 2018, https://medium.com/@devinelizabeth/my-other-me-f9a128281116.
67. Mari Herreras, "Ties That Bind: Internal Struggles in the UA Mexican American Studies Department Grow Due to Ties to TUSD," *Tucson Weekly*, May 3, 2012, www.tucsonweekly.com/tucson/ties-that-bind/Content?oid=3336109.
68. Jon Justice, "Word Bans and UNIDOS Gang," *My Nerd World with Jon Justice*, April 30, 2012, www.youtube.com/watch?v=yJxsV_Xp5-g, video: 9:35.
69. Ibid, 11:00.
70. Ibid, 11:14.
71. Howard Fischer, "FBI Says Horne Clipped Car, Drove Off, to Hide Affair," *Arizona Daily Star*, October 31, 2012, http://tucson.com/news/local/crime/fbi-says-horne-clipped-car-drove-off-to-hide-affair/article_3ebde4f1-a288-57d4-a363-114d4f3aad2c.html.
72. Stephen Lemons, "Tom Horne's Alleged Hit-and-Run at Address Listed for Carmen Chenal," *Phoenix New Times*, October 1, 2012, www.phoenixnewtimes.com/news/tom-hornes-alleged-hit-and-run-at-an-address-listed-for-carmen-chenal-w-update-6503680.
73. Ibid.
74. Ibid.
75. Howard Fischer, "FBI Says Horne Clipped Car."
76. Ibid.
77. Ibid.
78. Alexis Huicochea, "US Court Appoints 'Special Master' to Oversee TUSD Deseg," *Arizona Daily Star*, January 11, 2012, http://tucson.com/news/local/education/precollegiate/us-court-appoints-special-master-to-oversee-tusd-deseg/article_1d1beed4-da8f-5c39-b10b-065932004d94.html.
79. Nolan L. Cabrera, "Lies, Damn Lies, and Statistics: The Impact of Mexican American Studies Classes." In Cammarota and Romero, *Raza Studies*: 40–51; David F. Cappellucci, Christina Williams, Jeffrey J. Hernandez, Luanne P. Nelson, Teri Casteel, Glenton Gilzean, and Gershon Faulkner, *Curriculum Audit of the Mexican American Studies Department, Tucson Unified School District* (Miami Lakes, FL: Cambium Learning, 2011); Department of Accountability and Research, *AIMS Achievement Comparison for Students Taking One or More Ethnic Studies Classes: Initial Passing Rate versus Cumulative Passing Rate by AIMS Subject and Cohort Year* (Tucson, AZ: Tucson Unified School District, January 6, 2011); Department of Accountability and Research, *Selected Statistics – 2010 (Four Year) Graduation Cohort* (Tucson, AZ: Tucson Unified School District, January 6, 2011); Department of Accountability and Research, *AIMS Achievement Comparison*; Department of Accountability and Research, *Selected Statistics – 2010*. Department of Accountability and Research as cited by Alexis Huicochea, Ethnic Studies Claims in Question, *Arizona Daily Star*, March 15, 2011, http://azstarnet.com/news/local/education/ethnic-studies-claim-in-question/article_c316a3d0-7ff5-5f87-874e-6b7cf3b515f3.html; Augustine F. Romero, *Towards a Critically Compassionate Intellectualism Model of Transformative Education: Love, Hope, Identity, and Organic Intellectualism Through the Convergence of Critical Race Theory, Critical Pedagogy, and Authentic Caring*, Unpublished doctoral dissertation (Tucson, AZ: University of Arizona, 2008); Save Ethnic Studies, *Analysis and Evaluation of Mexican American Studies* (Tucson, AZ: Author, 2011) http://saveethnicstudies.org/.

80. Nolan L. Cabrera, Jeffrey F. Milem, and Ronald W. Marx, "An Empirical Analysis of the Effects of Mexican American Studies Participation on Student Achievement within Tucson Unified School District," Report to Special Master Dr. Willis D. Hawley on the Tucson Unified School District Desegregation Case (2012).
81. Ibid, 7.
82. *Mendoza et al. v. Tucson Unified School District No. One, Tucson Unified School District Unitary Status Plan (USP)*, February 20, 2013, http://deseg.tusd1.org/Portals/TUSD1/Deseg/docs/main/USP.pdf.
83. Ibid, 37.
84. Cabrera, Milem, Jaquette, and Marx, "Missing the (Student Achievement) Forest."

7 THE LAWSUIT

1. Michael Kiefer and Karina Bland, "Judge Respected Among Peers," *Arizona Republic*, January 9, 2011, http://archive.azcentral.com/news/articles/2011/01/08/20110108arizona-giffords-brk.html.
2. *Vicente v. Barnett*, No. 05-CV-157 TUC JMR, 2008 WL 11350243 (D. Ariz. 2008).
3. First Amended Complaint (April 12, 2011), ECF 17-1, at ¶ 5.
4. Order (August 15, 2011), ECF 83 (granting motion to amend complaint; denying defendants motion to dismiss Second Amended Complaint as now moot; and denying plaintiffs' motion for summary judgment without prejudice).
5. *Dred Scott v. Sandford*, 60 US 393, 403 (1856).
6. *City of Los Angeles v. Lyons*, 461 US 95, 97–98 (1983).
7. Ibid, 115.
8. Ibid, 115 (citing Complaint, Count V, ¶ 22).
9. Defendant Superintendent's Motion to Dismiss Third Amended Complaint (September 19, 2011) ECF 88.
10. Transcript of Motions Hearing Before the Honorable A. Wallace Tashima (December 21, 2011) ECF 242.
11. Declaration of Lorenzo "Larry" Lopez, Jr. (December 15, 2011), ECF 128-8, at 2 ¶ 8.
12. Exhibit A to Lorenzo "Larry" Lopez, Jr., Declaration, Tucson Magnet High School 2012–13 Junior Course Selection Worksheet, ECF 128-8,
13. Lopez Declaration, ECF 242, at 3–4.
14. Ibid, 19.
15. Order re Motion to Intervene (February 6, 2012), ECF 153.
16. *Schuette v. Coalition to Defend Affirmative Action, Integration and Immigrant Rights and Fight for Equality By Any Means Necessary* (BAMN), 572 US 291 (2014).
17. *Washington v. Seattle School District No. 1*, 458 US 457 (1982).
18. Order re Motions: (1) to Dismiss; and (2) for a Preliminary Injunction (January 10, 2012), ECF 138, at 16–17, n. 15.
19. *Kleindienst v. Mandel*, 408 US 753 (1972).
20. Ibid, 759.
21. Ibid, 762.
22. *Johnson v. Stuart*, 702 F.2d 193 (9th Cir. 1983).
23. *Meyer v. Nebraska*, 262 US 390 (1923).
24. Ibid, 396 (citing "An act relating to the teaching of a foreign languages in the state of Nebraska").
25. Ibid, 399 (quoting Fourteenth Amendment).
26. Ibid, 399–400.

27. Ibid, 401.
28. Transcript, Motion for Summary Judgment; Cross-Motion for Summary Judgment (March 19, 2012), ECF 203, at 2.
29. Ibid, 3.
30. Ibid, 7.
31. Ibid, 13.
32. Ibid, 13.
33. Ibid, 19.
34. Ibid, 20.
35. Ibid, 23.
36. ER 3.3. Candor Toward the Tribunal. A.R.S. Sup. Ct. Rules, Rule 42, Rules of Prof. Conduct.
37. *González v. Douglas*, 269 F. Supp. 3d 948, 972 (2017).
38. Transcript, Motion for Summary Judgment, ECF 203, at 20.
39. *Fisher v. United States*, Civ. No. 4:74–90 (D. Ariz.), ECF No. 1406-1 Joint Proposed Unitary Status Plan Noting Areas of Party Disagreement (December 10, 2012), at 33.
40. Motion for Immediate Status Conference and Placement on an Expedited Track (January 14, 2013) ECF 218.
41. Request for Hearing and Supplemental Filing of Exhibits to Motion for Preliminary Injunction (February 1, 2013) ECF 222.
42. ECF 222–4.
43. Memorandum Order (March 8, 2013), ECF 227.
44. Judgment (March 8, 2013), ECF 228.

8 THE APPEAL

1. Devon G. Peña, "Arizona Update: H2281 and Beyond," *mexmigration* (blog), March 24, 2013, http://mexmigration.blogspot.com/2013/03/arizona-update-hb2281-and-beyond-four.html.
2. Proposed Amici Curiae Brief of the National Association of Chicana & Chicano Studies, et al. (March 7, 2012), ECF 181-1.
3. R. Tolteka Cuautin, Miguel Zavala, Christine Sleeter, and Wayne Au, eds., *Rethinking Ethnic Studies* (Milwaukee, WI: Rethinking Schools, 2019).
4. Notice of Appeal (April 5, 2013), ECF 231.
5. Notice of Cross-Appeal (April 17, 2013), ECF 238.
6. *California v. Texas*, 593 U.S. (2021) (rejecting challenge on standing grounds and not reaching severability question).
7. Amy Goodman and Nermeen Shaikh, "Debating Tucson School District's Book Ban after Suspension of Mexican American Studies Program," *Democracy Now!*, January 18, 2012, www.democracynow.org/2012/1/18/debating_tucson_school_districts_book_ban; Amy Goodman and Juan González, "In Precedent-Setting Trial, Lawyers Say Arizona's Ethnic Studies Ban Is Discriminatory & Illegal," *Democracy Now!*, July 17, 2017, www.democracynow.org/2017/7/17/in_precedent_setting_trial_lawyers_say.
8. The twenty-six other organizations were: Association for Asian American Studies (AAAS); Hispanic Association of Colleges and Universities (HACU); the National Latino/a Education Research and Policy Project; the Mexican American Studies Department of San Jose State University; Chicano Studies Department of California State University-Northridge; the League of United Latin American Citizens (LULAC), a national 501(c)(3)

organization; Association of Raza Educators (ARE); Aztlan Libre Press; California Faculty Association (CFA); Coalición México-Americana (MXAC); Esperanza Peace and Justice Center (EPJC); For Chicana/Chicano Studies Foundation (FCCSF); Georgia Latino Alliance for Human Rights (GLAHR); Indigenous Women's Network/Alma de Mujer Center for Social Change; Latino Education and Advocacy Days (LEAD Organization); Mujeres Activas en Letras y Cambio Social (MALCS); Mujeres Activas en Letras y Cambio Social – Tejas (MALCS-Tejas); American Studies Association (ASA); Society for Applied Anthropology (SfAA), South Central Farmers (SCF); SouthWest Organizing Project (SWOP); Texas Association of Chicanos in Higher Education (TACHE); Texas League of United Latin American Citizens (Texas LULAC); the Acequia Institute (TAI); Unitarian Universalist Association – Pacific Southwest District.

9. Brief of Authors Rodolfo Acuña, Bill Bigelow, Richard Delgado, and Jean Stefancic as Amici Curiae in Support of Appellants (November 25, 2013), Ninth Circuit ECF 22.
10. Brief of Freedom to Read Foundation, et al. as Amici Curiae in Support of Plaintiffs-Appellants and Supporting Reversal (November 25, 2013), Ninth Circuit ECF 17.
11. Brief of the National Education Association and Arizona Education Association as Amici Curiae in Support of Plaintiffs-Appellants (November 25, 2013), Ninth Circuit ECF 18.
12. Brief for Amici Curiae 48 Public School Teachers in Support of Appellants' Request for Reversal (November 25, 2013), Ninth Circuit ECF 24.
13. Amici Curiae Brief on Behalf of Chief Earl Warren Institute on Law and Social Policy and the Anti-Defamation League, In Support of Plaintiffs-Appellants (November 25, 2013), Ninth Circuit ECF 21-2.
14. Brief of Amicus Curiae Latina and Latino Critical Legal Theory, Inc. Supporting Plaintiffs-Appellants Urging Reversal (November 25, 2013), Ninth Circuit ECF 23.
15. While we do not like the term "at-risk" and all of its political implications, we use it here to highlight arguments and framing the courts are sensitive to.
16. Cathryn Creno, "School Superintendent Huppenthal Acknowledges Anonymous Blog Posts," *Arizona Republic*, June 18, 2014, www.azcentral.com/story/news/arizona/politics/2014/06/18/huppenthal-acknowledges-anonymous-blog-posts/10749057/.
17. Tim Stellar, "On Blogs, Huppenthal Reveals His Inner Ugliness," *Arizona Daily Star*, November 9, 2017, https://tucson.com/news/local/column/steller-on-blogs-huppenthal-reveals-his-inner-ugliness/article_4446e245-9aaa-5b3c-9cf8-4737b5aa6c5f.html.
18. Laurie Roberts, "John Huppenthal Unmasked," *Arizona Republic*, June 24, 2014, www.azcentral.com/story/laurie-roberts/2014/06/19/john-huppenthal/10901575/.
19. Ibid.
20. Creno, "Anonymous Blog Posts."
21. Mary Beth Faller and Cathryn Creno, "Huppenthal Breaks Down in Tears Over Blog Posts," *Arizona Republic*, June 26, 2014, www.azcentral.com/story/news/arizona/politics/2014/06/25/arizona-huppenthal-blog-posts-tears-press/11373231/.
22. Ibid.
23. *Three Sonorans*, "MAS Teachers Forum at 2014 NAME," November 9, 2014, video, 58:50, www.youtube.com/watch?v=Iq67wE_NgFI&t=2s.
24. Doug MacEachern, "School Principal and Fellow Marxist in Public Brawl," *Arizona Republic*, November 18, 2014, www.azcentral.com/story/dougmaceachern/2014/11/18/tusd-marxists-romero-arce/19235097/.
25. Loretta Hunnicutt, "Romero Claims Mexican American. Studies Classes Never Left TUSD," *Arizona Daily Independent*, November 12, 2014, https://arizonadailyindependent.com/2014/11/12/romero-claims-mexican-american-studies-classes-never-left-tusd/.

26. *Three Sonorans*, "TUSD Principal Escorted Out of NAME Conference after Provoking a Fight, November 12, 2014," video, www.youtube.com/watch?v=SuGFWyXnsns.
27. Devin Boone, "My Other Me: A Community Saves Mexican American Studies. Can Mexican American Studies Save a Community?" *Medium*, November 16, 2018, https://medium.com/@devinelizabeth/my-other-me-f9a128281116; Mari, Herreras, "A Community Divided," *Tucson Weekly*, May 10, 2012, www.tucsonweekly.com/tucson/a-community-divided/Content?oid=3349554&showFullText=true.
28. Rojas, *Black Power*; Ed Wetschler, "After 50 Years, Ethnic Studies Still Controversial," *District Administration* 47, no. 7 (June 2011): 46–53.
29. *Three Sonorans*, "Arizona – Richard Martinez," January 15, 2015, video, www.youtube.com/watch?v=71OuZL1MMu4.
30. *Three Sonorans*, "Arizona – Lorenzo Lopez," January 15, 2015, video, www.youtube.com/watch?v=AdgT7pyj-F8.
31. *Three Sonorans*, "Arizona – Anita Fernández," January 15, 2015, video, www.youtube.com/watch?v=7R6WIzvw3yg.
32. *Three Sonorans*, "Arizona – Maya Arce," January 15, 2015, video, www.youtube.com/watch?v=Uf4mE5E4a5c.
33. *Three Sonorans*, "Arizona – Korina Lopez," January 15, 2015, video, www.youtube.com/watch?v=6etSYXhYSOA.
34. *Three Sonorans*, "Arizona – Nolan Cabrera," January 15, 2015, video, www.youtube.com/watch?v=YB-l4etipgg&t=43s.
35. Notice of Appearance of Leslie Kyman Cooper (January 22, 2013), ECF 219.
36. Ellman Acknowledgment of Hearing Notice (December 4, 2014), Ninth Circuit ECF 80.
37. *Arce v. Huppenthal*, Oral Argument, January 12, 2015, video, www.c-span.org/video/?323730-1/maya-arce-v-john-huppenthal-oral-argument.
38. Roque Planas, "Arizona Law That Banned Mexican-American Studies May Be Discriminatory, Court Rules," *Huffington Post*, July 7, 2015, www.huffpost.com/entry/arizona-mexican-american-studies_n_7748102.

9 A NEW HOPE

1. For more about the history of Borderlands Theater, please see www.borderlandstheater.org/about/history/.
2. More about Más and the production at the Tucson Borderlands Theater can be found here: www.borderlandstheater.org/productions/2015-2016-season/mas/.
3. Request for Leave for Telephonic Appearance: For Robert S. Chang (August 26, 2015), ECF 252.
4. Jim Quinn, *Don't Be Afraid to Win: How Free Agency Changed the Business of Pro Sports* (New York: Radius Book Group, 2019).
5. Plaintiffs' Request for Judicial Notice in Support of Plaintiffs' Reply to Defendants' Opposition to Plaintiffs' Request for Leave to File Fourth Amended Complaint (October 23, 2015), ECF 268, at 51.
6. Transcript of Proceedings, Pretrial Conference, *Arce v. Douglas*, 4:10-cv-623-AWT (April 13, 2017), at 50 (on file with Chang).
7. Taylor Hackford, *Blood in, Blood Out* (Burbank, CA: Buena Vista Pictures 1993), DVD.

10 TRIAL!

1. Transcript, Motion for Summary Judgment, Cross-Motion for Summary Judgment (March 19, 2012), ECF 203, at 13.
2. Transcript of Proceedings, Pretrial Conference, *Arce v. Douglas*, 4:10-cv-623-AWT (April 13, 2017), at 49–50 (on file with Chang).
3. *Washington v. Davis*, 426 U.S. 229 (1976).
4. Ibid.
5. Alan David Freeman, "Legitimizing Racial Discrimination through Antidiscrimination Law: A Critical Review of Supreme Court Doctrine," *Minnesota Law Review* 62, no. 6 (1978): 1049–1119.
6. Bonilla-Silva, *Racism Without Racists*; Haney López, *Dog Whistle Politics*.
7. Trial Day 1, 22.
8. Ibid, 23–24.
9. Ibid, 33.
10. Ibid, 43.
11. Ibid, 48.
12. Ibid.
13. Ibid, 49.
14. Ibid, 50.
15. Ibid, 45.
16. Ibid.
17. Ibid.
18. Ibid.
19. Ibid, 52.
20. Ibid, 61.
21. Ibid, 83.
22. Ibid, 92–93.
23. Ibid, 92.
24. Ibid, 93.
25. Ibid, 104–105.
26. Ibid, 105.
27. Ibid, 115.
28. Ibid, 116.
29. Ibid, 119–120.
30. Pretrial Conference, at 16.
31. Trial Day 1, 138.
32. Ibid, 139.
33. Ibid, 139–140.
34. Ibid, 142.
35. Ibid, 143–144.
36. Ibid, 144–146.
37. Ibid, 148.
38. Ibid.
39. Ibid, 148–149.
40. Ibid, 149.
41. Ibid.
42. Trial Day 3, 113–114.
43. Ibid, 114–115.

44. Ibid, 117.
45. Ibid.
46. Ibid, 118.
47. Ibid, 120.
48. Ibid, 121.
49. Ibid, 122–123.
50. Ibid, 124–129.
51. Ibid, 139.
52. Ibid, 144.
53. Ibid.
54. Ibid, 150.
55. Ibid, 151.
56. Ibid.
57. Ibid.
58. Ibid, 152.
59. Ibid, 158.
60. Ibid, 171–172.
61. 269 F. Supp. at 968.
62. Trial Day 4, 43.
63. Ibid, 74.
64. Ibid, 78.
65. Ibid, 79.
66. Ibid, 99.
67. Ibid, 101.
68. Ibid, 116–117.
69. Ibid, 117.

11 GOTCHA!

Portions of this chapter were previously published in Nolan L. Cabrera and Robert S. Chang, "Stats, Social Justice, and the Limits of Interest Convergence," *Association of Mexican American Educators Journal* 13, no. 3 (2019): 72–96. They are reproduced here with permission.

1. Stephen J. Pitti, *The Devil in Silicon Valley: Northern California, Race, and Mexican Americans* (Princeton, NJ: Princeton University Press, 2004).
2. Angela Valenzuela, *Subtractive Schooling: U.S.-Mexican Youth and the Politics of Caring* (Albany, NY: State University of New York Press, 1999).
3. Federal Rules of Evidence, 702.
4. *Daubert v. Merrell Dow Pharmaceuticals*, 509 US 579 (1993).
5. Defendants' Motion for Partial Summary Judgment on Plaintiffs' First Amendment Claim (September 26, 2016), ECF 355.
6. Defendants' Statement of Facts in Support of Their Motion for Partial Summary Judgment (September 26, 2016), ECF 356.
7. Response to Plaintiffs' Motion for Summary Judgment and Superintendent's Cross Motion for Summary Judgment (January 25, 2012), ECF 150, at 29.
8. Ibid, 6–8.
9. Order re Defendants' Motion for Partial Summary Judgment (February 7, 2017), ECF 374, at 4–6.
10. Order re *Daubert* Motions (February 10, 2017), ECF 375.

11. Ibid, 9–11.
12. Ibid, 125.
13. Ibid, 3–4.
14. Trial Day 4, 125.
15. Cabrera, "State-Mandated Epistemology."
16. Trial Day 4, 168.
17. Charles W. Mills, *The Racial Contract* (Ithaca, NY: Cornell University Press, 1999), at 18 (italics original).
18. Trial Day 4, 169.
19. Bonilla-Silva, *Racism Without Racists*; Haney López, *Dog Whistle Politics*.
20. Trial Day 4, 179.
21. Notice of Filing of Declaration of Rebuttal Expert Dr. Thomas M. Haladyna (May 12, 2017), ECF 394, at 6.
22. Trial Day 9, 48. Haladyna stated that "we don't know if the grades earned in the MÁS classes are disentangled from achievement in grades in other classes. So, there may have been an inflation."
23. Ibid, 41.
24. Ibid, 53–54.
25. Ibid, 64.
26. Ibid, 76.
27. Trial Day 7, 188.
28. Ibid, 197.
29. Declaration of Dr. Stephen Pitti, Ph.D. (May 12, 2017), ECF 392, at 6 ¶ 15(b).
30. Trial Day 4, 193–194.
31. Trial Day 7, 194.
32. Thomas S. Kuhn, *The Structure of Scientific Revolutions* (Chicago, IL: University of Chicago Press, 1962).
33. Day 7, 195–196.
34. Defendants' Motion to Exclude Expert Dr. Stephen Pitti's Report and Testimony (September 26, 2016), ECF 353, at 11.
35. Order Re *Daubert* Motions (February 10, 2017), ECF 375, at 8 (citation omitted).
36. Ibid, 8–9 (citation omitted).
37. 269 F. Supp. 3d at 967–968.
38. Day 7, 199.
39. Ibid, 208.
40. Ibid, 210.
41. Ibid, 209–210.
42. Trial Day 8, 23.
43. Ibid, 24.
44. Ibid, 24.
45. Ibid, 25.
46. Ibid, 28.
47. Ibid, 34.
48. Ibid, 39.
49. Ibid, 40–41.
50. Ibid, 41–42.
51. Trial Day 8, 82.
52. Ibid, 58.
53. Ibid, 60.

54. Ibid, 60.
55. Ibid, 60.
56. Ibid, 64.
57. Ibid, 72–73.
58. Ibid, 74.
59. Ibid, 82.
60. Pitti Declaration, ECF 392, at 9 ¶ 25.
61. Declaration of Dr. Angela Valenzuela, Ph.D. (May 12, 2017), ECF 391, at 4 ¶ 10.
62. Ibid, 9 ¶ 27.
63. Ibid, 10–13, ¶¶ 38–44.
64. Ibid, 16, ¶ 59.
65. Ibid, 16, ¶ 59.
66. Ibid, 10, ¶ 31.
67. Trial Day 8, 132.
68. Ibid, 152.
69. Ibid, 154–156.
70. Ex. D (May 12, 2017), ECF 391-4.
71. Ibid, 94.
72. Trial Day 8, 173.
73. Ibid.
74. Trial Days 9, 10, and 13.
75. Ibid, 21–22.
76. Ibid, 23.

12 DOUBLING DOWN ON RACISM

1. Trial Day 7, 119.
2. Ibid, 77.
3. Ibid, 12.
4. Ibid, 181.
5. Antidefamation League, "Hitler Salute (hand sign)," accessed February 29, 2024, www.adl.org/resources/hate-symbol/hitler-salute-hand-sign.
6. Trial Day 7, 18.
7. Ibid, 19.
8. Ibid.
9. A.R.S. § 38-231.
10. Trial Day 7, 14.
11. Ibid, 18, 19, 25, 32, 33, 70, 123, 142, 143, 162, 165, 167, 181.
12. Ibid, 28.
13. Ibid, 15.
14. Transcript, Motion for Summary Judgment; Cross-Motion for Summary Judgment, *Arce v. Huppenthal* (March 19, 2012), ECF 203, at 19.
15. Ibid.
16. Ibid, 54.
17. Ibid, 54.
18. Ibid, 65.
19. Ibid, 133.
20. Trial Day 7, 16.
21. Ibid, 126.

22. Ibid, 119.
23. Ibid, 156.
24. Ibid, 25.
25. Ibid, 83.
26. Ibid, 35.
27. Ibid, 34,
28. Ibid, 87.
29. Ibid, 88.
30. Ibid, 88.
31. Ibid, 57.
32. Ibid, 74.
33. Ibid, 101.
34. Ibid, 109.
35. Ibid, 115.
36. Ibid.
37. Ibid, 114. Heavy accents in this instance meant heavy Spanish accents. Teachers with heavy French or English accents were not targeted.
38. Ibid, 123.
39. Ibid, 149.
40. Ibid, 121.
41. Ibid.
42. Ibid, 123.
43. Ibid.
44. Ibid, 171.
45. Associated Press, "KKK Members Insist They're Not 'White Supremacists,'" Associated Press, December 11, 2016, www.cbsnews.com/news/kkk-insists-theyre-not-white-supremacists/.
46. Defendants' Preliminary Proposed Findings of Fact and Conclusions of Law (June 21, 2017), ECF 426, at 28.
47. Trial Day 7, 124–126. Though in his direct testimony, Horne referred to this group as "Hispanics for the Children," on cross-examination, he referred to the group as "English for the Children" and the plaque as having "a picture of a bunch of Hispanic students and their parents." Ibid, 126.
48. Ibid, 173.
49. Ibid, 150.
50. Ibid, 153.
51. Ibid, 151.
52. Haney López, *Dog Whistle Politics*.
53. Trial Day 7, 166.
54. Ibid, 172.
55. www.facebook.com/cesar.teolol/videos/10203283142554923
56. Trial Day 2, 189–190.
57. Ibid, 102–103.
58. Ibid, 87–88.
59. Transcript, Superintendent John Huppenthal's Western Free Press Interview, February 29, 2012, Ninth Circuit ECF. 12–3, at 273–274.
60. For an example of this rhetoric, see the following op-ed Huppenthal penned in the *Arizona Daily Star* just after the final ruling was announced. His argument, as the headline reads, was literally that he could not be racist because he is from South Tucson.

See John Huppenthal, "I Am Not a Racist – I Grew Up in South Tucson," *Arizona Daily Star*, August 26, 2017, https://tucson.com/john-huppenthal-i-am-not-a-racist—i-grew-up-in-south/article_b9f8d679-45f9-5003-93bf-b211369b98ee.html.
61. Trial Day 2, 111.
62. John Huppenthal, "I Am Not a Racist."
63. Trial Day 1, 183.
64. Ibid, 156.
65. Ibid, 157.
66. Ibid.
67. Ibid, 158.
68. Ibid.
69. Ibid, 198.
70. Ibid, 40.
71. Ibid, 209.
72. Ibid, 192.
73. Ibid, 161.
74. Trial Day 7, 35.
75. Trial Day 1, 176–177.
76. Haney López, *Dog Whistle Politics*.
77. Trial Day 2, 41.
78. Ibid, 42.
79. Ibid, 41.
80. Ibid, 50.
81. Ibid, 161–163.
82. Ibid, 52.
83. Ibid, 45.
84. Ibid, 85.
85. Ibid, 54.
86. Ibid, 83.
87. Ibid, 57.
88. Ibid, 57–58.
89. Ibid, 91.
90. Ibid, 86.
91. Ibid, 94.
92. Ibid, 95.
93. Ibid, 98.
94. Ibid.
95. Ibid, 99.
96. Ibid.
97. Ibid, 103.
98. Ibid, 104.
99. Ibid, 105.
100. Ibid, 106.
101. Ibid, 108.
102. Ibid, 109.
103. Ibid, 110.
104. Ibid.
105. Ibid, 111.
106. Ibid, 112.

107. Ibid, 114.
108. Ibid, 124.
109. Ibid, 130.
110. Ibid, 131.
111. Ibid, 137.
112. Ibid, 157.
113. Ibid, 164.
114. Ibid, 166.
115. Ibid, 189.
116. *González v. Douglas*, 269 F. Supp. 3d 948, 969, 973 n. 27, 972, 974 (D. Ariz. 2017).

13 THE S.S. VIOLATION AND THE CLOSE OF TRIAL

1. Defendant's Preliminary Proposed Findings of Fact and Conclusions of Law (June 21, 2017), ECF 426.
2. Trial Day 3, 10.
3. Ibid.
4. Ibid, 12.
5. Ibid, 30.
6. Ibid, 44–47.
7. Ibid, 46.
8. Ibid, 52–57.
9. Ibid, 43.
10. Ibid.
11. Ibid, 57.
12. Trial Day 6, 142–144.
13. Ibid, 149–150.
14. Ibid, 157.
15. Ibid, 158–159.
16. Ibid, 164–165.
17. Ibid, 108.
18. Order re Motions in Limine (June 16, 2017), ECF 422, at 3–4.
19. Trial Day 6, 112.
20. Ibid, 117.
21. Ibid, 132.
22. Ibid.
23. Ibid, 132–133.
24. Defendants' Preliminary Proposed Findings of Fact and Conclusions of Law (June 21, 2017), ECF 426, at 4.
25. Trial Day 1, 24.
26. Trial Day 5, 5–8.
27. Ibid, 12.
28. Ibid.
29. Ibid, 15–19.
30. Ibid.
31. Ibid, 41–42.
32. Ibid, 44–45.
33. See Chapter 6.
34. Trial Day 5, 48.

35. Ibid, 47.
36. Ibid, 80.
37. Ibid, 83–84.
38. Ibid, 84–85.
39. Ibid, 87.
40. Ibid, 94.
41. Ibid, 96.
42. Sally Rusk in discussion with author Robert Chang, July 1, 2017.
43. Rene Martinez in discussion with author Robert Chang, July 8, 2017.
44. Trial Day 6, 7–8.
45. Ibid, 8 (quoting Trial Day 5, 47).
46. Ibid, 14.
47. Ibid, 34–35.
48. Joyce Appleby, Alan Brinkley, Albert S. Broussard, James M. McPherson, Donald A. Ritchie, *The American Vision* (New York City, NY: Glencoe and McGraw-Hill, 2007), 490.
49. Ibid, 491.
50. Trial Day 6, 42.
51. Ibid, 42–43.
52. Ibid, 43.
53. Ibid, 47.
54. Ibid, 101.
55. Ibid, 103.
56. Trial Day 9, 96.
57. Ibid, 97.
58. Ibid.
59. Ibid.
60. Ibid, 124.
61. Ibid, 136.
62. Ibid, 136–137.
63. Ibid, 139.
64. Ibid, 148.
65. Hibbs Deposition, 47.
66. Trial Day 9, 173.
67. Luna Barrington, email message to Robert Chang, David Fitzmaurice, and James Quinn, July 20, 2017.
68. Jim W. Quinn, email message to MAS Legal Team, June 30, 2017.
69. Trial Day 9, 173.
70. Trial Day 10, 5.
71. Ibid, 71.
72. Ibid, 82–83.
73. Ibid, 76.
74. Ibid, 79.
75. Ibid, 84.
76. Ibid, 88–89.
77. Ibid, 91.
78. Ibid, 95.
79. Say the bar's name out loud.

14 VICTORY AND NATIONAL RENAISSANCE AMIDST BACKLASH

1. Madison Park, "Trump Hints at Potential Pardon for Ex-Sheriff Joe Arpaio," *CNN*, August 23, 2017, www.cnn.com/2017/08/22/politics/joe-arpaio-sheriff/index.html.
2. *González v. Douglas*, 269 F. Supp. 3d 948 (D. Ariz. 2017).
3. Ibid, 973.
4. Ian Haney López, *Dog Whistle Politics: How Coded Racial Appeals Have Reinvented Racism and Wrecked the Middle Class* (Oxford: Oxford University Press, 2015).
5. Ibid, 178.
6. *González v. Douglas*, 967
7. Ibid.
8. Ibid, 958–962.
9. Ibid, 951 and 951 n. 3.
10. U.N.I.D.O.S., "Official Statement Regarding Federal Court Decision," *Facebook*, August 22, 2017, www.facebook.com/UNIDOSYC/posts/1568645883157397
11. Loretta Hunnicutt, "Arizona Schools Now Free to 'Promote Resentment Toward a Race or Class of People,'" *Arizona Daily Independent*, December 27, 2017, https://arizonadailyindependent.com/2017/12/27/arizona-schools-now-free-to-promote-resentment-toward-a-race-or-class-of-people/.
12. Robert Robb, "If a Bigot Bans Ethnic Studies, the Law Is Unconstitutional?" *Arizona Republic*, September 4, 2017, www.azcentral.com/story/opinion/op-ed/robertrobb/2017/09/04/ethnic-studies-ruling-sets-troubling-precedent/626842001/.
13. Ulises Bella, interview with Nolan Cabrera, January 28, 2020 (on file with Cabrera): 19:00 and 19:52.
14. Tony Diaz, "Opinion: Arizona's Mexican American Studies Victory Gives Nation Some Hope for Future," *Latino USA*, August 25, 2017, www.latinousa.org/2017/08/23/opinion-arizonas-mexican-american-studies-victory-gives-nation-hope-future/.
15. Rupa Shenoy, "After a 10-Year Saga, Tucson Teachers Are Validated When a Judge Calls State Law Racist," *The World*, August 25, 2017, https://theworld.org/stories/2017-08-25/after-10-year-saga-tucson-teachers-are-validated-when-judge-calls-state-law.
16. Maggie Astor, "Tucson's Mexican [sic] Studies Was a Victim of 'Racial Animus,' Judge Says," *New York Times*, August 23, 2017, www.nytimes.com/2017/08/23/us/arizona-mexican-american-ruling.html.
17. Valerie Strauss, "Arizona's Ban on Mexican American Studies Was Racist, U.S. Court Rules," *Washington Post*, August 23, 2017, www.washingtonpost.com/news/answer-sheet/wp/2017/08/23/arizonas-ban-on-mexican-american-studies-was-racist-u-s-court-rules/.
18. Jaweed Kaleem, "Federal Judge Blocks Arizona from Banning Mexican American Studies Classes," *Los Angeles Times*, December 27, 2017, www.latimes.com/nation/la-na-mexican-american-studies-20171227-story.html.
19. Julie Depenbrock, "Federal Judge Finds Racism Behind Arizona Law Banning Ethnic Studies," *NPR: All Things Considered*, www.npr.org/sections/ed/2017/08/22/545402866/federal-judge-finds-racism-behind-arizona-law-banning-ethnic-studies.
20. Associated Press, "Racism Was Behind Arizona's Ban on Mexican-American Studies, Judge Says," *NBC News*, August 23, 2017, www.nbcnews.com/news/latino/racism-was-behind-arizona-s-ban-mexican-american-studies-judge-n795131.
21. Associated Press, "Judge Rules Racism Behind Arizona Law Banning Mexican-American Studies Classes," *ABC15*, August 22, 2017, www.abc15.com/news/region-central-southern-az/tucson/judge-rules-racism-behind-arizona-law-banning-mexican-american-studies-class.

22. Roque Planas, "Arizona Unconstitutionally Banned Mexican-American Studies Classes, Judge Rules," *Huffington Post*, August 22, 2017, www.huffpost.com/entry/unconstitutional-arizona-ban_n_599cd201e4b0d97c3fffdc9d
23. Bella Interview, 17:57.
24. Defendants' Response to Plaintiffs' Remedy Brief (September 25, 2017), ECF 475, at 7.
25. Plaintiffs' Remedy Reply Brief (September 25, 2017), ECF 474.
26. Ibid, 16.
27. Final Judgment, Declaration, and Permanent Injunction (December 27, 2017), ECF 487.
28. Lin-Manuel Miranda and Jeremy McCarter, *Hamilton: The Revolution* (New York: Grand Central Publishing, 2016), 72.
29. www.facebook.com/UNIDOSYC/photos/a.1475747639113889/1689870231034961/ (capitalization original)
30. Derrick A. Bell, Jr., "Brown v. Board of Education and the Interest-Convergence Dilemma," *Harvard Law Review* 93, no. 3 (1979): 518–533.
31. Ibid, 523.
32. Ibid, 524.
33. See generally Gerald N. Rosenberg, *The Hollow Hope: Can Courts Bring about Social Change?*, 2nd ed. (Chicago: University of Chicago Press, 2008).
34. Rachel Sedgwick, "Arizona, TUSD, and Plaintiffs: Why They Should All Just Get Along (The Students)," unpublished paper, University of Arizona (2016), www.academia.edu/34124584/Arizona_TUSD_and_Plaintiffs_Why_They_Should_All_Just_Get_Along_The_Students?uc-g-sw=26962740.
35. Evan Schreiber, "TUSD Board Does Not Vote to Re-Integrate Mexican American Studies," *KOLD13*, January 31, 2018, www.kold.com/story/37389970/tusd-board-does-not-vote-to-re-integrate-mexican-american-studies/.
36. Hank Stephenson, "TUSD Board Majority Sidesteps Effort to Resurrect Aspects of Mexican American Studies," *Arizona Daily Star*, January 31, 2018, https://tucson.com/news/local/tusd-board-majority-sidesteps-effort-to-resurrect-aspects-of-mexican/article_620f0e1b-6b09-57c3-ae4c-342130d3b612.html.
37. Schreiber, "TUSD Board."
38. Stephenson, "Majority Sidesteps Effort."
39. Ibid.
40. Ibid.
41. Ibid.
42. Adelita Grijalva, "Mexican American Studies Program Was Targeted by Racists, and Should Be Recognized for Its Success," *Arizona Daily Star*, February 4, 2018, http://tucson.com/opinion/local/adelita-grijalva-mexican-american-studies-program-was-targeted-by-racists/article_5f69ebed-534a-524e-95fd-af02616c16fb.html?utm_medium=social&utm_source=twitter&utm_campaign=user-share.
43. Phil Villareal, "TUSD Board: Counts, Grijalva In; Hicks Out," *KGUN9*, November 7, 2018, www.kgun9.com/news/political/elections-local/tusd-board-counts-grijalva-in-hicks-out.
44. Duncan Moon, "TUSD Governing Board Member Mark Stegeman Resigns," *Arizona Public Media*, October 3, 2019, https://news.azpm.org/p/news-topical-edu/2019/10/3/159438-tusd-governing-board-member-mark-stegeman-resigns/.
45. Stephenson, "Majority Sidesteps Effort."
46. Alexis Huicochea, "TUSD's Arce Voted Out Amid Protest," *Arizona Daily Star*, April 11, 2012, https://tucson.com/news/local/education/precollegiate/tusd-s-arce-voted-out-amid-protest/article_0c151184-f523-540f-8f94-ad95f48777ca.html.
47. Sally Rusk Circle K Teacher Award, https://arizonawildcats.com/sports/2014/1/23/209384336.

48. Acosta Educational Partnership, www.acostaeducationalpartnership.com.
49. Curtis Acosta, Faculty Profile, UA College of Education, https://coe.arizona.edu/person/curtis-acosta.
50. Mexican American Student Services Department, *TUSD*, accessed March 2, 2024, www.tusd1.org/mexican-american-student-services-dept.
51. Stephenson, "Majority Sidesteps Effort."
52. Alexis Huicochea, "TUSD Names New Director of Culturally Relevant Pedagogy and Instruction," *Arizona Daily Star*, December 10, 2014, https://tucson.com/news/blogs/ednotes/tusd-names-new-director-of-culturally-relevant-pedagogy/article_55188567-0728-5da5-a994-33a11247e668.html.
53. XITO: Xicanx Institute for Teaching & Organizing, www.xicanxinstitute.org.
54. Valerie Cavasos, "Pueblo Teacher Comes Forward on Grade Changing," *KGUN9*, August 2, 2016, www.kgun9.com/news/investigations/pueblo-teacher-comes-forward-on-grade-changing.
55. Roberto "Cintli" Rodríguez, *Our Sacred Maíz Is Our Mother* (Tucson, AZ: University of Arizona Press, 2014).
56. "UA MAS Department Statement on Documentary Precious Knowledge," February 17, 2019, https://mas.arizona.edu/news/ua-mas-department-statement-documentary-precious-knowledge.
57. Gonzales, *Message to Aztlán*, 93.
58. Glaude *Begin Again*.
59. Wayne Au, "California Vetoed Ethnic Studies Requirements for Public High School Students But the Movement Grows," *The Conversation*, November 25, 2020, https://theconversation.com/california-vetoed-ethnic-studies-requirements-for-public-high-school-students-but-the-movement-grows-148486.
60. Gonzales, *Message to Aztlán*; Muñoz, *Youth, Identity, Power*.
61. *Precious Knowledge*.
62. Though this phrase is often misattributed to Albert Einstein, this version of the quote appears in LGBTQ activist Rita Mae Brown's novel, *Sudden Death* (New York: Bantam Books, 1983), 68, though it appears that she was also paraphrasing a known quote.
63. Bettina L. Love, *We Want to Do More Than Survive: Abolitionist Teaching and the Pursuit of Educational Freedom* (Boston: Beacon Press, 2019).
64. Jeff M. Duncan-Andrade and Ernest Morrell, *The Art of Critical Pedagogy: Possibilities for Moving from Theory to Practice in Urban Schools* (New York: Peter Lang, 2008).
65. Phillip S. Foner and Yuval Taylor, eds., *Frederick Douglass: Selected Speeches and Writings* (Chicago: Chicago Review Press, 2000), 358.
66. Subini Annamma, *The Pedagogy of Pathologization: Dis/abled Girls of Color in the School-Prison Nexus* (New York: Routledge, 2018).
67. Michelle Alexander, *The New Jim Crow: Mass Incarceration in the Age of Colorblindness*, rev. ed. (New York: The New Press, 2020).
68. Nancy Acevedo-Gil, "New Juan Crow Education as a Context for Institutional Microaggressions: Latina/o/x Students Maintaining College Aspirations," *Urban Education* 57, no. 8 (2018): 1358–1386.
69. Acuña, *Occupied America*; Blackwell, *¡Chicana power!*; Muñoz, *Youth, Identity, Power*.
70. Foner and Taylor, *Frederick Douglas*, 358.
71. Biggers, *State Out of the Union*; Cabrera, Meza, Rodríguez, "The Fight for Ethnic Studies"; Cammarota and Romero, *Raza Studies*.
72. Gomez-Quiñones, "To Leave to Hope or Chance."

EPILOGUE

1. Tiafha Alexander, LaToya Baldwin Clark, Kyle Reinhard, and Noah Zatz, "CRT Forward: Tracking the Attack on Critical Race Theory, UCLA School of Law, Critical Race Studies," https://crtforward.law.ucla.edu/wp-content/uploads/2023/04/UCLA-Law_CRT-Report_Final.pdf.
2. Ibid, 5 (discussing Executive Order 13950).
3. Sarah Mervosh, "Florida Scoured Math Textbooks for 'Prohibited Topics.' Next Up: Social Studies," *New York Times*, March 20, 2023; Alexandra Petri, "Opinion, Excerpts from a Civics Textbook I Assume Would Be Welcome in Florida," *Washington Post*, March 20, 2023, www.washingtonpost.com/opinions/2023/03/20/florida-school-textbook-curriculum-review-satire/.
4. Lisa Tolin, "Revised Florida Textbooks Left Race Out of Rosa Parks History," *Pen America*, March 16, 2023, https://pen.org/florida-textbooks-rosa-parks-history/.
5. Brenda Álvarez, "Florida's New History Standard: 'A Blow to Our Students and Nation,'" *NEA Today*, August 3, 2023, www.nea.org/nea-today/all-news-articles/floridas-new-history-standard-blow-our-students-and-nation.
6. Francis Ford Coppola, *The Godfather, Part III* (Hollywood, CA: Paramount Pictures 1990), DVD.
7. Elias Weis, "Tom Horne Won Again: Here Are Four of His Sexiest Scandals in Public Life," *Phoenix New Times*, November 18, 2022, www.phoenixnewtimes.com/news/tom-horne-won-again-heres-four-of-his-sexiest-scandals-in-public-life-14930644.
8. Final Judgment, Declaration, and Permanent Injunction, *González v. Douglas* (December 27, 2017) ECF 487, at 2.

Index

104.1 *The Truth*, 26, 93, 126, 239

A.R.S. §15-112, 99, 108, 137, 211, 229, 235–236
Abu-Jamal, Mumia, 154
Acosta, Curtis, 4, 16, 32, 42, 68–70, 88, 97, 124, 126, 143–145, 149–152, 154–155, 157–159, 174–175, 179, 194–195, 198, 202, 222, 238
  trial testimony, 145–148, 150
Acosta v. Horne, 97
Acosta v. Huppenthal, 99
Acuña, Rudy, 8, 31, 33–34, 80, 197
African American Studies, at TUSD, 88, 95, 160–161
Alcaraz, Lalo, 35–37
American Educational Research Association (AERA), 34, 45
American History – Mexican American Perspectives
  MAS class, 10–11, 23, 102, 130, 151, 180
American Vision, The, 213–216
Anderson, Mark, 204–206
anti-Brown, 186–187, 191–192
anti-Mexican American racism, 24, 27, 29, 35, 65, 164, 171, 178, 192–193, 205, 207–208
Arce, Maya, 4, 99–101, 103–107, 126, 137–138, 150, 152
  trial testimony, 150–152
Arce, Sean, 4, 12, 25, 75–76, 97, 99, 104, 124–125, 131, 134, 137, 145, 149, 159–163, 166–167, 180–181, 210, 239
  ALJ hearing testimony, 75–76
  trial testimony, 157–158, 161–163
Arce v. Huppenthal, 105
Arizona Department of Education, 62, 123, 196, 204, 206–207, 209–214, 216, 218–219, 221
Arizona Republic, 126
Arpaio, Joe, 192, 228, 233, 281
Aztlán, 176–178, 200

Baldenegro, Salomón, 10, 59
Baldwin, James, 1, 3, 240, 284
banned or divisive concepts, 2, 13, 19, 116, 245
Barcelo, Julian, 138, 143
  trial testimony, 155–157
Barcelo, Manuel, 4, 138
Barrington, Luna, 136, 140, 150–152, 182–183, 206
Beck, Glenn, 26, 50, 52–53, 242
Bell, Derrick A., Jr., 18, 71, 138, 236, 238
Bella, Ulises, 40, 232–233
Biden, Joseph R., 245
Borderlands Theater, 133
Bradbury, Ray, 1–2
Breitbart.com, 71
Brown Berets, 187
Brown Scare, 14, 18, 145–146
Brown v. Board of Education, 10, 236
Burns, Judy, 47, 49, 79

Cabrera, Nolan, 14, 16, 60, 126, 129–130, 133, 139, 147, 163–164, 166–171, 230, 234
  trial testimony, 166, 168–169
Cambium, 62, 190, 196, 198–199, 202, 206, 209, 211–213, 216, 218–219
Cambium Audit, 62, 166, 181, 190, 211–214, 216, 218–219
Carrion, Dolores, 4, 97, 220, 239
Chang, Robert, 22, 45, 105, 108, 112, 116–117, 119–120, 122, 131, 133–135, 138–140, 142, 151, 155, 158, 160–161, 167, 171–175, 177–179, 182–183, 210, 213–214, 220, 229
Chavez, Cesar, 149
Chemerinsky, Erwin, 119, 128–129, 131
Chicana/o Studies, 7–8, 11–12, 33–35, 120
Chicano blowouts, 1960s, 10, 17, 59, 83
Churchill, Ward, 52–53, 67
Civil Rights Movement, 7–8, 45, 57, 66, 70, 80, 243, 247
Clifton, Richard R., 127–133

Coalition of Neighbors for Mexican American Studies (CONMAS), 11
code words, 28, 139, 164, 172–173, 176, 179, 193–194, 197
communism, 161
Cooper, Leslie, 128–131, 141, 151–152, 157, 160–163, 166–169, 171, 180–184, 201–202, 206, 210–211, 215, 221–222, 224–225, 234
Critical Race pedagogy, 137
Critical Race Theory, 13, 18, 53, 71, 73, 138
  attack on, 2–3, 18, 29, 71, 74–75, 116, 138, 145, 245–247
  in graduate education, 71
Cuevas, Miguel, 48–49, 59, 91, 242

DACA, 191
Daily Show, The, 28, 66, 87–88, 90–91, 93, 96, 121, 186, 211, 237
Delgado, Richard, 13, 80, 134
DeSantis, Ron, 2, 138, 245
Diaz, Tony, 131, 233, 281
dog whistle politics, 1–2, 193, 197, 229, 245
Dominguez, Nicholas "Nico," 4, 103–105, 136, 138, 143, 150
Douglas, Diane, 136–137, 235
Dugan, Margaret Garcia, 20, 88, 150, 187–188, 209
Dyson, Michael Eric, 23

El Plan de Santa Bárbara, 7, 244
Ellman, Rob, 129, 177, 192–194, 205, 207–209, 212, 217–218, 234
Escamilla, Alexandro "Salo," 4, 97, 124–125, 238
Ethnic Studies, 2–3, 23, 25, 31–32, 34, 39, 68, 116, 120–121, 126, 134, 226–227, 231, 233, 238, 240–246
  renaissance, 5, 19, 241, 244

Falcon 9, 123, 200
Federico Brummer, Maria, 4, 97, 124, 125, 238
Fernández, Anita, 124, 126
First Amendment, 31, 98–99, 105–107, 112, 118, 121, 129, 188–189
  overbreadth, 108–109, 121–122, 132
  viewpoint discrimination, 118, 121–122, 132, 137, 165–166, 193, 205, 220, 225
Fitzmaurice, David, 136, 140, 153, 167, 198
Foster, Kristel, 236–237
Fourteenth Amendment, 98, 103, 107–108, 112, 122, 143, 220, 229
  due process void for vagueness, 63–64, 99, 109–110, 118, 122, 132
  equal protection, 98–99, 117–118, 122, 131, 137, 143, 165, 171, 205, 220
  equal protection political process, 31, 103–104, 122
  substantive due process, 99, 113, 117–118

Franciosi, Robert, 207–209
Freire, Paulo, 13–14, 75, 80, 87, 176, 179, 191, 197

Giffords, Gabrielle, 33, 97
Glaude, Eddie, 1, 3
Godfather, Part III, The, 246
Goldwater Institute, 208
Gomez-Quiñones, Juan, 12, 244
Gonzales, Rodolfo "Corky," 7, 66, 80, 240
González, Jesus, trial testimony, 153–154
Gonzalez, Jose, 4, 14, 25, 97, 124–125, 137, 143, 238
Gonzalez, Joseph, 137–138
González, Noah, 138
Gonzalez, Norma, 4, 97, 124, 238
González v. Douglas, 4, 138
Grijalva, Adelita, 47, 49, 91, 124, 133, 236–237, 282
Grijalva, Raúl, 10, 87, 133
Guevara, "Che," 148, 154, 174, 176, 202
Gutiérrez, José Angel, 11, 18

Haladyna, Thomas, 139, 166, 169–171, 206
Haley, Nikki, 2, 245
HB 2281, 97–98, 101–102, 104, 108, 111–112, 114–115, 118, 121, 164, 167–168, 193, 195, 204–206, 229, 231
  legislative effort to pass, 4, 19, 191, 204–206
Hibbs, Elliott, 207, 211–212, 214, 217–219, 280
Hicks, Michael, 48–49, 65–66, 79, 87–91, 93, 96, 121, 186, 237, 242, 282
  ALJ hearing testimony, 65–66
Hitler, Adolf, 70, 148, 174, 192, 200
Hobbs, Katie, 3
Horne, Tom, 19–20, 97–99, 109–111, 116, 120–121, 128, 134, 142, 144, 147–148, 150, 158, 160–162, 168, 171, 174, 176–177, 185–186, 190–197, 200–207, 209–210, 217, 220–222, 230–231, 234, 239–240, 242, 246–247
  trial testimony, 186–192
Hrabluk, Kathryn, 157, 161–162, 180–181, 209–210, 212–213, 217–219, 221
  trial testimony, 210–216
Huckabee Sanders, Sarah, 2, 138, 245
Hu-DeHart, Evelyn, 8
Huerta, Dolores, 4, 20–21, 147, 187
Hunnicutt, Loretta, 26–27, 51, 126, 231, 242, 281
Huppenthal, John, 9, 62–64, 99, 102, 104–105, 109, 120–123, 134, 136, 142, 144, 147–148, 153, 158, 160–162, 165–166, 168–169, 174, 185–187, 194, 198–202, 205–206, 209–210, 213, 215, 217–222, 226, 230–231, 235, 239–240, 242
  blog posts, 123, 189, 198, 200–201, 207, 217–218, 221–222, 230
  trial testimony, 194–202

Immortal Technique, 6, 30, 243
In Lak'ech, 69, 156, 231

Jim Crow, 187
Justice, Jon, 26–29, 77, 126, 232, 239, 242

Kendi, Ibram X., 20, 28
Kid Frost, 226–227
King, Martin Luther, Jr., 10, 22, 24, 47, 59, 70, 192–193, 242
Korematsu, Fred, 245
Korematsu Center, 45, 105–107, 109, 111–112, 116, 119, 122, 127, 135
Kowal, Lewis, 64, 68, 73, 76–78, 96–97, 104–105, 165, 229
Ku Klux Klan, 70, 110, 123, 187, 189, 193–194

La Raza, 25, 28, 46, 77, 102, 149, 192, 196–197, 200, 226, 230
La Raza, by Kid Frost, 27, 226–227
La Raza Studies, 161
Latino Literature, MAS class, 6, 102, 105, 147–148, 154, 175
Lopez, Korina, 4, 99–107, 126, 136, 138, 150
Lopez, Lorenzo, 4, 97, 99, 102, 104, 126, 238

MacEachern, Doug, 25–26, 28, 53, 72, 126, 220, 232, 242
Madrigal, Al, 87–89
Malhotra, Anjana, 106, 108, 111–112
Martinez, Elizabeth, 80
Martinez, Rene, 4, 97, 213, 220, 239
Martinez, Richard, 23, 31–32, 44, 97, 99, 102–112, 116, 119, 126, 133–135, 139–140, 142–143, 149, 155, 157–163, 167, 169, 207–208, 220
Marxism, 25, 52, 76, 126, 146, 161, 191, 199
MAS courses, 13–14, 16, 47–48, 54, 61, 65, 79, 88, 94, 100, 105, 111, 129, 145, 152, 158, 180–182, 187, 216
MAS legal team, 22, 42, 111, 114, 116, 118, 127–132, 134–144, 146, 149–150, 153, 155–156, 158–163, 167, 169, 171, 174, 176–177, 180, 183, 208–210, 213, 216–221, 228–229, 234–235
MAS program, 21, 191, 204
 as anti-American, 10, 25–29, 40, 71, 77, 188
 as anti-White, 25, 72, 76, 89, 145, 148, 180
 attacks by conservative media, 25–26, 50, 52–53, 77, 93, 126, 242
 creation of, 4, 6–7, 11–14
 efficacy, 15–16, 25, 31, 64–65, 94, 139, 164, 166, 207, 222, 230, 241
 as fostering racism, 16
 as Marxist or Communist, 14, 23, 29, 144, 146, 176, 197, 219

MEChA, 10, 32, 66, 176–178, 189
MEChistas, 11, 178, 189
Mein Kampf, 149
Message to Aztlán, 7, 66, 80
Mexican American Legal Defense and Educational Fund, 106, 111
Mexican American Liberation Committee (MALC), 10
Mexican American Student Association (MASA), 10
Mexican American Studies, 98–99, 102–104, 107, 126, 137, 246–247
Milem, Jeffrey, 15, 70–73, 77, 94
 ALJ hearing testimony, 72
Mills, Charles, 168
Morales, David "Abie," 32–33, 53, 90, 124–125, 231, 239
Morley, Stacey, 206, 217

National Association of Chicana and Chicano Studies (NACCS), 35, 45, 114–115, 120
National Education Association, 120–121
Nazis, 70, 188–189
Noonan, John T., Jr., 127–129, 131

Obama, Barack, 52, 71, 123, 128, 178
Occupied America, 31, 33–34, 80, 197
Open Letter, by Tom Horne, 9, 13, 22, 25, 109, 186, 189
Ortiz, Milta, 133
Ozomatli, 40–41, 232

Palos, Ari, 115
Pan Asian Studies, at TUSD, 160–161
Parks, Rosa, 89, 245
Paulo Freire Freedom School, 191, 197, 199
Pedagogy of the Oppressed, 191, 197
Pedicone, John, 15–16, 39, 49–54, 56, 58–60, 65–67, 94, 149–150, 242
 ALJ hearing testimony, 66–67
Pinate, Marc, 133
Pitti, Stephen, 139, 164, 166, 171, 174, 176–177, 179, 193, 197, 229
 trial testimony, 171–179
Potemkin Village, 190–191, 197
Precious Knowledge, 15, 41–45, 114–116, 133, 143, 181, 187, 195–196, 202, 227, 239

Quinn, James, 136, 140, 143, 145–150, 157–158, 186–188, 190–194, 204–205

Rabago, Vincent, 120
racial animus, 144, 164–165, 167, 173, 186, 192–193, 195, 205, 210, 222, 229–230

Rakoff, Jed S., 127–128, 130–131
raza, 8, 27–28, 77, 233
red scare, 76, 146, 197
Reiss, Steven, 136, 140, 142, 155, 157, 167–171, 184, 195–197, 200–201, 206, 210–216, 218–221, 225, 228–229, 234
Rodríguez, Roberto "Cintli," 7, 51–53, 59, 90, 115, 239, 242
Roll, John M., 97–98, 106
Romero, Augustine, 12, 124–125, 162, 230, 238–239
Rusk, Sally, 4, 65–66, 97, 124, 143, 213, 226, 238

Santa Ana, Otto, 29
Save Ethnic Studies, 32, 34, 40, 45–46, 90, 136
SB 1070, 19, 32, 35, 40, 233
Sedgwick, Rachel, 236, 238
segregation in Arizona schools, 4, 10
Sleeter, Christine, 15, 124
Sotelo, Yolanda, 4, 97, 239
Stand and Deliver, 169
Stefancic, Jean, 13, 80
Stegeman, Mark, 39, 47–50, 54, 56, 59–60, 67–70, 77, 79–81, 91, 123–124, 150, 237, 242, 282
    ALJ hearing testimony, 68–70
Stegeman Resolution, 47–48, 50–51, 54, 57, 59, 61
Stollar, John, 209, 211–212, 214, 217
Stotsky, Sandra, 72–73, 75, 77
    ALJ hearing testimony, 73–75
Structure of Scientific Revolutions, The, 172
subtractive schooling, 179–180, 246
Subtractive Schooling, 179

Takaki, Ronald, 8
Tashima, A. Wallace, 19, 42, 62, 97–98, 103, 105–112, 116–118, 120, 124, 127, 129, 131–132, 139, 142, 148, 150–152, 155–163, 165–167, 169, 173–175, 179, 186, 189, 193–194, 198, 203, 207–208, 210, 215–217, 221, 225–226, 228–231, 235–237, 247
Tempest, The, 6, 147–148
Three Sonorans, The, 32–33, 53, 90–91, 125, 231, 239
Trump, Donald, 1–2, 13, 98, 127, 138, 191, 227–228, 232–233, 245, 249, 281
Tucson 11, 31–32, 44–45, 92, 96–97, 114–115, 238
Tucson Police Department (TPD), 56–57, 59–61
TUSD administrative appeal, 63–64, 78, 97
    hearings, 65–68, 70–74, 76, 94
TUSD Board, 11, 34, 47, 49, 60–61, 65, 68, 90–91, 238
TUSD board meeting, 25, 47–48, 50, 89, 91, 134
TUSD desegregation lawsuit, 4, 94, 111, 124, 152, 164, 240

UNIDOS, 44, 46–57, 61, 81, 83–84, 91–93, 95, 142, 231, 235, 237
    School of Ethnic Studies, 83–87
Urrea, Luis Alberto, 38–39

Valdez, Luis, 69
Valenzuela, Angela, 139, 147–148, 164, 166, 171, 179, 182–184, 202, 210, 221–222
    trial testimony, 179–183

Ward, John, 23–25, 28, 220
Weil, Gotshal & Manges, 136, 139–140, 142, 153, 158–159, 196, 226–227, 229
white supremacy, 9, 168, 243

Youngkin, Glenn, 138

www.ingramcontent.com/pod-product-compliance
Ingram Content Group UK Ltd.
Pitfield, Milton Keynes, MK11 3LW, UK
UKHW020639030125
452982UK00012B/125